The Old Testament Hebrew Scriptures in Five Minutes

Religion in 5 Minutes

Series Editors
Russell T. McCutcheon
University of Alabama
Aaron W. Hughes
University of Rochester

Published

Religion in Five Minutes
Edited by Aaron Hughes and Russell T. McCutcheon

Atheism in Five Minutes
Edited by Teemu Taira

Buddhism in Five Minutes
Edited by Elizabeth J. Harris

Hinduism in Five Minutes
Edited by Steven W. Ramey

Indigenous Religious Traditions in Five Minutes
Edited by Molly Bassett and Natalie Avalos

Forthcoming

African Diaspora Religions in Five Minutes
Edited by Emily D. Crews and Curtis J. Evans

Ancient Religion in Five Minutes
Edited by Andrew Durdin

Christianity in Five Minutes
Edited by Robyn Faith Walsh

Islam in Five Minutes
Edited by Edith Szanto

Jainism in Five Minutes
Edited by Steven M. Vose

Judaism in Five Minutes
Edited by Sarah Imhoff

Mormonism in Five Minutes
Edited by Daniel O. McClellan

Pagan Religions in Five Minutes
Edited by Suzanne Owen and Angela Puca

The Old Testament Hebrew Scriptures in Five Minutes

Edited by
Philippe Guillaume and Diana V. Edelman

SHEFFIELD UK   BRISTOL CT

Published by Equinox Publishing Ltd.

UK: Office 415, The Workstation, 15 Paternoster Row, Sheffield, South Yorkshire S1 2BX

USA: ISD, 70 Enterprise Drive, Bristol, CT 06010

www.equinoxpub.com

First published 2024

British Library Cataloguing-in-Publication Data

A catalogue record for this book is available from the British Library.

ISBN-13   978 1 80050 451 6   (hardback)
          978 1 80050 452 3   (paperback)
          978 1 80050 453 0   (ePDF)
          978 1 80050 469 1   (ePub)

Library of Congress Cataloging-in-Publication Data

Names: Guillaume, Philippe, 1960- editor. | Edelman, Diana Vikander, 1954- editor.
Title: The Old Testament Hebrew scriptures in five minutes / edited by Philippe Guillaume and Diana V. Edelman.
Description: Bristol, CT : Equinox Publishing Ltd., 2024. | Series: Religion in 5 minutes | Includes bibliographical references and index. | Summary: "This book deals with the essentials anyone entering the fascinating world of biblical scholarship needs to master. Concise and jargon-free chapters present the nature of the biblical texts and the different methodologies that have been developed to understand it. In addition, major issues that standard introductions tend to dodge are considered in a balanced way, providing the pros and cons for each position"-- Provided by publisher.
Identifiers: LCCN 2023035492 (print) | LCCN 2023035493 (ebook) | ISBN 9781800504516 (hardback) | ISBN 9781800504523 (paperback) | ISBN 9781800504530 (pdf) | ISBN 9781800504691 (epub)
Subjects: LCSH: Bible. Old Testament--Introductions. Classification: LCC BS1140.3 .O425 2024 (print) | LCC BS1140.3 (ebook) | DDC 221.6/1--dc23/eng/20231205
LC record available at https://lccn.loc.gov/2023035492
LC ebook record available at https://lccn.loc.gov/2023035493

Typeset by Scribe Inc.

Contents

Themes

Issues

Selected Biblical Figures

Methods and Approaches

Preface

Diana V. Edelman and Philippe Guillaume

The present volume belongs to Equinox's successful Religion in 5 Minutes series. After *Religion in Five Minutes*, *The Five-Minute Archaeologist in the Southern Levant*, and the *Five-Minute Linguist*, *The Old Testament Hebrew Scriptures in Five Minutes* covers the first and by far the largest part of what has become known as *the* Bible.

An all-time bestseller constantly being translated into new languages while old translations continue to be updated, the Bible is not a book at all. It is a collection of at least thirty-nine books and writings for the Jewish Bible and close to a hundred books and writings for the largest Christian biblical canons. Thus, *the* Bible exists as a crucial concept in the minds of those who venerate it, but there are, in fact, dozens of different kinds of bibles—that is, as many bibles as there are religious groups who differentiate themselves from others by adding or rejecting certain books from their Bible.

"The Bible" is venerated as holy writ; the Scriptures by Jews and Christians alike. Many of its stories and characters are discussed in the Qur'an as well. Given the authority half of the present human community grants to biblical writings, the Bible can hardly be ignored, even by those who contest its authority and consider, often rightly so, that it is misinterpreted or misused to support an ideology they reject.

To make things more intricate, the Bible as a whole is a treasure trove of mythical compositions, laws, stories, genealogies, oracles, hymns, proverbs, and quasi-philosophical writings produced two or three millennia ago in historical and cultural contexts vastly different from our own. Hence, reading the Bible is a baffling experience for anyone who ever ventured to open a Bible and read it as if it were an ordinary book. Such readers typically make it through the fifty chapters of the initial book (Genesis) and the first half of the second (Exodus), but then regulations and the intricate descriptions of rituals in what comes next get the better of even the most dedicated readers.

Like the thrills experienced by climbers of the highest peaks, to reach the Bible's summit, readers need guides to avoid crevasses and impassable precipices. This volume is one such guide, designed for a readership interested in learning about scholarly approaches, though the casual reader will also find much help in these eighty-three chapters. Each chapter is succinct enough to be covered in some five minutes. They provide key information in jargon-free language, without distracting footnotes, to all readers, even those with no previous knowledge of what the Bible is or what it contains.

While the initial chapters set the overall tone by delineating the parameters of any scholarly approach to the Bible in a scientific world, each chapter is a self-contained unit that can be read in any order. To facilitate their retrieval, the chapters are grouped into ten parts:

1. General Matters
2. Authorship, Audiences, Organization
3. Genres in the Hebrew Bible
4. Dating the Bible and the Bible as History
5. The Hebrew Bible and Archaeology
6. Translation and Transmission
7. Themes
8. Issues
9. Selected Biblical Figures
10. Methods and Approaches

Each chapter is written by a scholar whose research on the subject at hand has been or is being published in an academic venue where it underwent peer review. Each chapter provides cross-references to other relevant chapters that touch upon aspects raised in that piece.

Each chapter closes with a list of further readings to help the reader navigate the sea of scholarly literature. The volume is thus particularly designed for Bible instructors who can assign individual chapters as required reading.

Diana V. Edelman, professor emerita in Hebrew Bible/Old Testament, Faculty of Theology, University of Oslo.

Philippe Guillaume, holds a doctorate in theology from the University of Geneva.

General Matters

1

How Does One Read the Bible from a Scholarly Perspective?

Diana V. Edelman

Biblical studies is a discipline within the humanities, whose researchers usually hold a doctorate degree (PhD or ThD). The field recognizes that the Hebrew Bible forms all or part of the canons of Judaism (Tanak) and Christianity (the Old Testament) and is read in those contexts as a document of faith containing divinely inspired or revealed truths. However, as an object of scholarly investigation, the Hebrew Bible is seen to be a collection of ancient writings intended to provide an origin story for a religio-ethnic group, which included a shared history, belief system, and customs. One need not be a believing Jew or Christian to pursue biblical studies; anyone of any faith or none can read and study these texts, applying the range of theories and methods that are embraced by the discipline. These methods are grounded in the application of logic; the conclusions of an analysis undertaken using one or more of these methods are considered not truths but contingent results. Different answers can be given to a question depending on the method used to answer it.

A scholarly approach to the Hebrew Bible assumes that the anonymous books now collected together were written by humans, master scribes, using conventions current at the time of composition within their culture. They expected their readers to be familiar with those conventions and to share many elements of a common world view. Even so, the texts themselves indicate that certain aspects of what today would be called religious belief and practice were under dispute among the leading members of society.

Although the subject of this collection of books is humanity's relationship to the divine, there is no underlying presumption by a biblical scholar that every text was divinely inspired and no room for the view that they were written directly by God. Certainly, prophetic statements claim to convey direct divine revelation, but the point is, they are always mediated through a human. A scholarly approach does not rule out the possibility of divinely inspired master scribes, but this is not a necessary or preferred prerequisite. Rather, like other literary masterpieces, the books of the Hebrew Bible are to be viewed as creations by very talented individuals. Of course, one might want to debate whether the book of Leviticus qualifies as a masterpiece, but the point applies more generally to the collection.

Biblical studies is multidisciplinary. Questions and approaches that traditionally have been the focus of other recognized disciplines are also being applied by biblical scholars to the corpus of ancient texts. They include other traditional branches of the humanities, such as literary studies, history, linguistics, law, politics, philosophy, ethics, religion, classics, visual arts, geography, anthropology, and sociology. In addition, they include psychology, communication studies, trauma studies, gender studies, migration studies, memory studies, ritual studies, postcolonial studies, reception history, and disability studies.

It frequently is the case that certain approaches cannot be used effectively or questions pursued because the texts do not contain the necessary information. Even when the master scribes did not directly address a particular issue, however, indirect clues can be found in the biblical texts that allow the formulation of preliminary postulations. In addition, the results of archaeological excavations at various sites mentioned or not present in the Hebrew Bible can provide insight into daily life practices and point toward aspects of the world view at the time. These can sometimes supplement information present in the texts or even help scholars better grasp what likely is an ideal to be strived for in the writings rather than the reality at the time of writing.

Currently, biblical scholars can approach the biblical texts from a number of angles and situations. They can place the biblical books in their originating contexts in the ancient Near East and try to understand the literary conventions and world view(s) within them by comparing them with texts from surrounding cultures. We have access to texts from Egypt, from the Hittites, from Syria, from Mesopotamia, from Canaan, and from the Achaemenid Persians to accomplish this task. They also can study the reception of the books over time, including views expressed by the rabbis and church fathers in medieval commentaries during the Renaissance and Enlightenment, or narrow their focus to study their use or influence only in contemporary cultures. How an artist has interpreted a biblical text in a painting, mural, mosaic, or sculpture is fair game, as is how a musician has done the same by setting a text to music or how a politician draws on a specific text or invokes the Bible more generally as a source of authority.

As the subject of academic study, the Hebrew Bible is approached as humanly composed literature that can be situated in the past or the present and analyzed using a range of logic-based methods. When engaging in an academic approach to biblical studies, those for whom it also serves as a document of faith are expected to apply standard methods and follow them to their logical conclusions, regardless of what religious truths they might believe the texts to reveal.

About the Author

Diana V. Edelman holds a doctorate of philosophy (PhD) in biblical studies from the University of Chicago and is Professor Emerita in Hebrew Bible at the Faculty of Theology, University of Oslo. She has published widely on many aspects of the Hebrew Bible in its ancient Near Eastern context and has taught in humanities programs at various universities and in numerous seminaries.

Suggestions for Further Reading

In This Book
See also chapters 3 (religious in a scientific world), 5 (canons), 8 (anonymity), 13 (genres), 24 (Kings and Chronicles), 26 (conquest of Canaan), 79 (memory studies), 80 (social anthropology), 81 (gender studies), 82 (postcolonial studies), and 83 (reception criticism).

Elsewhere
Conroy, Charles. "Reflections on the Present State of Old Testament Studies." *Gregorianum* 73(4) (1992): 597–609.

Jonker, Louis. "Communities of Faith as Texts in the Process of Biblical Interpretation." *Skrif en Kirk* 20(1) (1999): 79–92.

Noll, Mark A. *Between Faith and Criticism* (2nd edition). Vancouver: Regent College Publishing, 2004.

2
What Is Religion?

David McConeghy

The Hebrew Bible is used by both Jews and Christians as part of their sacred canons; hence, it commonly is classified as a "religious text." What does this mean, exactly? What does the term "religion" connote?

The modern English word "religion" has ancient origins in the Latin term *religio*, which began to be used around the first century BCE by Roman writers. It may have roots in two different verbs: *religare*, "to bind fast," and *relegere*, "to consider carefully." The use of both terms is complex, but *religio* first appears in discussions by the philosophers Cicero (106–43 BCE) and Lucretius (ca. 99–55 BCE) about the ceremonial duties humans owe to the gods to avoid the wrath of forces beyond our control.

Today, it is more common to trace "religion" to *religare* in the sense of binding or connecting, but in the fourth century CE, Christians were comfortable using both meanings. *Religio* meant a person's scruples (or second thoughts) but was used equally to describe the proper worship that brought humans closer to each other and their god(s). The Christian theologian Augustine (354–430 CE), for instance, argued it was important for religion's worship to be focused on the correct object: God as opposed to statues. If you were going to bind yourself to God to avoid damnation, then you had better consider your options and choose wisely.

Augustine and many others who followed him wrote about Christianity and Judaism using terms from other languages that were not direct synonyms for *religio*. Latin was the primary language of Christian scholars for hundreds of years, but the Bible was translated from Greek and Hebrew. The Greek word *threskeia* dealt more directly with ritual worship, but there were also Hebrew terms that had cultural significance, like *ioudaismos*, referring to the Judeans or Jews, *ḥag*, "pilgrimage festival," *zebaḥ*, "sacrifice," and *torah*, "teaching, law." After the middle of the seventh century CE, it was necessary to have a serious discussion regarding Islam and what Muslims meant when they used the Arabic word *din*, "judgment, custom." With all these issues of translation, "religion" became a lens for cross-cultural understanding. Did both Christians and Jews have religion? What about rituals performed by Romans? Religion emerged as an analytical tool for description, identification, comparison, and classification. This process continued for hundreds of years, with growing contributions beyond the Mediterranean.

By the colonial and modern era beginning in the nineteenth century, "religion" was emerging as the catchall term for those in Europe and America to describe Buddhism, Christianity, Hinduism, Islam, Judaism, Taoism, and more. Definitions of religion struggled to identify the core of the term that mattered when comparing these traditions. Did it mean belief in one god? Was action or belief primary? Translation continued, as in the use of "Hindu" for Indian followers of Sanatana Dharma or the eternal law. For many in Asia, using a more generic Western term offered a trade-off: a reduction in the meaning(s) of expansive and complex native terms in favor of cohesion and recognition as "world religions" alongside Judaism, Christianity, and Islam.

That trade-off is unresolved, so what religion is or what counts as religious varies. The word's primary use remains as a tool of classification to describe an incredibly diverse class of objects, ideas, practices, and institutions. Definitions that have modeled themselves on the legacy of the use of *religio* in early Christianity have been attacked for coercing non-Christians to use a term developed to elevate Christianity and even to denigrate the beliefs and practices of other cultures. These challenges have been exacerbated by the legacy of religion's connection to colonial governance, because control of the term's scope and meaning influences a range of issues, such as the extent of legal protections for religious freedom. The self-evidence of many claims about religion (i.e., "I know it when I see it") remains a fundamental hurdle for the term's ongoing development. If it once described what Romans did to appease their gods, then today it is a battleground over identity: Can what seems self-evident to one group about what defines religion be used by others who see the world differently? Appropriately, the fight over the term's use connects us. We must all carefully consider how cross-cultural translation offers more than synonyms for foreign words. Thus, the origins of the word "religion" remind us that definition and translation are extraordinary powers that shape our connections to others.

About the Author

David McConeghy holds a PhD in religious studies from the University of California, Santa Barbara. For a decade, he taught religious ethics, world religions, and American religious history at colleges in California and Massachusetts. He now works as a freelance software developer in Greater Boston. He published "Narrating the USA's Religious Pluralism: Escaping World Religions through Media," pages 1–27 in *After World Religions,* edited by Christopher R. Cotter and David G. Robertson (London: Routledge, 2016).

Suggestions for Further Reading

In This Book
See also chapters 4 (sacred books), 5 (canons), 14 (myths), 32 (cultic context), 40 (holiness), 46 (afterlife), 49 (Torah), and 50 (magic).

Elsewhere

Masuzawa, Tomoko. *The Invention of World Religions: How European Universalism Was Preserved in the Language of Pluralism.* Chicago: University of Chicago Press, 2005.

McCutcheon, Russell T. *Manufacturing Religion: The Discourse on Sui Generis Religion and the Politics of Nostalgia.* Oxford: Oxford University Press, 1997.

Nongbri, Brent. *Before Religion: A History of a Modern Concept.* New Haven, CT: Yale University Press, 2013.

3
Can One Be Religious in a Scientific World?

Adrien Chauvet

Science is often said to be superior to religion because of science's apparent objectivity. Beyond superiority, it is even said that science is real because it works. To glorify science, however, illustrates a misunderstanding of what science is and how it works. Indeed, science does not work by itself. Science is made to work by a specific view and expectation of the world. And in a very similar way, religion can be made to work as effectively. Hence, instead of setting science against religion, a better approach is to explore their complementarity and define the purpose of each.

Science corresponds to a set of universal laws based on the universal language of mathematics. Science is universal in the sense that it is expected to transcend culture, time, and space. Technology derives from the advances of science: we find cures to diseases and we travel through space. Because of the apparent technological progress of our times, it is said, as Richard Dawkins famously stated at the Sheldonian Theatre in 2013, that "it [science] works, b*****s." The question that prompted such a crude answer referred to the problem posed by induction.

As discussed long ago by David Hume (1748, 25–39), the problem with induction is the following: The observation of repeated experiments steers us to believe that every cause leads to a specific effect. In turn, these relations of cause and effect provide the basis for scientific laws. For example, every time a rock is let go in the air, it falls back to the ground. Accordingly, we infer that masses attract each other. But without experience, it would be impossible to infer such a law simply by looking at either the earth or the rock. Furthermore, no experiment can ever prove that the derived law will forever be valid. From a philosophical point of view, there is no purely rational argument that can prove a physical law and its continuity.

The method of induction, which implies the continuity of these relations of cause and effect, is thus lacking rational justification. At most, inductive inquiry is the best possible assumption we can make, as discussed by James Ladyman (2002, 209–229). While being considered humanity's greatest material achievement, induction also is said to be the failure of human philosophy. The justification for inductive inquiry is indeed the apparent effectiveness of the technology derived from scientific laws. For example, the effective working of our mobile phones proves that the theories of electromagnetism that underlie wireless communication must be true. And the more these technological advances are valued, the more science is viewed as the ultimate way of describing the world. Science becomes the lens through which everything is explained and evaluated. Science thus shapes the way the world is valued. In turn, that way of valuing the world makes science prevail over any other means of knowing the world. In other words, science becomes a self-nurturing paradigm.

Besides the philosophical flaws discussed above, science also suffers from inherent biases. In accordance with the scientific paradigm, our technological societies nurture a specific hierarchy of values. For instance, we are taught to value scientific precision, numerical application, material benefits, and novelty over thankfulness, generosity, compassion, and tradition. This second set of values is not dismissed, but they are not granted the same weight. It is more common, for example, to treat symptoms rather than focus on a holistic approach to health care. It is also more common to value the profits generated by a new technology than the quality of life it provides. And whenever that quality of life is assessed, it is usually in material terms: access to medicine, access to information, disposable income, efficiency of transportation systems, and so on. These assessments tend to omit the related wider environmental impact, the related infringement of human rights, and the related consequences on mental and physical health, all of which are important measures of the well-being of a population. The fact that we focus on the positive consequences of technology and accept the negative ones as unfortunate corollaries shows a will to see technology, and thus, science, as inherently beneficial.

The scientific paradigm, with its inherent flaws and biases, is therefore not ideal. Yet, advocating a return to premodern lifestyles is hardly an option. It is also unfair to hold science responsible for all the ills of the world. But it is equally unfair to ignore the problems science generates. One of the dangers of upholding a scientific paradigm is the devaluation of alternative paradigms. In other words, the fact that many societies today are based on a hierarchy of values that is designed to make science prevail implies that any nonscientific ways of looking at the world will be devalued. This hierarchy of values creates a bias in favor of materiality. Hence, within a scientific paradigm, alternative philosophies of life, including those promoted by the Judeo-Christian-Muslim religions, cannot match science simply because they ask us to seek benefits that are mostly immaterial. As a result, these alternatives are deemed prone to prejudices. They are often accused of advocating for an improbable historicity, of being complicit in political instrumentalization, and of being responsible for the wrongdoing of some of their adherents. Yet, science can be accused of the same ills.

It is important to be aware of this hierarchy of values when assessing Judaism, Christianity, and Islam because they arose when the hierarchy of values was different. More specifically, when assessing their relevance to our current context, it is important to be mindful of the overall objective of these religions and to overlook our cultural barriers. For example, the creation of the universe is described in Genesis 1 and Qur'an 7:54 as taking place in six days of presumably twenty-four hours, and humankind is described in Genesis 2:7 and Qur'an 15:28–29 as having been directly molded from earthy material. Modern science, however, describes these same events in terms of the big bang, the standard model, and evolution. Read through lenses polished by centuries of scientific and technological advances, the scriptural passages might seem very odd and naïve. But when these passages are read as understandings of the position of humanity within the universe, the descriptions retain their full relevance: God is the creator, the universe is God's creation, and the universe is made subservient to our own creation. Thus, the differences between scriptural and scientific descriptions of the world are indicative of differing objectives.

The biblical and Qur'anic descriptions of the world are not meant to be sources of scientific theories. The scarcity of such descriptions in the texts is evidence that the scriptures were not intended to be scientific textbooks. The prime purpose of the scriptures is to teach about a divine entity, about ourselves, and about the relationship between the two. It is to teach about improving oneself to get closer to what, in English, we call God.

But even if the scriptures were written in a different cultural paradigm and for purposes that are not scientific, their adherents often consider that the theology and the morals conveyed transcend cultures and are relevant to all—scientists and nonscientists alike, across the ages. Hence, we have seen the scriptures read in many contexts, including various scientific paradigms. And the widespread use of imagery in the scriptures ideally suits metaphorical readings by scientifically oriented readers. For example, when the universe is described in Job 38:4–7 and in Qur'an 79:27–30 as an extended plate vaulted by the sky, the verses could well have been interpreted in terms of a temple-shaped universe by medieval readers. But they can also be read in modern times in terms of an Earth smoothed via the accretion within a constellation of stars. The chosen interpretation only reflects the cultural imagination of the translators and commentators. But the core message remains the same: it teaches about humanity's place and responsibilities within that universe.

Therefore, if one wants to experience the benefits derived from adhering to faith in the modern world, one must reset the current hierarchy of values. And by asking questions that are faith relevant, one will surely find appropriate answers. In other words, just as science is made to work within a scientific paradigm, one must adopt a religious paradigm to benefit from religion. In short, adopting a religious paradigm makes religion work. And the more benefits are derived from this religious world view in various aspects of our lives, the more effective and valuable religion becomes.

One might, therefore, wonder if both science and religion can work simultaneously or if one needs to be dismissed for the other to flourish. Such a question stems from the apparent notion that religion opposes science. This opposition is most vivid when discussing miracles. One might indeed take the biblical and Qur'anic concept of miracles as unacceptable in a society where the scientific paradigm dominates. Miracles are here defined as a divine alteration of the laws that science takes as immutable. Science, however, is limited to the study of the usual laws of nature. Experimental science is, indeed, not conducive to the study of exceptions, whether these exceptions correspond to direct divine actions or simply to a more fundamental physical law that takes effect only once, such as the big bang. Accordingly, to believe in miracles affects neither the aims nor the practice of science.

In conclusion, science and religion are distinguished by having their own logic and their own specific set of values. Both are, however, helpful to understand the world and its dynamics. The two are complementary once it is acknowledged that the scriptures are not a source of scientific truths and that science is not the ultimate and only way of knowing the world. In general, while science helps respond to our material needs, religion helps navigate this materiality to fulfill our spiritual and psychological needs. Accordingly, science and religion are complementary because they both fulfill some fundamental human needs.

About the Author

Adrien Chauvet holds a doctorate of philosophy (PhD) in biophysics from Purdue University and is currently a lecturer in physical chemistry at the University of Sheffield as well as an active member of the Sheffield Centre for Interdisciplinary Biblical Studies (SCIBS). His research includes the interplay between science and religion. On the same topic, he previously published *Scientifically Religious: Using Science to Rationalize Faith* (Markfield, UK: Kube, 2023).

Suggestions for Further Reading

In This Book
See also chapters 2 (religion), 4 (sacred books), 41 (symbolic numbers), 42 (Nephilim), 50 (magic), and 53 (creation).

Elsewhere
Hume, David. *An Enquiry concerning Human Understanding.* London, 1748.

Kuhn, Thomas. *The Structure of Scientific Revolutions.* Chicago: University of Chicago Press, 1962.

Ladyman, James. *Understanding Philosophy of Science.* London: Routledge, 2002.

Walton, John. *The Lost World of Genesis One.* Downers Grove, IL: Inter-Varsity, 2010.

4

Do All Religions Have Sacred Books?

Russell T. McCutcheon

Do all religions have sacred books? Well, yes and no. Such a question contains a number of key terms that sometimes, for scholars, contain little land mines. Given this or that way of talking about such a technical term like "sacred," not to mention "book," we might answer the question in rather different ways. No doubt many readers are familiar with the Bible and its place in Christianity, or maybe the role of the Hebrew Scriptures in Judaism and the Qur'an in Islam. These are, therefore, probably prototypes for such readers who work under the assumption that if "we" have books of consequence, we presumably will find the same thing when we start doing our cross-cultural comparisons. If the question translates as "What do they call their bible?" anyone posing such a question will have to take a step back and reconsider a few things.

First off, in many cases, we do, indeed, find written texts (which might not necessarily be what some readers mean by "books") in many of those systems we commonly know as religions. But before we go any further, the long-standing distinction between written and oral literature is important to think about. The ease with which we take reading and writing to be self-evident things we do naturally is part of the problem. In fact, there's a large body of work on the history of literacy and how the invention of alphabets and writing may have impacted not only the way we organize ourselves socially but also how we actually think about and perceive or interact with the world.

So, if we instead take seriously that such things as reading and writing have a history (i.e., humans haven't always done them and how we do them changes over time), we'll have to pause. We need to consider that before human beings developed systematized ways to represent information in public symbol systems outside their own brains, they had little choice but to talk to one another. Perhaps they did so in a rhythmic, ritual manner—in which their actions and gestures were no less important—to increase the memorability of what they were saying for both the speakers and the listeners.

What's more, it would be an error to assume orality was a mark of just ancient human beings. It's not difficult to find examples in the scholarly literature of small-scale societies that have only fairly recently encountered those of us who take writing for granted. In such situations, anthropologists working on an ethnography of the people have been known to transcribe the tales they're told once they've learned the language. Consequently, they produce texts that, over time, may actually come to be authoritative sources not just for scholars but for the people themselves. The cultural encounter of insider and outsider that takes place during fieldwork has the structure of a feedback loop, whereby a group's onetime oral literature ends up being transformed by the curious observer into a group's own written texts. The end result, perhaps unintended, is the invention of their so-called sacred book.

So, granting that, sooner or later, groups generally codify the stories they tell, we also have to consider that the items we find in such texts are hardly all similar. It might not even be accurate to call them all stories. Most simply, a story (or more technically, a narrative) is sometimes defined in a rather minimal fashion as a tale with a beginning, middle, and end—a narrative arc with some kind of climax or resolution. The Hebrew Bible tells the tale of a chosen people's calling and destiny across a sequence of books written by various ancient scribes. But then there are parts of the Old Testament that seem more concerned not with telling a story but, instead, with listing and thereby communicating the proper way to carry out what we'd today call rituals. Once recognized, this difference in texts opens the door to a large alternative body of texts that we find throughout the study of religion. Calling such texts "books" might, therefore, not be all that accurate; they could more accurately be understood as collections of rules, formulas, and ritual instructions, used primarily and sometimes even exclusively by ritual specialists but almost never read by laypeople, most of whom were illiterate.

Thus, if it is indeed the Bible that's being used as the model to pose a question about the books of other religions, we quickly land in the middle of some problems. You would never expect to see texts written by and for ritual specialists to be, let's say, in the drawer of a bedside nightstand of a motel. While some may be read for inspiration or consolation, others are more akin to either philosophical treatises thought to contain the wisdom of the ancients or instructional manuals on how specially trained people might maintain order in the universe.

Although there may be a variety of texts across world religions, talking about them as a coherent grouping of so-called sacred books—as late nineteenth-century scholars did when translating many of them into English, French, and German for the first time—is problematic. We need to keep in mind the challenge of holding within one and the same idea, on the one hand, a Brahmin ritual specialist in Hinduism, being watched perhaps by a small circle of local villagers who do not speak or read Sanskrit, the language in which his ancient texts are written and which he recites, performing his ritual gestures over a small fire and, on the other, a small child learning all about the exploits of, say, King David, by means of Bible stories in Hebrew or in Sunday school.

About the Author

Russell T. McCutcheon received his PhD from the University of Toronto in the study of religion. He is a professor and the former longtime chair of the Department of Religious Studies at the University of Alabama. His work is on the theories of religion and approaches to the study of myth. He also focuses on the history of the study of religion and the practical effects of classification systems. He has published *"Religion" in Theory and Practice* (Sheffield, UK: Equinox, 2018); and coedited *What Is Religion? Debating the Academic Study of Religion* (New York: Oxford University Press, 2021).

Suggestions for Further Reading

In This Book
See also chapters 1 (scholarly perspective), 2 (religion), 7 (who wrote the Bible?), 11 (Pentateuch), and 49 (Torah).

Elsewhere
Molendijk, Arie L. *Friedrich Max Müller and the Sacred Books of the East.* New York: Oxford University Press, 2016.

Sawyer, John. *Sacred Languages and Sacred Texts.* New York: Routledge, 1999.

Smart, Ninian, and Richard Hecht, editors. *Sacred Texts of the World: A Universal Anthology.* New York: Brécourt Academic, 2007.

5
Why Multiple Biblical Canons?

Jean Claude Loba-Mkole

A historical approach is necessary to understand the diversity of biblical canons. The word "bible" comes from the plural Greek noun *biblia*, meaning "scrolls, books." By definition, the Bible is an anthology. The term "canon" comes from the Greek noun *kanon*, a loanword from the Semitic noun *kaneh*, "a reed," and, by extension, a measuring rod. A canon is a precise standard or norm to guide the evaluation of a reality for which the type of chosen measurement is applicable. Thus, a biblical canon constitutes a collection of books (intrinsic canonicity) or a list of sacred books (extrinsic canonicity) acknowledged as authoritative and binding by a past or living Jewish or Christian community.

Ultimately, the authority of those writings is established on the belief that they record the word that goes out of God's mouth and does not return to the deity before it has accomplished its purpose (Isaiah 55:10–11). For Christians, once established as authoritative, biblical texts, together with related traditions, constitute the deposit of faith (2 Timothy 1:13–14). The religious community interacts with God's word through its members and leaders in different ways, such as liturgical rites, instructions, ethical norms, and legal codes. The recognition of the authority of a given text and the fixing of the boundaries of the list by appointed leaders in a given Jewish movement or Christian denomination were the result of a long, complex process.

Tradition played a decisive role in determining the criteria for canonicity. Different community leaders progressively recognized as authoritative the books their community used and read publicly on a regular basis, which were considered to derive from leaders of old such as Moses, the prophets, the sages, or the apostles. The study of this process pertains to historical research that deals with the different stages of the formation of the lists of authoritative books, codices (actual manuscripts), and catalogs.

The Hebrew Bible is called Tanak in rabbinic Jewish tradition. That is an acronym made from "T" for *Torah* (meaning "teaching"), "N" for

Nevi'im (Prophets), and "K" for *Ketuvim* (Writings), with vowels added to make the noun pronounceable. The Torah includes Genesis, Exodus, Leviticus, Numbers, and Deuteronomy. The Prophets are made up of Joshua, Judges, Samuel, Kings, Isaiah, Jeremiah, Ezekiel, and the twelve minor prophets. The Writings now contain Psalms, Job, Proverbs, Ruth, Song of Songs, Qohelet/Ecclesiastes, Lamentations, Esther, Daniel, Ezra, Nehemiah, and Chronicles. This arrangement resulted from the authority community members attributed to leaders like Moses, prophets, and sages, respectively. Scholars frequently refer to the first subdivision, the Torah, as the Pentateuch (Greek for "five volumes"). This is the only part of the Bible that is accepted as canonical by all Jewish and Christian groups because the Samaritans and the later Karaites, who emerged in the ninth century CE, do not recognize the Prophets and Writings as authoritative.

The date and occasion when the rabbinic canon of twenty-four books was finalized are not known. The prologue (verses 8–12) to the Wisdom of Jesus Ben Sira (a.k.a. Ecclesiaticus) refers to the contents of what became the Writings as the "other books of our ancestors," confirming there was not yet an established canonical list for this section circa 180–175 BCE. In fact, Luke 24:44 refers to the Scriptures as the law of Moses (the Torah), the Prophets, *and the Psalms*, which shows that in the first century CE, the contents of the third part was not yet fixed.

Until the 1960s, it was thought that the final subdivision was agreed upon after the destruction of the temple in Jerusalem at a meeting of rabbis at the city of Yavneh (the Council of Jamnia) before 90 CE. On this occasion, it was supposedly decided that Song of Songs and Qohelet would be in the Writings, but nothing was decided about the status of Chronicles or Esther at Yavneh. This theory has fallen out of favor, as the Tanak in twenty-four books was fixed later than the early second century CE.

While manuscripts of individual books of the Tanak are found among the Dead Sea Scrolls, the earliest codices containing the entire Hebrew Bible (Aleppo and Leningrad) date much later, from the tenth century CE. Both use the Ben-Asher masoretic tradition of adding a secondary system representing vowels to the consonantal text to reflect the inherited pronunciation, called Tiberian pointing; accents to mark divisions in verses; and concise marginal notes about the spelling of words and how many times a certain letter or word has appeared so far in an attempt to prevent scribal errors in the text.

The precanonical Hebrew Tanak was translated into Koine Greek (the type of Greek used as the lingua franca in Hellenistic and Roman times), probably in Egypt. The Torah is likely to have been produced in the mid-third century and the remaining books in the second century BCE. That collection of writings was called the Septuagint (LXX) and was subdivided into four sections: Pentateuch, Historical Books, Wisdom Books, and Prophetic Books. Surviving manuscripts of the LXX also contain some works that were not part of what became the rabbinical Masoretic Text: 1–3 Maccabees, Tobit, Judith, the Wisdom of Solomon, Sirach, Baruch, the Epistle of Jeremiah, and additions to Esther and Daniel. Some copies additionally include the Wisdom of Solomon, 4 Maccabees, the Epistle of Jeremiah, the Book of Odes, the Prayer of Manasseh, Psalm 151, the Prayer of Azariah, the Song of the Three Young Men, Susanna, and Bel and the Dragon. All these writings likely were composed between 200 BCE and 50 CE.

The main difference with the rabbinical canon is the chronological organization that places Ruth after Judges in the "historical" subsection that continues after 1–2 Kings, with 1–2 Chronicles (Paraleipomena), Esdras A and B (corresponding to Hebrew Ezra–Nehemiah), Esther, and then Judith, Tobit, and 1–3 Maccabees (sometimes also 4 Maccabees) as witnesses to Israel's past from the entry in Canaan to the Roman era.

The LXX became part of the Christian canon, preceding the four Gospels, Acts, Epistles, and Revelation relating to the apostles and other eminent followers of the Jesus movement. The Christian theologian Marcion of Sinope (ca. 110–160 CE) had attempted to remove the books in the Tanak from Christian bibles. As reported in the *Africanae Ecclesiae Canonum Codex* dating to 419 CE, however, it was at the Third Synod of Carthage, which took place in 397, that the bishops first confirmed a more exhaustive list of the authentic canonical books in the Western part of the Christian world. The first codices (rather than scrolls) of Christian bibles (Vaticanus, Sinaiticus, and Alexandrinus, all in Greek) date from the fourth century CE.

Though the early church synods had not considered the Hebrew language a criterion for canonicity, Luther and subsequent Protestant groups did. As Martin Luther (1483–1546), the founder of Protestantism, made a fresh translation of the Latin Catholic Bible into German, he moved the books with no original Hebrew counterparts to a new, noncanonical section. This move to return to the sources is known as the *ad fontes* interpretation principle or *hebraica veritas*; it assumed that the texts written in Hebrew were the truer ones. It resulted in a Bible containing the Old Testament and the New Testament, both canonical, and a third division, the Apocrypha (hidden things).

In response, at the Council of Trent in 1546, the Catholic Church reaffirmed the canonical status of the books that were in the Septuagint and the Latin Vulgate but rejected by Luther and Jews.

More so than Judaism, Christianity has generated many different canons. The Orthodox churches follow the list established at the Synod of Laodicea in 363/4 CE combined with the list of Trullo in 692/3 CE and have a total of seventy-six books. The Roman Catholic Church acknowledges a list of seventy-three books established in the Synod of Rome in 382 CE, confirmed by the Third Synod of Carthage in 397 and reaffirmed at the Council of Trent in 1546. Protestant and Anglican churches have a canon of sixty-six books in total. The early Syriac Peshitta of the Syrian churches and the canon of the Armenian Orthodox Church have seventy books, excluding 2 Peter, 2 and 3 John, Jude, and Revelation. The scholarly New Revised Standard Version provides a convenient translation of these canonical and deuterocanonical books, including some found in Slavonic and Latin bibles.

The Ethiopian Orthodox Tewahedo Church holds its "biblical canon" as neither open nor closed, though it recognizes eighty-one biblical books, following the statement of Fetha Nagast in 1240 that led the Ethiopian Orthodox church leaders to add eight more books to the sacred literature related to Jesus's movement. In African contexts, a biblical canon can even be more encompassing when Jesus is viewed as the protoancestor who spoke to the ancestors long before his incarnation and resurrection. In this case, biblical and nonbiblical religious texts may be regarded as authoritative once they are placed under the ultimate authority of this protoancestor.

At this point, it is important to note that there is no such thing as the biblical canon or biblical codex. Once a faith community has established its biblical canon, all the books therein are canonical; the excluded ones are noncanonical. To designate these books as deuterocanonical is erroneous. A biblical book is either part of the canon or excluded from it. A canon with half-canonical books is not a canon anymore. Yet, every faith community has a fixed and an open-ended set of authoritative books.

About the Author

Jean Claude Loba-Mkole holds a doctorate from the Catholic University of Leuven. He is a lay Dominican from Sainte Catherine of Siena Fraternity, Nairobi, where he works as a global translation advisor with the United Bible Societies. He is also a research fellow at the University of the Free State. His research includes Bible translation studies and intercultural hermeneutics. He has published "Biblical Canons in Church Traditions and Translations," *Bible Translator* 67 (2016): 108–119; *Bible and Orality in Africa: Interdisciplinary Approaches*, edited by Albert Ngengi Mundele,

Emanuel Wabandu, and Jean Claude Mkole (Nairobi: Biblical Centre for Africa and Madagascar, 2021); and "Jesus: The Apex of Biblical Canons," *HTS Theological Studies* 78(4) (2022): 1–9, http://dx.doi.org/10.4102/hts .v78i4.7189.

Suggestions for Further Reading

In This Book
See also chapters 4 (sacred books), 10 (Tanak), 33 (Septuagint), 34 (Dead Sea Scrolls), 38 (Samaritans), 48 (twelve tribes), 49 (Torah), 64 (Ruth), and 68 (Jeremiah).

Elsewhere
Auwers, Jean-Marie, and Henk Jan de Jonge, editors. *The Biblical Canons.* Leuven: Leuven University Press, 2003.

Collins, John J., Craig A. Evans, and Lee Martin McDonald. *Ancient Jewish and Christian Scriptures: New Developments in Canon Controversy.* Louisville, KY: Westminster John Knox, 2020.

Krisel, William. "The Place of Ruth in the Hebrew Canon: A New Hypothesis." *Estudios bíblicos* 79 (2021): 63–76.

McDonald, Martin L. *The Formation of Biblical Canon* (2 volumes). London: Bloomsbury, 2017–2018.

Papadopoulos, John K. "Canon Creation/Destruction and Cultural Formation: Authority, Reception, Canonicity, Marginality." Pages 3–34 in *Canonisation as Innovation: Anchoring Cultural Formation in the First Millennium BCE.* Edited by Damien Agut-Labordère and Miguel John Versluys. Leiden: Brill, 2022.

6

What Is Biblical Exegesis?

Pauline A. Viviano

"Exegesis," or "reading out," is often used today as a synonym for "interpretation," but as the term emerged in the field of biblical studies in the nineteenth century, it referred to a critical or more rigorous form of interpretation used by those who employ the historical-critical method. It is commonly recognized that we are conditioned by the historical and cultural periods in which we live. The way we think, the thoughts we have, the language we speak, and the way we compose documents and understand them rests on our experiences in the times and places in which we have lived.

As the scientific method developed in the modern era, it led to explosions of knowledge in various academic disciplines; of particular interest here was the great progress in our understanding of past civilizations. With advances in the field of archaeology, we moved forward in our knowledge of how ancient peoples lived, were governed, and composed documents. The result was more data with which to understand the historical context of the written material of the biblical text, and this led to the historical-critical method. Exegetes adopted this method as a way to interpret biblical texts "objectively." To determine the meaning of biblical texts, it became important to study the language, culture, social and political structures, religions, and philosophies—indeed, everything that formed the distinctive history of the people of the ancient Near East and the Greco-Roman world, from which the biblical texts emerged.

The counterpoint of exegesis is eisegesis. Where exegetes attempt to "read out" from a text what the author intended, those who "read into" a text practice eisegesis—that is, they read into a text their own ideas without consideration of the historical context in which the text was written or how the original audience would have understood the text. Where exegetes strive for "objectivity" by situating a text in its own time and place, those who practice eisegesis give prominence to their ideas, and even their biases, drawn from the present. These are two extremes, but most interpreters fall somewhere in the middle. Exegetes seek to read texts in their historical context, but our knowledge of the past is limited, especially the distant past. It is difficult to set aside our own ideas and biases in the task of interpreting. This is especially true of the interpretation of the biblical texts, as the Bible is seen by many as a sacred text in which God speaks a relevant message for their lives today. Exegetes are concerned with what the text *meant* when written; many believers today are interested in what the text *means* for their lives.

In spite of its claims, biblical exegesis is not more "objective" than "eisegesis"; in the current postmodern word, it is recognized that objectivity is an unattainable human ideal. Whether speaking with another or reading a book, we are immersed in the process of interpretation. We cannot escape seeing and interpreting the world through our own eyes and experiences, so objectivity is a pipe dream. Where, then, in the interpretative process is meaning to be found? Contemporary communication theory holds that three components are necessary for communication to take place: a sender, a message, and a receiver. In a written document, the sender is the author, the message is the text, and the receiver is the reader. Exegetes search for meaning in written documents, but where in these three components is meaning found?

Is meaning from the *author*? From the perspective of a historical-critical scholar, meaning is to be found in the intent of the author and the historical context that has shaped that author. These scholars seek to enter the "world behind the text" to understand what the author wants to convey. This method draws on a variety of disciplines: the study of biblical manuscripts and the languages of these manuscripts, which need to be translated for most readers (text criticism); the analysis of the remains, both material and written, uncovered by archaeologists, determining the sources used by authors (source criticism); the recovery of ancient forms or genres, such as saga, history, letters, call forms, and so on that betray the intent of an author (form criticism); the examination of how forms are changed as they are passed on (tradition criticism); and the comparison of similar documents focusing on editorial changes to determine the distinctive perspective of the final editor (redaction criticism). These "criticisms" refer to methods subsumed under the historical-critical model. Each method is a tool used by an exegete to determine the meaning of a text. Here, interpretation seeks to be objectively grounded on facts drawn from the best knowledge available to the scholar.

Is meaning in the *text* itself? Perhaps the author's intent has not been clearly represented in what the author wrote. Nothing is known of most biblical authors, which makes it difficult to determine their intent. The dating of biblical material remains disputed, so the determination of an exact historical context is elusive. Furthermore, as a text becomes the property of a specific community, it may take on meanings never considered by its author. Whatever the author intended, written material has a life of its own once it is passed on. These problems led biblical scholars toward the last third of the twentieth century to focus on the literary features of the text (new literary criticism or rhetorical criticism) to determine meaning. They sought to "enter the world of the text" and so focused on literary techniques such as structure, repetition, and style to determine the meaning. It should be noted that in dealing with ancient texts, we cannot move completely away from historical considerations, but the focus is not on the history behind the text or the author's intent but on how the text says what it says.

Is meaning created by the *reader*? Toward the end of the twentieth century, questions began to be raised about the role of the reader in the determination of meaning, leading to reader-response criticism or ideological criticism. The reader lives in "the world in front of the text" with questions and issues characteristic of their age, not the age that produced the Bible. Feminist criticism has emerged to deal with the role of women in the biblical world, but it also deals with how women today interpret texts written in a patriarchal world. One's socioeconomic position plays a role in their interpretation of the Bible, as is evidenced by the emergence of liberation criticism. Reader-response scholars take into consideration the perspectives and biases of contemporary readers in the determination of meaning, but they may use critical methods to find the answers to those questions.

My suspicion is that meaning results from the interaction of the three components involved in communication: the author, the text, and the reader. If such is the case, it may explain why the term "exegesis" is more recently being used as a synonym for "interpretation" and has moved away from its original meaning as a critical analysis using the historical-critical method.

About the Author

Pauline A. Viviano holds her PhD in biblical languages and literature from St. Louis University. She is Associate Professor Emerita from Loyola University. Her areas of specialization include the Deuteronomistic History (Deuteronomy, Joshua, Judges, 1–2 Samuel, 1–2 Kings), biblical poetry (especially the book of Jeremiah), and the history of biblical interpretation. Her publications in the field of biblical interpretation are "Source Criticism," pages 35–57 in *To Each Its Own Meaning: An Introduction to*

Biblical Criticisms and Their Application (revised and expanded edition) (Louisville, KY: Westminster John Knox, 1999); and "The Senses of Scripture," pages 1–4 in *The Word of God in the Life and Mission of the Church: Celebrating the Catechetical Year 2008–2009 with Resources for Catechetical Sunday 2008* (Washington, DC: Committee on Evangelization and Catechesis, United States Conference of Catholic Bishops, 2008), publication no. 7-028.

Suggestions for Further Reading

In This Book

See also chapters 1 (scholarly perspective), 3 (religious in a scientific world), 7 (who wrote the Bible?), 9 (audiences), 13 (genres), 21 (dates), 28–29 (archaeology), 72 (synchronic vs. diachronic), 73 (source criticism), 75 (historical criticism), 76 (redaction and text criticism), 77 (literary and form criticism), 78 (ideological criticism), 80 (social anthropology), 81 (gender studies), 82 (postcolonial studies), and 83 (reception criticism).

Elsewhere

Hayes, John H., and Carl R. Holladay. *Biblical Exegesis: A Beginner's Handbook*. Louisville, KY: Westminster John Knox, 2022.

Lohfink, Gerhard. *The Bible: Now I Get It! A Form-Criticism Handbook*. New York: Doubleday, 1979.

Stuart, Douglas. *Old Testament Exegesis: A Handbook for Students and Pastors* (5th edition). Louisville, KY: Westminster John Knox, 2022.

Authorship, Audiences, Organization

7
Who Wrote the Hebrew Bible?

Diana V. Edelman

How do we get behind the anonymity of every book in the Hebrew Bible to the real men who conceived and penned each scroll? (I say men specifically because it is generally thought that professional scribes in Israel and Judah were males only.) Well, basically, we cannot. But we can and should think about what being a scribe involved. And this is not easy because there is almost no information about that in the texts themselves.

During the monarchies, it appears the main term for a scribe was *sofer*, which meant, literally, "one who counts or recounts." Once Israel became an imperial province of Neo-Assyria (721 BCE) and Judah of Neo-Babylonia (587 BCE), and both continued as provinces under Achaemenid, then Ptolemaic and Seleucid control and eventually Roman domination, the preferred term for a scribe became *shoter*, meaning, literally, "one who writes." It likely was borrowed from Aramaic, the language of imperial administration in the Levantine territory of all these empires.

The scribal profession probably ran in families. Details of three generations of one such family have been preserved in the biblical texts, including, in some cases, their specific offices within the administration. In the closing days of the kingdom of Judah, Shaphan occupied the office of scribe (of the king). He had two known sons, Ahikam and Gemariah. Gemariah served in the temple administration (Jeremiah 36:10), and his son, Micaiah, had access to both the temple and palace complexes (Jeremiah 36:12) but perhaps was based in the temple, like his father. Ahikam appears to have worked as a court scribe, like his father (2 Kings 22:14; 2 Chronicles 22:20). His son, Gedaliah, was appointed overseer of the newly created province by the Babylonians (2 Kings 25:22; Jeremiah 40:5–16; 43:6).

Beyond this, we must turn to surrounding nations to gain possible insight into the education of scribes and their power and influence and assume that while there would have been differences from culture to culture, the general patterns of training and levels within the profession would have been similar. We have useful evidence from Mesopotamia, Egypt, and Hatti. Literacy was a privilege. In the Old Babylonian period, schools were established to train scribes, but these disappeared after the profession tended to become closed and hereditary, passed down from father to son or nephew. At that point, scribes tended to be trained by their own immediate or extended families. In Babylonia, they followed a progression from junior apprentice to apprentice to junior scribe to scribe, with the upper echelon consisting of senior or chief scribes and, at the very top of the profession, master scribe scholars, a title that only a few managed to attain. It is unlikely, therefore, that scribal schools existed in Israel or Judah. They had long disappeared in neighboring countries in favor of intergenerational training at home, even if, from time to time, a scribal family agreed to educate the son of a wealthy or influential person.

The educational process entailed work with selected examples of literary genres and, no doubt, a lot of memorization. But, more importantly, it inculcated a common way of thinking, shared attitudes and values, and a body of knowledge within a restricted group that set them apart from the ordinary, illiterate masses. At most, 10 percent of the population would have been literate, and scribes would have constituted the vast majority of those who had been taught to read and write, with sons of the wealthy and the royal house likely having undergone some basic education that included reading and writing. Even though a twenty-two-character alphabet would have been easy for an ordinary person to learn, it took years of practice and working with texts to become truly literate and a professional scribe.

Israelite and Judahite scribes wrote primarily on papyrus rolls, an organic material that deteriorates rapidly. We have no "school texts" like the wax tablets found in Mesopotamia, which sometimes contain samples of copied set texts. The tablets could be "erased" and reused. As a result, we have no idea if there had been a set of standard exemplary texts used by all scribal families or if each family covered the same range of genres but produced their own sample texts, including, perhaps, extracts from certain "masterpieces" of their day. It seems that passages from the Gilgamesh epic were used in teaching scribes cuneiform script, for example. By the middle of the Hellenistic period (323–31 BCE), when the majority of the books of the Hebrew Bible had been written, scribes appear to have drawn on biblical figures and excerpts to train the succeeding generation (see the book of Ben Sira).

Scribes worked in the bureaucracy, performing a range of clerical tasks as accountants, recorders, tax collectors, and census takers, for example. It is likely that cultic specialists also underwent at least basic literacy education before they moved on to specialized ritual training, although we cannot be sure of this. Scribes not only could be associated with the temple or the palace but also could be employed by wealthy private individuals. They even could be sought out by ordinary people who needed help composing a written petition to an official, as indicated by the draft of a letter found on an ostracon, a piece of a broken ceramic pot, at the ancient fort of Mesad Hashavyahu near the coast, close to the Philistine city of Ashdod. Those who worked in the royal bureaucracy and any royally sponsored temple most likely would have been subject to a formal contract that included the swearing of an oath of loyalty to perform all its stipulated terms and conditions.

Only master scribe scholars, who may have numbered one or perhaps two in a generation, would have been engaged in composing the literary masterpieces now included in the collected works forming the Hebrew Bible. Elsewhere, this was not a hereditary office; it was awarded based on talent and accomplishment, which meant it passed among rival scribal families. The same is likely to have held in Israel, Judah, and their successor provinces, Samerina/Samaria and Yehud/Judea, respectively. Master scribes would have had the ability to draw on inherited oral traditions and palace and temple archives to create new compositions that addressed the needs of their time. They could incorporate older materials by paraphrasing or even quoting verbatim, but they combined them with their own fresh ideas and ideological agendas to produce first editions of each of the books we have today.

Since none of their potential source material outside the Bible has survived the ravages of time, we cannot easily be certain when a master scribe was quoting an older source. When quoting another text in the collection, however, he used a technique where he reversed the order of the sentence, beginning with the closing of the earlier material and ending with what previously had opened it as a signal that it was a quotation. The scroll of the minor prophet Obadiah is a good example of citation and allusion. The scribe who created it has worked with a number of prophetic sayings concerning the destruction of Jerusalem and its hoped-for restoration from other books—especially Jeremiah 18:17; 25:15–29; 49:7, 9, 10, 12, 15–16, 22; Ezekiel 25:14; 35:5, 10, 15–16; 36:2; and Joel 4:3–6, 17, 19—into a short, twenty-one-verse composition that imagines the reader present and watching the events as they unfold. It is a creative reimagining that condemns Edom for having actively participated in the destruction and looting of Jerusalem and goes beyond all the earlier sources it cites.

Then, over time, those scrolls were recopied and additions were made, often to explain obsolete terms, challenge or alter an older idea, or "update" the text to address the concerns of a new generation. Copying errors also inevitably made their way into the manuscripts.

More substantive additions of entire chapters occurred in some cases. The original scroll dedicated to the prophetic figure of Isaiah dealt with the crisis of the Assyrian siege of Jerusalem in 701 BCE, which ended miraculously with the withdrawal of enemy troops, sparing the capture of the city. Yet, it was expanded to add chapters 40–55 to have that same figure predict the return of those deported from Jerusalem and Judah in 592, 587, and probably 582 BCE by the Neo-Babylonians. And it was expanded even further, in chapters 56–66, to deal with the issues some descendants of those exiled encountered after their return to Jerusalem and Yehud. Chapters 9–14 of the book of Zechariah are similarly considered by many to have been added by a later scribe, and the Greek translation of Jeremiah is much longer than the Hebrew version.

The dating of the initial composition of biblical books is highly disputed. It seems that most of the books were composed during a period of religious transition, as an inner dialogue among scribal families who endorsed different understandings of how Yhwh was to be conceived and the cult was to be carried out. There are plenty of polemics and ideologies present! Some seemed to have wanted to continue the Yahwistic cult that had prevailed during the monarchy, while others were pushing for a single, invisible, universal deity. At the same time, the families seemed to agree that there was a pressing need to create an origin story for Israel that could underscore a group identity for Yhwh worshippers whose historical homelands had been in Cisjordan and Transjordan. The kingdoms of Israel and Judah had disappeared, but these scribes were interested in maintaining an inherited cultural heritage and providing a divinely endorsed power base for themselves, as Levitical priests and Levitical scribes, within a provincial setting, where they now became middlemen between the local masses and the distant imperial ruler—but in reality, they were the local leadership on the ground.

Who the scribes wrote the various books for remains another hot issue. With literacy so restricted, the original intended audience might well have been other scribes, both within the same extended family and in rival families, with the hope of reinforcing one's held views and persuading others to adopt them. However, it needs to be asked whether any of the books might also have had a wider, illiterate audience in mind, to whom the scrolls or excerpted "episodes" could be read or possibly even performed. This would be the case particularly for not only Genesis and Exodus but also Ruth and Judges.

About the Author

Diana V. Edelman holds a doctorate of philosophy (PhD) in biblical studies from the University of Chicago and is Professor Emerita in Hebrew Bible at the Faculty of Theology, University of Oslo. She has published "The Text-Dating Conundrum: Viewing the Hebrew Bible from an Achaemenid Framework," pages 7–38 in *Stones, Tablets, and Scrolls: Periods of the Formation of the Bible*, edited by Peter Dubrovský and Federico Giuntoli (Tübingen: Mohr Siebeck, 2020); "Scribes (*šōṭᵉrîm*) in Deuteronomy," *Scandinavian Journal of the Old Testament* 21 (2023): 34–57; and "Creating Israelite Cultural Hegemony in the Persian Period: Shared Strategies and Points of Dispute among the Literati," in *Cultural Hegemony in Second Temple Judaism*, edited by Benedetta Rossi and Daniel Verde (Leuven: Peeters, forthcoming).

Suggestions for Further Reading

In This Book

See also chapters 1 (scholarly perspective), 4 (sacred books), 8 (anonymity), 20 (genealogies), 21 (dates), 25 (Deuteronomistic History), 27 (Josiah's scroll), 28 (archaeological proofs), 47 (monotheism), 51 (prophets), 56 (polemics), 63 (Moses), 67 (Isaiah), 68 (Jeremiah), and 72 (synchronic vs. diachronic).

Elsewhere

Allon, Niv, and Hana Navrátilová. *Ancient Egyptian Scribes*. London: Bloomsbury, 2017.

Ben Zvi, Ehud. "The Urban Center of Jerusalem and the Development of the Literature of the Hebrew Bible." Pages 194–209 in *Aspects of Urbanism in Antiquity*. Edited by Walter G. Aufrecht, Neil A. Mirau, and Steven W. Gauly. Sheffield, UK: Sheffield Academic, 1997.

Carr, David M. *Writing on the Tablet of the Heart*. New York: Oxford University Press, 2005.

Quick, Laura. "Recent Research on Ancient Israelite Education: A Bibliographic Essay." *Currents in Biblical Research* 13(2) (2014): 9–33.

Robson, Eleanor. *Ancient Knowledge Networks*. London: UCL Press, 2019.

8
Why Are There Anonymous, Pseudonymous, and Fictitious Texts in the Bible?

Philippe Guillaume

Can you imagine authors composing texts and allowing them to circulate without marking them as their work? Can you imagine authors quoting fictitious authors of their own creation? This is exactly what scholars face when studying any biblical text.

Not knowing who wrote a text and when hinders attempts to understand why it was written and which contexts motivated the writer. For anyone who is interested in trying to understand what a biblical author might have meant when he wrote (i.e., authorial intent), not knowing who the author was, having no idea about his origins, his education, or the challenges he faced—in short, his biography—seriously impairs the aim of interpretation.

Yet, almost all biblical books are anonymous. Qohelet (alias Ecclesiastes) at first glance would seem to be the exception; the initial verse identifies its author as Qohelet, son of David, king in Jerusalem (Ecclesiastes 1:1). Although *Qohelet* is a feminine participle form in Hebrew, the book is traditionally attributed to Solomon. Whether or not she was a woman, Qohelet is a personification of Wisdom, a feminine figure playing or dancing before the creator (Proverbs 8:30). There is no escaping the suspicion that Ecclesiastes is a pseudonym. If so, Ben Sira may well be the first biblical writer to have signed his work (Ecclesiasticus 50:27).

Many psalms are introduced with the so-called authorial lamed: *leDawid, leAsaf,* and so on. Given the grammatical function of the Semitic preposition lamed, *leDawid* should be rendered "attributed to David," which then begs the question "Attributed by whom?" and its corollary, "Why attribute certain psalms to David and others to Asaf, to the sons of Korah or to Moses (Ps 90:1)?" Though English Bibles tend to ignore the titles of the psalms, they indicate the literary heritage the writers understood their work to belong to and that they sought to perpetuate. For instance, Deuteronomy presents itself as Moses's lengthy testament pronounced before Israel's entry into the promised land. Then a copy of this speech was supposedly rediscovered in the temple of Jerusalem (2 Kings 22; 2 Chronicles 34).

The anonymous writer of the books of Chronicles, often referred to as "the Chronicler," claims to be quoting other chronicles by Samuel the seer, Nathan the prophet, and Gad the seer (1 Chronicles 29:29). These are likely fictitious creations, like the "book of the Chronicles of the Kings of Media and Persia" in Esther 10:2, possibly the "Book of Jashar" in Joshua 10:13 and 2 Samuel 1:18, and the scroll supposedly found in the Persian archives recording a decree issued by King Cyrus to rebuild the house of God in Jerusalem (Ezra 6). That this decree is transcribed in Aramaic rather than in Hebrew is proof of the linguistic proficiency of the scribe, not of the authenticity of the decree. The case of the annals of the kings of Israel and Judah quoted throughout the book of Kings (starting at 1 Kings 14:19 until 2 Chronicles 33:18) is less clear. The synchronic presentation of the reigns of Israelite and Judahite kings presupposes access to some kind of record. In any case, anonymous writers bolstered the authority of their work by claiming to quote famous authors or compositions. Today, this would be a case of plagiarism aggravated by forgery. In the ancient world—before Bishop Athanasius (*Festal Letters* 39; 367 CE) denounced those who produced books in the name of biblical figures as heretics—such practices were tools available to skillful scribes.

Attributing one's writing to an authoritative biblical figure goes beyond anonymity. It is pseudonymity, a trait of biblical production as much as the rule in the production of literary texts in the ancient Near Eastern world, if not beyond. Contracts, of course, were different. They included the name of the scribe, the parties involved, and the names of witnesses. The end of cuneiform tablets recording literary and scientific works often named the copyist and the owner of the tablet, but not the author.

The author is necessarily an individual. Coauthors retain their individuality, as it establishes authenticity and originality and enables each individual to claim intellectual property. Conversely, writing in the ancient world, including the Bible, was not a matter of individuals. It was a collective effort across generations. Our modern-day focus on the individuality of the author downplays the fact that even our authors immersed themselves for decades in the stream of tradition, the classics, or the authoritative textbooks of their branch of learning before becoming authors. Creation necessarily begins as imitation until the combination of parental traits evolves into something new.

Still, anonymity is uncomfortable. Until recently, scholars tried to overcome it. Without going as far as publishing "new" revelations in the form of unprovenanced artifacts of doubtful authenticity (papyri, ostraca, etc.), biblical writers or redactors were conceived of as individuals whose originality was such that their work could be distinguished from the mass of material into which their text was eventually set. Towering theological figures of the last centuries came to believe they were looking over the shoulder of the Yahwist or of the Deuteronomistic Historian, with whom they felt much affinity.

In fact, the anonymity of biblical texts is a prerequisite for texts containing the formula "Thus said the Lord . . ." A culture where different gods were vying with one another for supremacy had no room for human authors. Ascribing authorship to divine words would make the writer the author of the words of a god of his own making. The decisive question was how to create an authoritative text that made audiences feel that God was on their side.

Anonymity is also the recognition that the writer is a link in a chain of anonymous writers, imitators, and glossators. The links in that chain need not be innumerable if the addition of new material in a given manuscript occurred when it had deteriorated to the point that a new copy had to be produced to replace it. Still, such occasions to modify the contents of the previous copy would present themselves once or twice per century before some sort of canonical process that attempted to prevent the modification of Yhwh's commands (Deuteronomy 4:2; 12:32). Hence, a half dozen hands involved in the production of the largest biblical books can be expected, with an equivalent number of redactional layers, some of which are easier to identify than others. For instance, resumptive formulae such as "These are the stipulations, decrees and verdicts that Moses spoke to the people" (Deuteronomy 4:45) are often taken as indicating the beginning of a literary block that ends with a postscript "These are the terms of the covenant which Yhwh commanded Moses to conclude with the Israelites in the land of Moab, in addition to the covenant he had made at Horeb" (Deuteronomy 28:69; 29).

Other writers, however, may have preferred to imitate the language and style of their predecessors to make the identification of their own work less visible. In this case, our ability to recognize their contribution becomes as illusory as the quest for the original version.

Consequently, biblical scholars have grown wary of identifying authors and redactors. The "historical Isaiah" has waned as much as the once popular descriptions of his life and times. The superscriptions of prophetic books are less viewed as authorial. At most, the Hosea named in the first verses of Hosea could have first referred to the days of King

Hoshea, son of Elah (2 Kings 15:30; 17:1–4). If so, this would only give us an idea of when some of the oracles recorded in the book of Hosea were transcribed onto a separate scroll that eventually came ascribed to a man named Hosea, son of Beeri. Set at the beginning of the collection of Minor Prophets, this impersonation of the prophetic figure set the tone for all prophetic scrolls, each one introduced by a superscription that ascribes it to an individual who we eventually confused as the author.

In fact, it is the prophetic scroll that produced the man, while no single man ever wrote the scroll. This reversal of our understanding of the role of the author as the producer of a prophetic book is given a vivid illustration in Ezekiel 3:1–3, where an anonymous son of adam is ordered to ingest a scroll before speaking to Israel, who will not listen, though the prophet speaks their language. The scroll generates the prophet, whose speech remains inaudible.

The eclipse of the author led to a loss of interest in authorial intent and a focus on reader response—that is, in the meaning the reader constructs regardless of what the writer intended, which in turn produces new challenges. Replacing the meaning the writer intended with the meaning generated by each reader is not conducive to the debate between opposite views. Instead of the single authoritative meaning of the writer—which, indeed, we can never be sure to recover correctly—every individual reader can claim to possess the correct meaning. The production of meaning is restricted to closed circles of like-minded readers within which the text becomes a mere pretext at the service of the ideology of the group. This may well have been the situation in which the text arose, as scribes were recruited within a narrow circle of like-minded priests, which in turn makes the individuality of each writer irrelevant. Yet, in some cases, opposite views—or at least views that appear hardly reconcilable to us—are simply juxtaposed, which suggests a desire to retain different understandings, sometimes due to the sacrality granted to writing that made editors wary of simply deleting opinions they disagreed with.

In any case, the term "author" is a misnomer for every genre of biblical literature and should be avoided when referring to whoever actually produced (rather than merely copied) a text that ended up in the Bible.

Remember, though, that anonymity in no way undermines the authority of Scripture! Except in rare cases of first-person narratives, the biblical narrator is the most authoritative voice, the master of the tale.

About the Author

Philippe Guillaume holds a doctorate in theology from the University of Geneva. His research interests include the use of prophetic scrolls in divination. He has published "Nahum 1: Prophet, Senet and Divination," pages 129–160 in *A Palimpsest: Rhetoric, Ideology, Stylistics, and Language Relating to Persian Israel*, edited by Ehud Ben Zvi, Diana V. Edelman, and Frank Polak (Piscataway, NJ: Gorgias, 2009).

Suggestions for Further Reading

In This Book
See also chapters 1 (scholarly perspective), 4 (sacred books), 16 (Psalms), 25 (Deuteronomistic History), 27 (Josiah's scroll), 51 (prophets), 52 (covenant), 56 (polemics), 67 (Isaiah), 72 (synchronic vs. diachronic), and 74 ("P").

Elsewhere

Ben Zvi, Ehud. "Matters of Authorship, Authority, and Power from the Perspective of a Historian of the World of Yehudite/Judean Literati." Pages 93–114 in *Authorship and the Hebrew Bible*. Edited by Sonja Amman, Katharina Pyschny, and Julia Rhyder. Tübingen: Mohr Siebeck, 2022.

Foucault, Michel. "What Is an Author?" Pages 101–120 in *The Foucault Reader*. Edited by Paul Rabinow. New York: Random House, 1984.

Knauf, Ernst Axel. "Prophets That Never Were." Pages 451–456 in *Gott und Mensch im Dialog: Festschrift für Otto Kaiser zum 80. Geburtstag*. Edited by Markus Witte. Berlin: De Gruyter, 2004.

Reed, Annette Yoshiko. "Pseudepigraphy, Authorship, and the Reception of 'the Bible' in Late Antiquity." Pages 467–490 in *The Reception and Interpretation of the Bible in Late Antiquity*. Edited by Lorenzo DiTommaso and Lucian Turcescu. Leiden: Brill, 2008.

Reinhartz, Adele. *"Why Ask My Name?" Anonymity and Identity in Biblical Narrative*. New York: Oxford University Press, 1998.

Van der Toorn, Karel. *Scribal Culture and the Making of the Hebrew Bible*. Cambridge, MA: Harvard University Press, 2007.

Van Seters, John. "Creative Imitation in the Hebrew Bible." *Studies in Religion / Sciences Religieuses* 29 (2000): 395–409.

9
Who Are the Audiences of the Bible?

Jason M. Silverman

All communication requires an audience. This is as true for speech as it is for writing. The purposes of communication include conveying information and forming relationships, two functions that require an audience. Such audiences vary dramatically—from oneself to mass audiences—but they are an essential aspect of understanding any form of communication. Unlike interpersonal communication, however, texts such as those in the Bible are not tied to a specific situation and thus have multiple real and potential audiences.

This insight has been central to the field of communications and has long been part of the rhetorical tradition within scholarship. It entered biblical studies through hermeneutics, which is the philosophical and theological study of how to read the biblical text; reader-response approaches, which focus on an audience's response to texts; and poststructural approaches, which are reactions to theories of stable or universal meanings in language in critical theory. More recently, performance-critical approaches study how texts interact with their audience.

Whether one is interested in the historical origin of a text, in its use in popular culture, or even in scholarship, there are three levels on which the audience is important for any given text: the background of the text, the writing of the text, and the various receptions of the text.

The Background of the Text. Any given text was written at a point in time in response to real or imagined events. This historical moment provided the social and material conditions for an author to write. The language, genre, topics, and ideas the writer utilized were shaped by a tradition of *previous* audiences. The cultural expectations and assumptions available to the writer as well as his or her reasons for and expectations in writing the text depended on a history of interaction between storytellers and writers and their audiences. In biblical studies, the tradition of form criticism attempted to analyze these historical backgrounds for specific genres.

Unlike today, the vast majority of audiences interacted with stories, poems, and other genres by listening to them spoken aloud (oral-aural interaction) rather than through reading them (literacy). When the biblical texts were written, no more than 10 percent of the population could read and write. This means that the number of *readers* of any text would have been few. In such contexts, the prized stylistic features are whatever fosters an audience's aural recognition, memory, and enjoyment. Repetitions, set phrases and forms, and story types are among such strategies. These strategies form a background to any biblical writer's text.

The Writing of the Text. When actually writing, the author had a specific audience in mind. In other words, writers chose their material and shaped it with the expectation that it would be read by or read to a specific audience. This is typically called the *intended audience*. Such authorial decisions dramatically impact a text. Consider the difference between a book written for children and one written for college students: The vocabulary, complexity, and likely topics will be different based on the intended audience. The choice of allusions, references, idioms, rhetorical techniques, and topics was shaped with this intended audience in mind. For biblical texts, the few people who could read them likely shared very similar social, economic, and political circumstances with the writer. Thus, there is an important question as to whether any given text was intended for other literate writers of the time, for being read aloud to a wider oral audience, or merely for the benefit of the supernatural realm. Examples of the latter are probably rare in the Bible itself, but good examples would be foundation deposits uncovered during archaeological excavations. These are inscriptions that were buried in the foundation trenches of buildings and were thus only for the gods to read. It must be emphasized that while the intended audience is very important for how and why a text is written, there is also an implied reader.

The implied reader is how a given text's language and forms shape how a reader might respond to the text. It is neither the intended audience nor any real audience but a function of how a text shapes the ability of the reader to engage with it. Within the world of the biblical writers, this would include an assumption of other scribes who were trained in a similar way to themselves. Thus, the reader was somewhat familiar with the content of the text, and they would likely read the text aloud—even if only to themselves (reading aloud was common) or to apprentice scribes.

The Reading of the Text. Unlike oral speeches or interpersonal dialogue, where speech and listening are simultaneous, great distances in time and space can separate the intended audience and the implied reader of a text. Every single reader of the text is a new audience, regardless of whether their historical context is similar to or vastly different from that imagined by the author. Within the study of the Bible, concern generally falls on several different types of audiences: on the "original" audience, insofar as that might be reconstructed; on subsequent readers within the history of the development of the texts in Judaism and Christianity; on the receptions of more recent audiences through various media; and lastly, on scholarly reading itself.

In the historical study of biblical texts, assessing the intended and earliest audiences is crucial for breaking with modern assumptions to better understand the texts as historical artifacts. Considering the intended audience and the reception by likely audiences provides important insights into why the texts may have been written as well as the kinds of historical information they are likely to provide the historian. Key elements for this are the genre of a text, which is one way authors construct an implied reader and provide clues for their intended audience, and archaeological data, which provide contexts for where actual texts were found, used, and reused in real life.

Studies concerned with the formation of the Jewish and Christian communities and their canons are also concerned with who was reading these texts. Why these texts became important, why they were cited, copied, and rewritten, and how they became standardized into canons are all questions of this later audience for the texts.

The Bible continues to be read by scores of readers in various contexts. To understand how the Bible is interpreted and used by such readers requires explicit awareness of these new contexts. This is as true for rabbinic interpretations of the Torah as for uses of the Bible by the Protestant reformers and within contemporary popular culture. It also requires being keenly aware of the distance between modern readers and the earliest audiences of the texts—intended or real.

Lastly, it is important to remember that scholars are also a particular audience of the Bible. Some scholars are interested in the text as a historical source, some as a background to other media, and some in its usefulness for modern communities. All scholars, however, are still audiences of the text. The main difference between scholarly and nonscholarly audiences is an attempt at being rigorous in one's reading and in providing evidence and substantiation for one's approach to the text.

The latter point—that scholars attempt to be a rigorous and informed audience—highlights that every audience of the material engages with it differently. While scholars seek to control their interpretation through a close reading of the original languages, grammar, structure, historical contexts, and theoretical concerns, others read the text through the lens of a particular faith community and its presuppositions. Still others merely use it as a launching pad for concerns entirely external to the text.

When students and scholars pick up the biblical text, they are a brand-new audience for it in a context far removed from anything the author or editors could have imagined. Methods of dealing with this fact depend on the purpose of the reading—whether historiographical or creative—but it is essential and inevitable. One's appreciation for and use of the texts greatly improve through a conscious reflection on the space between previous audiences (intended, implied, and/or actual) and oneself.

About the Author

Jason M. Silverman earned a PhD from Trinity College Dublin. His research includes communication and social history in the Persian Empire and the Bible in film. He authored "Pseudepigraphy, Anonymity, and Auteur Theory," *Religion and the Arts* 15(4) (2011): 520–555.

Suggestions for Further Reading

In This Book
See also chapters 1 (scholarly perspective), 5 (canons), 8 (anonymity), 13 (genres), 35 (Philo), 28–31 (archaeology), 77 (literary and form criticism), and 83 (reception criticism).

Elsewhere
Esler, Philip F. *Sex, Wives, and Warriors: Reading Biblical Narrative with Its Ancient Audience*. Eugene, OR: Cascade Books, 2011.

Havea, Jione, and Monica Jyotsna Melanchthon. "Culture Tricks in Biblical Narrative." Pages 563–572 in *The Oxford Handbook of Biblical Narrative*. Edited by Danna Nolan Fewell. Oxford: Oxford University Press, 2015. https://doi.org/10.1093/oxfordhb/9780199967728.013.49.

Iser, Wolfgang. "Interaction between Text and Reader." Pages 1524–1532 in *The Norton Anthology of Theory and Criticism* (2nd edition). Edited by Vincent B. Leitch. New York: W. W. Norton, 2010.

Ong, Walter J. *Orality and Literacy*. London: Routledge, 2004.

Perry, Peter S. "Biblical Performance Criticism: Survey and Prospects." *Religions* 10(2) (2019): 1–15. https://doi.org/10.3390/rel10020117.

10
What Does "Tanak" Stand For?

Elaine Adler Goodfriend

The Hebrew Bible is an anthology of Israelite literature that was composed over a period of perhaps one thousand years from its earliest to latest works. While the Hebrew canon includes thirty-nine books, the traditional Jewish count is twenty-four, but this reflects a different way of counting the same works: the twelve minor prophets were considered as one, as they were all included in the same scroll, while Samuel, Kings, Ezra-Nehemiah, and Chronicles were considered as one book each and not two, as in later Bibles. While Hebrew is the primary language of the canon, Aramaic (a Semitic language of Syrian origin) is also found, mostly in the books of Ezra and Daniel.

While Christians generally refer to the Hebrew Bible as the Old Testament, the name preferred by Jews for the canon is Tanak (also written Tanakh), with each of the three consonantal letters standing for a distinct category of texts. The first is *Torah*, which means "teaching" or "law." It is composed of the five books traditionally viewed as God's revelation to Moses, hence its other designation as the Pentateuch (the five-volumed work). The second subcategory, the "N" of Tanak, stands for *Nevi'im*, or "Prophets," a diverse collection of works, both historical and poetic, yet all attributed to prophetic authorship. The "K" of Tanak stands for *Ketuvim*, "Writings," an appropriate designation for an assorted collection that includes narrative, poetry, wisdom sayings, and historical texts.

The original threefold division of Hebrew Scriptures is effaced somewhat in the Christian Bible, which is based on the order found in the Septuagint, the Greek translation of the Hebrew Bible that dates to the third through first centuries BCE. The Septuagint, a translation originally made by Jews for Jews, later became the official Bible of the Christian movement. There are many differences between the Septuagint and the Tanak, as the Greek version includes books and supplements to books (all of Jewish origin) that are absent from the Hebrew collection. Only the category of Torah, God's unique revelation to Moses, remains the same five works in both canons. Further, the subdivisions found in the Septuagint are fourfold and based on the more rational categories of literature and chronology. These divisions are Pentateuch, Historical Books, Wisdom Books, and Prophetic Books. For example, books with historical content (such as Chronicles or Esther) that the Tanak places in Writings are relocated in the Septuagint to its Historical Books section. The book of Ruth, which begins with the words "In the days when the judges ruled," is placed in the Septuagint immediately after the book of Judges, while in the Tanak, it is placed in Writings, the third section. Perhaps the Prophets was placed last in the Septuagint (in contrast to its central position in the Tanak) because it speaks of future events or because its immediate placement before the New Testament was considered meaningful for the Christian movement.

The three-part designation for the canon of Hebrew Scriptures is reflected in several references in Greek-Jewish writing to "the Law, the Prophets and the other Writings" (see Luke 24:44). While these earliest references date to the second century BCE, the tripartite division is likely centuries older. Unlike the Septuagint, this division is independent of genre or the period of history under discussion. Rather, the tripartite division represents three distinct and progressive stages of canonization, the process by which a collection of literary works is considered divinely inspired and authoritative. While we know little about the process of canonization, modern scholarship assigns the first of its three phases (the Torah) to the early Persian period (post 540 BCE) and its second phase, the closing of the Prophets section, to the late Persian period (fourth century BCE). The category called Ketuvim was more fluid and perhaps remained open into the early Roman period. Consider the book of Daniel, which contains miracle tales as well as visions of the distant future. Despite the fact that it presents itself as a product of the Babylonian/Persian periods (sixth century BCE), modern scholars assign it to the second century BCE because of allusions to later events. While the Christian canon includes Daniel in its Prophets collection (a reflection of its contents), the Tanak places Daniel in Writings, no doubt because Daniel's late date precluded it from finding a home in Prophets, a collection that was already closed. Another example is the historical work called Chronicles, which comes after Kings in the Septuagint's History section but, because of its relatively late date (fourth century BCE), was relegated to Writings in the Tanak. Keep in mind that while an individual book in the Ketuvim (for example, the Song of Songs) may be relatively early (perhaps dating to the period of the Israelite monarchy, 1000–587 BCE), this group as a whole was the last to be canonized, and other members of this group are generally later, dating to the Persian or Hellenistic periods (post 540 BCE). Thus, the date of the canonization of the group is not necessarily correlated with the dating of an individual work.

Within the last two categories of the Tanak, the Prophets and Writings, several subcategories are evident. The Prophets section consists of the Former Prophets, which is composed of narrative and historical texts with no mention of authorship. Jewish tradition, however, assigns to each of these works prophetic authors, which justifies their inclusion in the canon. Thus, the Talmud (*Baba Batra* 14B) records that the book of Samuel was written by Samuel even though he dies halfway through the work (1 Samuel 25:1), while Kings was written by the prophet Jeremiah. The second section of the Prophets, called the Latter Prophets, consists largely of the poetic orations of named prophets. Within this category, a distinction is generally made between "major" and "minor" prophets. This division is based on length and not importance: the Minor Prophets contains a total of sixty-seven chapters, about the length of the book of Isaiah alone. While the Prophets section is arranged in chronological order, the order of the eleven works found in the Writings varies according to the manuscript.

The thirty-nine works found in the Tanak were not the whole literary production of ancient Israel. Other books cited by the authors of the Tanak are the "Book of the Wars of the Lord" (Numbers 21:14), the "Book of Jashar" (Joshua 10:13; 2 Samuel 1:18), and various other royal annals no longer extant. The loss of this literature can be attributed to various factors: the absence of mass literacy, the perishability of writing materials, the change of script in the Persian period, and the various conquests visited upon the land of Israel.

About the Author

Elaine Adler Goodfriend holds a PhD in Near Eastern studies from the University of California, Berkeley. She writes about biblical and Jewish law. Her recent publications include "The *Qatlanit* ('Killer Wife') in Jewish Law: A Survey of Sources," *Women in Judaism: A Multidisciplinary E-journal* 17 (2020): 1–17; and "Why Is the Torah Divided into Five Books?," TheTorah .com, https://thetorah.com/why-is-the-torah-divided-into-five-books.

Suggestions for Further Reading

In This Book

Elsewhere

Brettler, Marc Z. "The Canonization of the Bible." Pages 2153–2158 in *The Jewish Study Bible* (2nd edition). Edited by Adele Berlin and Marc Z. Brettler. Oxford: Oxford University Press, 2004.

Brettler, Marc Z. "Canons of the Bible." Pages 453–458 in *The New Oxford Annotated Bible* (3rd edition). Edited by Michael D. Coogan. Oxford: Oxford University Press, 2001.

Sarna, Nahum M. "Bible Canon." Pages 814–836 in *Encyclopedia Judaica* (volume 4). Edited by Fred Skolnik and Michael Barenbaum. Jerusalem: Keter, 1972.

11
What Are the Pentateuch, Hexateuch, and Enneateuch?

Jean Louis Ska

The Sense of an Ending is the title both of the most celebrated work by the literary critic Frank Kermode (1967) and of a more recent novel by the British author Julian Barnes (2011). The title captures a basic human insight—namely, that we all try to make sense of our lives by looking at the end, sometimes at the "end of times." The same holds true in classical Western drama, where conflicts are resolved in the final act and the audience walks away with a sense of moral clarity. Without the resolution, the audience would not achieve any new understanding, and the play would likely have a short run. Similarly, readers might expect the first nine books in the collection known as the Tanak to deliver narratives with endings corresponding to its threefold division. The problem is that the narratives seem to overlap, and the endings are not where they might be expected.

Scholars have identified three possible metanarratives being told over the course of the first nine books in the Tanak. One runs from Genesis to Deuteronomy and is designated the Pentateuch because it covers five books. Another runs from Genesis to Joshua and is designated the Hexateuch (six books). The final one begins in Genesis and runs through the last chapter of Kings. This is called the Enneateuch (nine books), adding Judges, 1–2 Samuel counted as a single book, and 1–2 Kings counted as a single book to the Hexateuchal collection. All are modern constructions that do not coincide with the threefold division of the Tanak. All illustrate how our perception of the focus and meaning of the metanarrative changes depending on where we set its perceived ending.

Deuteronomy 34:10–12, for instance, is a watershed that gives unique importance to the first five books of the Old Testament. The statement "And there has not arisen a prophet since in Israel like Moses, whom the Lord knew face to face" (Deuteronomy 34:10) places Moses above all other prophets and grants the revelation he received from God a distinctive quality. With Moses's death, we reach the conclusion of the most important phase of God's revelation to Israel. Other texts are perhaps difficult to reconcile with this affirmation—for instance, Deuteronomy 18:15, 18, where God promises to raise a prophet like Moses in Israel, or Joshua 4:14, where it is said, "On that day the Lord exalted Joshua in the sight of all Israel, and they stood in awe of him just as they had stood in awe of Moses, all the days of his life." But Deuteronomy 34:10-12 is placed at a strategic point, right after the report of Moses's death and just before the beginning of Joshua's mission (see Joshua 1:1). We have good reason to assert that Deuteronomy 34:10-12 creates what has become the Pentateuch.

Something similar can be found at the end of the book of Joshua, which closes with a report of the deaths of Joshua and the priest Eleazar (Joshua 24:28-33). In Numbers 27:12-22, God had told Moses to appoint both of them, with different tasks, to lead Israel after Moses's death. Their deaths end another important phase of Israel's history—namely, the conquest of the land and its distribution to the different tribes. This phase is characterized by a special fidelity to Israel's God: "Israel served Yhwh all the days of Joshua and all the days of the elders who outlived Joshua and had known all the work that Yhwh did for Israel" (Joshua 24:31). The next phase, the period of Judges, is different according to Judges 2:7-9, which repeats Joshua 24:28-32 but adds, "And there arose another generation after them who did not know Yhwh or the work that he had done for Israel. And the people of Israel did what was evil in the sight of Yhwh and served the Baals" (Judges 2:10-11). This sentence sharply separates the golden age of Joshua from the ensuing period, a period of growing decadence.

The connection with the preceding Pentateuch is not as clear, but Joshua 1:1-2 informs the reader that Joshua had received from God the mission of completing Moses's task and conquering the land. For the informed reader, the conquest or the possession of the land is the fulfillment of a promise made to the patriarchs. To speak of a Hexateuch—a Pentateuch plus the book of Joshua—comes from a reading of the latter book in the light of the promises to the patriarchs present in Genesis, repeated in another form in Deuteronomy, and fulfilled by Joshua when taking possession of the promised land. But the biblical texts themselves are more implicit than explicit in this respect.

The most essential elements in favor of the idea of a Hexateuch are summaries starting with the patriarchs and ending with the conquest of the land, such as Exodus 6:2-6, Deuteronomy 6:20-25, 26:1-11, and Joshua 24:1-12. The reader, therefore, feels a necessity to read Joshua after the Pentateuch. But the book of Joshua refers only in general terms to older promises—for instance, in Joshua 23:14,

And now I [Joshua] am about to go the way of all the earth, and you
know in your hearts and souls, all of you, that not one word has failed
of all the good things that Yhwh your God promised concerning you.
All have come to pass for you; not one of them has failed.

Nowhere do we find a sentence about the possible fulfillment of what God
said to Moses in Exodus 6:8: "I will bring you into the land that I swore
[with lifted hand] to give to Abraham, to Isaac, and to Jacob. I will give it to
you for a possession." On the contrary, we read the following in Numbers
14:30: "Not one shall come into the land where I swore [with lifted hand]
that I would make you dwell, except Caleb the son of Jephunneh and
Joshua the son of Nun."

One more element may allow one to speak of a Hexateuch, but this
element is not exactly part of the substance of these books. I am speaking
of Joseph's bones. Joseph asks his brothers to bury his bones in Shechem
on the plot of land he received from his father (Genesis 50:25). Moses,
therefore, takes Joseph's bones with him when leaving Egypt (Exodus
13:19), and Joshua eventually buries these bones in Shechem after the
conquest of the land (Joshua 24:32). Nevertheless, as important as they can
be, three verses do not create a real plot. There is more in these six books
than the fate of Joseph's bones.

Another possible reading of the first part of the Hebrew Bible is as an
Enneateuch. In this case, however, only a few linguistic markers or clear
structural elements support the idea. For instance, 1 Samuel 12:1–12 is
another summary of Israel's past that begins, this time, with Moses, Aaron,
and the exodus and concludes with the choice of the first king, Saul. Israel's
monarchy is, therefore, one step more in the longer history of the people of
Israel. We find another clear allusion to the exodus in 1 Kings 6:1 in the
form of a date:

In the four hundred and eightieth year after the people of Israel went
out of the land of Egypt, in the fourth year of Solomon's reign over
Israel, in the month of Ziv, which is the second month, he began to
build the house of Yhwh.

These notations, however, are merely chronological. We are not told that the
monarchy or the building of the temple by Solomon are related to anything
particular in the Pentateuch. For instance, it is never said that the ark of the
covenant, built in the desert, finds its definitive dwelling place in Solomon's
temple or that this temple is a construction destined to substitute for the
(provisional?) tent of meeting that was built by Moses in the wilderness.

There are references to some elements in Exodus, however. For instance, in 1 Kings 8:9, in Solomon's prayer during the consecration of Jerusalem's temple, the following statement occurs: "There was nothing in the ark except the two tablets of stone that Moses put there at Horeb, where Yhwh made a covenant with the people of Israel when they came out of the land of Egypt." Again at the end of the same prayer, in 1 Kings 8:51–53, one reads,

> For they are your people and your heritage, which you brought out of Egypt from the midst of the iron furnace. Let your eyes be open to the plea of your servant and to the plea of your people Israel, giving ear to them whenever they call to you. For you separated them from among all the peoples of the earth to be your heritage, as you declared through Moses your servant, when you brought our fathers out of Egypt, O Yhwh Elohim.

This means that the people of Israel who are now celebrating God in Jerusalem's temple are the descendants of the people the same God brought out of slavery in Egypt, who are now living in the promised land. There is continuity in Israel's history and in Israel's worship.

The books of Kings end with the fall of Jerusalem, the exile in Babylon, and perhaps a note of hope with the restoration of Jehoiachin, king of Judah, by the king of Babylon (2 Kings 25:25–30). One important key to understanding these books is the importance of the covenant and the law. Unquestionably, not everything can be explained with the help of this key. Nonetheless, the tragic fate of both kingdoms, the kingdom of Samaria and the kingdom of Judah, is justified in some texts, especially in 2 Kings 17, by an explicit reference to the unfaithfulness of both kingdoms to God's covenant.

In the so-called Enneateuch, a few short texts that insist on the importance of the written law of Moses, often divine oracles, have been inserted into existing documents (e.g., Joshua 1:7–9; 23:1–16; 1 Kings 2:1–4). These texts are placed at strategic points in Israel's history: the conquest of the land and the first succession to the Davidic throne. The conquest of and the existence in the land as well as the stability of David's dynasty depend explicitly on faithfulness to the law. The book of the law is discovered in the temple under King Josiah (2 Kings 22–23). At this stage, the reader is invited to remember that the monarchy, the temple, the priesthood, and even prophecy will undergo the tragic events of the exile but that the law explains this course of events and, moreover, will survive and be the cornerstone of Israel's reconstruction. Other texts go in this direction: Joshua 24:1–28; Judges 2:1–5; 6:7–10 (absent from a Qumran fragment of Judges);

1 Kings 6:11–13 (absent from the Greek translation of the Septuagint); and 2 Kings 17:7–41.

Over time, scribes added a number of texts like those already discussed to the existing narratives and sequenced books that introduced new interpretations or new ways of understanding the events recounted. The additions also reinforced the sense of a longer, coherent metanarrative, whether intentionally or not. As elsewhere in the Old Testament, biblical writers did not completely rework their sources as Greek or Latin historians usually did; they added shorter or longer reflections to existing documents, adding new elements to older edifices rather than building new structures.

About the Author

Jean Louis Ska earned a doctorate in biblical exegesis from the Pontifical Biblical Institute. He is now emeritus in the same institute. His research includes studies on the Pentateuch and Old Testament narratives. He has published *Introduction to the Reading of the Pentateuch* (Winona Lake, IN: Eisenbrauns, 2006); *A Basic Guide to the Old Testament* (Mahwah, NJ: Paulist, 2018); and "Plot and Story in Genesis-Exodus and Joshua-Judges," pages 401–410 in *Book-Seams in the Hexateuch I: The Literary Transitions between the Books of Genesis/Exodus and Joshua/Judges*, edited by Christoph Berner and Harald Samuel (Tübingen: Mohr Siebeck, 2018).

Suggestions for Further Reading

In This Book
See also chapters 5 (canons), 10 (Tanak), 22 (periodization), 24 (Kings and Chronicles), 25 (Deuteronomistic History), 33 (Septuagint), 49 (Torah), and 52 (covenant).

Elsewhere
Barnes, Julian. *The Sense of an Ending*. London: Jonathan Cape, 2011.

Berner, Christoph. "The Attestation of the Book-Seam in the Early Textual Witnesses and Its Literary-Historical Implications." Pages 5–20 in *Book-Seams in the Hexateuch I: The Literary Transitions between the Books of Genesis/Exodus and Joshua/Judges*. Edited by Christoph Berner and Harald Samuel. Tübingen: Mohr Siebeck, 2018.

Kermode, Frank. *The Sense of an Ending: Studies in the Theory of Fiction*. Oxford: Oxford University Press, 1967.

Schmid, Konrad. "The Emergence and Disappearance of the Separation between the Pentateuch and the Deuteronomistic History in Biblical Studies." Pages 11–24 in *Pentateuch, Hexateuch, or Enneateuch: Identifying Literary Works in Genesis through Kings*. Edited by Thomas B. Dozeman, Thomas Römer, and Konrad Schmid. Atlanta: SBL, 2011.

12
Is There a "Book of the Twelve" or Are There Twelve Booklets of Minor Prophets?

Elena Di Pede

The books of the so-called Major Prophets (Isaiah, Jeremiah, and Ezekiel in the Hebrew Bible, plus Daniel in the Septuagint) are followed by twelve shorter prophetic writings that are considered a coherent whole, a book, in the Hebrew tradition: Hosea, Joel, Amos, Obadiah, Jonah, Micah, Nahum, Habakkuk, Zephaniah, Haggai, Zechariah, and Malachi (here in the Hebrew order). Since those writings are relatively short compared to the first group, they are called the Minor Prophets; the longest are Hosea and Zechariah, each with fourteen chapters, and the shortest is Obadiah, with only a single chapter. The notion of a single book, dubbed the Book of the Twelve/XII, is questioned in contemporary exegesis, at the levels of both the formation of the whole and its reception. Therefore, can we really speak of a "book" when referring to these twelve texts? Should we not consider each one a book(let) in itself?

Scholars have long focused on heterogenous elements within the collection and studied the twelve booklets separately. Each begins with a superscription naming the prophet, sometimes giving his ancestry (Zephaniah), his place of origin (Nahum), or his occupation (Amos). These "titles" reinforce the uniqueness of each booklet in relation to the others.

Thanks to the chronological indicators provided by the superscripts, some scholars thought they could reconstruct the career of each prophet and the historical development of Israelite prophecy and theology. Even when they noted the presence of shared vocabulary and themes among the XII, the focus was essentially on the editorial history, composition, and theology of each minor prophet. This exegetical approach, still practiced today, is not interested in the impression of unity—intended or not—that the whole can generate in the reader.

The emphasis on the unity of the whole as a "book" is recent. Its starting point is the overall unity of the prophetic books that goes beyond the complex history of their formation, which applies particularly to Isaiah. This approach seems to be rooted in scribal practice.

Ancient Hebrew and Greek manuscripts of the "scroll of the twelve prophets" have been used to argue in favor of a unity of the Twelve: Hebrew manuscripts are 4QXII from Cave 4 of Qumran and Mur88 from the caves at Wadi Murabba'at, written in the first century CE. In Greek, we have scroll 8HevXIIgr from the cave at Nahal Hever, also dating to the first century CE. Those manuscripts gather the Twelve on a single scroll. This is not necessarily a sign that they were considered together as a single book, because practical reasons would suffice to explain that they were copied on a single roll, but this fact is significant in itself.

The ancient Jewish tradition also testifies to a form of unity. The Talmud treaty *Baba Batra* (chapters 13–14) considers the Twelve to be a fourth prophetic book, in addition to Isaiah, Jeremiah, and Ezekiel, instructing the scribe (13b) to copy the Twelve together on a single scroll so that the smallest will not get lost. The Talmud of Babylon recommends separating the minor prophets with three blank lines instead of the four for the other biblical books, a sign of their close proximity. Sirach 49:10, written circa 200–175 BCE, refers to the Twelve Prophets as a coherent group, and the traditional counting of the biblical books attested in 4 Ezra 14:44–45 suggests that the Twelve are one of the twenty-four books dictated and read by Ezra. In his *Contra Apionem* (1:38–42), Flavius Josephus (ca. 37–100 CE) considers the Twelve to be one book, and Eusebius of Caesarea (flourished in the fourth century CE) reports that Meliton of Sardis, in the second century CE, spoke of the "twelve in one book" (*Historia ecclesiastica* IV, 26,14). All these elements plead in favor of the Twelve forming an anthology, where the order of the writings could vary.

The order of the first six booklets is slightly different in the Hebrew and in the Greek. The Greek order (Hosea, Amos, Micah, Joel, Obadiah, Jonah) seems more consistent from a geographical point of view: Hosea and Amos target the north, Joel focuses on the south, and Micah addresses both. The Hebrew Masoretic Text order reflects another theological elaboration that allows a pause, with Micah, between the salvation of Nineveh (Jonah) and the announcement of its destruction (Nahum).

The scribes who finalized the shape of the Hebrew Bible—the Masoretes—seem to have considered the Twelve a unit, without erasing the individuality of each booklet. They closed each biblical book with a colophon reporting the total number of verses and indicating the center of the book to avoid errors in copying. To respect the individuality of each prophet and the unity of the whole, they added a colophon at the end of each booklet and a global colophon at the end of Malachi that applied to the Twelve together.

Diachronic exegesis underlines the complexity of the editorial history of the corpus of the Twelve, which was probably preceded by "collections" gathering some of the booklets, possibly in forms different from those we know. Some scholars postulate that there was a desire for coherence of the whole at the editorial level. James D. Nogalski, for instance, examines the collection in the Hebrew order and proposes an interpretative model in which themes, quotations, and catchwords weave strong links that connect the end of one booklet to the beginning of the next. The titles are part of this editorial work that provides a historical frame: the different writings compose a history of prophecy from Hosea to Malachi, from the fall of the northern kingdom to the Persian era. This hypothesis highlights the importance of the insertion of Joel between Hosea and Amos and suggests that Joel is like a cameo that concentrates in itself the fundamental themes of the other booklets. According to Nogalski, the addition of Nahum, Habakkuk, and Obadiah is part of that same redactional work.

Ehud Ben Zvi and David J. A. Clines propose a different model. They disagree with the hypothesis of an editorial unification and believe instead that this unity takes place at the level of the receivers, the readers for whom the booklets were intended. Because these literati were attached to prophecy and prophetism, whose heritage they wished to maintain, they perceived the emergence of a unity and were able to recognize a form of coherence in the corpus. Thus, if the Twelve form a book, it is "by default" and not voluntarily. Other scholars, like David Petersen, think that one cannot speak of a deliberately unified whole and prefer to use the expression "thematized anthology." While drawing attention to common themes, the two models are limited to antiquity and the history of redaction, or of the first readership.

Another exegetical model has been developed in the field of synchronic exegesis. Paul House formulated the most original and most controversial hypothesis, studying the whole as a book in its own right, characterized by a unifying plot, a specific structure, and a literary genre. Using as a basis Aristotle's definition of "comedy"—a construction in which a character overcomes the adverse elements he or she encounters—House identifies an overall trajectory, a kind of plot that allows us to reread the history of Israel in three movements: Hosea–Micah (sin), Nahum–Zephaniah (punishment), and Haggai–Malachi (restoration). Without going as far as House, other scholars have studied the thematic links pinpointed by exegetes who seek to explain editorial history as a coherent and unified work. They put forward an overall chronological principle that seems to explain the Hebrew arrangement as well as important themes such as the "day of the Lord," *yôm Yhwh* (T. Collins; R. Rendtorff; J. D. Nogalski; P. House; M. Beck) or that of conversion (C. Bowman; J. LeCureux), which are, in fact, related themes.

The expression "day of the Lord" runs through the whole; it is present in each booklet except Jonah and Nahum. Its meaning is ambiguous because depending on the historical circumstances, it designates a happy or unhappy day. The expression provides a key to the temporal interpretation of the history of Israel. Its very ambiguity allows for an exploration and understanding of the reasons for the devastation and judgment as well as for the identification of what makes it possible to consider life still possible, beyond the destruction. All of this is obviously not unrelated to conversion, especially that of Israel, which, in the Twelve, unlike Nineveh, never repents (Jonah 3). The supporters of the unity of the Twelve believe that by exploring the theme of the "day of the Lord," this fourth prophetic book adds its own way of understanding the history of the covenant.

Whatever the adopted perspective, the question of the unity of the Twelve is not viewed unanimously. Depending on whether one considers the Twelve to be a set of individual and disparate booklets or a coherent literary whole, the approach is fundamentally different. From a canonical and theological point of view, perhaps it is not necessary to choose between these two paradigms, which enrich each other. Thus, to answer the question "A book of the Twelve or booklets of the minor prophets?" perhaps we should reply "Both, inseparably."

About the Author

Elena Di Pede holds a doctorate in theology from the University of Louvain. She teaches Old Testament exegesis and biblical languages at the University of Lorraine. Her research includes the prophetic books, especially Jeremiah, Ezekiel, Amos, and the Twelve as a book, about which she has edited and published a number of articles in French.

Suggestions for Further Reading

In This Book

Elsewhere

Ben Zvi, Ehud. "Remembering Twelve Prophetic Characters from the Past." Pages 6–35 in *The Book of the Twelve: One Book or Many? Metz Conference Proceedings 5–7 November 2015*. Edited by Elena Di Pede and Donatella Scaiola. Tübingen: Mohr Siebeck, 2016.

House, Paul R. *The Unity of the Twelve*. Sheffield, UK: Almond, 1990.

Knauf, Ernst Axel. "Kings among the Prophets." Pages 131–149 in *The Production of Prophecy: Constructing Prophecy and Prophets in Yehud*. Edited by Diana V. Edelman and Ehud Ben Zvi. London: Equinox, 2009.

Nogalski, James D. "Preexilic Portions of the Book of the Twelve: Early Collections and Composition Models." Pages 3–52 in *The Books of the Twelve Prophets: Minor Prophets—Major Theologies*. Edited by Heinz-Jozef Fabry. Leuven: Peeters, 2018.

O'Brien, Julia M., editor. *The Oxford Handbook of the Minor Prophets*. Oxford: Oxford University Press, 2021.

Petersen, David L. "A Book of the Twelve?" Pages 3–10 in *Reading and Hearing the Book of the Twelve*. Edited by James D. Nogalski and Marvin A. Sweeney. Atlanta: SBL, 2000.

Scaiola, Donatella. "The Twelve, One or Many Books? A Theological Proposal." Pages 180–194 in *The Book of the Twelve: One Book or Many? Metz Conference Proceedings 5–7 November 2015*. Edited by Elena di Pede and Donatella Scaiola. Tübingen: Mohr Siebeck, 2016.

Genres in the
Hebrew Bible

13
How Do We Determine Biblical Genres?

Diana V. Edelman

In school we are taught about different types of writing, called genres, and the conventions and expectations that go with them. So, for instance, a story that opens "Once upon a time" is instantly identifiable as a fairy tale, and the audience has no expectation that it will reflect actual events that took place in the past. We are familiar with categories like prose and poetry, fiction and nonfiction, historiography, lyrics, short stories, legends, epics, sagas, myths, contracts, speeches, legal briefs, recipes, and lists, to name a few. In each case, there will be typical features or contents that will allow us to recognize what genre is being used, and once we do, our minds will trigger an accompanying set of expectations.

The biblical writers seem to have worked with a different but overlapping range of genres than we have today, even if it is likely that more existed than the ones mentioned by name in the texts comprising the Old Testament / Hebrew Bible. Most interesting is how, on the one hand, some of their categories include a range of types we would separate into distinctive genres or subgenres and, on the other hand, how they lack terminology altogether to describe categories that are important today. Let us consider the main ones.

The *mashal* is basically a pithy saying; some translate it as "wisdom saying," others "proverb" or "byword." It often is a short, easy-to-remember aphorism that expresses a general truth. Examples include "Is Saul also among the prophets?" (1 Samuel 10:12) and "The parents have eaten sour grapes and the children's teeth are set on edge" (Ezekiel 18:2). The larger collection of sayings contained in the book of Proverbs is characterized as the *meshalim* (plural) of Solomon (1:1; 25:1). The uses of this term in Numbers 24:20–21 and 23 to describe the words that Balaam, son of Beor, immediately utters are additional examples, even if the earlier uses in 23:7, 18; 24:3, 15 do not provide direct quotes of short pithy sayings. In

Job 27:1 and 29:1, the term introduces much longer speeches that are not particularly pithy. A related category is the *hidah*, or "riddle." In Judges 14:12–14, Samson relates the following riddle to thirty young men at his wedding feast: "Out of the eater came something to eat. Out of the strong came something sweet."

The *shir* (masculine) or *shirah* (feminine) designates a poetically formulated composition. This includes psalms, love poetry, taunts, and a range of songs relating to drinking, the harvest, marriage, military victory, and work. What is unclear is whether all were set to music and sung aloud (thus songs) or some were recited as poems, which might be the case in Deuteronomy 31:19, 21–22, 30. The scribes recognized what we would likely make a subcategory in this genre known as the *qinah*, or "lament/dirge." It is marked by the use of "Alas" (*eyk* or *eykah*) as the opening word. Whether they would have considered it a separate category altogether is unknown.

The *'iggeret*, "letter," is a late term, probably a loanword from Assyrian *egirtu*. It occurs only in the books of Esther (9:26, 29), Nehemiah (2:7–9; 6:5, 17, 19), and 2 Chronicles (30:1, 6), all in the context of official correspondence or private letters written between officials, not letters written by ordinary people to other ordinary people. We do not know what the native Hebrew term was, even though we have examples of letters written on ostraca (pottery sherds) from the later part of the kingdom of Judah from the sites of Lachish and Arad, for example. The noun *miktav* means, literally, "that which is written" or "writing" more generally, not a letter specifically.

The *berit* is an agreement that seems to involve written terms, which also often was sealed with an oath. It typically is translated as "covenant" or "treaty," but it also can include written contracts and probably directives or instructions for royal employees. The word seems to be used to refer to both the larger bond established between the two parties involved and the written document that creates that bond by spelling out the conditions of its existence and, in the case of treaties, the consequences for the failure to uphold one of them.

Torah is usually translated as "law" but actually means "teaching." It can refer to a single instruction given by a priest, which might be oral (e.g., Leviticus 7:7, 37; 14:54; Numbers 19:14), or collectively, to a body of written teaching associated with Yhwh as its source (e.g., Exodus 24:12; 2 Kings 17:34) or Moses as the mediator of divine teaching (e.g., Deuteronomy 4:44; 31:9, 24, 26; Joshua 1:7; 22:5; 2 King 21:8; Nehemiah 8:14; 2 Chronicles 25:4). Something closer to what we consider a law or a regulation is a *mitzvah*, "that which is commanded/commandment," or a *hoq/huq*, "that which is inscribed," often rendered "statute." A *mishpat*, on the other hand, "that which is judged/judgment," might represent a sample case and its verdict, formulated conditionally. For example,

> If someone at enmity with another lies in wait and attacks and takes the life of that person, and flees into one of these cities [of asylum], then the elders of the killer's city shall send to have the culprit taken from there and handed over to the avenger of blood to be put to death. (Deuteronomy 19:11–12)

Various ancient Near Eastern cultures had written collections of such cases used to teach legal principles and phrasing but not what we call a "law code" today.

Finally, *devar Yhwh*, "word of Yhwh," is used to introduce a divine "direct quote" in prophetic books. Such words are written as poetry, not prose, like the *mashal* and *shir/shirah*. The noun *davar* has multiple meanings besides "word"—these include "speech," "matter," "affair," "act," and "thing"— but when used in a prophetic book, the term probably is meant to refer to a spoken word or words collectively. Prophets would receive divine messages in multiple forms; the ecstatics tended to experience visions and auditions while in an altered state of consciousness. Visions with no accompanying sound would need to be interpreted; auditions perhaps not. All experiences that resulted from actual acts of prophecy in the prophetic books would have been secondarily written down; scholars think some of the "divine words" have been composed as expansions or elaborations of older recorded words of prophecy. Thus, a case can be made that the written *debar Yhwh* was an intentional ancient Hebrew genre.

While we can distinguish the conventions of poetic and prose writing in Hebrew, no terms have been identified that describe either category. Similarly, there are no terms in Hebrew for fiction and nonfiction and for story or historiography. It seems that Hebrew scribes were taught a set of formulas and templates that were expected to be used in specific contexts. The conventions associated with poetry or heightened speech were used to convey wise aphorisms and bywords, lyrics, and divine speech in a memorable way, while prose was used for narrating stories or past events; for treaties, contracts, royal annals; and for official correspondence. The scribes knew what formats were appropriate in which contexts and used them as expected within their small circle of literate specialists.

Would the majority of the population, who were illiterate, have known and shared the same expectations as trained scribes when they encountered various genres? It is logical to suspect that the *mashal* and the *sir/sirah* were used at home orally and in local group settings to enculturate children, teach morality, and celebrate various happy events or alleviate the pain of unhappy events. Elders and perhaps traveling or local entertainers would also likely have told or performed stories, sagas, folktales, and legends at local village gatherings, so some of the conventions associated with prose would have been understood, even if encountered orally. Royal edicts may have been read out from time to time by messengers, and myths or "the mighty deeds of Yhwh" may have been read, told, or acted out at local or regional religious festivals during the monarchy.

The nonelite, general population likely would not have been familiar with written contracts, treaties, court annals, or letters. If asked, they probably would not have been able to list conventions for these forms. However, in a story or folktale, if they encountered a scene involving one or more women at a well, they would have been primed to expect a possible betrothal to follow. Or if the main character were introduced with a genealogy that made him a member of the seventh or tenth generation, they would have expected him to be destined for greatness.

When we read the collection of books comprising the Old Testament / Hebrew Bible, we read through the lenses of our own cultures and their genres, literary conventions, and the expectations that accompany them. We construe meaning on that basis, combined with personal experience. Awareness of the fact that the Hebrew writers did not share the same set of conventions or genres hopefully will spur a reader who encounters something that does not make sense in a biblical book to dig deeper into Hebrew and ancient Near Eastern literary conventions, genres, and accompanying expectations. By doing so, he or she may discover a plausible explanation that can render the nonsensical sensical. At the same time, an astute reader might wonder from time to time if the sense they have construed would also have been construed by an ancient audience member in light of these cultural differences and the expectations they trigger.

About the Author

Diana V. Edelman holds a doctorate of philosophy (PhD) in biblical studies from the University of Chicago and is Professor Emerita in Hebrew Bible at the Faculty of Theology, University of Oslo. She has published on various aspects of the Hebrew Bible in its ancient Near Eastern context, including some of its genres. One example is "Deuteronomy as the Instructions of Moses and Yhwh vs. a Framed Legal Code," pages 25–75 in *Deuteronomy in the Making: Studies in the Production of Debarim*, edited by Diana V. Edelman, Benedetta Rossi, Kåre Berge, and Philippe Guillaume (Berlin: De Gruyter, 2021).

Suggestions for Further Reading

In This Book
See also chapters 4 (sacred books), 9 (audiences), 24 (Kings and Chronicles), 51 (prophets), 52 (covenant), and 72 (synchronic vs. diachronic).

Elsewhere

Alter, Robert. *The Art of Biblical Narrative* (revised and updated edition). New York: Basic Books, 2011.

Carr, David M. *Writing on the Tablet of the Heart: Origins of Scripture and Literature*. Oxford: Oxford University Press, 2005.

Eissfeldt, Otto. *The Old Testament: An Introduction*. 1965. Reprint, New York: Harper & Row, 1974.

Niditch, Susan. *Folklore and the Hebrew Bible*. Eugene, OR: Wipf and Stock, 2004.

Pardee, Dennis. *Handbook of Ancient Hebrew Letters*. Chico, CA: Scholars, 1982.

14

Are There Myths in the Hebrew Bible?

James R. Linville

Whether the Hebrew Bible contains myths has concerned scholars for well over a century. Many passages in the Hebrew Bible have elements that closely resemble the mythology of Mesopotamia and Canaan. Still, biblical scholarship has systematically ruled out or downplayed the possibility of myth in the Hebrew Bible for much of its history. However, scholars are more likely to answer yes to this question in the modern world.

In the larger world of religious studies, anthropology, and related disciplines, scholars tend not to use a firm list of genre characteristics to determine whether a story is a myth. This term is used for countless kinds of stories, both long and involved and short and to the point, be they presented orally or in written form, in prose or poetry. Myths may or may not be used in rituals, and some may be acted out in drama or dance. Some myths may have a specific canonical text, yet a public recital may include countless expansions and improvisations by a master storyteller. Myths are not necessarily even religious in nature. Scholars often label stories of ethnic, national, or political significance as myths. The study of mythology, therefore, has many points of contact with the study of culture, politics, and social memory studies.

Every culture is unique, and each has its repertoire of narrative, poetry, or other texts telling its story, enshrining its values, and helping assert its identity over and against others. Each society has its system of categorizing and labeling its many kinds of narratives and other texts. Few, if any, of those labels may translate into English neatly as "myth," "legend," "saga," "fairy tale," or "history." "Myth" is a convenient academic label for the socially significant narratives of diverse societies, regardless of the genre categories those cultures may use. Regarding the Hebrew Bible, scholars are unsure how the ancient Israelites categorized their texts about the past.

Many scholars in the broader study of the world's religions use functional criteria to determine the applicability of the term "myth," looking at how a story may embody a society's sense of identity, purpose, values, and distinctiveness. Myths are generally regarded as stories people use to think about who they are, what they view as reality, and what makes a meaningful life. Such stories are frequently about the origins of the world or critical aspects of culture like kinship, leadership, laws, and customs. Deities, cosmic forces, or spirits are often given starring roles, but sometimes the divine has little role. Thus, a scholar might say such and such a story is a myth not because it has certain literary features but because it is used as a myth in a specific culture. Given this, one could argue that large portions of the Hebrew Bible may have served as a mythology for ancient Israelites and Judeans and continue to do so as well for modern Jews and Christians, because these texts are so central to how these people understood their world and societies. In this context, myth carries no negative connotations of untruth or irrationality.

Having said all of this, biblical scholarship has typically been reluctant to use the term about the Hebrew Bible. Much of this concerns religious and cultural biases that led European scholars to affirm the sharp distinction between the world views that produced the Bible and those of ancient Israel's neighbors. The Hebrew Bible itself is at pains to warn readers against doing as the foreign nations do, and scholars often sought to find evidence of that implied distinction at deep levels of the biblical text. Much of biblical scholarship grew out of liberal Christian theology that sought to bring religious belief in line with Enlightenment ideals that scorned superstition and fantasy in favor of applying critical reason to all areas of study. The result was that the Bible and myth were often understood as inherently incompatible. For some biblical scholars, myths were stories about multiple gods. Since ancient Israel only had one deity, their writings about that deity could not be myths.

Some scholars still hold that myth properly names stories set in a primordial epoch outside of historical time. For them, the Bible operates primarily in historical times, except for the creation accounts. Yet, it is frequently pointed out that the patriarchal narratives immediately follow these creation stories, so creation is more or less historicized. Additional arguments are made based on selective readings of work in comparative religion. Scholars such as Mircea Eliade (1954) noted how myth and ritual worked together in societies, including ancient Babylon, and brought together the world in which the practitioners lived and formative, primordial events. By performing a creation myth in a sacred time and place, the world itself would be renewed for another year. For many Bible scholars, the cyclical pattern of creation, breakdown, and re-creation seems fundamentally opposed to the onetime creation narrative in Genesis and its interconnected narratives that tell the story of Israel from Abraham to the end of the exile.

Countless pages have been written juxtaposing the myths of the Canaanites, Mesopotamians, and others against the supposedly historical mindset of the Israelites. The title of the famous study by Frank Moore Cross, *Canaanite Myth and Hebrew Epic*, implies the conflict the author saw between mythic modes of thought and the historical or epic perspective in much of the Old Testament. Thus, it was widely understood that Israelite scribes did theology in the context of writing history and scrupulously avoided mythmaking. Many scholars argued that the biblical passages that paralleled other ancient Near Eastern societies' myths were only superficially mythic or were deliberately "demythologized." Genesis 1:1–2:24 tells how a single deity creates all there is in six days and then has a day of rest. A general scholarly consensus grew that the Priestly writer appropriated many tropes from existing mythology but systematically reshaped them to eliminate their mythic character and illustrate the superiority of the Israelite God. Thus, the sun and the moon were demoted from being gods in their own right to inconsequential, inanimate creations of one god. Several passages outside Genesis's creation accounts refer to creation and a primordial period; some include references to Yhwh's slaying a dragon or defeating the sea (e.g., Psalm 74:12–17), motifs in Mesopotamian and Canaanite mythology. Yet, their appearance in the Hebrew Bible was explained as mere poetic figures of speech, "fragments of myth," or "faded" mythological references that suited poetic or imaginative styles but were hardly living Israelite mythology.

While the old way of thinking persists in many quarters, the denial of myth in the Hebrew Bible has become less popular over the past several decades, and excellent studies of the subject are not hard to find. Some in the new wave of biblical myth scholars claim that the notion of a myth-less Israel standing against its neighbors' mythic delusions is a modern myth that affirms some current religious claims to uniqueness.

With a non-genre-based definition of "myth" and one that emphasizes social function and status, none of these attempts to protect the biblical texts from accusations of including myths are valid. The creation narratives of Genesis say a lot about how an ancient society understood its deity and its complex relationship with flawed humans. The expression "charter myth" often labels narratives that establish or legitimize cultural institutions like political structures, kinship patterns, and rituals. The Bible has numerous such myths. The ancient Israelite and modern Jewish

Shabbat (Sabbath) is established by the Hebrew Bible's creation week story of the first day of rest. Exodus 20:2-17 contains the first recitation of the Ten Commandments. The longest of the ten demands that the people rest every seventh day (verses 8-11), as God did after creating. Many scholars point out the association between the Priestly creation account and later texts concerning the tabernacle and temple ideology. A connection between creation and ritual was common in the ancient Near East. One could also point to the book of Exodus and the first Pesach (Passover) story. The text is at pains to stress that the Israelites must remember the flight from Egypt by maintaining the prescribed rituals. To this day, Jews ritually recall how they, and not merely their ancestors, were slaves in Egypt. The original event becomes a recurring reality.

Because each society is unique and may have particular genres of stories that serve as myths, we should not regard biblical stories as myths only when they resemble those of other ancient Near Eastern cultures. Egyptian mythology differs in many ways from Babylonian mythology, and scholars need to inquire into what was unique about Israelite and Judean mythology. The Hebrew Bible is evidence that ancient Judah developed a concern with long-connected historical narratives to express national and religious identities and values. The scope of these narratives should not prevent us from recognizing this as mythology. The Japanese texts Nihon Shoki and Kojiki trace the imperial family back to the creation of the universe and the Japanese islands (Isomae 2010). This is a clear parallel to the kind of connection the Bible makes between the creation accounts and the patriarchal narratives in Genesis, the Israelite monarchies, and the exile. We should regard these as serving mythic purposes for their initial audiences (and later ones too).

The Israelite/Judean turn to an interconnected prose narration of the past represents a transformation of myth, not its replacement. Creation leads to the selection of Abraham and from him to an enslaved nation. In Exodus to Deuteronomy, one reads of the escape of the Israelites, the establishment of a priesthood, sacrificial services, annual pilgrimages, and interventions by God. Rules of purity and taboo are laid out, and a complex system of marking the sacred from the profane is outlined. Another great mythic complex in the Hebrew Bible is that of the exile, how the promised land was lost due to Israelite sin and their refusal to heed the prophets' warnings. That end is foreshadowed in numerous places in Joshua-2 Kings and rehearsed in Chronicles (with some level of resolution). Lamentations is woven around the tragic aftermath of the fall of Judah. Any other collection of stories with such essential religious and cultural elements would be called mythology by scholars of religion. The issue, then, is not whether there is mythology in the Hebrew Bible but how it served as a repository of mythology for its ancient audiences as they sought to build a world of meaning for themselves.

About the Author

James R. Linville received a PhD in Hebrew and Old Testament from the University of Edinburgh and is currently an associate professor of religious studies at the University of Lethbridge. He has written on myth in the Hebrew Bible's prophetic and historiographical writings—for example, "On the Authority of Dead Kings," pages 203–222 in *Deuteronomy-Kings as Emerging Authoritative Books: A Conversation*, edited by Diana V. Edelman (Atlanta: SBL, 2014); and "Myth of the Exilic Return: Myth Theory and the Exile as an Eternal Reality in the Prophets," pages 295–309 in *Concept of Exile in Ancient Israel and Its Contexts*, edited by Christoph Levin and Ehud Ben Zvi (Berlin: De Gruyter, 2010).

Suggestions for Further Reading

In This Book
See also chapters 3 (religious in a scientific world), 5 (canons), 7 (who wrote the Bible?), 13 (genres), 24 (Kings and Chronicles), 40 (holiness), 47 (monotheism), 48 (twelve tribes), 60 (Abraham), 53 (creation), and 74 ("P").

Elsewhere
Callender, Dexter E., editor. *Myth and Scripture: Contemporary Perspectives on Religion, Language, and Imagination*. Resources for Biblical Study. Atlanta: SBL, 2014.

Cross, Frank Moore. *Canaanite Myth and Hebrew Epic*. Cambridge, MA: Harvard University Press, 1973.

Csapo, Eric. *Theories of Mythology*. Oxford: Blackwell, 2005.

Eliade, Mircea. *The Myth of the Eternal Return, or Cosmos and History*. Princeton, NJ: Princeton University Press, 1954.

Isomae, Jun'ichi. *Japanese Mythology: Hermeneutics on Scripture*. London: Equinox, 2010.

Machinist, Peter. "The Problem of Myth in the Hebrew Bible." Speech given March 14, 2012, at the 2012 Annual Clifford Lecture, Boston College

School of Theology and Ministry, Continuing Education. https://www
.youtube.com/watch?v=9Un13LOBDFA.

Wyatt, Nick. "The Mythic Mind Revisited: Myth and History, or Myth
versus History, a Continuing Problem in Biblical Studies." *Scandinavian
Journal of the Old Testament* 22(2) (2008): 161–175.

15

Is There Apocalyptic Literature in the Hebrew Bible?

Emmanouil Gkinidis

The adjective "apocalyptic" is most familiar to readers of the Bible as a label for the last book of the Christian Bible, the Revelation of the Apostle John, or Apocalypsis in Greek. Revelation is an example of a wider scholarly genre labeled "apocalypse" or "apocalyptic literature," and examples of it are also found in the Hebrew Bible. Daniel 7–12 displays all the literary strategies and motifs that are distinctive to the genre. Yet, other passages such as Isaiah 24–27; 33–35, Jeremiah 33:14–26, Ezekiel 38–39, Joel 3:9–17, and Zechariah 12–14 use limited apocalyptic elements that had emerged before the Greco-Roman period (323 BCE–480 CE), which saw a vast production and circulation of apocalyptic texts. Recognizing the presence of exemplars of this genre in the Hebrew Bible allows us to understand responses generated during periods of crisis aimed at uniting a community to share a common mindset or galvanizing them into action.

John J. Collins (1979, 9) defines apocalypse as "revelatory literature with a narrative framework, in which a revelation is mediated by an otherworldly being to a human recipient, disclosing a transcendent reality which is both temporal, insofar as it envisages eschatological salvation, and spatial insofar as it involves another, supernatural world." An apocalypse narrates the journey of a human hero to otherworldly realities where he encounters a variety of creatures, divinities, and events he describes in great detail. In this journey, the hero is always accompanied by an immortal, supernatural being that is more than human but less than divine; it explains everything the hero sees, hears, and feels. To access these otherworldly realities, the hero goes through some sort of ritualistic death before receiving an eschatological prophecy.

A text is thus considered apocalyptic when it displays one or more of the basic literary motifs of the genre apocalypse. This realization has opened up brand-new fields of research in apocalyptic literature among texts from various epochs and cultures that share these features, even though they come from spatially and temporally diverse literatures.

The journey of the hero to other worlds stands out as the most basic apocalyptic feature. For every person in antiquity, the answers to the hard questions they asked themselves during their lifetimes, such as the meaning of life and the nature of injustice and hardships, would be answered after death and an assumed judgment that would take place in the afterlife. The other world—Hades, Sheol, heaven, or hell—was the real one, while the world in which they lived and died was a fictional one, a place of ephemeral joy, pain, and suffering.

The real world was the residence of the gods, the rulers of the universe and keepers of all the knowledge (gnosis). In an attempt to acquire some of this knowledge before death, every ancient Mediterranean and Near Eastern civilization developed religious and oracular techniques. Descriptions of the rituals used to ensure contact between humans and the divine and records of the gods' answers and advice dominate their religious literature.

The world view just described stands at the basis of every apocalyptic text, from the descent of Gilgamesh to hell, written in the second millennium BCE in Mesopotamia, to the late first millennium BCE Katabasis of Odysseus and Aeneas to Hades, the journey of Enoch to the end of the world in 1 Enoch, Isaiah's visions in his ascension, and the Revelation of John. In every apocalyptic narrative, the information that the hero acquires at the end, in either revelatory or prophetic form, stands out as the main reason the text was produced. The divine knowledge, a gift from the deities to their chosen one, the hero, leaves no space for criticism and doubt; it is the only fundamental truth, presented as a precious treasure to the faithful. They should follow it without hesitation or second thought.

Almost every apocalyptic narrative ends with an *ex eventu* prophecy— that is, a prophecy foretelling events that have already taken place but are presented as though they are still to come. The audience can confirm that the prophecy has been fulfilled. The credibility of the prophet is thus greatly enhanced, since he seems to have received knowledge about future events.

Besides *ex eventu* prophecies, apocalyptic narratives transmit moral teachings and the instructions of the divine for the moral and ethical guidance of believers. This realization becomes more apparent in the case of the monotheistic religions of the Greco-Roman world, which were characterized by the ever-growing influence and final prevalence of personal religion over the previously dominant communal type. This is when monotheism dominated over polytheism and when dualism as a profound and essential religious concept made its way into all aspects of daily life in every religion and mystical community.

However, such an important development in religions worldwide was far from random. The unification of the eastern Mediterranean and ancient Near Eastern worlds by Alexander the Great (338–323 BCE) marked an essential point in history when the coexistence of populations of diverse ethnical, cultural, and religious backgrounds led to a growth in the phenomenon of religious syncretism. Such syncretism had already begun under the previous Neo-Assyrian (911–609 BCE), Neo-Babylonian (626–539 BCE), and Achaemenid Empires (538–332 BCE). The apocalyptic way of thought and textual production were among the most significant features and values that the various ethnically separate groups of people lent to one another. The presence of major apocalyptic scenes and literary illustrations in Sumerian, Egyptian, and Greek literature testifies to the importance they had in the everyday life and religious traditions of those ethnic groups; notwithstanding, it is specifically in the Hellenistic (323–31 BCE) and Roman periods (27 BCE–480 CE) that apocalyptic literature was destined to grow and thrive as a main medium of ritual communication among the believers of the rapidly growing, or already present, monotheistic movements and religions, such as the Gnostics, the Hermetics, the Orphics, the Jews, the Christians, and later, the Muslims.

The prevalence of apocalyptic writing as one of the most influential and broadly used religious scribal styles lies in the distinctive character of its nature. Supernatural worlds, the judgment of the dead, otherworldly scenes, the luminous reality of heaven, and the eerie atmosphere of hell all allow the writers' imaginations to be set free and thrive without literary limitation. Apocalyptic language, or apocalyptic discourse, is the center of every apocalyptic activity, the instrument that sets in motion every part of the apocalyptic narrative.

This fact was well known to all apocalyptic writers, who always attempted to exploit the power of religiously oriented language. The main goal of every apocalyptic text is to prove to its audience the truth of its messages, advice, and prophecies—in other words, to persuade them about it. As primarily a tool of persuasion, apocalyptic language is bound to strict narrative and literary techniques that constitute a distinctive part of rhetorical language. Much like the ancient Greek rhetoric described by Aristotle, apocalyptic rhetoric also aims to convince its audience through depictions and illustrations rather than merely through the power of speech itself. Much pathos is obtained through descriptions of the fate of the righteous and the everlasting torments of the sinners to manipulate the emotions of the believing audience and prepare them for the voluntary acceptance of the sermons at the end of the narration.

A literary genre with such influence and power was not confined to community sermons, where it only would be heard by a few at a time in churches, synagogues, or temples in order to save their immortal souls from the bonds of their mortal bodies. On the contrary, it was produced primarily in order to affect the thoughts and actions of entire religious and ethnic groups in periods of crisis, when the collective mind needed to be rekindled, the defeated or those in mourning needed consolation, or the eschatological hopes of certain groups of people, scorned by their broader religious families, needed to be ignited. Such are the cases of Daniel 7–12, written to encourage Jews to maintain their religious beliefs and suffer martyrdom during the religious persecutions by Antiochus IV (168–67 BCE); 4 Ezra and 2 Baruch, texts that were produced to console the Jews over the destruction of the temple of Jerusalem in 70 CE; the Shepherd of Hermas, which was circulated in order to unite the Christians of Asia Minor against their persecutors during the second century CE; and the various texts of the apocalyptic sect of the Essenes, who constantly fought to keep their religious beliefs against mainstream Jewish Scripture.

As a primarily sociopolitical literary phenomenon, apocalyptic literature both influenced and was influenced to a great extent by various historical events while it helped shape the religious history and development of the major monotheistic religions in the Greco-Roman period. The power of its rhetoric was such that a large number of apocalyptic texts continued to be written during the Middle Ages, the Renaissance, and into our day and age.

About the Author

Emmanouil Gkinidis holds a doctorate of philosophy from the Democritus University of Thrace. His research includes apocalyptic rhetoric and discourse. He has published "Role Models as Moral Means of Persuasion in Apocalyptic Literature," *Marburg Journal of Religion* 21 (2019): 1–17, https://archiv.ub.uni-marburg.de/ep/0004/article/view/7819/8035; and "'To the Top of the World': Ascending Mountains in Apocalyptic Literature," *Marburg Journal of Religion* 21 (2019): 1–7, https://archiv.ub.uni-marburg.de/ep/0004/article/view/7818/8036.

Suggestions for Further Reading

In This Book
See also chapters 13 (genres), 34 (Dead Sea Scrolls), 43 (angels), 45 (heaven and hell), 46 (afterlife), 47 (monotheism), 51 (prophets), 61 (Melchizedek), and 70 (Satan).

Elsewhere

Carey, Greg, and L. Gregory Bloomquist, editors. *Vision and Persuasion: Rhetorical Dimensions of Apocalyptic Discourse*. St. Louis, MO: Chalice, 1999.

Collins, John J. *Apocalypse: The Morphology of a Genre*. Atlanta: Scholars, 1979.

DiTommaso, Lorenzo. "Apocalypses and Apocalypticism in Antiquity (Part 1)." *Currents in Biblical Research* 5(2) (2007): 235–286.

Portier-Young, Anathea E. *Apocalypse against Empire: Theologies of Resistance in Early Judaism*. Grand Rapids, MI: Eerdmans, 2001.

16
What Are Psalms Doing in the Hebrew Bible?

Bernard Gosse

The 150 poems in the book of Psalms employ the ancient Near Eastern principle of parallelism that typifies heightened speech throughout these cultures. The resulting repetition can make reading this biblical book tedious to anyone unfamiliar with Egyptian and Mesopotamian hymns and praises. Psalm 6:1, for instance, builds two synonymous half verses, stichs, or cola:

> O Lord, do not rebuke me in your anger, or discipline me in your wrath. (NRSV)

The second part of the verse simply repeats the first part with different words. The beginning of Psalm 96 is based on the same principle extended to three stichs:

> Sing to Yhwh a new song;
> sing to Yhwh, all the land;
> sing to Yhwh, bless his name (96:1–2; my translation)

Chiasmus is another poetic structure with three units, A-B-A' (B in the center framed by A and A')—for example, in Psalm 54, we have the following:

> Verses 3–5: Cry for help against enemies
> Verse 6: Confidence in Yhwh's support
> Verses 7–9: Thanksgiving for the victory

Chiasmus can be extended to larger blocks as A-B-C-B'-A' (in which case, the C stich forms the center), as in Psalm 58:

Verses 2–3: Injustice everywhere
Verses 4–6: Description of the evil ones
Verse 7: Calling out for God's help
Verses 8–10: A curse on the evil ones
Verses 11–12: Triumph of justice

This principle is even used to structure the entire Psalter into five books, with book 3 at the center, books 2 and 4 forming an inner frame, and books 1 and 5 the external frame.

Sometimes the poem is organized with refrains that repeat the same chorus, such as "Hope in God; for I shall again praise him" in Psalm 42:6, 11[5, 10] and 43:5, which shows that they are twin psalms.

Other psalms are built on the acrostic principle, using the first letter of each verse or line to convey a "hidden" message, such as "for Yannai and his wife," which dedicates Psalm 2 to the wedding of King Alexander Jannaeus (Yannai) and Salome Alexandra (ca. 100 BCE). Alphabetic acrostics are, however, the most common. Psalms 9–10 together; 25; 34; 37 in book 1 and Psalms 111; 112; 119; 145 in book 5 (see also Proverbs 31:10–31; Lamentations 1–4) cover the entire alphabet from *aleph* to *tav*. Each line starts with a letter of the Hebrew alphabet in the present order or in the ancient *pe-ayn* sequence attested in abecedaries (with the letter *pe* before *ayn*), as was probably the case in Psalms 9–10.

Psalm 119 is a scribal feat that pushes the alphabetic principle to the extreme, with 8 verses for each of the twenty-two letters, making it the longest psalm. All 176 verses express a single idea: the praise of the Torah. The word "torah" occurs twenty-five times in Psalm 119 (originally twenty-four?) besides seven synonyms, producing a sheer repetitiveness. As is the case with the five-part architecture of the Psalter, it is the structure more than the explicit meaning of individual verses that conveys the theological message of alphabetic psalms: wholeness, creational order as a mirror image of Genesis 1, or something else.

Alphabetic anomalies are significant and should not be systematically explained to have resulted from textual corruption. For instance, Psalms 9–10 omit all the letters from *mem* to *sade*, and the last verse of Psalm 34 starts with *pe*. That the purpose of alphabetic anomalies is elusive to us today does not necessarily mean that these scribes were incompetent.

Unfortunately, acrostics are lost in translation, because the Hebrew alphabet has only twenty-two letters, and not all of them have a corresponding letter in other languages (i.e., *khet, tet, ayn, ṣade*). Nevertheless, the Greek and Latin translations of the Psalter remember the alphabetic structure by counting Psalms 9 and 10 as a single psalm. This has led to a difference in numbering between the Hebrew text, which contains Psalms 11–113, and the Greek and Latin versions, which number these same hymns as Psalms 10–112. Further numbering differences occur throughout the collection:

Hebrew	Greek, Latin, Orthodox and older Catholic
1–9	1–9A
10	9B
11–113	10–112
114	113A
115	113B
116	114–115
117–146	116–145
147	146–147
148–150	148–150

While English Bibles tend to follow the Hebrew numbering, Orthodox and older Catholic Bibles, lectionaries, and missals use the Greek (and Latin) numbers. Hence, after a psalm number, one sometimes finds a second number between square brackets—for instance, the famous verse "the Lord is my shepherd" may be referred to as Psalm 22[23]:1 or Psalm 23[22]:1, depending on which system is treated as primary.

In addition to acrostics, the Psalter displays other scribal techniques. Psalm 42 introduces the Elohistic Psalter (Psalms 42–83), thus designated because the term 'elohim (God) occurs some 210 times, whereas "Yhwh" occurs only 44 times, in contrast with the rest of the Psalter in which "Yhwh" predominates. The title of Psalm 42 makes it the first psalm ascribed to the "sons of Korah" and the first part of this collection (42–49), which begins forty-two psalms later at Psalm 84, to amount to the symbolic total of twelve.

More than a debate over theological issues, the differences are likely to reflect the rivalry between different guild-like groups of scribes who defended their prerogatives by evoking illustrious biblical figures. For instance, the titles of Psalms 73–83 are attributed to Asaph, a collection that precedes the second group attributed to the sons of Korah (Psalms 84–85; 87–88).

The mention of Korah's death in the aftermath of the revolt of Nathan and Abiram (Numbers 16), but whose sons did not perish (Numbers

26:11), may be posterior to Psalm 106:16–17. It would be the result of the opposition of the pro-Davidic Asaphites to the Korahites.

Scribal training involved mastering arithmetic to draw up ledgers and other economic records. Scribes displayed their accounting skills by including such numerical games in the psalms. There may even be an intentional reference to the forty-two psalms of Korah in the forty-two boys who jeered at Elisha's supposed baldness and were mauled by two she-bears (2 Kings 2:23–24). Scholars today tend to ignore such games because they lack the seriousness expected in an academic study of the Bible. Yet, ignoring the titles or superscriptions of the psalms misses some of the richness of the Psalter.

The evidence from the Dead Sea Scrolls shows that the attribution of certain psalms to King David was a contested issue because it involved a complete recasting of the figure of the great warrior and ruthless politician in the books of Samuel. Nevertheless, the metamorphosis of David ensured the success of the Psalter in Jewish and Christian literature; it allowed believers to identify with the figure of a meek David who suffered, for instance, from the machinations of enemies such as Saul. (Psalm 18 equates "She'ol" in verse 6 with "Saul"; the two words share the same consonants). The title of Psalm 51 even evokes the Bathsheba affair (2 Samuel 11) to make David the symbol of the repentant sinner thoroughly restored by God's mercy.

As a whole, the Psalter presents itself as a second Pentateuch. It is divided into five books; the end of each one is marked by a double amen (Psalm 41:13; 72:19; 89:53) or an alleluia (106:48; 150:6). This internal division is completed by a general introduction to the entire Psalter (Psalms 1 and 2) and a general conclusion represented by Psalms 146–150, all of which begin and end with an alleluia.

All the psalms of book 1 (3–41) have a title mentioning David to identify him with the figure of the poor under Yhwh's care (see Psalms 9:13, 19; 10:2, 9, 12; 12:6; 14:6; 18:28; 22:25; 25:16; 34:7; 40:18).

Book 2 (Psalms 42–72) is constituted of two groups: Psalms 42–49, attributed to the Korahites, followed by a first psalm of Asaph (50), which marks the transition to a second group attributed to David (51–72). Whereas the titles of Psalms 51–72 recall David's wars from the books of Samuel, the Korahite psalms shift the focus away from David toward Jerusalem and Zion, both of which were miraculously saved by the Lord of Hosts (Psalm 48:9).

Book 3 (73–89) begins with Asaph psalms (73–83) focused on the fall of Jerusalem (74; 79). Psalm 77:21 (or verse 20 in Greek and Bibles that ignore titles) has the sole mention of Moses outside book 4 to anticipate the function of Moses as a counterpart to David (78:70–72) in book 4. The second part of book 3 (particularly Psalms 84–85 and 87–89) underlines the failure of the promises made to David following the fall of Jerusalem and the destruction of the temple. Psalm 89 closes book 3 with a note on the demise of the Davidic dynasty while reaffirming Yahwism that is downplayed in the Elohist Psalter (42–83).

Moses is the central figure of book 4 (90–106), beginning with the title of 90:1: "A Prayer of Moses, the Man of God." Moses is then named in 99:6; 103:7; 105:26; and 106:16, 23, 32.

The first psalm of book 5 (Psalm 107) underlines Yhwh's steadfast love, which endures forever, to indicate that the eclipse of David in book 4 is not final. David reappears twenty-one times in the body of book 5. Though Yhwh had sworn to David that one of his sons would reign after him (Psalm 132:11), beginning in the third generation, dynastic continuity is conditional on the observance of Yhwh's covenant (Psalm 132:12). Whatever happens to David's line, Zion is Yhwh's choice forever.

The mention of musical indications in the titles of many psalms suggests that they were used in temple service in Jerusalem and elsewhere and that some, if not all, of the scribes involved in the complex history of the Psalter were involved there as musicians. Yet, the dearth of nonbiblical evidence for the actual performance of the worship of Yhwh prevents one from drawing firm conclusions regarding the function of the psalms before the rise of synagogues.

About the Author

Bernard Gosse earned a doctorate from the Sorbonne. He has published dozens of articles on the psalms, the latest in English being "Deuteronomy's Influence on the Formation of the Psalter," in *Deuteronomy: Outside the Box*, edited by Diana V. Edelman and Philippe Guillaume (Sheffield, UK: Equinox, forthcoming). He also has authored *David and Abraham: Persian Period Traditions* (Paris: Gabalda, 2010); and "David and Moses in Post-exilic Times," pages 43–58 in *Innovation in Persian Period Judah*, edited by Jill Middlemas (Tübingen: Mohr Siebeck, 2023).

Suggestions for Further Reading

In This Book
See also chapters 8 (anonymity), 11 (Pentateuch), 13 (genres), 33 (Septuagint), 47 (monotheism), 52 (covenant), 63 (Moses), and 65 (King David).

Elsewhere

Amzallag, Nissim. "The Cosmopolitan Character of the Korahite Musical Congregation: Evidence from Psalm 87." *Vetus Testamentum* 64 (2014): 361–381.

Brown, William P., editor. *The Oxford Handbook of the Psalms*. Oxford: Oxford University Press, 2014.

Mitchell, David C. "'God Will Redeem My Soul from Sheol': The Psalms of the Sons of Korah." *Journal for the Study of the Old Testament* 30 (2006): 365–384.

Orton, David E., editor. *Poetry in the Hebrew Bible: Selected Studies from Vetus Testamentum*. Leiden: Brill, 2000.

Schuller, Eileen M. "Psalms, Hymns, and Prayers in Late Second Temple Judaism." Pages 5–23 in *Functions of Psalms and Prayers in the Late Second Temple Period*. Edited by John Barton, Ronald Hendel, Reinhard G. Kratz, and Markus Witte. Berlin: De Gruyter, 2017.

17
Wisdom: Where Is It Found?

Michael C. Legaspi

Among things that many readers hope to find in the Hebrew Bible, wisdom surely ranks high. Though the path to understanding wisdom in the Hebrew Bible is not simple or direct, those interested in it will find there a good deal to consider. Whether "wisdom" is named explicitly by the noun *hokmah* and related verbal and adjectival forms or treated indirectly, wisdom features in all parts of the Jewish canon: Torah, Prophets, and especially, Writings. The Greek canon includes a book known as Wisdom of Solomon and another, Ecclesiasticus (Sirach), which is distinct from Ecclesiastes, whose Hebrew name is Qohelet.

What, first of all, *is* wisdom? Though often regarded as a virtue or personal endowment, wisdom was, in ancient Israel (and in ancient Greece, Egypt, and Mesopotamia as well), something that corresponds to the cosmos. Though the word "wisdom" does not appear in the opening chapters of Genesis, the creation accounts nevertheless provide a basic framework for understanding it. God brings forth the created world in a sequential, rational, and deliberate manner. Out of chaos comes a pleasing and hospitable structure to which creatures are especially suited. The world is ordered and harmonious, fit for life. In Genesis, aspects of this situation are described as "good" (Genesis 1:10, 12, 18, 21, 25, 31). Psalm 104, referring to this goodness, identifies wisdom as the hallmark of creation: "O Lord, how manifold are your works! In wisdom you have made them all; the earth is full of your creatures" (Psalm 104:24). The same link between wisdom and creation appears in the prophets as well (Jeremiah 10:12; 51:15). For this reason, wisdom might be likened to a kind of cosmic blueprint or, as James Kugel (1997, 10) writes, "the great set of master plans by which the world—the natural world, of course, but also human society—was governed."

Yet there is more to wisdom than the static order suggested by a blueprint or set of plans. The book of Proverbs contains a remarkable series of passages in which wisdom is personified (Proverbs 8–9). Because the noun *hokmah* is grammatically feminine, the personification of wisdom in Proverbs is often called Lady Wisdom. In accord with the idea of a world made in or by wisdom, she identifies herself as the first of God's creatures (Proverbs 8:22) and a master worker (Proverbs 8:30) who rejoiced by God's side when God brought forth springs, hills, sky, and sea (Proverbs 8:22–31). The point, however, is not merely cosmic order; the same Lady Wisdom sponsors precepts that guide social, political, and ethical life as well. As wisdom was identified with rulership in many ancient societies, so it is by Lady Wisdom that kings reign, princes rule, nobles govern, and rulers decree what is just (Proverbs 8:15). Yet Lady Wisdom is not only concerned with the political elite; she addresses ordinary people in the streets, on the paths, and at the city gates, urging them to forsake pride and dishonesty (Proverbs 8:13) and embrace piety ("the fear of the Lord"), diligence, and discretion.

In one sense, then, wisdom (or Lady Wisdom) is everywhere, at work both in cosmic oversight and in decrying everyday human folly. In another sense, wisdom is decidedly local, for the Hebrew Bible also describes wisdom as a divine grant, a kind of moral and intellectual faculty that God bestows on individuals in particular circumstances. Perhaps the most famous example is King Solomon. Given the opportunity to ask anything of God, Solomon, instead of requesting success, long life, or riches, asked for an "understanding mind" (1 Kings 3:9) by which to govern Israel. God then bestowed prodigious wisdom on Solomon (1 Kings 4:29), making him the biblical figure most renowned for wisdom and the inspiration for literary works devoted to wisdom.

Often overlooked, though, are the special grants of wisdom made to craftsmen who participated in the construction of the tabernacle in the wilderness (Exodus 31:1–11) and the temple in Jerusalem (1 Kings 7:14). Though *hokmah* is often translated as "skill" or "ability" in these passages, the Hebrew word used here is the same word used for "wisdom." Just as Solomon used wisdom to build the kingdom of Israel and govern it effectively, so wisdom was needed to build Israel's sacred spaces. Contact with God in cultic settings and via cultic objects was fraught with peril (Leviticus 10:1–7; 1 Samuel 5–6; 2 Samuel 6:1–11). Tremendous care was needed to ensure that the cultic apparatus was configured appropriately and that sacrifices were offered properly. In the world view of the biblical writers, failure to do these things would lead to the destruction that Proverbs identifies with folly. Conversely, the ability to do these things well was seen to arise from wisdom.

By noting the significance of wisdom in the religious as well as the cosmic, ethical, and political spheres, one sees that wisdom encompasses all of life. It has as much to do with the order of things as with the active power needed to bring diverse dimensions of life into ongoing conformity with that order.

Given the forbidding scope of wisdom, so understood, it is appropriate to ask how humans can attain such a thing. It seems fit to ask where wisdom can indeed be found (Job 28:12). The foregoing makes clear, in the first instance, that wisdom may be found with God. Wisdom is, so to speak, at God's disposal. Like God, who is said to be everywhere (Psalm 139:7–12) and yet especially present in certain places like the tabernacle or temple (for example, Exodus 40:34; Isaiah 6:1–5), the domain of wisdom seems to include the universal and the particular. Thus arises the paradox of wisdom; it may be "here" because it is everywhere but, at the same time, "not here" because a specific person lacks wisdom.

One of the most famous passages on wisdom in the Hebrew Bible is the Hymn to Wisdom found in chapter 28 of the book of Job. In this poem, the poet uses spatial metaphors to explore the paradox. The text takes the reader on a journey to the extremities of creation: from the depths where people seek precious metals, to high mountains where birds of prey soar, to seas that cannot be fathomed. Amid the splendid strangeness of these places, the reader learns that wisdom cannot be located. Not even the savvy denizens of the underworld know where to find wisdom; they know it only by rumor (Job 28:22). Yet it is present. God knows the way to it (Job 28:23). The inaccessibility of wisdom, portrayed here in geographic terms, suggests that wisdom takes a certain kind of effort to find. Wisdom is available (present) yet elusive (not obviously present).

The effort involved in obtaining wisdom is not like the determination of the entrepreneurial miners featured in the Hymn to Wisdom, who ultimately possess what they unearth. It is, instead, the effort of an explorer traveling through unfamiliar terrain in the dark, guided by someone whose instructions must be followed fastidiously. Though God knows the way to wisdom, the deity does not disclose its full extent—merely its beginning. The only counsel offered by the poet is to hew closely to God while underway: "Truly, the fear of the Lord, that is wisdom; and to depart from evil is understanding" (Job 28:28). In this way, one not granted wisdom may still arrive at it.

The sentiment is echoed in the book of Ecclesiastes. Like the book of Proverbs, the book of Ecclesiastes is connected to Solomon. The narrator of the book identifies himself as the "son of David, king in Jerusalem" (Ecclesiastes 1:1), who "acquired great wisdom" (Ecclesiastes 1:16). Thus, the narrator presents himself as a Solomon-like figure. He is a great sage who professes to search out wisdom and take on the difficult task of explaining what the ultimate point of human life is. But unlike the Solomon who commends wisdom in Proverbs, the narrator of Ecclesiastes is an anti-Solomon who questions the efficacy of wisdom. In a tortuous narrative that appears at times to follow his stream of consciousness, he comes repeatedly to the conclusion that life is vanity: "Vanity of vanities. All is vanity" (Ecclesiastes 1:2). Pleasure, wealth, power, and education yield no lasting benefit to humans.

Conventional notions of success based on received wisdom do not hold up in experience: time and death frustrate human attempts to discover lasting meaning, leave durable legacies, or transcend the mundane through piety. He reports,

> Again I saw that under the sun the race is not to the swift, nor the battle to the strong, nor bread to the wise, nor riches to the intelligent, nor favor to the skillful: but time and chance happen to them all. (Ecclesiastes 9:11)

The juxtaposition of Ecclesiastes and Proverbs, with their radically different perspectives, is one of the most striking features of the biblical canon.

Yet it would be a mistake to see Ecclesiastes simply as a book aimed at negating the value or efficacy of wisdom. The narrator commends wisdom, stating that it can be helpful in governing (Ecclesiastes 7:19), offsetting the military superiority of an opponent (Ecclesiastes 9:13–18), finding modest success in one's work (Ecclesiastes 10:10), incurring favor in social situations (Ecclesiastes 10:12), and in other limited ways. This does not mean that one can comprehend wisdom in any full or final way. One may *use* the teachings of wisdom, but no one can *possess* wisdom or *become wise* in a way that insulates them from frustration and finally solves the riddle of existence. As the narrator puts it, "All this I have tested by wisdom; I said, 'I will be wise,' but it was far from me. That which is, is far off, and deep, very deep; who can find it out?" (Ecclesiastes 7:23–24). As in Job's Hymn to Wisdom, the substance of wisdom is, for Ecclesiastes, inaccessible. The best course of action is to accept the inscrutability of life, embrace one's limits, and live modestly—in other words, to live according to the "fear of God" (Ecclesiastes 3:14; 8:10–13; 12:13–14).

About the Author

Michael C. Legaspi holds a PhD from Harvard University. His research includes the history of biblical scholarship and the concept of wisdom in ancient thought. He has published *The Death of Scripture and the Rise of*

Biblical Studies (Oxford: Oxford University Press, 2010); and *Wisdom in Classical and Biblical Tradition* (Oxford: Oxford University Press, 2018).

Suggestions for Further Reading

In This Book
See also chapters 10 (Tanak), 15 (apocalyptic literature), 18 (Proverbs), 19 (Job), 65 (King David), 68 (Jeremiah), and 71 (Qohelet).

Elsewhere
Brague, Rémi. *The Wisdom of the World: The Human Experience of the Universe in Western Thought.* Translated by Teresa Lavender Fagan. Chicago: University of Chicago Press, 2003.

Kugel, James. "Wisdom and the Anthological Temper." *Prooftexts* 17 (1997): 9–32.

Weeks, Stuart. *An Introduction to the Study of Wisdom Literature.* London: T&T Clark, 2010.

18

What Is the Purpose of Proverbs?

Sonny E. Zaluchu

Like the Psalter, the book of Proverbs does not record narratives or prophecies but short sentences that often stand by themselves. They deal with
very practical issues of daily life, offering teachings, advice, guidelines,
warnings, and reprimands about how to live wisely at home, on the streets,
at the market, in the court, and wherever humans interact with others. In
short, these proverbs encourage their readers to live wisely by choosing
the right path; the right choice will produce good things, while the wrong
choice will have detrimental effects.

The introduction relates wisdom, understanding, insight, justice, and
discernment with the fear of Yhwh (Proverbs 1:2–7). Wisdom (*hokmah*)
implies that knowledge and expertise are not enough for a successful life.
In the view of Proverbs, knowledge and expertise come from Yhwh, so
people have to fear the deity to get it. If not, humans who ignore Yhwh
have to rely on their strengths, which are insufficient to deal successfully
with life's challenges.

Proverbs warns that human knowledge and expertise are very limited
and that much remains mysterious. For instance, three, even four, things
are too wonderful to comprehend: the way of an eagle in the air, the way
of a serpent upon a rock, the way of a ship amid the sea, and the way of a
man with a young woman (Proverbs 30:18–19). Today, we can evoke simple physical laws to explain the first three examples: how bodies heavier
than air can fly, how legless animals can move, and how ships can float
despite their cargo. But their course and subsequent position cannot be
determined with certainty, despite knowledge of their previous trajectory.
The fourth example is equally shrouded in mystery; psychological science
cannot unravel the mysteries of life. As much now as in antiquity, men
remain baffled at the way women think and act. No law will account for
love, and thankfully so.

These four examples illustrate the pedagogy of proverbial wisdom,
which begins with somewhat trite observations but soon leads to profound

issues upon further reflection. Science is no different; each scientific advancement introduces new questions and possibilities, highlighting the fundamental uncertainty of knowledge and its intrinsically tentative nature. In this sense, uncertainty is one of the themes of the Bible that unites science and religion. Ignoring uncertainty leads to dogma.

The limits of the human mind become particularly obvious when it comes to predicting the future. There are simply too many variables to take into account. Nevertheless, it is wise to anticipate, plan ahead, and expect arbitrariness and irregularity. Proverbs makes a strong case for the necessity of wisdom from Yhwh to prevent humans from making foolish choices.

The entire collection is ascribed to King Solomon (Proverbs 1:1), the paragon of the wise man who, according to 1 Kings 4:32, composed three thousand proverbs. Only about eight hundred of them are recorded in the book of Proverbs. Yet, some proverbs present similarities with other proverbial traditions, in particular the Egyptian collection of Amenemope, estimated to have been written around 1240–945 BCE. An English translation and bibliography of these proverbs are provided in Itibari Zulu (2009, 18–33).

For instance, both Amenemope and Solomon point out the importance of choosing with whom to associate:

Make no friends with those given to anger, and do not associate with hotheads. (Proverbs 22:24)

Do not deal with an intemperate person, nor associate yourself with a disloyal party. (Zulu 2009, 25)

Do not get into a quarrel with an argumentative person, or incite with words. (Zulu 2009, 18)

Though the Bible insists that Solomon was wiser than anyone else (1 Kings 4:31), the similarities with Egyptian proverbs are consistent with the notion that he married an Egyptian princess (1 Kings 7:8). Claiming that the source of wisdom is Israel's God does not prevent an appreciation of the wisdom of neighboring people. If Yhwh is indeed the only God, it has granted wisdom to other people besides its own.

The international nature of wisdom is further displayed by the attribution of Proverbs 30 to an otherwise unknown Agur, son of Jakeh, and chapter 31 to King Lemuel, who was neither a Judahite nor Israelite monarch listed in the book of Kings. Agur's writings read as a veiled parody of the Teacher, the son of David, to whom the book of Ecclesiastes, or Qohelet, is ascribed (Qohelet 1:1). The words of Agur display a number of parallels with Arab proverbs, in particular numerical maxims (Proverbs 30:18, 21, 24). The similarities with Arab proverbial traditions tie up with the presentation of the hero of the book of Job as the greatest man of the East (Job 1:3) to broaden the biblical horizon that otherwise remains focused on a narrow portion of the Fertile Crescent, Israel, its laws, its kings, and its prophets. The so-called biblical wisdom literature (the books of Job, Proverbs, Ecclesiastes, and Song of Solomon, to which can be added Ruth) counters cultural chauvinism by inviting readers of the Bible to learn from other cultures and from other creatures: the mighty lion as well as less impressive ones like roosters, ants, and even leeches (Proverbs 6:6; 30:15, 25–31). Jesus's parables are equally steeped in proverbial tradition by evoking birds, lilies, grass, and righteous foreigners.

In addition to its international nature, the book of Proverbs under-lines wisdom's timeless and oral character by ascribing chapters 25–29 to the scribes of King Hezekiah, who ruled centuries after Solomon (Proverbs 25:1). This section contains much advice on how young elite men must behave appropriately at court, where the main enemy is one's own tongue, while self-control is crucial to avoid the common pitfalls that await young fools. This can only be achieved if one submits himself to the rod of formal education, not simply as part of parental upbringing, but also in the course of apprenticeship by a scribal master. In this section at least, proverbial wisdom goes beyond the traditional folk sayings drawn from the expe-rience of the natural seasonal rhythms in an agricultural community. It applies to the training of elites rather than ordinary people.

The moral stance of Proverbs is traditional and upholds the pillars of society such as marriage. Sexual ethics are prominent, with warnings against adultery and immoral women (Proverbs 2:16; 5; 6:20–7:27). Never-theless, mothers are given a crucial role in education. Proverbs 31:1 states that King Lemuel learned wisdom from his mother—again a royal court setting—while other parts of the book are presented as a father's address to his son.

Depicted as a young man, this son is easy prey for the enticing charms of an experienced woman (5:20; 6:24–35; 7). The depiction of other women as capable of destroying kings (31:3) contrasts with the unique depiction of Lady Wisdom as Yhwh's very first creature who served as some sort of architect for the entire creation (Proverbs 8:22–31). Proverbs closes with an acrostic poem describing the ideal wife as an industrious busy bee (Proverbs 31:10–31) or, better, the human counterpart of the ant of Prov-erbs 6:7. Though she has no boss telling her what to do, she stockpiles her sustenance. The poem presents a strict division of labor that gives the lie to portrayals of wives as submissive to their husbands. The wife is in charge of the economic side of the household, while the husband is responsible for the political activities at the gate of the city, where his position depends much on his wife's reputation (Proverbs 31:23, 31).

Regarding social relationships, Proverbs teaches how important it is to speak the truth and maintain trust through words: "Like a war club, a sword, or a sharp arrow is one who bears false witness against a neighbor. Like a bad tooth or a lame foot is trust in a faithless person in time of trouble" (Proverbs 25:18–19).

It is easy to lie, and bearing false witness is a grave matter because it causes havoc. Relations with others are destroyed, and the perpetrator is called a traitor. This advice is also common in other literature in the Near East. Amenemope, for example, writes, "Do not converse falsely with a person, for it is the abomination of God" (Zulu 2009, 24).

All in all, the message of the book of Proverbs can be summarized thus: Do not become a fool. Choose to be a righteous person by obeying your parents and then your master. Beware of women, alcohol, and laziness. Hold your tongue. The fool is portrayed as wild and stupid—a gossiper, a flatterer, and a scoffer—to urge the young addressee to learn wisdom.

About the Author

Sonny E. Zaluchu holds a doctorate (PhD) in theology from the Indonesia Baptist Theological Seminary and in sociology of religion from Satya Wacana Christian University Salatiga. He is a lecturer in the doctoral program at Indonesia Baptist Theological Seminary and a visiting professor of theology at several seminaries in Indonesia. His research includes themes in Old Testament studies and religion and society. With Jacob D. Engel, he has published "When Do Religion and Science Meet in Uncertainty?," *Verbum et Ecclesia* 43 (2022): 1–7.

Suggestions for Further Reading

In This Book

See also chapters 16 (Psalms), 17 (Wisdom), 47 (monotheism), 50 (magic), 55 (patriarchalism), 57 (pro-choice), and 71 (Qohelet).

Elsewhere

Black, James Roger. "The Instruction of Amenemope: A Critical Edition and Commentary—Prolegomenon and Prologue." PhD dissertation, University of Wisconsin–Madison, 2002.

Guillaume, Philippe. "Wonder Woman's Field in Proverbs 31: Taken, Not Bought!" *Ugarit Forschungen* 47 (2016): 85–102.

Kassis, Riad A. *The Book of Proverbs and Arabic Proverbial Works*. Leiden: Brill, 1999.

Lichtheim, Miriam. *The New Kingdom* (volume 2 of *Ancient Egyptian Literature*). Berkeley: University of California Press, 1976.

Shupak, Nili. "The Instruction of Amenemope and Proverbs 22:17–24:22 from the Perspective of Contemporary Research." Pages 203–217 in *Seeking Out the Wisdom of the Ancients: Essays Offered to Honor Michael V. Fox on the Occasion of His Sixty-Fifth Birthday*. Edited by Ronald L. Troxel, Kevin G. Friebel, and Dennis R. Magary. Winona Lake, IN: Eisenbrauns, 2005.

Zulu, Itibari, editor. *Axioms of Kemet: Instructions for Today from Ancient Egypt*. Los Angeles: Amen-Ra Theological Seminary Press, 2009. http://www.jpanafrican.org/docs/vol1no6/AxiomsofKemet_vol1no6.pdf.

19
Is the Book of Job a Theodicy?

Philippe Guillaume

While children are very sensitive to unfairness, growing into adulthood means learning to live with the hard fact that life is basically unfair. Only death, the great equalizer, corrects the glaring inequalities that begin at birth and continue throughout life.

The Bible provides little solace in the notion of a moral God ensuring fairness by punishing evildoers and rewarding good guys. The Psalms bemoan the fact that the wicked prosper (Psalms 10:5; 37:7; 73:3). The Bible even sports an entire book devoted to the matter of God's justice, a notion philosophers refer to as "theodicy"—literally, "God's justice." Theodicy is a branch of theology that defends God against suggestions of unfairness resulting from the existence of evil in the world. One way to deal with the persistence of evil is to downplay its existence by claiming that it merely represents a deficit of goodness, as Saint Augustine famously argued in his *Confessions*. Philosophical answers of this kind offer little comfort to anyone suffering from injustice, fatal diseases, or any other undeserved evil not attributable to one's own behavior.

Since Genesis 1:31 underlines the goodness of creation, Bible readers certainly expect Scripture to uphold the justice of God. The story of the fall (Genesis 2–4) shields God by attributing evil to the disobedience of the first humans—in particular, Eve. Against this approach, the book of Job warns that no justice can be expected from God.

The biblical Job starts off not as a Hebrew or an Israelite but as the greatest man of the East (1:3), a hint to the fabled Arabia Felix, which creates a safe distance from the hard truths expressed in the book. Contrary to the prophetic caricature of the rich as necessarily evil (for instance, Isaiah 3:14; Amos 5:11) and of the poor of the Psalms as naturally good (Psalm 35:10; 37:3–11), Job is both super rich and super just. He offers expensive sacrifices after each of his children's banquets just in case they had cursed God in their hearts (1:5).

Rich as he is, Job is not privy to what is going on in the heavenly spheres, where a council meets to hear the report of the satan, a kind of state prosecutor who scours the land to identify problematic situations. Blameless and upright (1:8), Job is the last person to be suspected of any mishaps, but the Lord's boast about Job's unique behavior initiates a fateful wager. The satan challenges the motivations of Job and asks whether Job fears God for nothing (Job 1:9). To test Job's piety, Yhwh allows the satan to strike Job's possessions and family, but to no avail. Job stands firm. Having lost his possessions and his children, he is as naked as when he came out of his mother's womb. Job stoically accepts that God has taken back what he had given, blessed be God.

In the next sitting of the divine council, the satan argues that the test is not conclusive, because as long as Job remains healthy, he is unlikely to curse God (2:5). The Hebrew text states "to bless" rather than "to curse," but translations correct the text, because "to bless" supposedly does not make sense. This apparent incoherence places translators in a quandary and evokes the differences between what is apparent and what actually is in and beyond the text itself.

Yhwh then allows the satan to strike Job himself, on condition that his life be spared. Afflicted with loathsome sores from head to toe, Job argues that misfortunes should be welcomed in the same way as good fortunes. Job rebukes his wife for suggesting that he should bless God and die. Again, translations correct "to bless" with "to curse." As the narrator insists that Job did not sin *with his lips*, it seems more logical for Job to die if he curses God than if he blesses him. The writer continues to play tricks with readers and translators. At this juncture, three friends arrive to comfort Job.

Baffled by their friend's hardships, they sit in silence for seven days before launching into a twenty-nine-chapter dispute in verse, where each takes his turn accusing Job. They advise him to repent from the evil he must have committed to deserve such a reversal of fortunes. Job upholds his innocence and blames God for the disaster.

As the friends are unable to convince Job, a young Elihu dares to barge in, angry as he is with Job's self-righteous stance and the failure of his three friends to placate him (Job 32–37). Elihu, however, repeats the same arguments as the friends with no more success. Job does not even bother to reply. Instead, Yhwh intervenes to argue his own case (chapters 38–41). This time, Job seems subdued. He confesses his insignificance, lays his hand over his mouth, and promises to say no more (Job 40:4–5).

Silence, however, is no answer. If Job is right, will God be in the wrong (Job 40:8)? The second divine speech seems to drive this lesson home. Job accepts that Yhwh can do all things and that humans have no understanding. He admits he had spoken from hearsay, but having now seen Yhwh (but with one eye only in the Hebrew text of 42:5!), he despises himself and repents in dust and ashes (Job 42:6). In fact, he has been sitting in dust and ashes since 2:8, which bodes ill for any great changes in the stalemate. Did Job buckle under the forceful display of divine power?

Not really. The concluding verses return to the prose of the introduction. Now it is Yhwh's turn to be angry and rebuke the three friends for not having spoken rightly, contrary to Job. Young Elihu is ignored again, either because he is a later addition or because only old, seasoned figures count.

In any case, Yhwh vindicates Job and admits that the man was attacked for nothing. Job was blameless and remained blameless throughout—even when he accused God of unfairness. Yet, instead of blaming the satan, God admits guilt by paying compensation for the damages incurred. Job's wealth is thus doubled (compare Job 1:3 and 42:12), including the number of sons: the Hebrew text reads the word for "seven" as a dual form; thus, fourteen sons. The daughters remain three in number; they represented a greater burden for fathers, who would have had to pay them a share of their estate when they married. In the world of the writer, six daughters would be less of a blessing than fourteen sons.

The morale of the book is that God is indeed all powerful but not necessarily just and fair. The divine speeches suggest that Job's troubles are negligible compared to the care of the universe. Divine power is brutal and indiscriminate. Its working out on the microlevel of individual human destinies excludes the notion of justice.

As God vindicates Job, the notion of Job's repentance is clearly erroneous. Translators are keen to paint a chastised Job, but Job simply throws in the towel. Arguing that Job repented because he was guilty ends up in one adopting the precarious position of Job's friends, whom Yhwh declares guilty of not having spoken rightly like Job (42:7–8). The only matter Job confesses is his inability to understand why the God he served so carefully could let him go through such an ordeal.

There is no explanation for evil, misfortunes, natural catastrophes, and diseases that strike evildoers and good persons alike. The satan leaves the scene after chapter 2, yet nothing disproves his innuendo that Job's piety is motivated by self-interest and that his blamelessness contributed positively to his wealth. As Job eventually recoups his losses with a profit, the morale of the morale is that at the end of the day, it is more profitable to toe the line, especially when the immediate rewards seem meager compared to the profit gained from twisting the rules.

The book of Job is the most thorough treatment of the matter of evil and injustice within an exclusive monotheistic framework that leaves no room for another deity to blame for misfortunes. Job placates the philosophical notion of theodicy by figuring the satan as an entity strictly under orders of the deity. It is only with God's permission that the satan strikes Job. Job does not go as far as Ezekiel 20:25 in ascribing both good and evil to Yhwh. He simply explains that we should receive evil as much as good from God (Job 2:10). Despite the inherent goodness of creation, wars, diseases, accidents, and disasters occur, but they should never ever be explained as divine punishments. To let God be God, we need to accept that we cannot fathom the divine realm. Whether as marks of capriciousness, irrationality, or the existence of a dark face in the divine, monotheism requires abstaining from explaining evil and maintaining a humble recognition of our failure to figure out God's plan. We can merely accept the hard truth of the irrelevance of the individual at the species level—and even the irrelevance of particular species (including humanity) within a given ecological niche.

About the Author

Philippe Guillaume holds a doctorate in Old Testament from the University of Geneva and a habilitation from the University of Berne. He has published "Caution: Rhetorical Questions," *Biblische Notizen* 103 (2000): 11–16; and "Dismantling the Deconstruction of Job," *Journal of Biblical Literature* 127(3) (2008): 491–499.

Suggestions for Further Reading

In This Book
See also chapters 16 (Psalms), 17 (Wisdom), 18 (Proverbs), 42 (Nephilim), 43 (angels), 47 (monotheism), 70 (Satan), and 74 ("P").

Elsewhere
Augustine. *Confessions* (book 7). Translated and edited by Albert C. Outler. Philadelphia: Westminster, 1955.

LaCocque, André. "The Deconstruction of Job's Fundamentalism." *Journal of Biblical Literature* 126 (2007): 83–97.

Ngwa, Kenneth Numfor. *The Hermeneutics of the "Happy" Ending in Job 42:7–17.* Berlin: De Gruyter, 2005.

Vieira, Celso. "The Capricious Gods Counterattack: On What the Empirical Method and the Rational Gods Model Miss." *Academia Letters* (June 2021), article 1183. https://doi.org/10.20935/AL1183.

20
Why Are There So Many Genealogies in the Bible?

Dexter E. Callender Jr.

Those familiar with the Bible often consider genealogies its least interesting parts, despite our modern obsession with ancestry. Yet, questions like "Are sixth cousins still family?" and the humor we find in sayings like "Mules are always boasting that their ancestors were horses" reflect what sociologist Eviatar Zerubavel (2012, 3) calls "our unmistakably social visions of genealogical relatedness." Approaching genealogies from this perspective illuminates how the genealogies in the Hebrew Bible reflect a grappling with fundamental questions of human identity and community in ways that reverberate in contemporary life. For the biblical writers, as for us, genealogies are devices that betray our interests in establishing social reality.

In the most basic sense, a genealogy is a kinship record, an account of a person or group's ancestry and descent. Genealogies are an expression of blood-based family relations. Biblical genealogies articulate class identities within a variety of larger narrative purposes. Our intuitive sense of kinship relations makes genealogy a metaphor applicable to other areas. Insofar as biology conveys a sense of natural process, genealogies are literary devices that suggest to us a sense of natural kinds, of true or reliable structure in the world.

Genealogies serve a range of functions. Cross-cultural study of genealogies has demonstrated a variety of settings in which they were used, including political, economic, domestic, and religious. The forms genealogies assume are similarly varied and appropriated. Two basic forms lie at the core. Linear genealogies recount descent from father to son to grandson to great-grandson, and so on, omitting siblings and spouses. This form normally appears in descending order from parent to child (e.g., Ruth 4:18; 1 Chronicles 9:39–44) but is also found in ascending order from child to parent (e.g., 1 Chronicles 9:14–16). Segmented genealogies, on the other hand, often name all sons in one generation and then trace the sons of each one, sometimes including the names of spouses as well (e.g., Genesis 4:19–23; 10:1–32; Genesis 35:22–26; Numbers 26:5–51). These offer structure to define and regulate social interaction in virtually any sphere of human relations and in hierarchical terms such as equality and inequality.

Genealogies can be elaborated in various ways. Genealogical lists can contain narrative notices. Likewise, narratives can be augmented by genealogies. The roughly twenty-five genealogies found throughout the Hebrew Bible are embedded in narrative frameworks. Moreover, a genealogy itself, apart from its specific form, betrays a kind of narrative progression, relating a story of kinship relations relevant to the scribes who preserved them. Thus, genealogies functioned hand in hand with their narrative frameworks for the scribal custodians and interpreters of tradition over time. In this sense, genealogies are an *ongoing* reflection of social reality.

Traditionally, biblical scholars have focused on the meaning of "the text itself" as a literary work or on the intentions of its authors, in contrast to many church theologians or orthodox rabbis who have sought its meaning as a divinely inspired document. The results of these approaches are contingent on the ideological commitments and interests of the interpreters, who are embedded within their own "social visions of genealogical relatedness," to quote Zerubavel again. Thus, whether one takes into consideration the growth and development of the text over time or chooses to focus on the "final" or "received" form of the text, the background concerns of the interpreter will shape the methods of inquiry and the results.

Although the genealogies at times appear schematic or exhibit changes that reflect a kind of fluidity, they can preserve some reliable historical information. The frequent appearance of the number twelve in tribal listings in, for example, the genealogies of Nahor in Genesis 22:20–24, Ishmael in Genesis 25:13–16, and Esau in Genesis 36:10–14 suggests the use of a schematic portrayal, an account of "the whole." The genealogies of twelve sons may reflect political alliances expressed as kinship ties. Yet, the internal consistency between the genealogical notices of the sons of Jacob (Genesis 29:31–30:23; 35:16–26) and the associated narratives suggests a sense of veracity behind the texts. Six of the sons mentioned in the birth narratives and their descendants are the featured actors in the associated narratives that follow the birth reports and continue through the conquest. These six tribes may have been the original descendants of Jacob. The other six sons mentioned in the birth narratives would reflect groups incorporated later on into a larger league. Their status as latecomers would be reflected in their birth circumstances, which presents them as sons of the handmaids Bilhah or Zilpah or as the later births of the unloved wife, Leah. Reconstructions of this sort involve a measure of speculation. If, however, the genealogies reflect the historical development of the Israelite league and the background of the monarchy, it would not be surprising that the birth circumstances would function as a mode of expressing social status.

Genealogies that portray a close association between a founding ancestor and a group appear more clearly as frames for providing social commentary on groups. The scribes of the Edomite genealogies of Genesis 36 include the explanatory gloss "Esau is Edom," explicitly equating the ancestor with the politico-ethnic group Edom / the Edomites (36:8). The rivalry of the twin brothers in the Genesis narratives appears to reflect the close but at times problematic relationship between the polities of Israel and Edom. In much the same manner, social commentary is evident in the unflattering birth narratives of the ancestors of the Ammonites and Moabites in Genesis 19:30–38, two groups that appear in adversarial roles with respect to the Israelite tribes. Elsewhere, genealogical relations frequently reflect contrasting social types or kinds, as in the case of Cain and Abel, who reflect pastoralists and agriculturalists, respectively (Genesis 4:1–2).

The genealogies of Genesis 4 and 5 trace human descent from Adam through Cain and Seth, respectively. The overlap in names between the two lists suggests a common tradition transmitted and elaborated for different purposes. The genealogy of Cain's descendants (4:17–23) emphasizes cultural origins, while the genealogy of Seth's descendants (5:1–32) emphasizes life spans and further segmentation. Seth's highly formulaic genealogy connects Adam to Noah and, after the flood (6:5–9:29), Noah to Abraham (11:10–32). The narrative elaborations that surround these genealogies (4:1–16, 23–26; 6:1–4; 10:1–11:9) portray various aspects of life before and after the flood. In this regard, these genealogies resemble Mesopotamian traditions like the Sumerian King List and lists recognizing culture heroes of the remote past.

One might conjecture that the narrative elaboration of the first genealogical relationships in Genesis functions within scribal tradition as a kind of commentary on genealogy and the idea of social reality itself—how we conceive of nature, natural kinds, and our relation to each. Thus, in the narrative elaboration of the first human family, social relations are problematized in terms of uneven power dynamics (3:16), fratricide (4:8), and internecine conflict as a generational legacy (4:14–15; 4:23–24). In the aftermath of the flood, a similar problematizing of social relations among the sons of Noah is articulated in "Noah's curse" (9:20–27). Here too, schematic or ideal presentation appears to be at work in the reckoning of three sons to Adam, Lamech, and Noah, a configuration seen elsewhere in the three sons of Deucalion in Greek tradition. Such embedded schematics and ideal presentations pose an additional challenge for interpreters of the genealogical relations and their narrative elaborations.

Genealogies appear most prominently in the book of Genesis and in the books of Chronicles and Ezra-Nehemiah. One might infer from this something of their general function in establishing social reality. The crucial themes in these books are the creation of humanity and its reconstitution following the flood (Genesis) and the reconstitution of the Israelite polity in the land following the chaos of the exile (Chronicles, Ezra-Nehemiah). Both reflect an underlying desire to depict the (re)establishment of a natural or created order.

Certain biblical genealogies have had a particularly strong impact on the formation of Western society. The genealogies of Genesis 1–11 have played a prominent role in current conceptions of human social reality, particularly in terms of notions of race and ethnicity. The Table of Nations (Genesis 10:1–32) and the Tower of Babel (11:1–32) give genealogical accounts of Noah's three sons spreading across the earth after the flood. These have been appropriated in a variety of ways. In the case of the Table of Nations, the differences in the branching of lines of the sons of Noah (languages, lands, and people groups) express the ideal brotherhood of humanity, which, by implication, involves innate equality and collective responsibility. Others, however, have interpreted this genealogy to emphasize the "natural" and absolute differences within humanity.

Gaps in the genealogies have given rise to other accounts of human ancestry. Isaac La Peyrere (1596–1676) used biblical and "pagan" sources to argue that some humans had been created prior to Adam, from whom Adam did not descend. For La Peyrere, the flood was local, and the biblical text properly accounted for the European descendants of Adam. The notion of pre-Adamism has been combined with evolutionary reconstructions of human origins to argue that Neanderthals were the ancestors of modern *Homo sapiens*. Alternatively, biblical texts have been combined with genomic studies to conclude that Neanderthals were human and made in the image of God. These attempts to reach into the past through genealogy to define the present can never be considered value-neutral. As Bruce Lincoln points out, primordial origins remain notoriously elusive. The shards of information and prior narratives they contain are converted into "fictions that satisfy . . . unattainable desires while doing . . . ideological work." Lincoln concludes that when students of myth engage in a discourse of origins, "they enter a recursive spiral, spinning their own myths while they sincerely believe themselves to be interpreting myths of others, others who may even be the product of their imagination and discourse"

(1999, 95). Lincoln's comments resonate in what Marianne Sommer (2016, 307) observed of one group of genomic researchers—namely, that "the belief in a politically neutral science blinded the project participants to the fact that population genetic studies also always coproduce the social and the natural order." The question of whether such concerns occupied the thoughts of the biblical writers in crafting and transmitting genealogies, although not easily answered, offers reason to take this genre seriously in reflecting on the ongoing human project of self- and social definition.

About the Author

Dexter E. Callender Jr. holds a doctorate (PhD) from Harvard University. His research investigates myth theory and cognitive approaches to the Hebrew Bible. He has published *Adam in Myth and History: Ancient Israelite Perspectives on the Primal Human* (Winona Lake, IN: Eisenbrauns, 2000); and *Myth and Scripture: Contemporary Perspectives on Religion, Language, and Imagination* (Atlanta: SBL, 2014).

Suggestions for Further Reading

In This Book

See also chapters 1 (scholarly perspective), 9 (audiences), 41 (symbolic numbers), 48 (twelve tribes), 77 (literary and form criticism), 78 (ideological criticism), 79 (memory studies), and 82 (postcolonial studies).

Elsewhere

Ingeborg, Löwisch. "Cracks in the Male Mirror: References to Women as Challenges to Patrilinear Authority in the Genealogies of Judah." Pages 105–132 in *What Was Authoritative for Chronicles?* Edited by Ehud Ben Zvi and Diana V. Edelman. University Park: Penn State University Press, 2011.

Johnson, Marshall D. *The Purpose of the Biblical Genealogies: With Special Reference to the Setting of the Genealogies of Jesus*. Cambridge: Cambridge University Press, 1969.

Lincoln, Bruce. *Theorizing Myth: Narrative, Ideology, and Scholarship*. Chicago: University of Chicago Press, 1999.

Rendsburg, Gary A. "The Internal Consistency and Historical Reliability of the Biblical Genealogies." *Vetus Testamentum* 40(2) (1990): 185–206. https://doi.org/10.1163/156853390X00352.

Sommer, Marianne. *History Within: The Science, Culture, and Politics of Bones, Organisms, and Molecules*. Chicago: University of Chicago Press, 2016.

Weasel, Lisa. "How Neanderthals Became White: The Introgression of Race into Contemporary Human Evolutionary Genetics." *American Naturalist* 200(1) (2022): 129–139.

Wilson, Robert R. *Genealogy and History in the Biblical World*. New Haven, CT: Yale University Press, 1977.

Zerubavel, Eviatar. *Ancestors and Cousins: Genealogy, Identity, and Community*. New York: Oxford University Press, 2012.

Dating the Bible and the Bible as History

21
Preexilic, Exilic, and Postexilic: Can We Date the Books of the Hebrew Bible?

Diana V. Edelman

Dating anonymous books is impossible to do with certainty. Without the name of an author and records of when he lived, we must turn to internal, circumstantial clues in the text to try to provide a context and date for any given book in the collection comprising the Hebrew Bible. This process, however, is subjective; what one person sees as a clear clue, another may reject as not having any relevance for dating. This is the case even when it generally is acknowledged that a book provides insight into the world view and assumptions that are current or being debated at the time of composition.

Another complicating factor is the recognition that every book has later intentional additions that have updated the text to make it relevant for new times and communities. This is in addition to inadvertent scribal errors made during copying. Estimates vary greatly as to how much of the present text would have been "original" and how much has been added later on.

A third, significant complicating factor is that while we know that a single individual would have created the first version of every narrative book, often drawing on older oral and written sources and planning its plotline and the literary devices that would develop the plot effectively, we will never be able to establish the exact wording of that composition. All we have are dozens of manuscript versions, each of which is slightly different, except for masoretic copies, which were standardized when a fixed text was adopted within rabbinic Judaism in the ninth century CE to prevent further corruption. Prior to that, we have only the various versions, including translations into other languages, so it is not possible to move from them to an "original."

Thus, in seeking to date a book, we need to ask what we are actually trying to attach a date and context of composition to: Is it a "final" version attested in a single manuscript? Is it the earliest material, which would be possible underlying sources that have been included in a book? Is it later editions to the text, especially if, as biblical scholars have proposed, there were systematic redactions done in ancient times to bind certain books in the collection together more closely? Or is it a hypothetical "original" or earliest version of a given book? None can be determined with certainty.

Within Hebrew Bible scholarship, there has been a long-standing tendency to use the internal biblical periodization scheme to talk about dating. In particular, this involves not only the categories "preexilic," "exilic," and "postexilic" but also a second, overlapping scheme with the categories "premonarchic," "monarchic," and "postmonarchic." "Preexilic" usually is equivalent to "monarchic" and "postexilic" to "postmonarchic." "Premonarchic" includes events that would have taken place in the periods of the forefathers, the exodus, the wilderness wanderings, or the occupation of Canaan. "Exilic" marks off a subdivision within the postmonarchic period that was of great significance to the biblical writers: the exile of segments of the population of Judah to Babylonia in 598 (2 Kings 24:1–17), 587 (2 Kings 24:18–25:12), and possibly 581 BCE (2 Kings 25:22–27) and the alleged return home of some of them under King Cyrus of Persia (Ezra 1:1–2:69). "Postexilic," then, deals with developments in the province of Yehud, the successor to the kingdom of Judah, after this purported return, even though Judeans continued to live outside the territory of Judah/Yehud in Babylonia as well as Egypt and possibly Transjordan.

Historians tend to use a dating scheme that is not specifically drawn from biblical texts but still is not 100 percent neutral. It adopts the archaeological dating scheme for the southern Levant, which mixes the categories of Late Bronze Age (ca. 1550–1200 BCE) and Iron Age (ca. 1200–587 BCE) with terminology linked to the subsequent progression of the Neo-Babylonian (ca. 587–539 BCE) and Persian or Achaemenid Empires (ca. 539–332 BCE), followed by the Hellenistic (ca. 332–63 BCE) and Roman (ca. 63 BCE–324 CE) periods. Some archaeologists now eliminate the Neo-Babylonian category altogether, recognizing that there is no break in the pottery tradition after 587 BCE and that while many settlements were destroyed, not all were; occupation continued in the territory of Benjamin and Judah. They extend the Iron IIc period to the late sixth century or speak of an Iron IId period.

It should be noted that while the Neo-Babylonians conquered the Assyrians and became the new imperial power in the ancient Near East circa 626 BCE, within biblical studies, the Neo-Babylonian period begins officially only when the kingdom of Judah was conquered in 587 BCE and incorporated into the Neo-Babylonian Empire. It corresponds largely with the "exilic" period. The ensuing Persian period covers, more or less, the biblical "postexilic" period, although the latter also extends into the Hellenistic period, in which the composition of certain books like Chronicles, Daniel, and Ecclesiastes are generally placed.

The creation of the earliest version of the majority of biblical texts of the Hebrew Bible that are set before the conversion of Judah to a Neo-Babylonian province has traditionally been dated primarily to the period when Judah was a kingdom, circa 980–587 BCE. Those who adopt this dating tend to assume this is most logical because scribes would have had access to records and archives at this time, but not after the end of the monarchy. However, the Neo-Babylonians made Mizpah the regional seat after they destroyed Jerusalem (2 Kings 25:22–23) and likely would have moved some archives from the former capital to the new one for administrative purposes. In addition, texts that had been part of the standard scribal curriculum would have been memorized and could easily have been reproduced. Many also assume that the details in the texts accurately reflect the events they describe. They similarly assume that the books set during the Persian period—like Haggai, Zechariah, Malachi, Ezra, Nehemiah, and Esther—were written close to the time of the events they portray and so are historically reliable.

Other scholars would place the composition during the period between the destruction of Jerusalem in 587 BCE and the reestablishment of Jerusalem as the regional seat by the Achaemenid rulers, circa 450 BCE. Still others opt for the bulk of the composition first after 450 BCE, while a minority argue for their composition in the Hellenistic period. Those who opt for the earliest dating scheme tend to see subsequent and systematic editing or redacting as having taken place in the subsequent two or three periods. Those who opt for the last two periods are more open to the possibility that some portrayals of the past are examples of what has been called "invented history" or "invented memory." All present arguments for the creation of the majority of the books that center on the desire to create a sense of communal identity in the given time period and circumstances.

Two examples illustrating these issues may help. The book of Genesis, with its folktale-like stories, has traditionally been seen to have been composed in Judah prior to 587 BCE, drawing heavily on oral tribal traditions to create a common descent for people in Judah from twelve tribes that had occupied the land of Canaan. In this case, one needs logically to place its composition after 721 BCE, when the kingdom of Israel became the Assyrian province of Samerina, as part of a royal initiative to incorporate its population into the kingdom of Judah eventually via annexation. This would account for the emphasis on Israel rather than

Judah and territory outside Judah proper. Genesis 1–11, however, which rejects a number of Neo-Babylonian religious beliefs and asserts instead that Yhwh is the only god and creator of everything, needs to be seen as a later addition.

If one focuses, however, on a number of issues relating to religious belief and practice, a later date, after the emergence of the ideas that will develop into early Judaism, is implied. Abraham builds altars (12:6, 8; 13:18) and in one case plants a tree (21:33) "to call on the name of Yhwh [only]," with no clear instances of offering animal sacrifice on any of the altars, only prayer. The deity is equated with four generic categories of god—"most high" (*'elyon*; 14:18–22), "seeing" (*ro'i*; 16:13), "of the hills or breasts" (*shaddai*; 17:1; 28:3; 35:11; 43:14; 48:11), and "eternal" (*'olam*; 21:33)—which points to a move to collapse the former pantheon and have Yhwh take over the roles of other deities once worshipped. In a similar vein, Yhwh alone controls the wombs of women (e.g., 16:1–2; 17:6; 20:17; 29:31; 30:2) and provides or withholds children and crops (26:12; not Asherah and Baal, respectively), and the burial of the teraphim associated with the former representation of divinized ancestors (35:1–4) is meant to become the norm. These ideas probably first developed among one or more deported elite families living in Babylonia but took some time to mature and spread. A focus on migration from Babylonia to Canaan, from Canaan to Paddan-Aram and back again, and from Canaan to Egypt and back again suggests a concern for both those in Canaan and diaspora communities of exiled Israelites and Judeans. Cumulatively, these clues logically suggest a date of composition in the Persian period and a hoped-for community that will adopt the new religious views, from Dan to Beer-sheba and in the diaspora.

The book of Esther is often assumed to be a court tale deriving from the Persian period that was written down in the same time frame. However, it displays a number of details that parallel accounts found in Greek writers about characters they situate in the Persian world as well as historiographical techniques distinctive to Hellenistic literature, like explaining exotic customs, quoting alleged archives, and using terms and names deriving from the Persian language. While some scholars would attribute some of these "Hellenisms" to subsequent editing, the cumulative observations make the most sense when one assumes that the writer of the book lived in the Hellenistic period, was familiar with Greek modes of writing about the Persians, and decided to use them when writing his story.

If you find a definitive date claimed for a book in the Hebrew Bible or even a unit of text within a book, you should be highly suspicious of how such a claim has been determined and can be made.

About the Author

Diana V. Edelman holds a doctorate of philosophy (PhD) in biblical studies from the University of Chicago and is Professor Emerita in Hebrew Bible at the Faculty of Theology, University of Oslo. She has published "Genesis: A Composition for Construing a Homeland of the Imagination for Scribal Circles or for Educating the Illiterate?," pages 47–66 in *Writing the Bible: Scribes, Scribalism and Script*, edited by Philip R. Davies and Thomas Römer (Durham, NC: Acumen, 2013); and "The Text-Dating Conundrum: Viewing the Hebrew Bible from an Achaemenid Framework," pages 7–38 in *Stones, Tablets, and Scrolls: Periods of the Formation of the Bible*, edited by Peter Dubrovský and Federico Giuntoli (Tübingen: Mohr Siebeck, 2020).

Suggestions for Further Reading

In This Book
See also chapters 8 (anonymity), 22 (periodization), 44 (ancestors), 47 (monotheism), 72 (synchronic vs. diachronic), 73 (source criticism), 76 (redaction and text criticism), 78 (ideological criticism), and 79 (memory studies).

Elsewhere
Macchi, Jean-Daniel. "The Book of Esther: A Persian Story in Greek Style." Pages 109–128 in *A Palimpsest: Rhetoric, Ideology, Stylistics, and Language Relating to Persian Israel*. Edited by Ehud Ben Zvi, Diana V. Edelman, and Frank Polak. Piscataway, NJ: Georgias, 2009.

22

How Did Scribes Periodize the Past in the Hebrew Bible?

Diana V. Edelman

In all cultures, the past is schematized as part of the process of making it meaningful for the present. The past is a continuum. When focusing on a discrete segment of the past, a starting point and ending point are set along the continuum. Ultimately, these "terminal points" are determined by contingent considerations relevant to those who are placing past events in a chain of cause and effect to assign meaning in the present to those events.

The master scribes who wrote the individual books now forming the Hebrew Bible, as well as later scribes who read and reread them and linked them more closely together into a chronological sequence by adding references and allusion both forward and backward in time, were well aware that they were schematizing their past.

There are multiple periodization schemes within the Hebrew Bible. Martin Noth noted that Deuteronomy to 2 Kings divides Israel's past into five periods: the Mosaic era (book of Deuteronomy), which closes with Moses's speech before his death and burial in chapter 34; the conquest under Joshua (book of Joshua), which closes with Joshua's speech in 23:1–16; the period of the judges (Judges 2:11–1 Samuel 12), which is marked by Samuel's concluding speech; the united monarchy under Kings Saul, David, and Solomon (1 Samuel 13–1 Kings 8), which ends with Solomon's speech in 1 Kings 8:14–53; and the period of the divided kingdoms of Israel and Judah until their respective demises (1 Kings 9–2 Kings 25), with a speech in 2 Kings 17:7–23 explaining why the kingdom of Israel was destroyed and a brief note in 2 Kings 25:27–30 about the release of King Jehoiachin from prison in Babylon after the destruction of the kingdom of Judah.

If one looks at the broader narrative presented in Genesis–2 Kings, however, the preceding periodization has additional subdivisions. It begins with the period of the patriarchs (the book of Genesis), which includes Jacob's deathbed speech about the future in Genesis 49, before his death and burial in chapter 50. The ensuing books of Exodus, Leviticus, and Numbers all deal, then, with events during Moses's lifetime and, as such, could be assigned to a Mosaic age. However, they also could be seen to detail two periods between the patriarchs and the conquest: the period of Israel's slavery in Egypt and subsequent liberation (books of Exodus and Leviticus), which has no concluding speech, and the wilderness wanderings (books of Numbers and Deuteronomy), which features Moses's farewell speech in Deuteronomy 33.

A totally different periodization scheme uses the motif of the creation of order from watery chaos to symbolize a new beginning. It marks four periods in Israel's formative past: from the creation of the universe to an overpopulous, corrupt humanity (Genesis 1:1–8:22); from Noah's family after the flood to the parting of the Red Sea, marking Israel's escape from Egypt (Genesis 9:1–Exodus 15:21); from Israel becoming God's people at Mount Sinai and on the plains of Moab before entering the promised land (Exodus 15:22–Deuteronomy 34:12); and from the conquest to the demise of the kingdoms of Israel and Judah (Joshua 1:1–2 Kings 25:30). This division of the past overlaps with the former in the time of the wilderness wanderings but would assign Exodus 15:22–Deuteronomy 34:12 to a single period, moving Exodus 1–15:21 to a period extending from the world after the flood, through the prepatriarchal generations and the patriarchs, to the twelve tribes enslaved in Egypt and their miraculous escape. This long period constitutes an "ancestral age." The two divine covenants with two subsequent generations of Israelites then belong to the same period outside the land, while the final period covers events in the promised land, from its conquest to the demise of the two kingdoms.

This way of subdividing the past emphasizes the role of divine covenants—first with all humanity (Genesis 9:12–17) and the patriarchs (Genesis 15:18; 17:1–22; 26:3–5; 28:13–15; Exodus 2:24; 6:5) in the second period and then with Israel (Exodus 19:5; 24:7; 31:6; 34:10, 17, 28; Leviticus 24:8; 26:9, 15; 25; 42; 44–45; Deuteronomy 5:2–3; 7:9; 9:9, 11, 15; 29:1, 9, 12, 14, 19, 21, 25; 31:16, 20); Aaron and his sons (Numbers 18:19–20); Phineas, son of Eleazar, son of Aaron (Numbers 25:12–13); and the Levites (Deuteronomy 10:8; 33:9) in the third. Speeches no longer mark the end of an age.

A third scheme for understanding the past uses the exodus from Egypt as the pivotal dating point. In 1 Kings 6:1, it is said that 480 years elapsed between the exodus from Egypt and the building of the temple by King Solomon in Jerusalem. This represents twelve cycles of forty years—a symbolic number representing "a long time"—one for each tribe of Israel.

A fourth scheme involves 430 years. According to Exodus 12:40–41, this was the length of time that the Israelites sojourned in Egypt. The biblical chronology in Kings also adds up to 430 years from the foundation of the temple to its destruction. In this scheme, both the exodus and the existence of the first temple during the time of the Judahite monarchy are highlighted as key events for those who identify with biblical Israel. No symbolic value is obvious for the figure of 430.

These internal periodizations do not correspond with the canonical subdivisions of the Tanak, however, or even of the books within the canon, as seen above for starting and ending verses for different eras or ages. Judaism established the threefold classification of texts into Torah (law; Genesis–Deuteronomy), Prophets (Joshua–Malachi), and Writings (Psalms–Chronicles), which was not based strictly on any chronological schematization of the past. The book of Ruth, for example, takes place in the so-called period of the judges, yet it is grouped among the Writings, although in the Greek version of the Old Testament, it is placed between the books of Samuel and Kings, in logical chronological order. The book of Chronicles ends the Writings, even though it deals with Israel from its origins to the destruction of Jerusalem by the Neo-Babylonians in 587 BCE. According to chronological logic, it should follow the books of Kings, as it does in the Greek version.

Some of the major and minor prophetic books open with statements known as superscriptions that place the career of the prophet within the reign of one or more kings, which links them more closely to the period of the divided kingdoms of Israel and Judah until their respective demises (1 Kings 9–2 Kings 25). They include Amos, Hosea, Isaiah, Micah, Jeremiah, and Zephaniah. Haggai and Zechariah, on the other hand, bear a series of date superscriptions placing them in the reign of one of the imperial Persian kings named Darius. This selective dating likely was done as part of a larger theological strategy of establishing an unbroken chain of prophets raised by Yhwh after Moses, who, during the united and divided monarchic eras (and earlier), warned both the kings and the people about their repeated disobedience to the Torah, simultaneously announcing signs and consequences for their actions. The destruction of Jerusalem and its temple and the exile of many of its inhabitants are seen to be the enactment of the prophetic messages.

All this is a very strong reminder that the Hebrew Bible collection is not formulated on the principles of modern historiography or our historical sensibilities, even though it deals with the past and memory. The past is a major concern for biblical writers as a form of collective memory that provides a basis for shared identity in their present and future. Subdividing the past into meaningful, discrete units can be done in a number of different ways, with or without consensus. The periodization in the texts comprising the Hebrew Bible need not be followed by modern readers, who are culturally conditioned to place events in a chronological sequence based on the Gregorian calendar and modern dating conventions. Readers are free to decide if they will adopt the conventions used by the writers of these ancient texts or apply more familiar ones; one system is not more inherently "correct" than the other. Either way, however, attention must be paid to how the ancients conceived of the past and the fact that they did not share our notions of history and historiography.

About the Author

Diana V. Edelman holds a doctorate of philosophy (PhD) in biblical studies from the University of Chicago and is Professor Emerita in Hebrew Bible at the Faculty of Theology, University of Oslo. She has published "Doing History in Biblical Studies," pages 13–25 in *The Fabric of History: Text, Artifact and Israel's Past*, edited by Diana V. Edelman (Sheffield, UK: Sheffield Academic, 1991).

Suggestions for Further Reading

In This Book

See also chapters 1 (scholarly perspective), 5 (canons), 10 (Tanak), 11 (Pentateuch), 24 (Kings and Chronicles), 36 (Old Testament theology), 39 (calendars), 49 (Torah), 51 (prophets), and 52 (covenant).

Elsewhere

Davies, Philip R. *The History of Ancient Israel: A Guide for the Perplexed.* London: Bloomsbury T&T Clark, 2015.

Jordanova, Ludmilla. *History in Practice* (2nd edition). London: Hodder Arnold, 2006.

Knauf, E. Axel. "Kings among the Prophets." Pages 131–149 in *The Production of Prophecy: Constructing Prophecy and Prophets in Yehud*. Edited by Diana V. Edelman and Ehud Ben Zvi. London: Equinox, 2009.

Knoppers, Gary N. "Periodization in Ancient Israelite Historiography: Three Case Studies." Pages 139–168 in *Covenant and Election in Exilic and Post-exilic Judaism: Studies of the Sofja Kovalevskaja Research Group on Early Jewish Monotheism* (volume 5). Edited by Nathan MacDonald. Tübingen: Mohr Siebeck, 2015.

Noth, Martin. *The Deuteronomistic History*. Sheffield, UK: Sheffield Academic, 1990.

23
What Was the Minimalist versus Maximalist Debate?

Emanuel Pfoh

The minimalist-maximalist debate(s) appeared as a prominent feature of discussions about the Hebrew Bible / Old Testament in Europe and the United States during the 1990s. The conceptual matter, however, can be traced back to the changes in the field during the 1960s, but especially during the 1970s. In the middle of this decade, two studies were published independently of each other, initiating a deconstructive mode of biblical historicity whose full impact emerged in the 1990s. Thomas L. Thompson (1974) and John Van Seters (1975) separately indicated that Abraham and the biblical patriarchs (Abraham, Isaac, and Jacob) were not historical figures, since no archaeological or epigraphic traces of them were available in the ancient Near Eastern record of the Bronze Age (ca. 3300–1200 BCE), and that the patriarchal traditions were posterior to that age, in effect belonging either to the period of the united monarchy in Israel (ca. tenth century BCE) or to the exilic period (ca. sixth century BCE). In any case, it was clear to these scholars that a history of Israel could not start with the patriarchs. Further developments in the late 1970s and the 1980s were also critical of the historicity of an Israelite exodus from Egypt, of the conquest of the promised land, and of the existence of a period of the judges in Israel—namely, of a considerable portion of the narratives in Genesis–Joshua. By the late 1980s, the then available critical histories of Israel would deem the united monarchy of David and Solomon as a safe historical period in which to start writing the history of the ancient Israelites. This consensus, however, was once again challenged in the early 1990s, consolidating the historiographical perspective we now know as "biblical minimalism."

In 1991, Niels Peter Lemche, from the University of Copenhagen, published a monograph on the ancient Canaanites, considering them to be not a clear ethnic and homogenous population during the Bronze Age but rather a loose conceptual element deriving primarily from comments about the peoples living in the western part of the southern Levant found in the biblical narrative. In other words, if the ancient Canaanites were literary enemies of the ancient Israelites in the Bible, the logical step was also to consider the biblical image of the Israelites as distorted by the biblical authors. Shortly after, in 1992, two studies were published, cementing the deconstructive mode initiated in the 1970s. Once again, Thompson (1992) was at the forefront. According to a critical interpretation of the archaeological, epigraphic, and biblical sources, there was no place for a united monarchy of David and Solomon in the tenth century BCE. The history of Israel began as two separate kingdoms in the ninth and eighth centuries BCE: the kingdom of Israel and the kingdom of Judah. This interpretation would be endorsed by the archaeologist Israel Finkelstein from Tel Aviv University in a series of publications also from the 1990s that would (unwittingly) place him among the minimalists during that decade. The other study was written by Philip R. Davies (1992), from the University of Sheffield. In it, Davies argued that we should understand "Israel" via three concepts: a *biblical Israel* found as a literary figure in the biblical narrative, a *historical Israel* found in the archaeology and epigraphic record of the Iron Age (ca. 1200–586 BCE) and subsequent periods of the first millennium BCE, and an "ancient Israel" (with quotation marks in the original), a historiographical invention of historical-critical studies and biblical archaeology through a rather uncritical blending of external sources and the biblical text.

The idea of an "invention" of ancient Israel caused considerable quarrels, especially in the more conservative quarters of biblical scholarship and among both text- and archaeology-oriented scholars. In fact, in 1996, Keith W. Whitelam, initially at the University of Sterling but later also at the University of Sheffield, published a critical monograph entitled *The Invention of Ancient Israel*, with the more controversial subtitle *The Silencing of Palestinian History*. Whitelam's argument rested on the idea that biblical scholarship's exclusive attention to the historicity of ancient Israel had obscured a wider history of the region, in effect silencing what he deemed Palestinian history. Whitelam also offered an explicit connection of the historiography of ancient Israel in the twentieth century to modern politics related to the Israel-Palestine conflict, which eventually caused the biblical minimalists to be accused of being politically motivated (i.e., anti-Bible and anti-Israel) by their scholarly opponents.

Reactions to biblical minimalism appeared rapidly, essentially against the somewhat misunderstood idea of an "invention" of ancient Israel. This term was wrongly thought to mean a fabrication out of nothing instead of a particular social and cultural creation. Reactions also were voiced against questioning the Hebrew Bible as a historical source for writing the history of the Iron Age in the region and against the implication of the existence of covert politics in the previous work of important figures of Old Testament studies like William F. Albright and Albrecht Alt. The opponents of biblical minimalism were then considered "biblical maximalists"—although, in fact, they were the ones coming up with the general tag of "biblical minimalists" for the Copenhagen and Sheffield scholars. The terminology should, then, be clarified.

Briefly stated, by the mid-1990s, the so-called biblical minimalists argued that a minimal amount of verified historical data could be found in the Hebrew Bible given its literary nature (more related to myth than to history) and also the fact that the biblical narrative was most probably composed during the Persian-Roman periods (ca. fifth–second centuries BCE), therefore being a secondary source to the history of Iron Age Israel. This history could only be written by attending to the primary sources of the period—namely, archaeology and epigraphy, together with other auxiliary historical disciplines (anthropology, sociology, demography, etc.). Moreover, this history differed considerably from the history written by closely following the historical sketch found in the Hebrew Bible and correcting it through archaeology, a procedure most appropriate by previous scholarship both in Europe and in the United States (i.e., biblical archaeology). On the contrary, the maximalist camp argued that the Hebrew Bible, even if it were a late composition, contained earlier historical memories that could, in fact, be used to write history in the Iron Age unless this data were explicitly contradicted by external sources.

So, in the end, the key discussion was between two historical epistemologies but also between two historical methodologies. Minimalism refrained from using Hebrew Bible data as the primary source for historical reconstruction because they were embedded in myth and literary production and because the Hebrew Bible belonged to a much later compositional period than the Iron Age. Instead, the biblical narrative was considered a primary source for the intellectual history of the Second Temple period (ca. 516 BCE–70 CE). Maximalism defended a primary use of Hebrew Bible data because sometimes they did refer to a corroborated context from the Iron Age, despite later literary redactions of the text, and because the Hebrew Bible was thought to have been produced or started being produced sometime between the tenth and seventh century BCE (depending on the scholar) and, therefore, contained historical memories from relatively recent periods.

By the early 2000s, the intensity of discussions and the number of exchanges between the original contenders in the minimalist-maximalist debates had mostly abated. The impact of so-called minimalism, however, left a clear mark on discussions about historical epistemology and methodology for dealing with the Hebrew Bible and the history of Iron Age Israel. One could argue that while minimalism did not completely shift the previous paradigm for history writing in Old Testament scholarship, it did produce an epistemological break that made an alternative history of the region of Israel/Palestine (or the southern Levant, in more comprehensive terms) certainly possible.

Currently, scholars have different opinions about the intensity of this legacy. More conservative scholars will state that minimalism has indeed changed the field. Now, hardly any critical scholar will speak of the biblical events of the exodus, the conquest of the land, or a period of judges as historically real, and the united monarchy of David and Solomon is represented in recent histories of Israel not as a big ("biblical") empire but instead as a kingdom of two highland chieftains. Furthermore, the focus of historical attention has moved from the late second millennium to the first millennium BCE, where more external correlations of the biblical texts with ancient Near Eastern sources can be made and, therefore, more secure historical facts can be asserted. On the other hand, scholars coming from a minimalist epistemological position will find that many earlier ("preminimalism") assertions remain utterly unchallenged in the field, perpetuating more traditional forms of history writing in relation to Davies's concept of "ancient Israel."

What is certain is that the minimalist-maximalist debates of the 1990s offered a necessary—and by that time, already dated—discussion about updating epistemologies and methodologies in biblical scholarship as many other disciplines in the humanities and the social sciences had already achieved it in the 1960s and 1970s. Even when "more traditional" ways of doing history with the biblical texts are still active in the field, by recalibrating our understanding of the literary and compositional nature of the biblical texts, biblical minimalism showed how an alternative mode of dealing with the past of the region was and still is possible.

About the Author

Emanuel Pfoh holds a PhD in history from the University of Buenos Aires. He is a researcher at Argentina's National Research Council and at the Centre of Excellence in Ancient Near Eastern Empires, University of Helsinki. He is the author of *Syria-Palestine in the Late Bronze Age: An Anthropology of Politics and Power* (London: Routledge, 2016); "On Biblical Minimalism in Hebrew Bible/Old Testament Studies," *Annali di Storia dell'Esegesi* 38(2)

(2021): 283–300; and "Introduction: Social and Cultural Anthropology and the Hebrew Bible in Perspective," pages 1–16 in *T&T Clark Handbook of Anthropology and the Hebrew Bible*, edited by Emanuel Pfoh (London: Bloomsbury T&T Clark, 2023).

Suggestions for Further Reading

In This Book
See also chapters 1 (scholarly perspective), 7 (who wrote the Bible?), 13 (genres), 14 (myths), 21 (dates), 22 (periodization), 24 (Kings and Chronicles), 26 (conquest of Canaan), 28–30 (archaeology), 48 (twelve tribes), 56 (polemics), 65 (King David), 73 (source criticism), 75 (historical criticism), 78 (ideological criticism), 79 (memory studies), and 80 (social anthropology).

Elsewhere
Ben Zvi, Ehud. "'Minimalists,' 'Maximalists,' Method and Theory in History, and Social Memory Lenses." Pages 15–27 in *Minimalists in Biblical Studies: From Rebels to Unsuspected Contributors*, Biblische Notizen 193. Edited by Florian Lippke and Philippe Guillaume. Freiburg: Herder, 2022.

Davies, Philip R. *In Search of "Ancient Israel": A Study in Biblical Origins*. Sheffield, UK: Sheffield Academic, 1992.

Grabbe, Lester L. "How the Minimalists Won! A Discussion of Historical Method in Biblical Studies." Pages 5–14 in *Minimalists in Biblical Studies: From Rebels to Unsuspected Contributors*, Biblische Notizen 193. Edited by Florian Lippke and Philippe Guillaume. Freiburg: Herder, 2022.

Lemche, Niels Peter. *The Canaanites and Their Land: The Idea of Canaan in the Old Testament*. Journal for the study of the Old Testament, supplement series 110. Sheffield, UK: JSOT, 1991.

Pfoh, Emanuel. "On Biblical Minimalism in Hebrew Bible/Old Testament Studies." *Annali di Storia dell'Esegesi* 38(2) (2021): 283–300.

Thompson, Thomas L. *Early History of the Israelite Peoples: From the Written and Archaeological Sources*. Leiden: Brill, 1992.

Thompson, Thomas L. *The Historicity of the Patriarchal Narratives: The Quest for the Historical Abraham*. Berlin: De Gruyter, 1974.

Thompson, Thomas L. "Is the Bible Historical? The Challenge of 'Minimalism' for Biblical Scholars and Historians." *Holy Land Studies* 3(1) (2004): 1–27.

Van Seters, John. *Abraham in History and Tradition*. New Haven, CT: Yale University Press, 1975.

Whitelam, Keith W. *The Invention of Ancient Israel: The Silencing of Palestinian History*. London: Routledge, 1996.

24
Why Are There Two Versions of Israel's Past in the Hebrew Bible?

Rodney K. Duke

The Hebrew Bible (HB) / Old Testament (OT) contains two different but complementary histories of ancient Israel. The first history, found in Samuel–Kings, is part of a larger collection of books that includes Joshua, Judges, 1 and 2 Samuel, and 1 and 2 Kings. This set of six books is often called the Deuteronomistic History (DtrH; explained below). This first history is noteworthy because it may well be the first recorded history of a people who reflected on the formation and the ebb and flow of their nation. The second history is often called the Chronistic History (ChrH) and is found in 1 and 2 Chronicles, Ezra, and Nehemiah. A remarkable feature of the OT is that contrary to the thinking of "modern" historians, the leaders of ancient (Second Temple) Judaism recognized the value of holding together two differing accounts of Israel's past.

A people's or a person's historical narrative implicitly reveals an ideology for life as they perceive it through three key aspects: (1) values are revealed through the selection of key characters and events, (2) emplotment and purpose are found as the narratives present events moving forward through time, and (3) "laws" of reality are communicated as they state or imply the relationships among the events of their story.

Both histories overlap a lot in their content. The DtrH surveys Israelite history from the conquest of Canaan to exile in Babylon with the following segments and emphases. It begins with the conquest of the promised land and its distribution, when Israel is obedient to God/Yhwh (Joshua). Then follows a succession of subjugations to foreign nations during the tribal years, when the people repeatedly "forget" God (Judges). Next is a transition from tribal rule guided by the judge and prophet Samuel to the beginning of a national state under the first king, Saul, who fails to obey God and will be replaced by the more faithful, anointed, successor-to-be King David (1 Samuel). Events in the life of David after he is crowned king ensue as he organizes a national state, but also recorded is his moral failure and its disruptive consequences in his family and kingdom (2 Samuel). The rise of David's son Solomon as his successor and his building of the temple in Jerusalem until his death (1 Kings 1–11) precedes the subsequent division of the unified nation into the northern kingdom (NK, which retains the name Israel) and the southern kingdom (SK, called Judah). The interconnected histories of the two kingdoms are then narrated, with a focus on the growing religious apostasy of the NK and stories about the great prophets Elijah and Elisha, who attempt to stop the apostasy that eventually leads to the destruction of the NK by the Assyrians, who scatter the people of the NK across their empire (1 Kings 12–2 Kings 17). Finally, the story of the SK continues, but it eventually also succumbs to apostasy and is destroyed by the Babylonians, who carry much of the population into exile and settle them as a community in and around Babylon (2 Kings 17–25).

One readily sees that the main characters are Yhwh, who is actively involved in the events; the faithful prophets, like Samuel, Elijah, and Elisha; and the nations' leaders, who set the tone for apostasy or obedience. Key events are particularly related to the promised land and the success or failure in obtaining it and defending it. Even when there is a microfocus on events in the lives of Saul and David, Saul's failure to be a faithful king serves as a foil to David's successful rise to power over the nation's enemies, although he too falters and brings turmoil into the royal house. As one tracks back and forth between the kings of the NK and those of the SK, one sees how the apostasy of the kings of the NK led to its subjugation to the Assyrian Empire and to ruin. Although there are more faithful kings in the Davidic lineage in the SK, it eventually follows a similar pattern—with the important difference that the people of the SK are settled together in and around Babylon. Still, the trajectory of emplotment for both the NK and SK is a downhill slide of apostasy and its results.

When one looks for the "laws" of reality at work behind this story, much is left implicit, and readers could come to differing conclusions except for a key literary feature. In the 1940s, Martin Noth identified key texts that create a unifying perspective throughout these books (with some modification: Joshua 1:23; Judges 2:6–23; 1 Samuel 12; 2 Samuel 7; 1 Kings 8:14–61; 2 Kings 17:7–41; but prefaced by Deuteronomy 31 and perhaps 29–30). Rather than being fast-moving narratives, these texts are primarily speeches by main characters or a narrator that generally summarize and evaluate events as the fulfillment of the curses for apostasy or blessings for obedience found in the covenant of Deuteronomy—hence the name, Deuteronomistic History. Noth theorized that the DtrH received its main shape with these inserted blocks while the exiled people of the SK were in Babylon. Further study suggests that there was at least an earlier and a later edition.

Were the whole material to be read aloud ("published") to those exiles, the key blocks might have served as introductions and/or conclusions to a segmented reading over a few days. Also, the act of reading aloud the explanatory speeches of the main characters would have the impact of directly addressing the listening audience of exiles and presenting them with an ideological lesson. Thus, one finds in the books of Joshua–2 Kings an ideological history aimed at the exiles in Babylon. It tells them that their God, Yhwh, did not abandon them to the Babylonians; rather, they and their leaders did not listen to the prophets but abandoned God and suffered the curses of the Deuteronomic covenant. Moreover, this national history could give those in exile a sense of continuing religious identity in the face of the loss of landed identity. Then, when a generation later those exiles had a chance to return and rebuild under the Persian Empire, many still held allegiance to Yhwh and to their national identity and came back to Israel/Judah to begin again.

The ChrH tells another history of Israel, starting with Adam and ending with the reforms of Ezra and Nehemiah, as they direct the establishment of the restored community in Yehud (the Persian name of the province formerly known as Judah) and launch what becomes known as Second Temple Judaism. This group seems to be the initial target audience. The history is composed primarily of four blocks of material: First is 1 Chronicles 1–10, mainly through lists and genealogies, with a brief narrative closing on King Saul's death (1 Chronicles 10). It "tells" the biblical history from Adam to Saul. Second is 1 Chronicles 11–2 Chronicles 9, which covers King David the nation builder and his son, King Solomon, the temple builder. Third, 2 Chronicles 10–36 surveys the history of the SK and its kings down to the Babylonian captivity. Finally, Ezra and Nehemiah narrate the trials of the community that went back to Jerusalem from Babylon and how they rebuilt the temple and started over as the people of Yhwh. Within these four blocks, the main subjects are "all Israel" (the faithful worshippers of Yhwh), the tribe of Levi and the priestly families, the tribe of Judah and the Davidic kings, and implicitly, Yhwh, who is involved in their fate.

Since this second history would have an overlapping audience with those who knew the DtrH, it makes sense that the Chronicler, whether a person or a group who formed the main narrative, appears to have worked strategically to create a portrait that a DtrH audience could accept while coloring it in new ways. The "laws" of reality are first developed after Saul's death through the microfocus on the stories of David and Solomon. At the

close of the narrative about Saul, the narrator states that Saul was unfaith-
ful to Yhwh and did not "seek Yhwh," which resulted in the loss of his kingdom. Such a direct evaluation would be acceptable from the perspective of
a DtrH audience. Afterward, for the most part, the narrator as evaluator
fades into the background and presents a detailed focus on an idealized
portrait of David and Solomon, who bring blessings on themselves and
the nation when they "seek Yhwh." However, "seeking Yhwh," while not
contradicting the laws of the DtrH, now focuses much more on establishing the proper worship of Yhwh. That is to say, the audience sees that
the blessings of success in war and the prosperity of the nation follow the
actions of a prayerful king who protects the cultic aspects of worshipping
Yhwh correctly. Having established this paradigm in the second block of
material, in the third block, the narrator tells the history of the nation, but
only from the perspective of the SK. Now one finds the narrator making
explicit judgments on the kings as ones who either sought Yhwh and were
blessed, like David, or failed to seek Yhwh and were cursed.

One also finds a shift in the emplotment in this block compared to the
DtrH. The DtrH's history of the kings of the NK and SK basically shows a
downhill slide. In the SK, there were good kings, but from Manasseh on,
even though he was followed by the good king Josiah, the audience can
see that Judah's fate is sealed; it is headed toward disaster. In the ChrH,
however, the reigns of the kings following Solomon, who belong to the
divinely ordained royal line, are more self-contained units in which each
generation chooses its fate. The king and people might start off in a state of
blessing and end up experiencing cursing due to not seeking God, or the
opposite might occur. It is not a downhill slide; each generation chooses.

The fourth block of Ezra and Nehemiah appears to be material added
later to the work of the narrator(s) of 1–2 Chronicles, with the merging
taking place after the first few chapters of Ezra, in which the Chronicler
tells of the return of the faithful people to Jerusalem under the Persians. The
laws of reality have not changed, but the narrator's explanatory comments
on the seeking paradigm are not present. Still, the focus is on the ups and
downs of the community as it sets aside self-focus to make its priority the
establishment of the city walls, the building of the temple, the worship of
Yhwh, and a new practice, the reading of the law.

In summary, in the ChrH, one finds an ideology appropriate for a
community that has returned from exile and is starting over again. Like
the DtrH, God is the primary agent in history, not controlling all things
but responding to the people's faithfulness or unfaithfulness with positive
or negative consequences. Similar to the DtrH, the laws of reality are connected to being faithful; however, they are more focused on (re)establishing

and maintaining the temple proper and the correct cultic practices as per the examples of David and Solomon, probably with the hope of a restored Davidic kingship in the future. Unlike the DtrH, the emplotment does not reveal a downhill slide over multiple generations. Rather, the individual, generational portraits of the Davidic kings following Solomon teach that each generation has its opportunity for blessing or curse depending on whether they seek God.

About the Author

Rodney K. Duke holds a PhD in Old Testament from the University of Emory. Besides Chronicles, his research interests include narrative theology and the use of the Hebrew Scriptures in the New Testament. He is the author of "The Ethical Appeal of the Chronicler," pages 33–51 in *Rhetoric, Ethic, and Moral Persuasion in Biblical Discourse: Essays from the 2002 Heidelberg Conference*, edited by Thomas H. Olbricht and Anders Eriksson (London: T&T Clark International, 2005); "Chronicles, 1 & 2," pages 161–181 in *Dictionary of the Old Testament: Historical Books*, edited by Bill T. Arnold and Hugh G. M. Williamson (Downers Grove, IL: Inter-Varsity, 2005); and "The Strategic Use of Enthymeme and Example in the Argumentation of the Books of Chronicles," pages in *Rhetorical Argumentation in Biblical Texts: Essays from the Lund 2000 Conference*, Emory Studies for Early Christianity, edited by Anders Eriksson, Thomas H. Olbricht, and Walter Übelacker (Harrisburg, PA: Trinity Press International, 2002).

Suggestions for Further Reading

In This Book
See also chapters 20 (genealogies), 22 (periodization), 25 (Deuteronomistic History), 27 (Josiah's scroll), 44 (ancestors), 49 (Torah), and 52 (covenant).

Elsewhere
Allen, Leslie C. *1 & 2 Chronicles: A Message for Yehud; Introduction and Study Guide*. London: T&T International, 2021.

Ben Zvi, Ehud. "Chronicles and Samuel-Kings: Two Interlacing Aspects of One Memory System in the Late Persian/Early Hellenistic Period." Pages 41–56 in *Rereading the Relecture? The Question of (Post)Chronistic Influence in the Latest Redactions of the Books of Samuel*, FAT 2.66. Edited by Uwe Becker and Hannes Bezzel. Tübingen: Mohr Siebeck, 2014.

Guy, Jordan. *United in Exile, Reunited in Restoration: The Chronicler's Agenda*. Sheffield, UK: Sheffield Phoenix, 2019.

Jonker, Louis C. "Melting Pots and Rejoinders? The Interplay among Literature Formation Processes during the Late Persian and Early Hellenistic Periods." *Vetus Testamentum* 70 (2020): 42–54.

Lynch, Matthew J. "A Theological Comparison of the Deuteronomistic History and Chronicles." Pages 266–283 in *The Oxford Handbook of the Historical Books of the Hebrew Bible*. Edited by Brad E. Kelle and Brent A. Strawn. Oxford: Oxford University Press, 2020.

25

Is There Such a Thing as a "Deuteronomistic History"?

Philippe Guillaume

Koenigsberg (modern Russian Kaliningrad) was the easternmost German university of the Third Reich. Some months after the German surrender at Stalingrad in February 1943, Martin Noth, professor of Old Testament at the local university since 1930, published a small book, *Überlieferungs-geschichtliche Studien* (*Studies in Reception History*). It presented two historical narratives in the Bible, the Chronicles and a Deuteronomistic History. Having no access to normal scholarly publications at the time, Noth drew conclusions primarily from the biblical text itself. Even so, his little book became remarkably influential in the microcosm of Old Testament scholars throughout the second part of the twentieth century.

Noth hypothesized that the biblical books from Deuteronomy to 2 Kings formed a unified history of Israel written by a single author, commonly referred to in English as "Dtr." In his view, Dtr redacted the existing first version of Deuteronomy and then compiled old traditions into four distinctive eras: the time of Moses, Joshua's conquest, the period of the judges, and the monarchy. To unify the available disparate traditions, Dtr formulated speeches for the main characters at key junctures: Joshua 1:1–9; 12:1–6; 23:1–16; Judges 2:11–3:6; 1 Samuel 12:1–15; 1 Kings 8:14–53; 2 Kings 17:7–23, each using characteristic language and ideology. Since Joshua 1 does not provide a suitable introduction for this hypothetical extended narrative, Noth searched for it in Deuteronomy—hence the designation "Deuteronomistic" for the purported history.

Noth suggested that Dtr wrote from Mizpah, the new capital set up by the Neo-Babylonians to replace Jerusalem in 586 BCE. From Mizpah, Dtr could meditate on the theological implications of Zion's smoking ruins around 562 BCE, after the date of the last recorded event—Jehoiachin's release from a Babylonian prison (2 Kings 24:27–30). He could explain to the Judeans and Israelites who continued to thrive in the Benjamin region after the destruction of Jerusalem that their brethren suffered in exile after the destruction of their kingdoms because of their lack of loyalty to Yhwh.

The many and contradicting modifications introduced by Noth's followers to make the Deuteronomistic History comply with the complexities of the biblical texts underline the oversimplistic aspect of the initial hypothesis. Additional editors were postulated—some prior to the exile (586 BCE) in the reign of Josiah, others later in the Persian era (586–332 BCE)—to account for the differences Noth overlooked. In addition, Noth's defining of Deuteronomy–2 Kings as a single, independent composition clashed with the traditional view that Genesis–Deuteronomy forms a planned metanarrative within the biblical collection, with a focus on Torah teaching (the Pentateuch), as well as the scholarly suggestion that there might once have been a metanarrative that extended from Genesis to Joshua.

Hartmut Rösel argues that the programmatic passages Noth attributed to Dtr are unlikely to have been produced by the same writer because they deal very differently with the themes scholars identify as typically Deuteronomistic: foreign gods, covenant, sin, and divine punishment. Similar themes and even vocabulary are attested outside the Hebrew Bible as far back as Hittite texts (second millennium BCE), in Neo-Assyrian treaties, and just on the other side of the Jordan, on the stele set up by King Mesha in Dibon around 850 BCE. Mesha attributes the ability of the Israelite kings Omri and Ahab to occupy the land of Moab to the anger of his god Kemosh. Without explaining how Kemosh's anger was placated, Mesha boasts of having slaughtered the population of an entire Israelite town as a sacrifice of thanksgiving for his success in expelling the Israelite invaders. To describe such a sacrifice, Mesha uses the term *ḥerem*, which also is deemed a mark of Deuteronomistic theology.

In Thomas Römer's popular revision of Noth's hypothesis, the original Deuteronomistic History was written in Babylonia, not Mizpah. It lacked the period of the judges, which, Römer argues, was created later, possibly as late as the Hellenistic era (323–31 BCE). This is, indeed, when interaction with a multitude of ethnic groups from all over the ancient Near East fostered a need to inquire into the origins of the Egyptians, Babylonians, and others. Works such as Manetho's *History of Egypt* and Berossus's *History of Babylonia* were produced then.

Following the rise of a significant Jewish diaspora in Egypt, Römer postulates that the need was felt in the megapolis of Alexandria to produce a similar compilation to trace the origin of the people who hailed from the highlands of what Herodotus deemed Palestina. The production of a history along the lines of those written by Manetho and Berossus to trace the history of the Jews makes sense in this context. The question is whether only the period of the judges was invented then to complete an older Deuteronomistic History or if the entire organization of the Israelite past from creation to the return of the Jews from Babylon in the days of King Cyrus occurred in the wake of the Alexandrian historians. If so, Noth's date for the invention of history several centuries earlier and away from the thriving intellectual scene of the Hellenistic era is quite remarkable, since it sets the invention of "history" a century or two before Herodotus, the "father of history" (around 450 BCE).

It is possible that Noth correctly perceived that "history" was somewhat invented in the wake of the destruction of Jerusalem, though one must take into account another factor at work when Noth formulated his famous hypothesis. Alfred Rosenberg (1930) argued that the original Christianity had been corrupted by Judaized influences. German theologians responded with the "history" catchword to counter Rosenberg's twentieth-century myth with a supposed biblical understanding of history, setting up a confrontation between "myth" and "history." "History" was in the air when Noth developed the hypothesis of a Deuteronomistic History. There is no indication that he was conscious that a Jewish history spanning six books of the Old Testament would, indeed, counter tendencies to disregard the Old Testament as an essential part of the Christian Scriptures.

The echo the Deuteronomistic History produced in the Western outlook after World War II contributed to the success of Noth's hypothesis. As Diane Banks (2006, 124) notes, Noth's conviction that Israel's unique destiny was designed by God made him particularly palatable to North American views of special destiny and God's active involvement in historical events. Noth was rector of the University of Bonn in 1947–1948 and in 1957–1958. He became the first German member of the editorial board of the new journal *Vetus Testamentum* and held important positions in the International Organization for the Study of the Old Testament, presiding at its fourth congress at Bonn in 1962.

That subsequent researchers introduced modifications in the original hypothesis is inevitable. The question today is whether the hypothesis itself is still tenable, given the major changes involved. If the period of the judges could have been elaborated in the Hellenistic era, there is a possibility that the understanding of Israel's past as distinct eras echoes Hellenistic historians. Today, one must be aware of the dangers of using the term and the notion of "Deuteronomistic History" as if it were a well-established hypothesis. It is not.

One valuable methodological lesson in Martin Noth's biography is that the acquisition of an intimate knowledge of a biblical passage in its original languages (Hebrew, Aramaic, Greek, Latin) is essential to scholarly excellence before plunging into the vast scholarly literature.

In conclusion, and to answer the question in the title, a Deuteronomistic History indeed existed in the minds of Old Testament scholars throughout the second part of the twentieth century CE. If it existed before, with a beginning somewhere in Deuteronomy, it was soon rejected and replaced by the notion of the Torah, with the book of Deuteronomy as the end of Moses's teaching rather than the introduction of a history. Most if not all of the stories that follow Moses's death were certainly written and known before the Hellenistic era, but they were not understood as building blocks of a history before they were translated into Greek.

About the Author

Philippe Guillaume holds a doctorate of theology (PhD) in Old Testament from the University of Geneva. He published "Philadelphus' Alexandria as Cradle of Biblical Historiography," pages 247–255 in *Ptolemy II Philadelphus and his World*, edited by Paul McKechnie and Philippe Guillaume (Leiden: Brill, 2008); and "From Philadelphus to Hyrkanus: An Alternative Approach to the Formation of the 'Deuteronomistic History,'" pages 186–202 in *Even God Cannot Change the Past*, edited by Lester L. Grabbe (London: T&T Clark, 2018).

Suggestions for Further Reading

In This Book
See also chapters 5 (canons), 11 (Pentateuch), 14 (myths), 22 (periodization), 33 (Septuagint), and 52 (covenant).

Elsewhere
Banks, Diane. *Writing the History of Israel*. New York: T&T Clark, 2006.

Begg, Christopher T. "Martin Noth: Notes on His Life and Work." Pages 18–30 in *The History of Israel's Traditions: The Heritage of Martin Noth*. Edited by Steven L. McKenzie and M. Patrick Graham. Sheffield, UK: Sheffield Academic, 1994.

Noth, Martin. *Überlieferungsgeschichtliche Studien* (3rd edition). Darmstadt: Wissenschaftliche Buchgesellschaft, 1967. Translated as *The Deuteronomistic History* (Sheffield, UK: JSOT, 1991).

Römer, Thomas C. *The So-Called Deuteronomistic History*. London: T&T Clark, 2005.

Rösel, Harmut N. "Does a Comprehensive Leitmotiv Exist in the Deuteronomistic History?" Pages 195–211 in *The Future of the Deuteronomistic History*. Edited by Thomas C. Römer. Leuven: Leuven University Press, 2000.

Rosenberg, Alfred. *The Myth of the Twentieth Century*. 1930. Newport, CA: Noontide, 1993.

26
Did the Hebrews Conquer Canaan?

Erin Darby

While it may appear that the answer to this question is a simple yes or no, both the Hebrew Bible and archaeology require reframing the query. The question is grounded in only certain biblical texts, like the narratives of conquest in Joshua 1–12. Likewise, it is informed by particular interpretations of the biblical text that may not take into consideration the history of composition or the aims of later biblical editors. As Avraham Faust (2022, 6) notes, irregularities in the biblical account of Joshua, not archaeology, originally prompted scholars to revisit the historical accuracy of Joshua's conquest narrative.

Before proceeding to the issue of "conquest," we must first address two related questions: Who were the "Israelites" and what did that name mean? In other words, did a unified ethnic or political group refer to themselves as Israelites in this early stage? While a variety of biblical texts postdating this period use the terms "Israelite" or "Hebrews" to describe a coherent group of interrelated tribes, no inscriptions from the inhabitants of the territory in question use "Hebrew," "Israelite," or "Israel" in the second millennium. This challenge is compounded by the fact that so few inscriptions from the Levant are preserved at all!

The only extrabiblical reference in this period to the "Israelites" is found in the Egyptian Merneptah Stele (thirteenth century BCE). The stele is an engraved stone that commemorates the victories of Pharaoh Merneptah while on a military campaign in the late 1200s BCE. Although the first attestation of "Israel" in reference to an ethnic group was written in Egyptian hieroglyphs, many scholars argue that the name had already been adopted by the inhabitants themselves. This suggests that an Israelite people group had already settled in the land by the end of the thirteenth century. Sadly, it tells us little about how large that group may have been or even where in modern Israel, Gaza, the West Bank, or Jordan they may have lived.

Complicating matters further, even the biblical text is inconsistent in relating the names of the tribes of Israel and the manner of their settlement (e.g., Genesis 49, Deuteronomy 27 and 33, Joshua 13–19, Judges 1 and 5). These texts were written and edited by various authors over a range of periods, mostly postdating the time during which the events purportedly happened. Many of the details of their composition are debated by scholars still today.

Several challenges impede us from using archaeological excavation to locate evidence for early Israelites. First, we would need to clearly identify the time periods relevant to the biblical descriptions of the exodus from Egypt, the wilderness wanderings, and the conquest of Canaan. Extensive scholarly debate has yielded various theories, largely ranging from the fifteenth to the twelfth centuries, but consensus on the historical accuracy of the biblical narratives remains elusive. As of today, very few of the archaeological sites from the Late Bronze (ca. 1550–1200 BCE) or Iron I (ca. 1200–1000 BCE) periods can be associated with locations or events in the biblical narratives, and very few of the sites or events mentioned in the biblical narratives have been confirmed through archaeological investigation.

A related issue is whether we would recognize distinctively "Israelite" material culture if we found it. This problem has enjoyed a long history of debate. Scholars may point to changes in building style, orientation, or pottery in the few cities that were reoccupied during the Iron I. These changes could indicate the influx of a new population, although without any inscriptions, scholars are left to conjecture who might be responsible for the next phase of occupation. In other cases, scholars have interpreted pottery styles, like the collared rim jar; foodways, such as the (near) absence of pig bones; and architectural forms, like the four-room house, as signs of a unique Israelite identity in the small settlements of the early Iron Age. Additional archaeological investigation, however, has demonstrated that most of these "ethnic markers" occur in several regions, including those associated with other people groups.

Are we any clearer about the "Canaanites" of the biblical texts? In the Hebrew Bible, the term refers to a broad range of people living in the southern Levant. Canaanites are predominantly portrayed as hostile to the resettling Israelites, and the religious practices attributed to the Canaanites are routinely denigrated. This pattern calls into question whether the pejorative tone in the biblical text overshadows accurate historical details.

The terms "Canaan" and "Canaanite" are found in a range of texts from the second millennium BCE, though none of these texts were written by the "Canaanites." As indicated by their own letters in the fourteenth century (the Amarna Tablets), they may have thought of themselves primarily as inhabitants or rulers of a particular city-state rather than as part of a single, regional entity. Nevertheless, building on the textual and archaeological evidence, most contemporary scholars use the term "Canaanite" to refer to inhabitants of what is today modern Israel, Gaza, the West Bank, Jordan, Lebanon, and southern Syria in the second millennium BCE.

Archaeology provides a great deal of information about the settlements across the southern Levant, where, according to the biblical stories, Canaanites eventually interacted with the fledgling Israelites. For most of the second millennium, the Canaanite city-states that formed the fabric of daily life were ruled by the Egyptians. This complex relationship was marked by periods of warfare and collaboration, by Levantine inhabitants being taken as slaves, as well as by Levantine elites accumulating wealth and status in Canaan and Egypt. Through trade and politics, many Canaanite urban settlements were connected with distant locations across the Near East and the Mediterranean. These cities have yielded evidence of socioeconomic stratification, including impressive temples and palaces. Their religious traditions probably revolved around a complex pantheon, with key figures, like El and Baal, at their center.

The archaeological record also confirms that city-states in the southern Levant experienced widespread societal turmoil that impacted the entire Mediterranean in the Late Bronze Age. This period saw the migration of different groups, like the Mediterranean Sea Peoples, who eventually settled along the Levantine coast. In the wake of that breakdown, some important cities in the lowlands of Canaan collapsed and were eventually reoccupied, and other cities on both sides of the Jordan experienced a period of turmoil but recovered and remained relatively strong from the twelfth through tenth centuries BCE. In still other regions, like the hill country, the Iron I saw the rise of new, unwalled, small-scale settlements in areas that had remained largely uninhabited for hundreds of years.

Did these new settlement patterns result from a military conquest of the type described in the biblical book of Joshua? Or were they the outcome of other societal forces? After over a century of archaeological exploration, we are still lacking evidence of widespread warfare associated with the influx of a new population. In some cases, like Jericho, earlier interpretations that identified destruction with possible Israelite conquest have been unanimously overturned due to improved methods for dating occupational layers. While some sites experienced destruction, like Hazor, they are in the minority. Even at Hazor, a significant gap separates the time between the site's destruction and its ephemeral reoccupation, suggesting that the new material culture associated with a different population is impossible to attribute to a conquering army. Finally, some sites have produced evidence for multiple, partial destructions and gradual decline throughout the Late Bronze and Iron I without any population change, like Megiddo. The absence of evidence is not the evidence of absence, of course, yet many years of archaeological investigation failed to corroborate the account in Joshua, which is the result of later editorial activity that long postdates the Late Bronze and Iron I periods.

The archaeological pattern of new agricultural settlements in the hill country more closely aligns with the account of the Israelite tribes in the book of Judges. Judges tells the story of individual tribes that unite when need dictates but largely operate autonomously in their own territories. Far from having successfully driven out all other inhabitants, these tribes interact with various local populations and, according to the stories, are, at times, dominated by them. This is not to say that Judges should be read as a script that directly recounts the historical events of the Iron I. It, too, has been shaped by later editorial hands. However, many scholars still draw attention to the similarities between what archaeology reveals and the picture the authors of Judges paint of a multiethnic region, a largely agrarian setting, and the diffuse tribal organization predating a system of government that emerges only in the tenth century or thereafter.

To account for the differences between the biblical and archaeological records, some scholars reconstructed the emergence of Israel with a peasant revolt model: the people who became the Israelites largely came from Canaanite lower classes, rebelling against the elites of their city-states. Many scholars argue for some variation of a migration model that approaches the emergence of Israel not as a conquest by a single people group but as a redistribution of various populations related to the turmoil of the Late Bronze period. Some of these groups could have come from Egypt, but others were likely the inhabitants of nearby Canaanite settlements. This model could account for the similarities in material culture across the Late Bronze and Iron I divide as well as the fact that settlement change occurred gradually, at different rates, and in different ways across the region. In this scholarly approach, the destruction of some Levantine Canaanite urban centers had little to do with an Israelite army but resulted from the various chaotic forces that characterized the Late Bronze Age, including environmental degradation, large-scale political decline and upheaval, internal unrest, and population movement. Resettlement by a diverse population in the highlands was an economic response to Late Bronze societal breakdown, and new hamlets survived through a combination of seminomadic pastoralism and small-scale agriculture.

Thus, if we ask whether archaeology confirms that the Israelites conquered the Canaanites as portrayed in the book of Joshua, the answer has to be no. Even when taken on its own, the Hebrew Bible's multiple perspectives and editorial history warn us against an overly simplistic interpretation. Instead, both the Hebrew Bible and archaeology present us with a complex picture of the emergence of Israel; its development as an ethnic, cultural, and political unit; and its interactions with other people groups.

About the Author

Erin Darby holds a doctorate of philosophy (PhD) in religion from Duke University and is currently an associate professor in religious studies and the faculty director of undergraduate research and fellowships at the University of Tennessee. Her research includes the Hebrew Bible, iconography, and ancient religion, and she serves as the codirector for the 'Ayn Gharandal Archaeological Project. She has published *Interpreting Judean Pillar Figurines: Gender and Empire in Judean Apotropaic Ritual.* FAT II 69 (Tübingen: Mohr Siebeck, 2014); and "What Is Primary vs. Secondary Use?" and "How Is Archaeology Used to Support Nationalism?," pages 86–88 and 235–238 in *The Five-Minute Archaeologist in the Southern Levant*, edited by Cynthia Schafer-Elliott (London: Equinox, 2016). She served as the coeditor with Izaak J. de Hulster of *Iron Age Terracotta Figurines from the Southern Levant in Context*, CHANE 125 (Leiden: Brill, 2022).

Suggestions for Further Reading

In This Book

See also chapters 1 (scholarly perspective), 2 (religion), 3 (religious in a scientific world), 7 (who wrote the Bible?), 21 (dates), 22 (periodization), 24 (Kings and Chronicles), 25 (Deuteronomistic History), 28–30 (archaeology), 44 (ancestors), 48 (twelve tribes), 54 (genocide), 47 (monotheism), and 56 (polemics).

Elsewhere

Burke, Aaron A. "New Kingdom Egypt and Early Israel: Entangled Identities." Pages 537–548 in *The Ancient Israelite World*. Edited by Kyle H. Keimer and George A. Pierce. London: Routledge, 2022.

Cline, Eric H. *1177 B.C.: The Year Civilization Collapsed: Revised and Updated.* Princeton, NJ: Princeton University Press, 2021.

Doak, Brian R. *Ancient Israel's Neighbors*. Oxford: Oxford University Press, 2020.

Faust, Avraham. "Between the Biblical Story and History: Writing an Archaeological History of Ancient Israel." Pages 67–81 in *The Ancient Israelite World*. Edited by Kyle H. Keimer and George A. Pierce. London: Routledge, 2022.

Faust, Avraham. *Israel's Ethnogenesis: Settlement, Interaction, Expansion and Resistance*. London: Routledge, 2006.

Finkelstein, Israel, and Neil Asher Silberman. *The Bible Unearthed: Archaeology's New Vision of Ancient Israel and the Origin of Sacred Texts*. New York: Free Press, 2001.

Gadot, Yuval. "The Iron I Settlement Wave in the Samaria Highlands and Its Connection with the Urban Centers." *Near Eastern Archaeology* 82(1) (2019): 32–41.

Killebrew, Ann E. *Biblical Peoples and Ethnicity: An Archaeological Study of Egyptians, Canaanites, Philistines, and Early Israel, 1300–1100 B.C.E.* Atlanta: SBL, 2005.

27
Was Josiah's Scroll Lost and Found Twice?

Diana V. Edelman

In 2 Kings, during temple repairs ordered by King Josiah (ca. 640–609 BCE), it is said that Hilkiah the high priest found "the scroll of the teaching [torah]" (22:8, 11), which subsequently is called "the scroll of the covenant [*berit*]" (23:2). The king is then said to have made a covenant (*berit*), which the people of Judah and Jerusalem joined into, to enact the words/matters of the covenant written in "this scroll" (23:3). Josiah's subsequent actions described in the ensuing verses logically detail covenantal stipulations in the scroll that were not being followed (23:4–24), which he set about to correct. All are religious reforms. He is said to have removed the symbols, paraphernalia, personnel, places of worship, and cult of Asherah and Baal; the sun and the moon and the constellations and all the hosts of heaven; and Molech in Judah and the neighboring province of Samaria. He also orders the celebration of Passover and removes (those who consult) spirits and familiar spirits as well as household gods (teraphim) and idols. Thus, according to 2 Kings 22–23, King Josiah reformed official and household religion not only in his kingdom but in the adjoining Assyrian province of Samaria as well.

Scholars continue to debate what the contents of the scroll in question would have been as well as if these events ever happened. The two issues are interrelated. Some scholars propose that the scroll contained most of the contents now found in Deuteronomy 12–26, which they label *Ur-Deuteronomium* and which also is frequently dubbed the Deuteronomic Law Code. Others suggest the scroll was the book of Deuteronomy itself, while still others see it to be similar to Deuteronomy but not Deuteronomy. Another proposal is that the scroll included the first five books, Genesis, Exodus, Leviticus, Numbers, and Deuteronomy, which come to be designated the Torah in rabbinic Judaism.

The arguments concerning the contents are influenced in part by the Chronicler's account of Josiah's reign. It places the beginning of his religious reforms in Judah and Jerusalem six years before the scroll is found during temple repairs (2 Chronicles 34:3–8, 15). It refers to the contents of the scroll as the teaching (torah) of Yhwh through Moses, not just the teaching, as in Kings, and subsequently, as the scroll of the covenant (34:30), as in Kings. After Josiah and the people in Jerusalem and Benjamin join in a covenant to perform the words of the covenant written in the scroll, the people in Jerusalem allegedly follow the covenant of Elohim, the god of their fathers, and Josiah removes all the abominations from all the territories belonging to the children of Israel and makes them serve Yhwh, their god.

The second influencing factor consists of the claims made in the book of Deuteronomy that Moses personally wrote the teaching/torah of Yhwh in a scroll (31:9, 24; 29:21; 30:10). However, he also was to have commanded the Levites to place it beside the ark of the covenant in 34:26. While the first set of verses would seem to have led the Chronicler to think some or all of Deuteronomy was what was found during Josiah's temple repairs, it needs to be noted that the book does not contain the text of a formal covenant document, which seems to be envisioned by the writer of 2 Kings.

Deuteronomy presents itself as a series of first-person speeches made by Moses on the plains of Moab right before his death. Moses conveys Yhwh's teaching, adding additional comments meant to impress on the Israelites the consequences of obedience and disobedience. Typical of teaching or instructions, the majority of the precepts to be followed are delivered in the second-person singular and plural, not the third person, like so-called ancient legal codes. The narrator also makes comments in the third person. We are told incidentally that a covenant was established that day on the plains of Moab between Yhwh Elohim and the people of Israel (Deuteronomy 26:17–19), however, so it still might be appropriate to characterize some or all of Deuteronomy as "the scroll of the covenant."

But then, how could such an important scroll that should have been located in the holy of holies beside the ark have gotten lost or mislaid? The high priest was the only person authorized to enter this space (Leviticus 16:2–24), and he was only to do so once a year to purify it. Surely he would have noted if the scroll had gone missing.

Once allegedly found during temple repairs, the scroll seems to disappear again, along with the ark, when Jerusalem is captured by the Neo-Babylonians in 587 BCE and the temple is looted and burned. Unlike the ark, however, the scroll or something similar allegedly reappears with Ezra, the scribe of priestly descent who returned home from exile in Babylonia.

It is "reintroduced" in what now has become the province of Yehud and Jerusalem as the teaching of Moses that Yhwh, the God of Israel, had given (Ezra 7:6, 10; also 3:2; 6:18; Nehemiah 8:1, 14; scroll of Moses in Nehemiah 13:1). The Persian king Artaxerxes refers to it instead as "the teaching [torah] of the God of heaven" (Ezra 7:12, 14, 25–26), while the narrator in Nehemiah 8:8 and 10:28–29 calls it the teaching of God and the scroll of the teaching of God (verse 18). So in the social memory reflected collectively in the various books comprising the Hebrew Bible, the scroll of teaching/torah allegedly went to Babylonia with the exiles and returned home with them as well, in the care of the scribe and priest Ezra.

On closer inspection, the story of the returning scroll of the teaching/ torah associated with Yhwh, Elohim, and Moses is part of a larger rhetorical argument designed to link the Persian-era rebuilt temple, priesthood, and its practices with the monarchic-era, Solomonic temple, its priesthood, and vessels (Ezra 1:7–11; 5:14–15; 6:5) in a direct line of continuity in spite of a number of changes that were introduced. The books of Haggai and Zechariah emphasize how the rebuilt temple is to be for Yhwh Ṣebaʾot, the name used in Jerusalem for Yhwh during the monarchy, although it is actually for Yhwh Elohim, the preferred name in the Persian period. The new high priest Yeshua is allegedly the grandson of the last high priest who was exiled in 587 BCE, Seraiah (Nehemiah 3:2; 12:1, 7, 26; 1 Chronicles 6:14–15). The scroll of the law of Moses that was beside the ark replaces the lost ark. It allegedly is the same scroll found during Josiah's temple repairs, even though Moses is not named in 2 Kings.

Toward the end of the Hellenistic period (323–31 BCE), this idea of continuity is further enhanced by the idea that the fire from the monarchic-era temple that had descended from heaven to dedicate the temple of Solomon (2 Chronicles 7:1) was hidden in a dry well when the temple was destroyed. When retrieved by order of the Persian governor Nehemiah, it had turned into petroleum oil (*naptha*), which was poured on the wood at the rededication of the temple, and the sun miraculously lit it (2 Maccabees 1:10b–2:18).

The innovative emphasis on the scroll of teaching/torah associated with Yhwh Elohim in the Persian period as central for defining normative behavior logically would have required the invention of the story about the scroll finding late in the monarchy to serve as a "historical" precedent to create a memory of continuity with the past in the face of an actual break/change. Some scholars have suspected that the scroll was written by a scribe belonging to Josiah's court to justify cultic reform and the anticipated political annexation of Samaria at that time. By placing it in the temple to be "found" during the repairs, its assumed authority as a venerable religious document would provide divine endorsement for those plans. A few scholars accept the story of finding the scroll as historically reliable. The date one prefers to assign to the writing of the book of Deuteronomy and the ideas it endorses is ultimately affected by one's understanding of the evolving memory of the scroll of teaching/torah and how that relates to real events in the past.

About the Author

Diana V. Edelman holds a doctorate of philosophy (PhD) in biblical studies from the University of Chicago and is Professor Emerita in Hebrew Bible at the Faculty of Theology, University of Oslo. She has published *The Origins of the "Second" Temple: Persian Imperial Policies and the Rebuilding of Jerusalem* (London: Equinox, 2005); and "Deuteronomy as the Instructions of Moses and Yhwh vs. a Framed Legal Code," pages 27–75 in *Deuteronomy in the Making: Studies in the Production of Debarim*, edited by Diana V. Edelman, Benedetta Rossi, Kåre Berge, and Philippe Guillaume (Berlin: De Gruyter, 2021).

Suggestions for Further Reading

In This Book
See also chapters 10 (Tanak), 24 (Kings and Chronicles), 44 (ancestors), 47 (monotheism), 49 (Torah), 51 (prophets), 52 (covenant), 56 (polemics), and 63 (Moses).

Elsewhere
Ben-Dov, Jonathan. "Some Precedents for the Religion of the Book: Josiah's Book and Ancient Revelatory Literature." Pages 43–62 in *Constructs of Prophecy in the Former and Latter Prophets and Other Texts*. Edited by Lester L. Grabbe and Martti Nissinen. Atlanta: SBL, 2011.

Ben Zvi, Ehud. "Imagining Josiah's Book and the Implications of Imagining It in Early Persian Yehud." Pages 193–212 in *Berührungspunkte. Studien zur Sozial- und Religionsgeschichte Israels und seiner Umwelt. Festschrift für Rainer Albertz zu seinem 65. Geburtstag*. Edited by Ingo Gottsieper, Rüdiger Schmitt, and Jakob Wöhrle. Münster: Ugarit Verlag, 2008.

Berge, Kåre. "Dynamics of Power and the Re-invention of 'Israel' in Persian Empire Judah." Pages 293–321 in *Levantine Entanglements: Local Dynamics of Globalization in a Contested Region*. Edited by Terje Stordalen and Øystein LaBianca. Sheffield, UK: Equinox, 2011.

Davies, Philip R. "Josiah and the Law Book." Pages 65–77 in *Good Kings and Bad Kings*. Edited by Lester L. Grabbe. New York: T&T Clark, 2005.

Rossi, Benedetta. "Torah in Deuteronomy." In *Deuteronomy: Outside the Box*. Edited by Diana V. Edelman and Philippe Guillaume. Sheffield, UK: Equinox, 2022. https://www.equinoxpub.com/home/view-chapter/?id =44618.

The Hebrew Bible
and Archaeology

28
Can Archaeology Prove the Truth of Biblical Texts?

Tammi J. Schneider

If you have ever wondered if archaeology can prove the truth of the biblical texts in the Hebrew Bible, this entry is for you. When we unpack, even briefly, the notions of "truth," "biblical texts," and "archaeology," it becomes clear that putting them together misses the point of all of them. Two examples will illustrate why.

Truth. According to Wikipedia (I use Wikipedia here not because it is the best dictionary but because it is the one more people turn to, and therefore, more people accept its definitions than those of any other dictionary), truth means, first, "that which is true or in accordance with fact or reality." While there are "facts" and a certain reality behind both the biblical text and archaeological finds, both depend heavily on interpretation to contextualize the meaning behind them. A second meaning for truth is "a fact or belief that is accepted as true." It is possible this cuts a bit closer to the issue inherent in finding the truth using archaeology to prove the Bible in that in this case, "truth" is a fact or belief accepted as true. It leaves open the possibility that the fact or belief is not true, but everyone accepts it, somewhat like Wikipedia definitions.

Biblical Texts. There are numerous articles in this volume grappling with what the biblical text is, what it means, how it should be read, who wrote it, who was/is the audience, and how it should be interpreted. These entries suggest that there are many people interpreting the text in different ways, some that may or may not be in agreement with each other. To prove any truth behind such a complex text, there would have to be some agreement concerning what its wording suggests about anything.

For many, the Bible is a religious and/or theological document. As far as we know, none of the texts included are intended to be historical documents providing clear details to prove their veracity. Proving belief is difficult. In the context of something that could be proved archaeologically, there would have to be some specific reference inside the text that scholars in general agree is an intentional "fact." In general, to prove something in the biblical text, one would have to assume the text was written by someone who intentionally wrote it to be dated and/or proved and that it was passed on without change through the entire biblical process of transmission. It is a tough scenario to envision.

Archaeology. Again, following Wikipedia, archaeology is "the study of human history and prehistory through the excavation of sites and the analysis of artifacts and other physical remains." Archaeology is focused on physical remains left behind by previous civilizations. Archaeological remains are silent: they are artifacts found in the ground and must be interpreted. While the field of archaeology has advanced considerably since its inception, it is the role of human archaeologists to take the finds and analyze them using the most scientific methodological approaches available to come up with a good analysis of those remains. It is not a pure science because it cannot be replicated. As a result, just like trying to understand the biblical text, archaeology concerns humans using their best tools to interpret the text, meaning any archaeological assessment of what a site or artifact means is an interpretation.

Two examples should suffice to demonstrate how difficult it is to use archaeology to prove the accuracy of any biblical text. The first example concerns Noah's ark, found in Genesis 6–9, depending on where one wants to end the story. People are constantly finding Noah's ark. It is usually found in modern Turkey, in the mountains, because someone flying over-head sees something made of wood jutting out of the snow, and someone sneaks up there—usually in violation of some country's laws—and steals some wood and takes photographs that prove "archaeologically" that it must be Noah's ark. Sir Leonard Woolley also claimed to have found evidence of the flood at the site of Ur in modern-day Iraq.

Numerous problems emerge from such things. First, the biblical text is not consistent about how many animals boarded the vessel or how long it rained. The text does not say why the deity sent the flood, nor does it state precisely where the ark landed. The fact that the story ends with a rainbow as a sign of a covenant suggests that the point of the story is not to be proved archaeologically at all; instead, it is about longer-term issues concerning the relationship of humans to the earth and, probably, their deity. An atmospheric phenomenon infused with theological notions concerning the future of the planet cannot be proved with an archaeolog-ical artifact.

Similar problems emerge with the Battle of Jericho. Joshua 2–6 recounts the battle, and the site of Jericho has been excavated. Configuring the timeline for when the Israelites leave Egypt and enter the land (if it happened) involves a complicated bit of sleuthing. The problem for Jericho is that if the Israelites leave Egypt around the end of the Late Bronze Age (1550–1200 BCE), then they capture a city that was abandoned a few hundred years before their arrival. The story of Jericho ends with the Israelites violating a proscription the first time they are in a battle in the land, suggesting that maybe the story was not about Jericho after all but about the Israelites' relationship to their deity and how they should behave in their land.

By briefly examining truth, biblical texts, and archaeology, it seems clear that if one needs to prove the Bible through archaeology, one is not really grappling with what the biblical text is.

About the Author

Tammi J. Schneider received her PhD in ancient history (including the fields of archaeology, history, and languages of the Bible and Mesopotamia) from the University of Pennsylvania and holds the Danforth Chair in Religion at Claremont Graduate University. She has twenty-eight years of archaeological experience in Israel, serving as staff in various capacities or directing excavations at the sites of Tel Miqne / Ekron, Tel Safi, Tel Harassim, Tel el-Far'a (South), and Akko. She has published *Bible and Archaeology: Where Have We Been and Where Are We Going?*, Occasional Papers 49 (Claremont, CA: Institute for Antiquity and Christianity, Claremont Graduate University, 2006); and "Jezebel: A Phoenician Princess Gone Bad?," pages 123–132 in *Partners with God: Theological and Critical Readings of the Bible in Honor of Marvin A. Sweeney*, edited by Shelley Birdsong (Claremont, CA: Claremont Press, 2017).

Suggestions for Further Reading

In This Book
See also chapters 1 (scholarly perspective), 6 (biblical exegesis), 7 (who wrote the Bible?), 9 (audiences), 14 (myths), 23 (minimalism), 26 (conquest of Canaan), 27 (Josiah's scroll), 28–31 (archaeology), 48 (twelve tribes), 52 (covenant), 72 (synchronic vs. diachronic), and 75 (historical criticism).

Elsewhere
Collins, John J. *Introduction to the Hebrew Bible with CD-ROM*. Minneapolis: Fortress, 2004.

Ebeling, Jennie, J. Edward Wright, Mark Elliot, and Paul V. M. Flesher. *The Old Testament in Archaeology and History*. Waco: Baylor University Press, 2017.

Miller, Maxwell J., and John H. Hayes. *A History of Ancient Israel and Judah* (2nd edition). Louisville, KY: Westminster John Knox, 2006.

Steiner, Margreet L., and Ann E. Killebrew. *The Oxford Handbook of the Archaeology of the Levant c. 8000–332 BCE*. Oxford: Oxford University Press, 2014.

29
How Should We Read the "Archaeological Evidence"?

Raz Kletter

In Israel in the 1980s, students in the humanities made use of inexpensive, xeroxed compendia of articles compiled by teachers rather than expensive textbooks. In the introduction to one such compendium, the teacher strongly advised students, when reading an article, to distinguish carefully among facts, assumptions, and conclusions. However, the teacher did not explain how to do it.

It is easy to determine how an author presents facts, assumptions, or conclusions in a text. In 1905, $E = mc^2$ was a new conclusion by Einstein; others considered it an assumption, while we today tend to speak about it as fact. But it is not easy to determine whether assumptions and conclusions are true—or put more exactly, reasonable or convincing—because there are no absolute, eternal truths in science. The student or the biblical scholar who reads an archaeological article does not necessarily have the required expertise to judge the author's claims but cannot trust that the archaeologist's claims are valid.

Let me demonstrate why with a case study concerning Shiloh. In 1 Samuel 1–4, Shiloh is a religious center of the Israelites in the days of the judges. The prophet Samuel, who led Israel in recovering the ark of God and choosing a king, was a priest at Shiloh.

Shiloh (Tel Seilun in Arabic) is located in the West Bank. It was excavated by a Danish team in the 1920s and 1930s and in the 1980s by Israel Finkelstein. Finkelstein viewed Shiloh as a "biblical site," as the title of his 1983 excavation report announced. Shiloh was also central in his *Archaeology of the Israelite Settlement*, where he concluded that "we have been able to shed new light on the special position of Shiloh as the first religious center of Israelite population in the hill country" (1988, 234).

In fact, no Iron Age sanctuary was discovered. Two small fragments of a cultic stand were found, but cultic stands are also found in domestic

contexts. The animal bones found "may have been the remains of offerings," but animal bones are commonly found in excavations, and no proof
was shown for their use as offerings at Shiloh.

Finkelstein's conclusions about Shiloh "proved" much of the biblical
story—because they were based on it, a common approach that archaeologists and biblical scholars gradually came to recognize as problematic.
Finkelstein (2005, 19) later explained that he was "not yet fully liberated
from a somewhat naïve reading of the biblical text" when he wrote that
the archaeology hints that Shiloh was a cultic place: "The architecture is
quite common, and so is the pottery. The size of the site and the settlement
pattern around it are unexceptional, and there are almost no finds that can
be directly associated with cult."

This 180-degree turn cannot be explained on the basis of archaeological facts, since nothing has changed at Shiloh. Rather, it relates to changing historical circumstances. During the Oslo peace process (1993–2000),
under the influence of the "minimalist" scholars from Copenhagen, it was
fashionable to doubt the historicity of the Bible. "Biblical archaeology"
was passé. To be viewed as "scientific," the archaeology of biblical sites had
to distance itself from the Bible.

Yet, this new trend proved less enduring than biblical archaeology.
Finkelstein (2019, 10–11) argued that more recent excavations shed new
light on Shiloh:

> The Iron I site was bigger than previously estimated, with more
> extensive storage facilities; it could have reached up to 2.5 ha, far
> larger than the average Iron I habitation site in the highlands. To
> judge from the biblical tradition and long-term history of the site,
> its focus and raison d'être was probably a cult place on the summit.

These new excavations were made with the explicit aim of "demon-
strating the historical reliability of the Bible" (Associates for Biblical
Research, n.d.). However, they have not demonstrated the presence of
any religious center in Shiloh. Additional storage buildings are just additional storage buildings. Estimations of the sizes of sites are notoriously
inaccurate, and size does not prove religious centrality. Archaeology can
conclude, so far, that perhaps there was a regional sanctuary at Shiloh, but
perhaps there was not, because the subsequent excavations added nothing
new about a possible sanctuary.

The reasons for the shift are again rooted in modern, not ancient,
history. Gone are the Oslo years. Generous budgets are channeled now for
projects in places like East Jerusalem, and there is a growing radicalization

of the public in terms of viewing the nation's past. It is no longer politically correct to cast doubts on the historicity of the biblical portrayal of Israel, so it is preferable to make Shiloh great again.

We can learn from this case study that the archaeological "facts" about the past are not absolute and eternal but malleable and related to present ideologies and circumstances. The same excavator presented three contrasting, incompatible sets of facts and conclusions about Iron I Shiloh—proving, disproving, and again proving the biblical stories about it. At first, Shiloh was an Israelite religious center, but only of four to five tribes, not twelve. Then, there was no religious center at Shiloh (and no united monarchy and no early Philistines). Finally (so far), the religious center at Shiloh was resurrected. Chieftain Saul became an important historical figure (replacing David and Solomon), and many biblical verses, even if "late," regained their early historical kernels.

As Father Roland de Vaux has written, archaeology cannot "prove" the text, whose truth is of a religious order. It can offer important cultural background, but each archaeological fact may have several historical interpretations. Judging the "archaeological evidence" requires a tedious process of reading, of comparing different views, of acquiring the necessary tools (like terminology), and of being skeptical about authoritative claims and jargon. If you still believe that there is an easy shortcut, perhaps you have wasted five minutes on reading this article.

About the Author

Raz Kletter completed his PhD at Tel Aviv University. He is an archaeologist of the Bronze and Iron Ages of the southern Levant, focusing on religion, economy, identity, and the history of archaeology. He directed and published excavations from varied periods for the Israel Antiquities Authority and is currently a member of the Centre of Excellence Ancient Near Eastern Empires at the University of Helsinki. His extensive publishing record includes *Just Past: The History of Israeli Archaeology* (London: Equinox, 2006); and *Archaeology, Heritage and Ethics in the Western Wall Plaza, Jerusalem: Darkness at the End of the Tunnel* (New York: Routledge, 2019).

Suggestions for Further Reading

In This Book

See also chapters 1 (scholarly perspective), 2 (religion), 3 (religious in a scientific world), 7 (who wrote the Bible?), 23 (minimalism), 26 (conquest of Canaan), 28–31 (archaeology), 48 (twelve tribes), 56 (polemics), and 82 (postcolonial studies).

Elsewhere
Associates for Biblical Research. "The Shiloh Excavations." https://bible archaeology.org/research/topics/shiloh.

de Vaux, Roland. "On Right and Wrong Uses of Archaeology." Pages 64–80 in *Near Eastern Archaeology in the Twentieth Century*. Edited by James A. Sanders. New York: Doubleday, 1970.

Finkelstein, Israel. *Archaeology of the Israelite Settlement*. Jerusalem: Israel Exploration Society, 1988.

Finkelstein, Israel. "First Israel, Core Israel, United (Northern) Israel." *Near Eastern Archaeology* 82(1) (2019): 8–15.

Finkelstein, Israel. "From Canaanites to Israelites: When, How and Why." Pages 11–27 in *Convegno Internazionale: Recenti Tendenze nella Ricostruzione della Storia Antica D'Israele*. Edited by Mario Liverani. Rome: Accademia Nazionale dei Lincei, 2005.

Long, Burke O. *Planting and Reaping Albright: Politics, Ideology, and Interpreting the Bible*. University Park: Penn State University Press, 1997.

Pfoh, Emanuel. "The Need for a Comprehensive Sociology of Knowledge of Biblical and Archaeological Studies of the Southern Levant." Pages 35–46 in *Biblical Narratives, Archaeology, and Historicity: Essays in Honour of Thomas L. Thompson*. Edited by Emanuel Pfoh and Lukasz Niesiołowski-Spanò. London: T&T Clark, 2019.

Sherrard, Brooke. "Mystical Unification or Ethnic Domination? American Biblical Archeologists' Responses to the Six-Day War." *Journal of Biblical Reception* 3(1) (2016): 109–133.

30
How Is Archaeology Used to Support Nationalism?

Erin Darby

By its very nature, archaeology in the Levant has always been political. In the simplest terms, archaeologists are not allowed to excavate or survey without permission from a political body. Thus, from its outset, Levantine archaeology was mired in the various nationalistic and political aspirations of the countries from which excavators originated as well as the countries governing the territories where excavators wished to work.

The same situation applies today. National governing bodies control all of the policies affecting archaeological research and cultural heritage preservation, and archaeologists cannot help but interact with this level of nationalism. Moreover, the situation is supported by international institutions and legal infrastructure, such as UNESCO and the Hague Conventions, which tie the management and preservation of archaeological remains to the national entities governing areas where the remains are found.

Yet, there are other senses in which archaeology has been used to support nationalism. Historically, the rise of Levantine archaeology corresponded with the development of colonial territories and postcolonial nations in the region, bridging the gap between vassals and sovereign national bodies. As such, archaeology played an important role at the end of the nineteenth and into the middle of the twentieth centuries. During this time, the right to manage antiquities played prominently into a variety of nationalist propagandas, whether Ottoman, British, Jordanian, Israeli, or otherwise. In some cases, knowledge gained through archaeological surveys was then used in military engagement and national politics, particularly during the First World War.

In other cases, like the Dead Sea Scrolls, studying the history of their discovery and dissemination provides a veritable world history lesson, exemplifying the extent to which archaeological exploration is tied to the rise and fall of governing bodies and the shifting territorialization of various states within the region.

A further argument is that archaeology, as a discipline, arose in a particular period of Western scientific discourse and, as such, has a powerful influence on nationalism in the modern period. In other words, archaeology and modern nationalism were born around the same time and share certain traits. As a "science" that produces "facts," archaeology can be wielded to lend an air of authenticity and authority to the experts who generate that data and the subsequent use of that data by nonarchaeologists. Of course, this requires that the "interpretive" aspects of archaeology be downplayed and the "scientific" aspects be accented.

Another factor that ties archaeology and nationalism together in this region is the degree to which history has been co-opted for modern nationalistic agendas. To take Israel as an example, the extent to which archaeologists can "verify" or "prove" the connection between ancient Israel and modern land ownership has long been a center point in debates over modern Israel's claim to particular territories. Archaeology may be combined with various texts like the Bible or Josephus in attempts to demonstrate Israelite or Jewish sovereignty. Alternately, the co-option of Nabataean identity by the modern nation of Jordan also demonstrates the way archaeology comes into service for larger national goals, like generating tourist income and fashioning a common ancestry.

Similarly, religion has also occupied pride of place in nationalistic discourse, producing texts and traditions that are then verified or denied based on the interpretation of archaeological materials. Because religiocultural forces play a strong role in the formation of modern national identity, the connection between the archaeology of the region and religious traditions remains an influential link between archaeology and nationalism. Thus, the study of temples, synagogues, churches, and mosques often carries nationalist overtones, as many of these sites feature prominently in modern territorial disputes, claims to land ownership, or theological justifications for modern political activities.

Cultural resource management (CRM) throughout the region also directly relates to nationalist agendas. For example, where to excavate and who can excavate remains contested, as the ongoing violence over excavations on and nearby the Haram al Sharif / Temple Mount makes clear. The 'Ir David archaeological park, Herodium, and Qumran all represent other examples. Some argue these sites should not be excavated because the current national body managing the territory is illegitimate, while others claim that the absence of any other viable governing body and the danger of looting make immediate excavation and preservation necessary. Additional arguments focus on sites that share an intimate connection with a contemporary religious or ethnic group, regardless of where the sites are located.

Another CRM element rife with nationalistic conflict is the decision to create archaeological parks and even which structures to preserve, which to dig through, and which to backfill. In some cases, the construction of an archaeological park may radically change a local community's access to the land for other purposes. Within parks, excavators and cultural resource managers must decide what structures to leave standing, which betrays both the research bias of the excavation team and the political, social, or economic aims of governing bodies. Monumentalizing remains often serves a present national, cultural, or religious function.

Finally, museum displays and acquisitions have also tended toward nationalistic ends. From their inception, Western museums became the nexus point where imperial superiority as curators of non-Western antiquities was played out in Western communities. So, too, museums in the Levant display a particular interpretation of history to visitors and interact with national and international laws in their various acquisition policies.

Thus, Levantine archaeology and nationalism are intimately bound together for a variety of reasons. Historically, archaeology incorporates some of the same modernist versions of reality that are responsible for nationalism and was operating in the Levant during the fall of colonial powers and the rise of autonomous states. Archaeology has played a role in the justification of certain territorial borders, social hierarchies, religious perspectives, and political objectives and has been used to help solidify national identity. The preservation of cultural heritage in excavation, archaeological parks, and museum displays likewise is affected by various national and international entities and has been used to help undergird nationalist narratives across the Levant.

About the Author

Erin Darby holds a doctorate of philosophy (PhD) in religion from Duke University and is currently an associate professor in religious studies and the faculty director of undergraduate research and fellowships at the University of Tennessee. Her research includes the Hebrew Bible, iconography, and ancient religion, and she serves as the codirector for the 'Ayn Gharandal Archaeological Project. She has published *Interpreting Judean Pillar Figurines: Gender and Empire in Judean Apotropaic Ritual* (Tübingen: Mohr Siebeck, 2014); and "What Is Primary vs. Secondary Use?" and "How Is Archaeology Used to Support Nationalism?," pages 86–88 and 235–238 in *The Five-Minute Archaeologist in the Southern Levant*, edited by Cynthia

Schafer-Elliott (London: Equinox, 2016). She served as the coeditor with Izaak J. de Hulster of *Iron Age Terracotta Figurines from the Southern Levant in Context*, CHANE 125 (Leiden: Brill, 2022).

Suggestions for Further Reading

In This Book
See also chapters 28 (archaeological proofs), 29 (archaeological "evidence"), 31 (contested areas), and 82 (postcolonial studies).

Elsewhere

Abu el-Haj, Nadia. *Facts on the Ground: Archaeological Practice and Territorial Self-Fashioning in Israeli Society*. Chicago: University of Chicago Press, 2001.

Luke, Christina, and Morag M. Kersel. *U.S. Cultural Diplomacy and Archaeology: Soft Power, Hard Heritage*. New York: Routledge, 2013.

Meskell, Lynn, editor. *Archaeology Under Fire: Nationalism, Politics, and Heritage in the Eastern Mediterranean and Middle East*. London: Routledge, 1998.

Meyers, Eric M., and Carol Meyers, editors. *Archaeology, Politics, and the Media: Proceedings from the Duke University Conference, April 23–24, 2009*. Duke Judaic Studies 4. Winona Lake, IN: Eisenbrauns, 2012.

Rowan, York, and Uzi Baram, editors. *Marketing Heritage: Archaeology and the Consumption of the Past*. Walnut Creek, CA: AltaMira, 2004.

Silberman, Neil Asher. *Between Past and Present: Archaeology, Ideology, and Nationalism in the Modern Middle East*. New York: Henry Holt, 1989.

31

Is It Ethical to Excavate
in Contested Areas?

Laura Wright

Have you ever wished you could participate in an excavation yourself? Many projects throughout the world welcome students and nonspecialists. If you stumble upon a project in a politically contested region or an intriguing new find from a volatile area, you may wonder about the ethics of excavation in those regions and the means whereby knowledge was created. Archaeologists have similar questions as they choose their projects.

While earlier twentieth-century archaeologists considered their pursuit of scientific and pure knowledge to be separate from political narratives, many archaeologists now have come to realize that their work is inherently bound to the narratives and people of a region. Archaeologists contribute to knowledge creation that structures a region's own narratives and self-understanding.

Archaeologists in Cyprus have denounced the destruction of sites in northern Cyprus, occupied by Turkey since 1974. They recognize that archaeological projects can be co-opted to produce the systematic removal of one people's history in what has been called "cultural cleansing" by the occupier. In another instance, newly formed states, like Kurdistan, issue excavation permits that may not be recognized by other sovereign states.

How does the archaeologist understand the ethics of excavation in these contested regions? For my own work, the question of excavation in the occupied territory of the West Bank is relevant. We will use it as a short case study here.

The West Bank is the land west of the Jordan River and east of the 1949 Armistice Line—also called the Green Line after the ink used in making the agreement. (East Jerusalem is also on the east side of the Green Line, but its political status is even more problematic. This short essay cannot include it.)

The West Bank has been occupied since the sixteenth century by four successive foreign militaries: the Ottoman Empire, the British Mandate,

Jordan, and now Israel. Since the nineteenth century, the Hague Regulations set out to govern occupying regimes. This body of international law was initially an agreement between elite regimes, not groups of local people. It identified the occupying regime as financially and legally responsible for public order and civil life until the ousted regime returned. The application of the Hague Regulations to the West Bank was problematic. There was no ousted regime, exiled due to a military defeat. After all, the territory had been occupied for centuries. In the aftermath of the Second World War, international law—the Fourth Geneva Convention—shifted its focus to the people rather than ruling regimes.

As the emphasis shifted, a people's right to self-determination became a central concern for the international community. Following the 1967 war, Israel's military seized the West Bank from Jordan and set up a military apparatus to rule the region, as international law specified. The Palestinians were not granted citizenship or the right to vote because this would have implied annexation. In short, they were denied the right to full self-determination.

In the 1990s the Oslo Accords, a set of agreements between the government of Israel and the Palestine Liberation Organization, changed the legal and archaeological landscape of the West Bank. It granted partial self-determination to the Palestinian people by dividing the occupied territory into three regions—Areas A, B, and C—which continue to this day. Each region is governed by different sets of laws. Area C is the biggest, with more than 60 percent of the West Bank. It is under Israeli military law. Area B is under a combination of Israeli military law and Palestinian civil law. The smallest of the regions, Area A, is where many Palestinians live. It is under the civil and military control of the Palestinian Authority; however, the Israeli military can still enter and arrest residents.

Along with changing the authorities in charge of the West Bank, the Oslo Accords also fundamentally changed archaeology there. Prior to Oslo, an Israeli military official called the Staff Officer of Archaeology controlled all cultural heritage in the region. After Oslo, the Palestinian Department of Antiquities and Cultural Heritage, which traced its roots to its British predecessor, was formed. Following the broader division of the region into three areas, cultural heritage in Area A fell under the Palestinian department, while Israel's Staff Officer of Archaeology continued to control Area C.

Palestinian archaeologists have critiqued the drawing of Oslo's lines, noting that a number of major archaeological sites were kept under sole Israeli control, though they were in areas that would otherwise have been given to the Palestinian Authority because of their large Palestinian population. The ancient tell of Samaria is one example. Thousands of

Palestinians live on and around the ancient city, yet Israel retains sole control of the upper tell, where Israelite remains were excavated. This convoluted legal and archaeological landscape is further complicated by settlements scattered over the hills of the West Bank. These settlements contain only Israeli citizens. They are considered illegal under the Fourth Geneva Convention because they transfer the occupier's population to the region under military control. However, in the late 1970s, Israel's Supreme Court ruled these settlements lawful. Incrementally, Israeli law was applied to its citizens in the West Bank, and a broad, two-tier legal system—one for citizens and another for noncitizens—emerged.

As settlements grew in size and number, settler groups, such as the influential Gush Emunim, saw the West Bank as Israel's by divine right, yet the largely secular society of Israel did not accept this narrative. In order to gain legitimacy for their settlements, the Gush Emunim settlers and others emphasized that the West Bank was part of ancient Israel—as if to say they were there first. Settlers emphasized the antiquity of their land claim by locating settlements on ancient Israelite tells from the Bible—Hebron, Bethel, and Shiloh. They used scientifically grounded archaeology to legitimize their narrative before a secular Israeli society that had incorporated archaeology as a part of its civil religion. Numerous other excavations were done by the Staff Officer of Archaeology to create infrastructure to support the settlements, though the 1954 Hague Convention forbids all damage to cultural heritage in occupied territory, unless militarily necessary. Archaeology became one of the tools settlers used to control the political landscape of the West Bank. In response, the average Palestinian came to view archaeology as part of the occupier's system.

In response to the Israeli occupation, Palestinian archaeologists sought to counter the settlers' narratives with their own national archaeology. Some connected Palestinians to Canaanites, as if to say their land claim was even older than the settlers' claim. Another group of Palestinian archaeologists argued that this narrative was wrong because archaeology could not soundly make this ethnic claim. They sought, instead, to emphasize the continuity between centuries of inhabitants and current Palestinians.

As someone outside of the conflict, you may wish to remain neutral. Many Western scholars have presented themselves as neutral agents of scientific inquiry who can rise above political claims as they tell the broader story of human history. Yet every excavation requires a government permit that embeds the scholar in the political narratives of a region.

If you are considering excavating in a contested area, you may ask yourself the following questions: How does my participation in this excavation make me part of the political narrative of the region? Was the site chosen because it contributes to only one people's narrative? Does the excavation encourage all people around the site to participate in the history of that site? After all, every resident of the region will need to protect its cultural heritage and share in its history. As we struggle with these questions, I encourage you to read scholars from all perspectives. Each will raise new and unexpected ethical questions as we work to live justly with all our neighbors.

About the Author

Laura Wright is an assistant professor at Luther College. She is a researcher of seals from the Late Bronze and Iron Ages and uses them to explore the religious practices in death from the period before and after Israel first emerged. She has worked with excavations in Israel for almost a decade.

Suggestions for Further Reading

In This Book

See also chapters 28 (archaeological proofs), 29 (archaeological "evidence"), 30 (nationalism), and 82 (postcolonial studies).

Elsewhere

Feige, Michael. "Recovering Authenticity: West-Bank Settlers and the Second Stage of National Archaeology." Pages 277–298 in *Selective Remembrances: Archaeology in the Construction, Commemoration, and Consecration of National Pasts*. Edited by Philip Kohl, Mara Kozelsky, and Nachman Ben-Yehuda. Chicago: University of Chicago Press, 2007.

Kersel, Morag M. "Fractured Oversight: The ABCs of Cultural Heritage in Palestine after the Oslo Accords." *Journal of Social Archaeology* 15(1) (2015): 24–44.

Knapp, A. Bernard, and Sophia Antoniadou. "Archaeology, Politics, and the Cultural Heritage of Cyprus." Pages 13–43 in *Archaeology Under Fire: Nationalism, Politics, and Heritage in the Eastern Mediterranean and Middle East*. Edited by Lynn Meskell. London: Routledge, 2002.

Ziadeh-Seely, Ghada. "An Archaeology of Palestine: Mourning a Dream." Pages 326–345 in *Selective Remembrances: Archaeology in the Construction, Commemoration, and Consecration of National Pasts*. Edited by Philip Kohl, Mara Kozelsky, and Nachman Ben-Yehuda. Chicago: University of Chicago Press, 2007.

32
How Do You Define Cultic Context?

Jonathan S. Greer

A "cultic context" may be defined simply as a place where religious activities are habitually practiced in the worship of a deity or deities. Identifying these installations in archaeological excavations in the southern Levant—the geographical setting for many of the religious practices described in the Hebrew Bible / Old Testament—is a notoriously difficult endeavor.

There is an old (pun intended?) archaeology joke that when something is discovered and the archaeologist doesn't know what it is . . . well, then it's "cultic"! In practice, however, archaeologists are far more sophisticated in their identification of such spaces even if there is a kernel (or sometimes a cob) of truth in the quip.

Traditionally, the first flag that an installation is "cultic" has been that of difference—that is, when a structure discovered differs in its architectural features and associated material culture from the context around it. Yet there are problems with this simplistic approach. For instance, one may rightly question a distinction based on "difference" as well as any attempt to draw clear lines between "secular" and "sacred." In fact, there are plenty of examples of cultic practices carried out within the context of the home even today, sometimes involving religious paraphernalia, thus "different" (e.g., the lighting of the *hanukkiah* in celebration of Hanukkah), but other times employing no material markers flagging "difference" at all (e.g., Catholic grace and making the sign of the cross before meals).

Indeed, archaeological evidence for ancient cultic practices is no less varied. Apparently "cultic" figurines and so-called incense altars have been discovered in domestic contexts, and conversely, material culture associated with everyday life—domestic cooking pots and eating vessels, for example—have been found in clearly cultic contexts such as temple precincts.

The point here is that there is not always a direct correlation between "difference" and cultic contexts, and interpretations need to be appropriately nuanced with evidence from a variety of different categories. While different archaeologists employ different methods, there are three main categories of evidence that are considered when identifying cultic contexts in the southern Levant: architecture, artifacts, and animal bones.

Architectural features are often recognized as cultic, according to the often-cited "archaeological indicators of ritual" paradigm developed by Colin Renfrew, if they serve to focus attention, reinforce a boundary zone between the physical and spiritual worlds, house a deity or deities (or symbols of such), and/or facilitate participation and offering. Some of the archaeological indicators that Renfrew correlates with these cultic aspects include locations near natural features that have supernatural associations (e.g., a cave, spring, or grove of trees), architectural installations that aid in religious focus (especially altars, but also sacred stones, benches, and hearths) or in mediating the boundaries between "clean" and "unclean" (e.g., pools or restricted areas of graded sacredness), and "conspicuous display" demonstrated in the magnitude and quality of the workmanship of the construction. Other archaeologists have further refined and applied these characteristics to map out ritual movements within sacred space.

To these characteristics, we may also add the continuity of veneration over time. In the southern Levant, and elsewhere even in contemporary contexts, once a site is considered sacred, it often remains a sacred location for long periods of time. Frequently, temples were built upon previous temples whether or not the deity worshipped there or the ethnicity of the worshippers remained constant—in a sense, once holy, always holy.

Renfrew's paradigm is also applicable to our second category: artifacts. Artifacts associated with cultic settings include attention-focusing items (e.g., lamps, bells, censers) as well as material objects associated with sacrifice and offering (e.g., altar kits containing shovels, forks, and ash pots). In some cases, discoveries in this category include a cultic image (or images) or other artistic representations of symbols and motifs often repeated throughout the space. Religious iconography in the southern Levant, though present, is limited in comparison to the iconographic repertoire of Mesoamerica, Mesopotamia, or Egypt, and scholars debate the reason for this (ideological, sociological, political, or simply an accident of preservation?). Interestingly, certain classes of symbolic images that have been discovered (e.g., so-called Judahite pillar figurines) are found most often, though not exclusively, in domestic contexts.

Evidence drawn from animal bones is a bit more complex and often misunderstood. Animal remains are one of the most frequent finds at archaeological sites, and when archaeologists discover a concentration of bones along with other indicators of cultic activity, they often call it evidence of "sacrifice." Of course, the term "sacrifice" can be applied in a number of ways, but most are referring to animals that were killed and given up to a deity through burning.

Though this was indeed a common practice in a variety of Levantine cultures, the problem is that this type of sacrifice leaves very little animal bone evidence behind, and the ash residue that does result, if it remains in close proximity to the place of sacrifice at all, is often missed in excavation. The bones that are found are rather much more frequently evidence of cultic meals. Even here, one must be careful in equating the location of the bones with the location of the meals, as bones were not always deposited in the same space as the eating events. That the bones provide evidence of meals rather than sacrifice (narrowly defined) does not, however, minimize their importance in defining cultic contexts, for cultic festivals were an essential (and remain an archaeologically accessible) characteristic of Levantine religious practice.

Thus, while complexity surrounding the task of defining a cultic context remains, a varied approach that incorporates evidence from architecture, artifacts, and animal bones—as well as ancient texts and textual traditions such as the Hebrew Bible / Old Testament—often yields reasonably secure identifications, even if a few "mystery items," alas, retain the classification of "cult objects" when nothing else fits.

This essay is adapted from "How Do You Define Cultic Context?," pages 178–181 in *The Five-Minute Archaeologist in the Southern Levant*, edited by Cynthia Shafer-Elliot (Sheffield, UK: Equinox, 2016).

About the Author

Jonathan S. Greer is an archaeologist and biblical scholar. He earned his PhD from the Pennsylvania State University. His research interests include ancient Israelite religion, sacrifice, and feasting. He is a visiting professor of archaeology at Grand Valley State University and associate director of excavations at Tel Dan, Israel. He has published a number of works on the relationship of the Bible to the ancient world—for example, "Feasting and Festivals," pages 299–320 in *The T&T Clark Handbook to Food in the Hebrew Bible and Ancient Israel*, edited by Janling Fu, Cynthia Shafer-Elliott, and Carol Meyers (London: Bloomsbury, 2012); "Drinking the Dregs of the Divine: Daniel 5 and the Motif of 'King and Cup' in Its Ancient Near Eastern Context," *Journal of Near Eastern Studies* 79(1) (2020): 99–112; "The 'Priestly Portion' in the Hebrew Bible: Its Ancient Near Eastern Context and Its Implications for the Composition of P,"

Journal of Biblical Literature 138 (2019): 263–284; "The Zooarchaeology of Israelite Religion: Methods and Practice," *Religions* 10(4) (2019): 1–19; and *Dinner at Dan: Biblical and Archaeological Evidence for Sacred Feasts at Iron Age II Tel Dan and Their Significance* (Leiden: Brill, 2013).

Suggestions for Further Reading

In This Book
See also chapters 23 (minimalism), 28 (archaeological proofs), 29 (archaeological "evidence"), 30 (nationalism), 31 (contested areas), and 82 (postcolonial studies).

Elsewhere

Horwitz, Liora Kolska. "The Contribution of Archaeozoology to the Identification of Ritual Sites." Pages 63–69 in *The Practical Impact of Science on Near Eastern and Aegean Archaeology*. Edited by Scott Pike and Seymour Gitin. London: Archetype, 1999.

Renfrew, Colin. "The Archaeology of Religion." Pages 47–54 in *The Ancient Mind: Elements of Cognitive Archaeology*, New Directions in Archaeology. Edited by Colin Renfrew and Ezra B. W. Zubrow. Cambridge: Cambridge University Press, 1994.

Zevit, Ziony. *The Religions of Ancient Israel: A Synthesis of Parallactic Approaches*. London: Continuum, 2001.

Translation and Transmission

33

The Septuagint: Why Was the Hebrew Bible Translated into Greek?

Ellen De Doncker

The Septuagint is the oldest translation of the Hebrew Bible, and its name, "Septuagint," originally designated the Greek translation of the first five books of the Bible (the Pentateuch). According to the legend transmitted by the second-century BCE Letter of Aristeas, King Ptolemy Philadelphus II (284–246 BCE) commissioned a translation of the sacred texts of the Jews for the famous Library of Alexandria. The task is said to have been accomplished by seventy-two translators—six translators for each of the twelve tribes of Israel. Over time, the number changed to seventy, *septuaginta* in Latin and "LXX" in roman numerals. While its authenticity is questioned, the Letter of Aristeas underlines the inspired character of the translation, which is advanced even further in later additions to the legend, and points to the need for a translation of the Pentateuch in the Hellenistic surroundings of the translators.

In the wake of the conquest of the Near East by Alexander the Great (332 BCE), postclassical Greek (Koine Greek) became the lingua franca of the East Mediterranean world. This must have been a major impetus for the translation of the Pentateuch, as Jews were living all over the increasingly Hellenized East Mediterranean world and beyond. Egyptian influences on the vocabulary and language of the LXX suggest that the translators were at work in the broader context of Ptolemaic Egypt, including contacts with nearby Palestine, which was under direct Ptolemaic rule from 300 to 200 BCE. In this Hellenistic context, the translation of the Pentateuch was completed, probably by the third century BCE. The bulk of the other books were gradually translated in the next century, as attested by the second-century BCE preface of the Wisdom of Ben Sira (Ecclesiasticus), while the translations of Qohelet (Ecclesiastes), Song of Songs, and Lamentations were probably only completed in the first century CE, as can be deduced from stylistic and lexical differences in the translations of those books.

These translational differences among the LXX books imply that each biblical book had its own translator(s). Intertextual parallels provide a remarkable level of homogeneity among the books, but none equivalent to that evoked by the term "Septuagint"; *the Septuagint* does not exist as a project undertaken by a single group of translators who collaborated to translate the entire Hebrew Bible systematically within their lifetimes. The Greek translation has been transmitted via manuscripts, versions, and recensions differing from one another, which form a heterogeneous corpus that now includes more books, the so-called deuterocanonical/ apocryphal books.

The order of the books also differs from Hebrew versions. Judges is followed by Ruth, then the poetical writings, and next the Latter Prophets, including Daniel. Within certain books—for example, Exodus and Psalms—the order of some chapters varies. Large differences in size also occur, in particular the shorter Greek text in Jeremiah and 1 Samuel (1 Kingdoms) 16–18.

Little is known about the actual origins of the LXX. The translation probably answered external and internal needs. A royal initiative to get acquainted with the Jewish law or the production of a translation of the law for the Alexandrian library reflects needs external to Jewish communities. The Pentateuch, however, is *more* than law, and legal reasons might not have been the primary motivation behind the translation. Liturgical or educational needs within Jewish communities were probably pressing reasons too. Little is known about Jewish liturgy at the time, but the translation shows important parallels with liturgical language. The use of the translation for educational purposes rests on the presupposition that the Jews of the diaspora no longer understood Hebrew but used Greek (Egypt, Alexandria) or Aramaic (Palestine). Yet, translation studies point to complex and well-studied word choices, which suggests that the LXX responded to educational needs broader than giving access to the Hebrew Scriptures to non-Hebrew-speaking audiences.

The translation was not completed once and for all. The Greek text continued to evolve, and individual books display a diversity of variant readings and sequencing. The so-called Old Greek (OG), an original Old Greek translation supposedly made from the Hebrew and later reworked by secondary revisions and recensions, can only be partially recovered through the careful evaluation of textual variants. Likewise, the Hebrew or Aramaic parent texts used by the Greek translators displayed textual diversity. The manuscripts found near the Dead Sea clearly indicate that there was no single, standardized biblical text until the end of the first century CE and that several forms of the biblical text circulated. It was only at the beginning of the second century CE that one text type imposed itself as the so-called textus receptus (received text), which meant that the Greek translation of Scripture was expected to conform to this generally accepted biblical text. Conformity occurred through adaptions of the LXX version to concur with the current Hebrew text (revisions) and through new translations of the Hebrew into Greek (recensions).

The *kaige* revision is the earliest known Jewish revision; it dates to the first century BCE. It is named after the use of the words *kai ge* (και γε), which are strange together in Greek but are a literal rendering of the Hebrew phrase *wegam* (וגם), first discovered in Dead Sea Scrolls found at Naḥal Ḥever. The process of revision and recension continued in the second century CE, when the Jewish revisors/translators Aquila (α´), Symmachus (σ´), and Theodotion (θ´) completed their works. These "three" were included in Origen's Hexapla, a third-century CE Christian edition of the Old Testament, now largely lost, that set six existing translations side by side for comparative purposes. The Hexaplaric revision was highly influential and left traces in many manuscripts. As a post-Hexaplaric revision, the Lucianic (Antiochene Christian) revision is important, especially in the books of Kings and Prophets, and seems to go back on an older textual recension. Later transmission is attested in the so-called daughter translations of the LXX—for example, the Vetus Latina, a Latin translation of the LXX made in the second through third centuries CE.

Besides the fact that the LXX represents the largest document in Koine Greek and is thus of immense value for lexicographic studies of postclassical Greek, the importance of the LXX for the study of the Hebrew Bible cannot be overstated. The complexity of the century-long processes that led to "the Septuagint" prevents us from considering the Greek texts as inferior, secondary translations of a superior, inspired Hebrew text, which had been the prevailing view. It is now understood that the Greek Bible reflects an intelligent and inspired translation of an evolving text. As a translation, the LXX offers glimpses of what one version of the many existing Hebrew texts looked like at a given time as well as clues about a given translator's interpretation of the Hebrew text.

The differences between the Greek and the Hebrew attest to more than the historical evolution of the text; they also reflect the theological, historical, and political views of the translators, since a translation always involves a degree of interpretation. Accordingly, the LXX is valuable not only for plotting the history of the Hebrew text but also for documenting the reinterpretation and contextualization of the text as early biblical exegesis. This last point connects the study of the LXX to studies in Hellenistic Judaism, providing clues about early Jewish ideology and theology.

Current research is moving away from using the LXX merely to reconstruct the possible Hebrew parent text toward other domains, such as the Hexapla and post-Hexaplaric revisions and studies to recover the influence and the significance of the Ptolemaic and Seleucid environments. Contemporary research also analyzes the Jewish reception of the Greek versions, as this reception not only attests to further interpretation of ideological elements of the LXX but also informs our understanding of Jewish-Christian relations.

In summary, that the LXX differs on some points from the Masoretic Text does not imply unfaithfulness or inferiority; rather, it shows how the Hebrew/Aramaic text and its interpretation evolved and left traces in the oldest translation. The LXX is a heterogeneous corpus of Greek texts, with traces of revisions and theological, sociopolitical, and lexicographic particularities. From its legendary origins to its dynamic transmission, the "translation of the Seventy" opens the door to innovative research fields and deserves due attention in the study of the Christian Old Testament as much as in that of the Jewish Scriptures.

About the Author

Ellen De Doncker, Aspirante FRS-FNRS, is completing a PhD in biblical studies (promoter Prof. H. Ausloos) at the Catholic University of Louvain and is a member of the Centre for Septuagint Studies and Textual Criticism (CSSTC). Her research interests include Septuagint, translation technique, modern and ancient Judaism, and material studies. She is the author of "The Lexeme *panîm* and Its Greek Rendering in Exodus 33: Between Grammaticalized Idiom and Playfulness," *BABELAO Electronic Journal for Ancient and Oriental Studies* 11 (2023); and with Anne Létourneau and Olivier Roy-Turgeon, "A Parade of Adornments (Isa 3:18–23): Daughters Zion in the Light of Gender and Material Culture Studies," *Open Theology* 8 (2022): 445–459.

Suggestions for Further Reading

In This Book

See also chapters 5 (canons), 10 (Tanak), 11 (Pentateuch), 22 (periodization), 34 (Dead Sea Scrolls), 35 (Philo), 72 (synchronic vs. diachronic), and 76 (redaction and text criticism).

Elsewhere

Ausloos, Hans, and Benedicte Lemmelijn, editors. *The Theology of Septuagint*. Gütersloh: Gütersloher Verlagshaus, 2020.

Jobes, Karen H., and Moisés Silva. *Invitation to the Septuagint* (2nd edition). Grand Rapids, MI: Baker, 2015.

Lust, Johan, Erick Eynikel, and Katrin Hauspie, editors. *A Greek-English Lexicon of the Septuagint* (3rd edition). Stuttgart: Deutsche Bibelgesellschaft, 2015.

Ross, William A., and W. Edward Glenny, editors. *T&T Clark Handbook of Septuagint Research*. London: Bloomsbury, 2021.

Salvesen, Alison, and Timothy Michael Law, editors. *The Oxford Handbook of the Septuagint*. Oxford: Oxford University Press, 2021.

Tov, Emmanuel. *The Text-Critical Use of the Septuagint in Biblical Research: Completely Revised and Expanded Third Edition*. Winona Lake, IN: Eisenbrauns, 2015.

34
What Do the Dead Sea Scrolls Reveal about the Biblical Text?

Sidnie White Crawford

The Dead Sea Scrolls (DSS), also known as the Judean Desert manuscripts, are ancient Hebrew, Aramaic, and Greek manuscripts found in several cave complexes along the western side of the Dead Sea (Qumran, Naḥal Ḥever, Wadi Murabbaʻat, etc.). Approximately 25 percent of these manuscripts reflect a version of a book that later became part of the Jewish canon of Scripture (Genesis, Isaiah, Psalms, etc.). These manuscripts range in date from the third century BCE to the second century CE, making them substantially older than the oldest complete masoretic codices, the Aleppo Codex (tenth century CE) and the Leningrad Codex (eleventh century CE). Thus, the manuscripts of the DSS reveal much about the history of the biblical text prior to its stabilization in the late first century CE and about the progress toward a canon of Scripture in the late Second Temple period. A canon is a fixed list of authoritative texts agreed upon and considered binding on a given community. It is important to remember that different communities have different canons; thus, the Samaritans recognize only the books of the Torah as their canon, while Jews recognize the books contained in the Tanak, and the Christian Bible contains the Old and New Testaments and, in some cases, the books of the Apocrypha.

The DSS biblical manuscripts demonstrate that during the late Second Temple period, the text of the biblical books was not fixed, as it later became, but fluid and subject to change. That is, each individual hand-copied manuscript of, say, the book of Deuteronomy, contains differences from other copies. These differences, known as variants, range in length from single words to phrases to whole paragraphs or sections. There are several types of variants. The first type are variants that affect the *accidents* of a text, its spelling or morphological forms. These variants do not change the meaning of a text. The spelling *'lhym* (אלהים, "God"), common in the Masoretic Text

(MT), reflects the same meaning as the spelling *'lwhym* (אלוהים, "God"), far more common in DSS manuscripts. A second type of variant is the inadvertent error, where a scribe might misspell a word or leave out a phrase from the text by accident. Sometimes these inadvertent errors continued to be copied by subsequent scribes and became fixed in the textual tradition. For example, 1 Samuel 13:1 according to MT reads, "Saul was one year old when he began to reign and he reigned over Israel two years." This is clearly an error, contradicted by the entire story of Saul as found in the masoretic version of Samuel. Two numbers have dropped out of the text: Saul's full age when he began to reign and the true number of years he ruled. The DSS biblical manuscripts contain many examples of both these types of variants.

Another type of variant, however, is the deliberate variant, where a scribe has purposefully intervened in the text he was copying in order to change it in some way. These changes can include linguistic updates, harmonizations, and theological revisions. For example, Deuteronomy 32:8 contains a deliberate variant between the Hebrew masoretic version and the Greek Septuagint version. The Hebrew reads, "When the Most High apportioned the nations, when he divided humankind, he fixed the boundaries of the peoples according to the number of the sons of Israel [*bny ysr'l*; בני ישראל]," while the Old Greek reads, "When the Most High apportioned the nations, when he divided humankind, he fixed the boundaries of the peoples according to the number of the sons of God [*uiôn theou*]." Some Greek manuscripts contain the variant "angels" of God (*angelôn*). The Greek variant "sons of God" is now supported by a Qumran manuscript, 4QDeut^j, which contains the phrase *bny 'lwhym* (בני אלוהים, "sons of God"). It is likely that a theological change was made in the precursor form of the MT, removing the theologically objectionable phrase "sons of God" and replacing it with the more acceptable "sons of Israel." Many of the DSS biblical manuscripts contain this type of deliberate variant.

At times, these deliberate variants can form a cohesive pattern and be so extensive that a new literary edition is created. The book of Jeremiah, for example, existed in two Hebrew literary editions in the late Second Temple period. The older version, reflected in two Qumran manuscripts, 4QJer^b and 4QJer^d, as well as the Septuagint, is shorter and has a different order of chapters than the later masoretic version (also reflected in 4QJer^a and 4QJer^c). Different literary editions also exist for the books of Exodus, Numbers, and Psalms. There is no indication among the manuscripts that one version was more authoritative or held in higher esteem than another.

This brings us to the question of canon in the Second Temple period. The first thing to state is that there was no canon of Jewish Scripture in the Second

Temple period in the commonly agreed usage of that term. The canon was a later development in Judaism that followed the defeat of the Jews and the destruction of the Jerusalem temple by the Romans in 70 CE.

However, the DSS, in particular those found in the caves opposite Qumran, do illustrate progress toward a canon of Scripture in the Second Temple period. The Qumran texts contained copies of every book of the Jewish Bible with the exception of Esther. Some of those books, such as the books of the Pentateuch, Psalms, and many of the prophetic books, are quoted as authoritative, have commentaries written on them, and exist in multiple copies. All these factors point to an authoritative, high status within the Qumran community and, without doubt, wider Judaism. However, the status of other biblical books, such as Ruth, Chronicles, and Song of Songs, is not transparent. They may simply have been part of Jewish religious literature of the period, carrying no particular authority or status. Further, there is evidence among the scrolls found at Qumran that certain books that were later excluded from the Jewish canon—that is, the books of Enoch and the book of Jubilees—had a high status, at least in that community. The DSS therefore demonstrate that while a nascent canon could be said to exist, no Jewish canon of Scripture actually existed in the Second Temple period.

Although the DSS, contrary to rumors throughout the decades since their discovery, do not contain any "smoking guns" that undermine the tenets of either Judaism or Christianity, they do teach us a great deal about the period before the development of rabbinic Judaism and early Christianity, including the history of the biblical text and canon. Thus, the scrolls fully deserve the attention they receive in the scholarly literature and in the popular imagination.

About the Author

Sidnie White Crawford holds a PhD in Near Eastern languages and civilizations from Harvard University and is Professor Emerita in Hebrew Bible at the University of Nebraska–Lincoln. Her research interests include textual criticism of the Hebrew Bible and the Qumran Dead Sea Scrolls. She has published *The Text of the Pentateuch: Textual Criticism and the Dead Sea Scrolls* (Berlin: De Gruyter, 2021); and *Scribes and Scrolls at Qumran* (Grand Rapids, MI: Eerdmans, 2019).

Suggestions for Further Reading

In This Book

See also chapters 5 (canons), 11 (Pentateuch), 16 (Psalms), 17 (Wisdom), 24 (Kings and Chronicles), 29–32 (archaeology), 47 (monotheism), 64 (Ruth), and 68 (Jeremiah).

Elsewhere

Tov, Emanuel. *Textual Criticism of the Hebrew Bible* (3rd and revised edition). Minneapolis: Fortress, 2012.

Ulrich, Eugene. *The Dead Sea Scrolls and the Developmental Composition of the Bible*. SVT 169. Leiden: Brill, 2015.

35

Was Philo of Alexandria the Earliest Biblical Commentator?

Maria Sokolskaya

The life span of Philo of Alexandria (or Philo Judaeus) matches almost exactly that of Paul the apostle, who was maybe some ten or fifteen years his junior and perhaps lived a decade longer, although we cannot be sure. But while Paul, a Greek-speaking Jew from Tarsus in Cilicia, received his education as a Torah teacher in Judea and Jerusalem "at the feet of [Rabbi] Gamaliel" (Acts 22:3), presumably in Hebrew and Aramaic, Philo spent his whole life in Alexandria in Egypt and received his Torah education there, presumably in Greek. Philo's literary output, like Paul's, is all in Greek; unlike Paul, however, he studied the Torah in a venerated Alexandrian Greek translation, at his time about three hundred years old, which was later named "the Septuagint"—that is, "the translation of the Seventy." Seventy was the number of the inspired translators according to a legend reported in the so-called Letter of Aristeas, an anonymous Alexandrian work written toward the end of the second century BCE. Philo himself tells a short version of the legend in his "Life of Moses," book 2, §§26–43.

Unlike Paul, Philo apparently never heard of Jesus of Nazareth or was not impressed by what he may have heard. But, again like Paul, he was read, venerated, and transmitted to later generations by early Christians. His reception within Judaism seems to have come to an end with the collapse of the great Greek-speaking Jewish communities outside Judea at Antioch in modern Turkey and Alexandria in Egypt after the destruction of the temple (70 CE) and the Bar Kochba Revolt (132–136 CE). Flavius Josephus (ca. 37–100 CE) is the only ancient Jewish author who mentions Philo; he does so briefly but with the highest respect (*Antiquities of the Jews*, book 18, §§259–60). Philo was not "rediscovered" by the Jews until the Renaissance, when he was reintroduced into Jewish intellectual life by the great physician and scholar Azariah ben Moses de Rossi (1511–1578).

In the formative years of rabbinic Judaism, which is still often perceived as *the* Judaism today, centers of Jewish cultural life moved eastward, and the common language of the Jews was now Aramaic, not Greek. The great achievements of the Hellenistic Jews, which included the Greek Torah of the Seventy, among many other works, were absorbed by Christianity. Christianity, which began as a Jewish religious movement, became the transethnic, dominant force in medieval Europe and overtly hostile to Judaism. For many centuries, Philo's exegesis, based on the Septuagint, remained on the Christian side of the dividing line, even though Philo had been a Jew.

Jewish and non-Jewish scholars alike have recently come to see Philo and the Greek-speaking Hellenistic Judaism as a whole as genuinely Jewish, not an inferior, syncretistic form of religious belief and practice. It is now understood that in the Roman and Hellenistic periods, the so-called diaspora (Jews living outside of Judea and speaking Greek) had strong connections with Jerusalem, whose learned elite, in turn, was thoroughly versed in Greek culture and language.

Philo is currently seen as a Jew of his time, no longer as a Hellenistic philosopher of Jewish descent who had a personal fancy to illustrate Platonic and Stoic philosophical teachings with biblical citations and allusions. It is now realized that with Philo's works, we possess an entire corpus of Jewish biblical commentaries from the age before the rise of Christianity.

So, what can we learn from Philo about how Scripture was perceived by a pious Jew at the turn of the first century CE? First of all, there was a sharp dividing line between the Torah (a.k.a. Pentateuch, or the five books of Moses) and the rest of the Tanak. The Torah was viewed as the authentic word of God, transmitted to humankind through Moses the Lawgiver, the greatest of prophets. The rest of what was recognized as Scripture at the time, the Former and Latter Prophets and Psalms, was held in great respect but did not possess the same sacral character that made the Torah *the* object of lifelong study and a specific kind of exegesis for a committed Jew.

Torah exegesis was based on the assumption that this text—the word of the eternal God—has an endless range of meanings. The meaning of a human word or statement is defined and confined through its context: in order to understand, we ask who has spoken, to whom, at what time, and under which circumstances. But the word of God is not confined by space or by time; it speaks to the whole of humankind in eternity. This universal status of the Torah is not an invention of Philo or an influence of Greek philosophy but an understanding developed by Jewish religious thought long before Philo's time. The plurality of meanings is the logical consequence of universality: as a human, you get from the Scripture what you need and are able to get at every particular moment. We must bear this in mind in order to understand Philo's multiple-meaning exegesis—the same phrase or figure of the Torah can have any number of different interpretations throughout his writings.

For Philo, the Torah has three levels of interpretation: literal, ethical, and allegorical meaning. All three are important, but there is a hierarchy of levels. The literal meaning is about the correct understanding of the story as it is told in the Mosaic writings and about literal obedience to the commandments. Although Philo offers elaborate allegorical interpretations of the commandments, especially of the dietary laws, he insists on the absolute necessity for a Jew to observe the Mosaic law literally in his daily life. In the same vein, Philo may translate biblical stories into allegories perceived by a modern reader as farfetched, but he is equally eager to show that inconsistencies in the literal story are only apparent. His privileged means for that is an extensive retelling of a biblical narrative, supplying missing links, smoothing contradictions, and providing psychological explanations. This approach is characteristic of one of Philo's commentary series, his "Exposition of the Law." For instance, the treatise "On the Life of Joseph" is such a retelling of the story of Joseph in Genesis 37–50. In Genesis 37:14, Jacob said to Joseph, "Go now, see if it is well with your brothers and with the flock; and bring word back to me." Since antiquity, readers have wondered how Jacob could send his beloved son alone to his brothers, knowing that they hated Joseph with all their hearts. In "On the Life of Joseph" §10, Philo reads the story as follows:

> Then, dreading lest continuous association should breed disturbance and broils among the brothers through the grudge which they bore against the dreamer for his visions, Jacob sent them away to tend the sheep, but kept him at home for such season as should prove needed. He knew that time is said to be the physician of the distempers and ailments of the soul and is able to remove grief, to quench anger and to heal fear, for time relieves everything, even what is naturally hard to cure. But when he guessed that they would have ceased to harbour enmity in their hearts, he sent him partly to salute his brothers and partly to bring him word how it fared with themselves and the flocks under their charge. (Colson 1959, 145–146)

The next level of meaning is ethical. The Holy Writ supplies models of righteous behavior we should ruminate over to perfect our conduct and thinking about moral issues. Modern readers often scoff at the long speech held by Philo's Joseph as Potiphar's wife grabbed his garment and tried to drag him into her bed (§§42–48). But Philo's exposition is not a modern romance, where the behavior of the characters must be psychologically convincing. It is a collection of sermons; the goal is to unfold the wealth of useful moral lessons hidden in laconic biblical statements. The sermon that Joseph addresses to Potiphar's wife is the earliest document we possess in Greek that exhibits the important moral notion of "conscience": even if nobody is ever to find out, says Joseph to the temptress, "all the same I shall turn informer against myself through my colour, my look, my voice, convicted . . . by my conscience" (§48). The third level, the allegorical, is also present in the "Exposition" series, making Joseph with his multicolored coat the symbol of a politician who must change colors every moment to stay In favor of the public. But the allegory here remains subordinate to the historical narrative.

Another series of Philo's writings is called "Allegorical Commentary." The focus there is not on the whole of a biblical story but on single verses or words containing deep, divine mysteries. The literal sense is now left far behind so that Joseph may not be righteous at all but is a symbol of conceit; his brothers who put him in chains symbolize reason restricting passions— as in the treatise *On Dreams* (Colson and Whitaker 2001, 485–492).

Least preserved is Philo's third commentary series, the "Questions and Answers on Genesis and Exodus." In it, he discusses difficulties in the biblical text, providing a brief solution that can be literal, ethical, or allegorical.

A striking feature in the entire Philonic corpus is the abundant use he makes of the Hebrew etymologies of biblical names. Even though he supposedly knew no Hebrew, he constantly reminds his readers of the original language of the Torah. The etymologies themselves, though mostly false in terms of modern linguistics, demonstrate a high level of linguistic competence in Hebrew. As many of these etymologies are closely connected with Philo's allegories, it stands to reason that Philo had predecessors who elaborated the etymologically backed allegories. This helps us understand Philo as a participant in the genuine Jewish tradition of biblical exegesis, which, in his day, was carried out in all three major languages of the Jews: Hebrew, Aramaic, and Greek.

About the Author

Maria Sokolskaya holds a doctorate in theology from the University of Berne. Her research includes the Septuagint, the Letter of Aristeas, and Philo of Alexandria. She has published *Die griechische Bibel in Alexandrien:*

Ihre Legende und die exegetische Praxis im hellenistischen Judentum (Leiden: Brill, 2022); "Meals in the Works of Philo of Alexandria," pages 9–18 in *T&T Clark Handbook to Early Christian Meals in the Greco-Roman World*, edited by Soham Al-Suadi and Peter Ben-Smit (London: Bloomsbury, 2019); and "Was Demetrius of Phalerum the Founder of the Alexandrian Library?," pages 81–95 in *Alexandria: Hub of the Hellenistic World*, edited by Benjamin Schliesser, Jan Rüggemeier, Thomas J. Kraus, and Jörg Frey (Tübingen: Mohr Siebeck, 2021).

Suggestions for Further Reading

In This Book
See also chapters 9 (audiences), 10 (Tanak), 11 (Pentateuch), 33 (Septuagint), 49 (Torah), 62 (Joseph), 63 (Moses), and 83 (reception criticism).

Elsewhere
Birnbaum, Ellen. "Exegetical Building Blocks in Philo's Interpretation of the Patriarchs." Pages 69–92 in *From Judaism to Christianity: Tradition and Transition; A Festschrift for Thomas H. Tobin*. Edited by Patricia Walters. Leiden: Brill, 2010.

Cohen, Naomi G. *Philo's Scriptures: Citations from the Prophets and Writings; Evidence for a Haftarah Cycle in Second Temple Judaism*. Leiden: Brill, 2007.

Colson, F. H., translator. *On Abraham. On Joseph. On Moses* (volume 4 of *Philo*). Loeb Classical Library 289. Cambridge, MA: Harvard University Press, 1959.

Colson, F. H., and G. H. Whitaker, translators. *On Flight and Finding. On the Change of Names. On Dreams* (volume 5 of *Philo*). Loeb Classical Library 275. Cambridge, MA: Harvard University Press, 2001.

Runia, David T. "How to Read Philo." Pages 185–198 in *Exegesis and Philosophy: Studies on Philo of Alexandria*. Edited by David T. Runia. Aldershot, UK: Variorum, 1990.

Sandmel, Samuel. *Philo of Alexandria: An Introduction*. New York: Oxford University Press, 1979.

36
What Is Old Testament Theology?

Pauline A. Viviano

On the surface, it seems that "What is Old Testament theology?" should be an easy question to answer, but it is not. What is theology? Simply put, "theology" means "words about God" or "the study of God," but there are many kinds of theology. It is clear from the opening question that we are dealing with biblical theology, which is to be distinguished from other theologies, particularly dogmatic/systematic theology, historical theology, and practical theology. Dogmatic/systematic theology focuses on the doctrines of the Christian faith. It draws on the Bible as a source, but also on philosophy, historical development, and other areas of knowledge. Historical theology studies how the church and its doctrines developed over time. Practical theology focuses on how faith is lived by believers and finds expression, for example, in one's ethics and spirituality. The focus of biblical theology is what the Bible has to say about the nature of God and God's actions in the Old and New Testaments. There are various related topics that can be addressed, such as the history of Israel; the prophetic movement; the life, death, and resurrection of Jesus; and the teachings and history of the early Christian community.

The "Old Testament" is a Christian designation of the sacred writings of the Jews that were adopted by the early Christians. By the end of the first century CE, Christians had privileged the Greek translation of those sacred writings, commonly called the Septuagint. With the formation and acceptance of the New Testament, Christians continued to revere the Old Testament and included it in their canon of Scripture. The Old Testament was understood to be about God's covenant with Israel; for Christians, the New Testament speaks of God's covenant in Christ that is extended to all of humanity, Gentiles and well as Jews.

Since Christianity grew out of Judaism, it is not surprising that the Old Testament, regarded as a collection of sacred texts by first-century Jews, also became sacred for early Christians, but its "theology" was not understood on its own terms or in its historical context. The surface meaning of the Old Testament may point to the nature of the God of the Old Testament, but for Christians, the importance of Old Testament texts rests in a deeper or spiritual meaning that points to Jesus as the fulfillment of messianic expectations. Yes, the nature of God was spoken of, but the focus was more on God as the Father of Jesus who brought about salvation through the death and resurrection of his son than on God as the God of Israel. As Christianity grew and spread throughout the Greco-Roman world, it developed its own theology, drawing heavily on classical and Hellenistic philosophical systems to understand and explain the nature of God and Christ. Tradition and the Bible remained important sources of authority for the Christian church, but the importance of the Old Testament continued to be in its pointing to Christ. Even Martin Luther, who treated Scripture as the only authority for Christians, still read the Old Testament in terms of what it revealed concerning Christ. He spoke of Christ as being fully present in his whole person (divine and human) in the Old Testament.

Rabbinic interpretation of the Hebrew Bible / Tanak has a different focus. It assumes the text is divinely inspired, internally coherent, meaningful in every detail, and relevant to people's lives. It moves from there to explain apparent contradictions and ethical problems, to provide textual bases for later Jewish theological developments, and to read texts in light of other texts (intertextuality).

Today, when scholars ask "What is Old Testament theology?" the answer—indeed, the answers—is very different than the one described above, which had been prominent in Christian communities for centuries. The change in perception began in the modern era with the rise of the scientific method, the privileging of reason in the Enlightenment, and the emergence of the historical-critical method. It continued in the twentieth century with a recognition of the limitations of the historical-critical method and a new set of questions being asked of the Old Testament.

The scientific method makes a claim to objectivity because its results are based on data that are available to all. During the Enlightenment, the authority of rulers and even church leaders began to lose its hold on citizens and believers. What is known by reason was opposed to what is known by faith. Scientific conclusions superseded traditions held for centuries, while archaeological discoveries led to greater knowledge of the past. One important result of this intellectual movement has been the development of a sense of history—the recognition that the social, political, religious, and philosophical categories of past civilizations were different and that one is defined by the place and time in which one lives. Questions were raised about the meaning of the Old Testament on its own terms, apart from the New Testament, and the historical-critical method became the dominant system of interpretation. Scholars sought "objective" answers to historical questions about the events of Israel's life as a people and, eventually, its rise and fall as a nation. The answers to these questions led to a search for traditions behind the narratives in the Old Testament and how these traditions were passed on orally and eventually became written documents. This discussion took place primarily in the academy and moved away from confessional considerations of dogmatic theology.

In the twentieth century, questions were raised about the presupposed "objectivity" of the historical-critical method. It was recognized that its conclusions regarding the dating of biblical material were influenced by an "evolutionary" philosophy that maintained that religious beliefs moved from a more primitive to a more advanced and sophisticated understanding of God and religion. Monotheism replaced polytheism, and ethical standards became more important than the rituals of the cult. The sources behind the Old Testament were dated based on this "evolutionary" movement. The Yahwist source was deemed the oldest because its God spoke and appeared directly to the ancestors. In the Priestly source, God does not interact directly but is met in dreams and in worship. The culmination of Old Testament theology was seen in the advanced theology of the prophets, whose God judged Israel based on higher moral standards but also would forgive this group if and when it repented. It became clear that these conclusions reflected the intellectual and confessional context of the scholars who argued for such a development in ancient Israel, not the reality of ancient Israel.

Scholars continued their search for an Old Testament theology, but one no longer based on a reconstruction of the history behind the text. Instead, scholars searched for the dominant depiction of God presented in the Old Testament. Two scholars of particular importance in this endeavor were Walther Eichrodt and Gerhard von Rad. Both wrote two volumes on the theology of the Old Testament, but they held different views on what was the most important feature of the God of the Old Testament.

For Eichrodt (1967), Israel's God is a deity who enters into a relationship with humans; that relationship is symbolized in God's covenant with Israel. It is not a one-sided relationship. The God of Israel is bound to Israel, but Israel is also bound to God. As covenant lord, God is to act on behalf of the people of Israel, but Israel is expected to live in accordance with the demands of the covenant. The character of the covenant relationship is expressed in Israel's laws, its cult, and its leaders. In his second volume, Eichrodt expanded his theology of relationship to include the cosmos and the nature of humanity.

In contrast, von Rad (1965) emphasized the God of Israel as a god who acts in history in his understanding of Old Testament theology. In a subsequent article, he referred to lists of God's acts in Israel's history, which he called credos (Deuteronomy 6:20–24; 26:5–9; Joshua 24:2–13). He thought these lists had been confessional statements recited in the context of worship that had provided a summary of the acts of God on behalf of Israel in its history. His second volume focused on the theology of the Old Testament as presented in the prophetic books.

As the search for an Old Testament theology moved into the 1970s, the positions of Eichrodt and von Rad began to recede into the background. Newer methods, like literary/rhetorical criticism, feminist criticism, and liberation criticism, among others, emerged. These newer methods created considerable diversity in the field of biblical study by asking new questions. In answering these questions, scholars became more sensitive to their own biases, especially their confessional beliefs, as they explored the Old Testament. They became more aware of the complexity of the Old Testament itself and now recognized that many "theologies" are present in the Old Testament, not one privileged view of the nature of Israel's God. These "theologies" are present in multiple levels of tradition in the Old Testament and vary over the centuries covered by the text. As a result, today there is no simple answer to the question "What is Old Testament theology?"

About the Author

Pauline A. Viviano holds her PhD in biblical languages and literature from St. Louis University. She is Associate Professor Emerita from Loyola University. Her areas of specialization include the Deuteronomistic History (Deuteronomy, Joshua, Judges, 1–2 Samuel, 1–2 Kings), biblical poetry (especially the book of Jeremiah), and the history of biblical interpretation. Her publications in the field of biblical interpretation are "Source Criticism," pages 35–57 in *To Each Its Own Meaning: An Introduction to Biblical Criticisms and Their Application* (revised and expanded edition) (Louisville, KY: Westminster John Knox, 1999); and "The Senses of Scripture," pages 1–4 in *The Word of God in the Life and Mission of the Church: Celebrating the Catechetical Year 2008–2009 with Resources for Catechetical Sunday 2008* (Washington, DC: Committee on Evangelization and Catechesis, United States Conference of Catholic Bishops, 2008), publication no. 7-028.

Suggestions for Further Reading

In This Book
See also chapters 1 (scholarly perspective), 3 (religious in a scientific world), 5 (canons), 28 (archaeological proofs), 33 (Septuagint), 37 (rabbinic interpretation), 47 (monotheism), 49 (Torah), 52 (covenant), 73 (source criticism), 74 ("P"), 75 (historical criticism), 77 (literary and form criticism), 81 (gender studies), and 82 (postcolonial studies).

Elsewhere
Birch, Bruce C., Walter Brueggemann, Terence E. Fretheim, and David I. Petersen. *A Theological Introduction to the Old Testament*. Nashville: Abingdon, 1999.

Eichrodt, Walther. *Theology of the Old Testament* (volumes 1–2). Philadelphia: Westminster, 1967.

Gerstenberger, Erhard S. *Theologies in the Old Testament*. Minneapolis: Fortress, 2002.

Hayes, John H., and Frederick C. Prussner. *Old Testament Theology: Its History and Development*. Atlanta: John Knox, 1985.

Perdue, Leo G. *The Collapse of History: Reconstructing Old Testament Theology*. Minneapolis: Fortress, 1994.

von Rad, Gerhard. *Old Testament Theology* (volumes 1–2). New York: Harper & Row, 1965.

Westermann, Claus. *Elements of Old Testament Theology*. Translated by Douglas W. Stott. Atlanta: John Knox, 1982.

37
What Is Rabbinic Interpretation?

Zev Farber

How one reads a book is partly dependent on the premises one has about the work. Let's take *Animal Farm* as an example. Given that we know a lot about George Orwell, the world he lived in, and his views, we generally understand it as a political allegory. Readers from a different culture with no such context could, in theory, read it as a history of a different reality when animals talked, as a sacred myth, or as science fiction or fantasy.

Readers of the Hebrew Bible are faced with the same issues. Critical scholarship is the attempt to uncover what the biblical works meant in their context by studying the material culture and comparative literature from the same period. In contrast, readers from different faith groups, from ancient times to the present, come with very different assumptions.

From early times, Christian readers saw the Hebrew Scriptures as prefiguring Jesus, and they continue to find oblique references to him, his life, his death, his saving grace, and other topics all over what they call "the Old Testament." Jews, however, see nothing at all related to Jesus in the Hebrew Bible / Tanak, but this does not mean that Jewish tradition is engaged in critical study either.

Rabbinic hermeneutic tradition is known as midrash. As James Kugel (1998) explains, midrash follows in the footsteps of Second Temple Jewish reading. It worked with four premises: Scripture is divinely inspired, internally coherent, meaningful in all details, and relevant to people's lives. In rabbinic midrash, these premises can be found with varying emphases depending on the type of text.

For example, in Exodus 2:18, Moses's father-in-law is named Reuel, but Jethro in Exodus 3:1, and Hobab in Numbers 10:29. The midrash solves this contradictory presentation by stating that Jethro had multiple names and that each teaches one something about the person (Mekhilta de-Ri, VaYishma §1).

Solving legal contradictions worked the same way. Numbers 18:24 requires Israelites to tithe their produce every year and give this to the

Levites. Deuteronomy 14:22–23, however, requires the tithe to be used on pilgrimage festivals. The rabbis solve this by saying that Israelites have to give two tithes, the first to the Levites and the second to celebrate in Jerusalem (Mishnah, Tractate Maasrot).

Midrashic solutions can be wildly creative. For instance, Genesis 1:27 states, "So God created the human in his image . . . male and female he created them." To explain the shift from singular "the human" to plural "them," the rabbis claim that God created the first human as a being with two fronts, one male and the other female, and then, at some point, separated them into two beings (Leviticus Rabbah 14:1).

Another example of a problem solved by a narrow reading of terms is that of Ruth. She is a Moabite woman whom Boaz marries, and yet, Deuteronomy 23:4 specifically forbids Israelites from marrying Moabites forever. Sifre Deuteronomy §249 interprets Deuteronomy's use of the male term *mo'abi* to mean "a Moabite but not a Moabitess."

Not every midrash is meant to solve contradictions. Often the rabbis are simply picking up on unusual features of language. For instance, Exodus 8:1 has God commanding Moses to have Aaron bring forth frogs as a plague on the Egyptians. The next verse states, "Aaron spread out his hand onto the waters of Egypt, and the frog came out and covered the land of Egypt." The term here, *tzefardea'*, is in the singular. While it may just be a collective usage here, like the English "fish," Midrash Tanchuma (Vaera §14) offers a fanciful literal reading: "Rabbi Akiva says: 'It was one frog, and when the Egyptians would hit it, it would spew forth many more frogs.'"

The frog example is playful, but sometimes the rabbis would use this same type of reading to deal with ethical problems in the text. For instance, Deuteronomy 21:19–21 legislates the public execution of a wayward son whose parents bring him to the elders and accuse him of gluttony, drunkenness, and disrespect. Apparently uncomfortable with this law, the rabbis (b. Sanhedrin 71a) pick up on the phrase "he doesn't listen to our voice" and state that the two parents must have the same voice—and indeed, the same height and appearance—in order for the law to apply.

Literal readings could also be used to push theological agendas. For instance, the Torah never discusses the resurrection of the dead, which became a core faith principle in later forms of Judaism. The rabbis, therefore, looked for hidden clues and found one in the opening of the Song of the Sea (Exodus 15:1), which says, "Then Moses [*yashir*]." The verb, in context, means "sang," but the form can also be understood as "will sing." Thus, the rabbis interpreted the phrase to mean that Moses will sing this song in his next life, "and from here we have a proof from the Torah of the resurrection of the dead" (b. Sanhedrin 91b).

Sometimes, the rabbis stretch the meaning of a simple text by interpreting a common term or grammatical feature. For instance, biblical Hebrew requires the use of the untranslatable particle *'et* to mark the direct object (i.e., the accusative case). Even so, in the command to "honor [*'et*] your father and [*'et*] your mother," the rabbis suggest that each *'et* teaches the need to honor one's respective stepparents and that the "and," also necessary in the sentence, teaches the requirement to respect one's older brother (b. Ketubot 103b).

Another important principle is intertextuality, which in midrash refers to reading a term or phrase in one place in light of its use elsewhere. For example, the phrase "when your son asks you tomorrow, saying" appears twice in the Torah. In Exodus 13:14, the son asks—referring to the offering of firstborn animals—"What is this?" In Deuteronomy 6:20, he asks, "What are the testimonies, statues, and laws that YHWH our God has commanded [us/you]?" The manuscript versions differ on the last word. The rabbis compare the questions and, noticing that one is very simple and the other detailed, suggest that the first was asked by a weak-minded child and the second by a wise one (Passover Haggadah).

In legal texts, this kind of comparison often takes the form of a *gezeriah shavvah*, a use of two identical words. For instance, Psalm 82:2 states that "God stands in the divine assembly [*'edah*]." The story of the ten sinful spies in Numbers 14:27 describes them as an "evil assembly [*'edah*]." Reading the passage in Psalms in light of Numbers, the rabbis suggest that God only appears in an assembly of ten, thus the need in synagogues for a *minyan* (prayer quorum) to recite certain special prayers such as the Kaddish.

There is no one collection of midrashim. In the Tannaitic period (first and second centuries CE), there were at least three schools of thought, each with their own style of midrash: the Rabbi Ishmael school and two versions of the Rabbi Akiva school (the regular and the *zuta*). Their respective schools collected their works in various *midrashei halakha* (legal midrash) on the books of Exodus through Deuteronomy, only parts of which have survived. In the Amoraic period (third–sixth centuries CE) and after, the methods seem to have been used without school specificity, and midrashim of all styles appear in both Talmuds, the minor tractates, and several collections of *midrashei aggadah* (narrative midrash), generally in the form of commentaries on the Torah, or the five scrolls, but also on a smattering of other biblical books.

About the Author

Zev Farber holds a PhD in Jewish religious cultures from Emory University and has advanced rabbinical ordination from Yeshivat Chovevei Torah Rabbinical School. He is the senior editor of TheTorah.com and is a research fellow at the Kogod Center of the Shalom Hartman Institute. He has published *Images of Joshua in the Bible and Their Reception* (Berlin: De Gruyter, 2016).

Suggestions for Further Reading

In This Book
See also chapters 1 (scholarly perspective), 2 (religion), 5 (canons), 6 (biblical exegesis), 9 (audiences), 10 (Tanak), 14 (myths), 33 (Septuagint), and 36 (Old Testament theology).

Elsewhere

Bakhos, Carol, editor. *Current Trends in the Study of Midrash*. Leiden: Brill, 2006.

Boyarin, Daniel. *Intertextuality and the Reading of Midrash*. Bloomington: Indiana University Press, 1990.

Kugel, James. *Traditions of the Bible: A Guide to the Bible as It Was at the Start of the Common Era*. Cambridge, MA: Harvard University Press, 1998.

Safrai, Shmuel, Zeev Safrai, Joshua Schwartz, and Peter J. Tomson, editors. *The Literature of the Sages* (part 2). Assen: Royal Van Gorcum and Fortress Press, 2006.

Yadin-Israel, Azzan. *Scripture as Logos: Rabbi Ishmael and the Origins of Midrash*. Philadelphia: University of Pennsylvania Press, 2004.

38

Who Were and Are the Samaritans?

Benedikt Hensel

Today, the Samaritans are one of the smallest religious minorities in the world. Their community currently numbers approximately eight hundred individuals, the majority of whom live on their holy mountain, Mount Gerizim, above the modern city of Nablus in the West Bank. In antiquity, this was the location of not only the metropolis of Shechem but also a city founded by Vespasian in 72 CE for Roman veterans called Neapolis.

The modern Samaritans identify themselves as "Israelites" and worship the God of Israel. However, their religious center is not in Jerusalem but atop Mount Gerizim. Their authoritative text is the so-called Samaritan Pentateuch, also known as the Samaritanus. This text is identical to the Jewish Torah except for certain deviations in content, orthography, and phonetics. The Samaritans consider only the Pentateuch (Genesis, Exodus, Leviticus, Numbers, Deuteronomy) to be authoritative; they do not recognize the Judean/Jewish texts that were included in the Hebrew Bible under the subheadings the *Nevi'im* (Prophets) or the *Ketuvim* (Writings).

The name "Samaritans" derives from the province of Samaria, established by the Neo-Assyrians after the fall of the northern kingdom of Israel (721 BCE). Contrary to what the comparatively small size of this community might suggest, the Samaritans of antiquity played a crucial role in the course of the histories of Israel followed by Samaria and Judah followed by Yehud and then Judea as well as in the formation of ancient Judaism.

The Traditional View: Samaritans as "Strangers" and a "Sect of Judaism"

The Samaritans have been firmly anchored in the cultural memory of modern times because of the parable of the good Samaritan in the New Testament in Luke 10:29–37. The theological point of the parable can be boiled down to the fact that back then, the Samaritans were seen as strangers. Thus, in the parable, a stranger becomes a neighbor to a stranger. Current research has been able to demonstrate that this classification of Samaritans as "strangers" is false; Samaritans are "Israelites" in their material heritage. Yet this characterization as strangers, which was imposed on the group by outsiders for polemical purposes, has shaped understandings of history for nearly two thousand years.

The Jewish historian Flavius Josephus (first century CE), for example, gives two origin stories for the Samaritans (see Josephus, *Antiquitates*, 11.297–347 in Spilbury and Seeman 2016): Some of the Samaritans were "apostates" who broke away from Jerusalem circa 334 BCE due to certain disputes about the Torah and who built a temple in the then province of Samaria (in the former territory of the northern kingdom) above the ancient city of Shechem. Thus, Mount Gerizim served as a rival temple to Jerusalem. Elsewhere, Josephus adds that the Samaritans were originally a multiethnic and multireligious population, coming from "Babylon, Cuthah, Avva, Hamath, and Sepharvaim" (here drawing on 2 Kings 17:18) in the area of the former kingdom of Israel after it was conquered by the Neo-Assyrians in 721 BCE. Josephus's description articulates the contemporary perception of this group: the origins of the Samaritans lie in a Jewish sect (of Jerusalem dissidents) who joined with the local population of the multiethnic melting pot of Samaria in the fourth century BCE.

Modern Research: Samaritans as Israelites

In recent years, historical research uses coins and images on coins, seals, bullae, administrative texts and property deeds written in Aramaic, and surface surveys of the settlement patterns in the province of Samaria to show that the Samaritans are the cultural and religious successors of the inhabitants of the northern kingdom of Israel (ca. 931–721 BCE). It is these people whose monarchy was absorbed by the Neo-Assyrians and whose heartland was occupied by the Assyrians and turned into the province of Samaria, which lasted into the Hellenistic period (323–31 BCE). The upheavals and the continuities of the Samaritans are similar to how we imagine the cultural, ethnic, and religious continuities of the Judeans in Judah after the destruction of Jerusalem in 587 BCE.

In fact, there is no evidence whatsoever for the frequent assumption of Samarian syncretism and the related processes of "foreign infiltration" traceable back to the Assyrians. On the contrary, the material cultures of Judah and Samaria correspond to each other rather significantly in the Neo-Babylonian and Persian periods.

The large-scale excavations on Mount Gerizim carried out between 1983 and 2006 under the direction of Yitzhak Magen on behalf of the Israeli military administration's Civil Administration in Judea and Samaria uncovered a remarkably large sanctuary that had actually existed from the Persian period; the earliest evidence, a coin found inside the complex, dates to circa 486 BCE. The temple continued to exist into the second century BCE.

Nearly four hundred inscriptions stemming from the Persian and Hellenistic periods were found in the context of the sanctuary and are religious texts ("dedicatory inscriptions") written primarily in Aramaic but in some cases also Hebrew and Greek. These indicate that the Samaritans on Mount Gerizim worshipped the God of Israel, Yhwh, probably as the only god and with an aniconic cult as in Jerusalem. These Samaritan worshippers of Yhwh called themselves "Israel," as first documented in two inscriptions from the Greek island of Delos from the third–second century BCE. Thus, they self-identified with the name of the former kingdom of Israel, in whose territory their most important cultic place atop Mount Gerizim was located.

The circumstances of the sanctuary's foundation had nothing to do with any separation from Jerusalem, as Josephus had assumed. None of the remains at the site indicate that Gerizim was considered a "rival sanctuary" to Jerusalem. In the Persian period, it was established as a sanctuary for those who lived in the province of Samaria and worshipped Yhwh—comparable to how the temple was (re)built in Jerusalem by 515 BCE, according to the books of Ezra and Nehemiah. The worshippers of Yhwh in the province of Samaria can only be seen as a *variant* form of the Yahwistic faith of that time. The Judean form of this faith, centered in Jerusalem, represents another, contemporaneous option alongside it.

To understand the Samaritans, it is crucial to recognize that they are not a sect of Judaism, since the *one authoritative tradition* from which the Samaritans could have split off—more or less the Judean/Jewish one in Jerusalem—only developed gradually after the temple was rebuilt and its theology was elaborated. These two groups can be described through a certain analogy from church history as two different *denominations* of "Israel" that slowly began to form in the Persian provinces of Samaria and Judah, each with their own religious center: one on Mount Zion and one on Mount Gerizim.

Coexistence and Exchange: On the Significance of the Samaritans in Antiquity

There is no evidence of major disputes between the Judeans and Samaritans during the Persian period. This is almost certainly due to the political situation, with each community existing within its provincial borders defined by Persian authorities and managing its own affairs at its own sanctuary to Yhwh.

Contrary to the widespread image, the Samaritans were not a marginal minority but were actually quite influential. The province of Samaria was immensely important in the Persian period; the provincial capital located at Samaria (modern Sebastiye) grew into the largest city in Palestine and exerted a relatively significant amount of influence. Under the Neo-Babylonians and then the Persians, Samaria was the administrative center of the southern Levant. It was the seat of the Persian governor, who ruled over the larger region. This center of political power also naturally drew inhabitants to it. In no other period in the entire history of the area in antiquity were there more settlements in the greater Samaria region than in the Persian period.

Judah was largely insignificant during this period, and its influence was limited to the provincial level. This difference in the importance of the two provinces is clearly recognizable in the material culture. For example, the rich, international iconographic program of the Samarian provincial coins is worlds apart from the provincial iconographic motifs of the coins from Judah, which contain a very limited repertoire.

There would have always been jealousies among one or another of the subgroups in Jerusalem or between certain individuals (Nehemiah 1–6). However, such sentiments and rivalries were not predominant during this period. There must have been a regular exchange between Judean and Samarian scribes on multiple levels, including religious matters. Several Aramaic papyri found on the island of Elephantine in the Nile that date to the fifth century BCE attest to the Judeo-Aramaic community on Elephantine being in contact with both Judean and Samarian officials (TAD A4.7–4.9).

The Parting of the Ways

The relations between Samaria and Judah began to deteriorate from the late fourth or early third century BCE for reasons that are not yet fully understood. The oldest attestation of this dispute is in the Greek version of Ben Sira (ca. 180 BCE): "Two peoples do I detest, and the third is not a people: those who live the Samarian hill country and the Philistines and the foolish people who live in Shechem" (Sira 50:25–26). The Samarians are not only classified as non-Israelites; they are denied a national identity altogether. From the late second or early first century BCE, there is a definitive parting of the ways between the Jews and the Samaritans. One catalyst for the festering conflict is the Jerusalem king John Hyrcanus I (134–104 BCE), who intended to extend his domain to Samaria and destroyed the Gerizim sanctuary sometime around 111 BCE (Josephus, *Antiquitates* 13.254–256; *Bellum Iudaicum* 1.62–64 in Mason 2008). An indication of the separation process is the formation of a separate Samaritan language, writing, vocalization, and reading tradition distinct from the Jewish/masoretic tradition.

The "Common Torah" and the "Samaritan Pentateuch"

The encroachments by the Jerusalem Hasmonean dynasty (ca. 140–37 BCE) spurred the process of self-demarcation. Whereas the Judean/Jewish version developed into the textual tradition that later merged into the Masoretic Text, the Samaritan version merged into the Samaritan Pentateuch.

Prior to this, both sibling communities likely shared a common Pentateuch. This Pentateuch would have been completed by the fourth century BCE at the very latest, and it is likely that representatives of the Samaritan community were also involved in the finalization of this central text—since in this period, there were no deep disputes between Samaria and Judah. Regulations, holidays, circumcision, and so on were recorded, while specific questions such as the place of worship were excluded.

This strategy is recognizable in the Torah, where cultic centralization laws in Deuteronomy never mention the location of the one legitimate place of worship for offering sacrifices to the God of Israel. Sacrifice is to be made only at the one place (*maqom*) "that Yhwh will choose" (Deuteronomy 12:14 and twenty further times in Deuteronomy). This openness made it possible for the two groups to read the Torah at their own sanctuaries and relate its texts positively to their own traditions.

About the Author

Benedikt Hensel is a full professor of Hebrew Bible at the Carl von Ossietzky University of Oldenburg. He holds a PhD (2011) and a habilitation (2016) in Hebrew Bible studies and archaeology from the Johannes Gutenberg University of Mainz. He specializes in the religious history, archaeology, and literary history of Israel, Judah, and Transjordan. He has published "On the Relationship of Judah and Samaria in Post-exilic Times: A Farewell to the Conflict Paradigm," *Journal of the Study of the Old Testament* 44(1) (2019): 19–42; "Debating Temple and Torah in the Second Temple Period: Theological and Political Aspects of the Final Redaction(s) of the Pentateuch," pages 27–49 in *Torah, Temple,*

Land: Construction of Judaism in Antiquity, edited by Markus Witte, Jens Schröter, and Verena M. Lepper (Tübingen: Mohr Siebeck, 2020); and "Ezra-Nehemiah and Chronicles: New Insights into the Early History of Samari(t)an-Jewish Relations," *Religions* 11 (2020): 1–24.

Suggestions for Further Reading

In This Book

See also chapters 5 (canons), 10 (Tanak), 11 (Pentateuch), 25 (Deuteronomistic History), 34 (Dead Sea Scrolls), 47 (monotheism), and 56 (polemics).

Elsewhere

Kartveit, Magnar. *The Origin of the Samaritans*. Leiden: Brill, 2009.

Knoppers, Gary N. *Jews and Samaritans: The Origins and History of Their Early Relations*. New York: Oxford University Press, 2013.

Mason, Steve. *Flavius Josephus: Translation and Commentary* (volume 1). Leiden: Brill, 2008.

Pummer, Reinhard. *The Samaritans: A Profile*. Grand Rapids, MI: Eerdmans, 2016.

Schmid, Konrad. "Overcoming the Sub-Deuteronomism and Sub-Chronicism of Historiography in Biblical Studies: The Case of the Samaritans." Pages 17–29 in *The Bible, Qumran, and the Samaritans*. Edited by Magnar Kartveit and Gary N Knoppers. Boston: De Gruyter, 2018.

Spilbury, Paul, and Chris Seeman. *Flavius Josephus: Translation and Commentary* (volume 6a). Leiden: Brill, 2016.

Themes

39

How Do the Moon, Month, and Sabbath Regulate Biblical Calendars?

Philippe Guillaume

Ever since humans started sowing grains and pulses to improve food security, they invented time-reckoning methods to follow the advancement of the seasons as precisely as possible. Reliance on the weather is not sufficient for farmers to decide when to sow. As Ecclesiastes 11:4 notes, "Whoever observes the wind will not sow; and whoever regards the clouds will not reap." Anticipation is essential to ensure that plants will mature before the drought in dry climates or before the winter in cold climates.

Counting days and moon cycles is too imprecise. Neither the yearly solar cycle of 365 days (and five hours, forty-eight minutes, and forty-six seconds) nor the moon cycle of approximately 29.530 days corresponds to a nonfractional number of twenty-four-hour days. After a few decades, most calendars lag behind the equinox, and it is necessary to correct the deviation. To do so, different calendar systems were invented, adding either a number of days or an entire month to certain years.

Mesopotamia favored the intercalation of an entire month at irregular intervals. The procedure was eventually standardized according to the so-called Metonic cycle that used years three, six, eight, eleven, fourteen, seventeen, and nineteen as long thirteen-month years (leap years), whereas the other years were ordinary twelve-month years.

One system used in Egypt was based on a 365-day year divided into three seasons of four 30-day months, plus an additional 5 days added at the end of each year ($3 \times 4 \times 30 = 360 + 5 = 365$ days).

The Bible displays influences from the surrounding cultures, with a mixture of time-reckoning systems, as is the case in rabbinic Judaism as well. Hence, it is impossible to identify a typically Hebrew or Jewish calendar. The Bible only names in passing a selection of months, some with West

Semitic names: Aviv (Exodus 13:4; 23:15; 34:18; Deuteronomy 16:1), Ziv (1 Kings 6:1, 37), Eitanim (1 Kings 8:2), and Bul (1 Kings 6:38). Others have Babylonian names: Nissan (Nehemiah 2:1; Esther 3:7; 11:2; 8:9; 1 Esdras 5:6), Sivan (Esther 8:9), and Elul (Nehemiah 6:15; 1 Maccabees 14:27). One should thus beware of taking modern practices as representatives of ancient biblical practices. For instance, in modern Israel, the Jewish New Year (Rosh Hashanah) is set in the autumn, while the best-attested beginning of the year in the Bible is in the spring (for instance, Exodus 12).

In the Hebrew Bible, the word for "month" is *yeraḥ*, "moon," an indication of the importance of the moon cycle. The Sabbath itself probably originates from Mesopotamia, where it designated the full (*shabatum*) moon (see 2 Kings 4:23) that split the month in two "weeks," from the first crescent to the full moon and from the full moon to the disappearance of the last crescent. The period of invisibility of the moon between the last crescent and the reappearance of the first crescent was a major challenge because it was impossible to predict how long it would last: A single night or up to three? The difference of three days was not negligible, as many loans were contracted for periods of a few months. Moreover, the days of the dark moon were considered dangerous, and the king was not to perform certain actions.

Today, the Sabbath is the seventh day, the beginning or the end of the week, not the middle of the month. Redefined as the seventh day, the Sabbath freed the calendar from the unpredictability of the moon. There was no longer any need to scrutinize the sky to spot the first crescent and determine the beginning of the new month. Anyone could count up to seven and know when the new week begins, irrespective of the weather and location. Mesopotamian scholars eventually worked out mathematical methods to predict the duration of the black or invisible moon, but the seven-day week made the moon mostly irrelevant for basic calendrical matters.

A calendar based on the 7-day week is designated as the sabbatical calendar, the Jubilee calendar, or the 364-day calendar. It consists of fifty-two whole weeks ($52 \times 7 = 364$ days). It is based on a Mesopotamian theoretical model (MUL.APIN in Sumerian) and is attested in some Dead Sea Scrolls, in the nonbiblical books of Jubilees and Enoch, and in the Bible, including the Gospel accounts of the Last Supper.

The sabbatical calendar is thus independent of the moon, with the length of months determined in advance with an invariable sequence of three thirty-day months and an additional day at the end of months three, six, nine, and twelve ($4 \times 91 = 364$ days; see 1 Enoch 72). Obviously, however, over a day and a half was missing annually from this calendar to keep it synced with the seasons. The problem was solved by adding an entire week at a time to preserve the sacred rhythm of the seventh-day Sabbath and to ensure that every year begins on a Wednesday (the fourth day, when the luminaries were created; Genesis 1:14–19). The result is a perpetual calendar in which all Sabbaths occur every year on the same date, and any date is forever fixed to a particular day of the week. The question of when to intercalate additional weeks and how many remains.

In fact, two Dead Sea Scrolls (4Q319 and 4Q503) use a two-step inter-calation method, with a whole week added every seventh year ($[364 \times 7] + 7 = 2{,}555$ days = 365-day mean years), plus an additional week every twenty-eighth year ($[365 \times 28] + 7 = 10{,}227$ days = 365.25 days per mean year).

Since the Bible begins with the creation of the seven-day week and the consecration of the Sabbath, it is hardly surprising that it uses the sabbatical calendar in most of its books. The problem is that nowhere does the Bible refer explicitly to intercalation. For this reason, the sabbatical calendar has been deemed impractical, and some have doubted its very existence.

In fact, the first books of the Bible transmit clues about intercalation—discreet ones because the control of the calendar is a matter of secret knowledge guarded often by priests, for whom it is a source of power.

Enoch's life span in Genesis is a first clue. Enoch represents the seventh generation and is raptured by God when he is "only" 365 years old (Genesis 5:23–24). His years at death underline the need to add an extra day in the mean year of the 364-day calendar. To ensure that the sacred rhythm of the Sabbath is not interrupted by the intercalation of a day each year, 365-day mean years are obtained by adding a whole week every seventh year: the first six years amount to fifty-two weeks, and the seventh has fifty-three weeks ($[364 \times 6] + [364 + 7] / 7 = 365$). A 365-day mean year is still about a quarter of a day too short.

Abraham's life span provides a second clue. He is graced with the most elaborate and complete life span notice in Genesis (compare Genesis 23:1; 25:7, 17; 47:28): "These are the days of the years of the life of Abraham, one hundred seventy-five years. He breathed his last. Abraham died in a good old age, old and full. He was gathered to his people" (Genesis 25:7–8; my translation). Abraham's "good and full" life span of 175 years establishes the length of the overall cycle during which the remaining weeks are to be intercalated to keep in sync with the seasons.

The exact rhythm of the insertion of the missing weeks is provided by the size of the curtains that surround the tabernacle Moses built in the wilderness. The curtains are embroidered with cherubim and are joined to one another with loops and hooks to ensure that the "tabernacle is one whole" (Exodus 36:13). Each curtain is 28 × 4 cubits (Exodus 26:2 // 36:9). Taking cubits for years, 28 indicates four seven-year cycles, at the end of which a second week is to be added. This means that a week is added at the end of every seventh year, plus a second week at the end of the twenty-eighth year. After six such twenty-eight-year cycles, thirty additional weeks have been intercalated between year 1 and year 168 (28 × 6 = 168). This, however, is not the complete cycle. As indicated by Abraham's perfect life span, a final week should be added at the end of year 175. Upon the completion of the cycle, the intercalation scheme reverts back to the beginning. Each cycle thus consists of 175 × 52 weeks + 31 intercalary weeks = 9,131 weeks. This number of weeks can be compared to the Julian calendar, in which every century is too long by about three-fourth days. For this reason, in 1582, Pope Gregory XIII advanced the calendar by ten days.

Over a period of 175 years, these calendars amount to the following:

Julian calendar (365.25-day year): 365.25 × 175 = 63,918.750 days
Gregorian calendar (365.2425-day year): = 63,917.4375 days
Intercalated sabbatical calendar: (175 × 364 days) + (31 days × 7) =
    63,700 + 217 = 63,917 days
Present reckoning of the tropical year: 365.2422 × 175 =
    63,917.385 days

With the three intercalations mentioned above, the sabbatical calendar is only 0.385 days short of the present reckoning of the tropical year. Hence, the sabbatical calendar achieved an impressive accuracy a millennium and a half before the Gregorian calendar reform.

That it is remarkably accurate does not prove that the sabbatical calendar was ever put into practice. Yet, rabbinical Judaism remembers the first two intercalations of the sabbatical calendar; a blessing of the sun is pronounced every twenty-eighth year.

Despite the apparent complexity of its intercalation schemes, the sabbatical calendar is not totally impractical, since the Gregorian calendar we use today also requires a correction at intervals that have not yet been decided. Hence, practicality is not the issue.

Most societies across the world cope with different calendars to regulate credit, taxation, and religious festivals. Intercalation is a major issue. Some calendars, like Islam's, reject all intercalation schemes, but the majority add days, weeks, or months. Intercalating whole weeks preserves the sacred rhythm of the Sabbath and prevents other festivals from falling on a Sabbath but nevertheless takes into account the function of the two luminaries set in the dome of the sky to serve as signs for festivals, days, and years (Genesis 1:14).

Ultimately, the choice of a particular calendar, like other means of communication such as languages and writing systems, is a political decision that reflects power struggles.

About the Author

Philippe Guillaume holds a ThD from the University of Geneva and a habilitation from the University of Berne. He published *Land and Calendar: The Priestly Document from Genesis 1 to Joshua 18* (New York: T&T Clark, 2009).

Suggestions for Further Reading

In This Book
See also chapters 1 (scholarly perspective), 3 (religious in a scientific world), 40 (holiness), 41 (symbolic numbers), 47 (monotheism), 53 (creation), and 74 ("P").

Elsewhere

Jaubert, Annie. *The Date of the Last Supper*. Translated by Isaac Rafferty. Staten Island, NY: Alba, 1965.

Klukowski, Michał. "The Tradition of the 364-Day Calendar versus the Calendar Polemic in Second Temple Judaism." *Verbum Vitae* 38 (2020): 79–105.

Saulnier, Stéphane. *Calendrical Variation in Second Temple Judaism*. Leiden: Brill, 2012.

Wagenaar, Jan A. *Origin and Transformation of the Ancient Israelite Festival Calendar*. Wiesbaden: Harrassowitz, 2005.

40

Does the Hebrew Bible Apply Holiness to Space or to Time?

Philippe Guillaume

Holiness is, of course, a central biblical concept. Most religions declare particular sites and certain days as sacred. Holy days are set apart from the daily routine to gather and construct identities, build social cohesion, and synchronize human activities. Holy sites such as springs, mountains, outdoor shrines, and elaborate temples are believed to provide privileged access to the divine realm. The Bible, however, favors mobility over root-edness and displays a consistent resistance to the sacralization of space.

Holiness (*qodesh*) evokes separation for purification and dedication to out-of-the-ordinary activities. Holiness concerns warriors who prepare themselves by staying away from women (1 Samuel 21:4–6), priests who are holy to their God and so must not marry certain women (Leviticus 21:7), or the entire Israel declared holy to the Lord (Leviticus 19:2; Deuteronomy 7:6). One could expect holiness to apply also to sanctuaries, cultic utensils, offerings, and to the Holy Land. Yet, Jacob Milgrom (2000, 1962) makes the astonishing claim that "never in Scripture do we find that God sanctifies space." Indeed, the various altars built by the patriarchs in Canaan are *not* declared holy sites, though the stone Jacob anoints at Bethel in Genesis 28 indicates that it was part of a famous shrine.

Exodus refrains from ascribing holiness to the shrine where Moses meets Yhwh, though curtains embroidered with cherubim surround it to mark out a restricted space (Exodus 36:8–13). The Tent of Meeting is not a holy place; it endowed no holiness to the sites where it was once erected. In fact, the wilderness that marks a forty-year era between Egypt and Canaan is less than a "desert" that may be located on a map. It is a wilderness in the middle of nowhere—that is, out of space or "beyond the wilderness," as Exodus 3:1 locates Moses's encounter with the burning bush. He must remove his sandals because he is told, "The soil [*'adamah*] upon which you stand is holy" (Exodus 3:5). The Bible never turns this soil into a sanctuary, though it likely remembers a particular shrine such as Mount Sinai, which was hailed as a sacred mountaintop before and after the Bible used it as the place of revelation. Zechariah 2:12 recalls this *'adamah* and identifies Judah as the Lord's share "on the soil of the holy."

Bringing the ark Moses built in the wilderness into the city of David does not turn Jerusalem into a holy city. Yhwh resists David's desire to build a temple (2 Samuel 7), and when Solomon eventually erects a house for the Lord, its inner part is the "holy of holies," not a room and even less the "most holy *place* [or space]," as it is commonly rendered in English (Exodus 26:34–35 and parallels). Though built and adorned with cedar and much gold, Solomon's temple contradicts the mobility of the wilderness tent, a mobility expressed already in Deuteronomy (e.g., 12:5, 11; 14:23), where the place chosen by Yhwh to set his name is never given a specific location. Scholars imagine that the place can be none other than Jerusalem, though Jerusalem is never named in the Torah.

Jerusalem is referred to as "the city of the holiness" (*'ir haqodesh*; Nehemiah 11:1) and the "city of your holiness" (*'ir haqodsheka*; Daniel 9:24). Ezekiel 48:35 reveals the name of the new Jerusalem as "the Lord is there." From the stomach of the great fish, Jonah evokes the "temple of your holiness," often mistranslated as "your holy temple" (Jonah 2:4–7), leaving the location of that temple open. It is in Greek intertestamental literature (Tobit 13:9 and in the books of the Maccabees) that Jerusalem becomes "the holy city"—that is, in texts not regarded as Scripture by Jews and Protestants.

The Hebrew avoidance of anchoring holiness to a specific place is likely a reaction to shrines erected "under every green tree" (1 Kings 14:23; 2 Kings 16:4), standing stones, and holy pillars. The biblical god is depicted to have an aversion to being tied down to a particular temple or city, a consequence of the sanctification of the seventh day of creation (Genesis 2:3). The Sabbath is the sole creature the creator sanctifies, the sole repository of holiness. The Sabbath is the crown of creation and the sacred measuring rod for what we designate as "time" (Exodus 31:14).

"Time" as an abstract notion was introduced in the Bible by the translators of the Septuagint. Instead of the Hebrew creation in seven days, the Greek text considers creation complete already on day *six* (Genesis 2:2). Humanity becomes the crown of creation, and the Sabbath is deprived of its creational status. It becomes a mere time of rest for a seemingly exhausted god.

Yet, the question of time and the difficulty of reconciling it with mobility was the subject of one of the paradoxes attributed to the Greek philosopher Zeno of Elea (490–430 BCE). With the image of the flying arrow, Zeno suggested that to be moving means to be nowhere—that is, beyond any knowable point in space. As Alba Papa-Grimaldi (1998, 108–123) shows, the human mind cannot grasp movement. We conceive of a flying arrow as a succession of stations. The arrow cannot be here and there at the same time. Space cannot account for movement. Zeno's arrow is either in movement and thus out of particular spaces or immobile in countless instances when it occupies a space identical to itself. Though the duration of the movement is obvious to our senses and is measurable, movement has to be segmented into infinitesimal instants to be conceivable. Divide time as much as you want; you only get more instances when the arrow occupies the same space and is not moving at all. Hence one needs to abandon the notion of time to conceive of motion. Zeno's paradox is highly relevant to the primacy the Bible grants to movement over space and rootedness that anchors and immobilizes holiness.

In the Bible, time is the privileged means to convey holiness in the world. This primacy of time over space remains highly relevant today. Letting holiness overflow into space to declare certain sites sacred can end up justifying violent means to protect them. Jerusalem is the parade example of such a process. Jerusalem is a flash point for crusades and jihads to liberate or purify its sacred shrines. Moreover, sacred spaces (holy land, holy temple) and any priesthood claiming for itself a "holier than thou" position introduce a gradation of holiness that contradicts the nature of holiness that pertains to the absolute. Apportioning holiness, even if it does not lead to hierarchy and exclusion, contradicts what holiness stands for: God.

The contradiction is avoided when holiness is reserved for time—time conceived of not as a physical entity but as a flow, a constant and unstoppable movement. Change and movement are often perceived as confusing and dangerous. Traditions are established to resist the chaos resulting from constant change. Instead of setting up rival sacred places to those already in existence, the Bible organizes chaos with the Sabbath, the crown of creation and the sole creature sanctified by the creator. As such, the Sabbath is the mathematical expression of the divine spirit that blew over the primordial waters at the onset of creation (Genesis 1:2). The seven-day rhythm produces regularity within constant flow, allowing tent-dwelling patriarchs to travel freely between Mesopotamia and Egypt, and Israel between Egypt and Canaan, worshipping their God everywhere without being tied to a particular place. The divine predilection for tents, for mobile shrines that leave no sacred leftovers behind, throws a dark shadow over the royal attempts to immobilize God and use religion for political purposes. The spirit of God is a wind: movement par excellence. The divine cannot be anchored somewhere (for instance, in a particular temple) or it loses the potential of movement—that is, being ever fresh, spurring worshippers to move ahead.

Practically, this means that any concept of holiness attributed to particular persons, objects, and places should be handled with much caution. Yet, ever since the Torah was rendered into Greek in Alexandria, Egypt, Bible translators—and even more, their readers who have no access to the Hebrew text—find it hard to resist the notions of "Holy Land," "Holy City," and "Holy Temple." Such categories are present throughout the world, and for this very reason, the Bible resists them.

About the Author

Philippe Guillaume holds a ThD from the University of Geneva and a habilitation from the University of Berne. He published *Land and Calendar: The Priestly Document from Genesis 1 to Joshua 18* (New York: T&T Clark, 2009).

Suggestions for Further Reading

In This Book
See also chapters 33 (Septuagint), 34 (Dead Sea Scrolls), 39 (calendars), 49 (Torah), 53 (creation), 65 (King David), and 69 (Jonah).

Elsewhere
Eynikel, Erik, and Katrin Hauspie. "καιρός and κρόνος in the Septuagint." *Ephemerides Theologicae Lovanienses* 73 (1997): 369–385.

Kimball, Charles. *When Religion Becomes Evil: Five Warning Signs.* New York: HarperOne, 2008.

Milgrom, Jacob. *Leviticus 17–22: A New Translation with Commentary.* New York: Doubleday, 2000.

Papa-Grimaldi, Alba. *Time and Reality.* Aldershot, UK: Ashgate, 1998.

Sasson, Jack M. "Time . . . to Begin." Pages 183–194 in *"Sha'arei Talmon": Studies in the Bible, Qumran, and Ancient Near East Presented to Shemaryahu Talmon.* Edited by Michael Fishbane, Emanuel Tov, and Weston W. Field. Winona Lake, IN: Eisenbrauns, 1992.

Stern, Sacha. *Time and Process in Ancient Judaism.* Oxford: Littman Library of Jewish Civilization, 2003.

41
Which Numbers Can Be Symbolic in the Hebrew Bible?

Elaine Adler Goodfriend

Numbers can convey qualitative ideas in addition to their quantitative values. For example, in common English usage, a number can express abundance in a nonliteral way ("a million"), excellence ("a ten"), or frequency ("a hundred times"). So too, several biblical numbers carry meaning and specific connotations that were conventional in the biblical world view and ancient Israelite society but are not shared by current societies. As a result, their symbolic usage is often overlooked in favor of a literal meaning, which can affect one's understanding of what is being conveyed in a given biblical passage.

The Number Seven

The number seven is the most important "symbolic" number in the Hebrew Bible and conveys the idea of wholeness and perfection and thus, in some cases, holiness, as the Israelite God is identified with perfection. The use of seven in this way is not restricted to the Bible, as many examples are found in ancient Near Eastern literature. Possible reasons for the significance of seven are as follows: there were seven heavenly bodies known to Babylonia astronomers, and because of their deification, seven became identified with holiness; the lunar month, while a continuum, is divided into four distinct phases, each with seven days so that a seven-day period was considered the basic passage of time (after a single day); among the digits from one to ten, the number seven (a prime) stands unique because it is allied with neither the even numbers (two, four, six, eight) nor other odd numbers (three, nine) nor five (half of ten and associated with the number of digits on a hand). Thus, the number seven stands alone. This is evident in the depiction of creation in Genesis 1, where the first six days of creation can be broken down into three corresponding pairs, while the seventh day, the Sabbath, is unmatched.

Further, as if to emphasize the holiness and wholeness of the seven-day pattern, Genesis 1:1–2:4 abounds with both words and elements that recur seven times or in multiples of seven. Genesis 1:1 contains seven words and twenty-eight letters, and Genesis 1:2 has fourteen words; the word "Elohim" (God) occurs thirty-five times, *'eretz* (land) appears twenty-one times, and *tov* (good) appears seven times. Genesis 2:1–3, which tells of the seventh day, has thirty-five words (hence, 7 × 5).

The seven-day pattern also appears in Israel's festival calendar, as Passover and the Feast of Tabernacles last seven days (Leviticus 23:6, 34). Boys are circumcised after seven days have passed, akin to an animal's readiness for sacrifice (Genesis 17:12; Leviticus 22:27). The consecration of the priesthood is a seven-day ritual (Leviticus 8:33, 35).

This notion of wholeness and holiness associated with the seven-day pattern extends as well to larger units of time. Shavuot (Pentecost) is seven weeks after Passover (Leviticus 23:15). The seventh month after the exodus from Egypt contains several of the Torah's most significant holy days, including the day later called "New Year" and the Day of Atonement (Leviticus 23:24). The Hebrew slave is freed in his seventh year of servitude, while every seven years, debts are canceled and the land lies fallow (Exodus 21:2; Leviticus 25:4; Deuteronomy 15:1). The patriarch Jacob works to acquire Rachel and Leah for seven years each, the same as the years of plenty and famine in Pharaoh's dreams (Genesis 29, 41).

The number seven also plays an important role in the biblical narrative. For example, Noah is commanded to bring seven pairs of clean animals into the ark (Genesis 7:2). Job has seven sons (Job 1:2), while Moses's father-in-law, Reuel, has seven daughters (Exodus 2:16). Sevenfold punishment is mentioned in the story of Cain and Abel (Genesis 4:15) and in God's chastisement of Israel for covenant violations (Leviticus 26:18). While nowhere explicit, the number seven accords with the number of the ancestors of Israel (four matriarchs and three patriarchs) and the generations from Abraham to Moses.

Because of its association with perfection and holiness, seven is the most prominent number in Israel's ritual life. The sanctuary's lampstand has seven lamps (Exodus 25:37). Rituals of purification make use of seven sprinklings or immersions, and the demand for seven animals is common in sacrificial rituals.

Multiples of Seven

Multiples of seven convey similar notions of wholeness and perfection. The square of seven, forty-nine, comprises the number of days from

Passover to Pentecost (falling on the fiftieth day), akin to the counting of years until the Jubilee, the fiftieth year (Leviticus 23:16; 25:8). The number seventy, the product of two numbers linked to perfection, is associated with the descendants of Jacob who went down to Egypt (Exodus 1:5), the number of nations that comprise humanity (Genesis 10, although the sum is not offered there), and the number of elders who represent Israel in its covenant with God (Exodus 24:1). Seventy years represents a prolonged period of punishment in prophetic literature and is associated with a life span that is both realistic and satisfactory—not ideal but fanciful like 120 years (Isaiah 23:17; Jeremiah 25:12; Zechariah 1:12; Psalm 90:10). Sevenfold punishment is harsh, but not as dramatic as seventy-seven-fold (Genesis 4:24).

The Number Ten

Ten is the number of fingers on both hands and thus the most obvious means of counting. Thus, we find the association between the number ten and the idea of completeness. The commandments given by God directly to Israel at Sinai are ten (Exodus 20:1–18; 34:28). God accuses Israel of testing him ten times in the wilderness (Numbers 14:22). When Hannah weeps because of her barrenness, her husband, Elkanah, responds incredulously, "Am I not better to you than ten sons?" (1 Samuel 1:8). The number of plagues inflicted on Egypt is ten, but the number is not specifically stated in the narrative (Exodus 7–11).

The Numbers Three and Forty

A period of three days appears over thirty times in the Hebrew Bible and conveys the notion of a short period of time. For example, after God calls Abraham to sacrifice his son, he arrives at the appointed place on the third day (Genesis 22:4). Moses tells Pharaoh that the Israelites are just taking a three-day excursion into the wilderness to sacrifice to their God (Exodus 5:3). God's presence descends on Mount Sinai on the third day after their arrival (Exodus 19:11). According to the prophet Hosea, the Israelite people imagine that God will "raise" them on the third day to live in God's presence (Hosea 6:2). The period of three days similarly appears in ancient Near Eastern literature.

In contrast to the number three, the number forty (regarding days or years) conveys the notion of a long duration. The element of forty days appears with this connotation regarding the following: the days of the flood

(Genesis 7–8), Moses's stay and Elijah's travel to Mount Sinai (Exodus 24:18; 1 Kings 19:8), Goliath's twice-daily blasphemous challenge to Israel (1 Samuel 17:16), and the prophet Jonah's call for repentance (Jonah 3:4). A woman remains impure after the birth of a child for forty days for a boy and eighty for a girl (Leviticus 12). Israel's punishment was forty years in the wilderness (Numbers 14:34; Deuteronomy 2:7). The reigns of both David and Solomon were forty years, a substantial period (1 Kings 2:11; 11:42). The chaotic era described in the book of Judges is similarly broken up into forty-year periods (3:11; 5:31; 8:28, 13:1; 1 Samuel 4:18). Mathematicians view forty as an "abundant number," as it is divisible by two, four, five, eight, ten, and twenty.

The Number Five

The number five reflects the number of fingers on the human hand and thus is easily countable. Further, the easiest multiplier of the numbers from two to nine is five because its products alternate between numbers that have the units digit of five or zero. Thus Abraham's test of divine justice in Genesis 18:16–38 begins the negotiations over Sodom's threatened destruction with fifty righteous people. Then Abraham adjusts his bargaining position to forty-five, then forty, followed by thirty and twenty and, ultimately, ten. The value of persons according to Leviticus 27:1–8 are multiples of five, and so is the redemption price of one's firstborn (Numbers 3:47; 18:16). The number five in these cases is probably not symbolic as much as convenient for the purpose of priestly bookkeeping. Only in the story of Joseph does the number five play a prominent role (Genesis 41:34; 43:34; 45:6, 11; 45:22; 47:2; 47:24), but its significance is unclear.

The Number Twelve

The number twelve is meaningful in the Hebrew Bible as the number of Israel's tribes (even when the identities of the twelve are fluid). Thus, the number twelve appears when the Bible emphasizes the equal participation of all the tribes: the twelve spies who surveyed the land of Canaan (Numbers 13), the twelve stones that the Israelites took from the Jordan River (Joshua 4:3), and the twelve stones in the altar the prophet Elijah built (1 Kings 18:31). The tabernacle's "Bread of Presence" contained twelve loaves (Leviticus 24:5). Other tribal confederations including six or twelve tribes are mentioned in the Hebrew Bible and play a role in ancient Greece as well (Genesis 17:20; 22:20–24; 25:13–16; 36:9–14). The fact that twelve is the number of lunar months in a year may serve as the basis for its importance, along with its divisibility (by two, three, four, and six) and its role in the Sumerian sexagesimal system.

The Number Seventeen

The number seventeen seems to have a symbolic significance in the flood narrative and the chronology of the Joseph narrative. Genesis 7:11 informs us that the flood began in the six hundredth year of Noah's life, on the seventeenth day of the second month (2/17/600), while according to Genesis 8:4, the ark came to rest on Mount Ararat on the seventeenth day of the seventh month (7/17/600). According to Genesis 37, Joseph is sold into slavery in Egypt when he is 17 years old, while Jacob comes down to Egypt and is reunited with his son when he is 130 years of age and dies at 147. Thus, Joseph spends his first 17 years with his father, while Jacob spends his last 17 years with his son. Otherwise, the number is insinuated in the ages of the patriarchs, where seventeen is the sum of the factors of the life spans of Abraham, Isaac, and Jacob:

Abraham: $175 = 7 \times 5 \times 5$ (or 5^2) $(7 + 5 + 5 = 17)$
Isaac: $180 = 5 \times 6 \times 6$ (or 6^2) $(5 + 6 + 6 = 17)$
Jacob: $147 = 3 \times 7 \times 7$ (or 7^2) $(3 + 7 + 7 = 17)$

Note that the first multiplicand in each case decreases by two, while the multipliers increase by one, thus creating a pattern. The pattern created by these numbers suggests that the events of Israel's ancient history are neither random nor haphazard but rather ordered by God's grand design. On an obvious level, seventeen is the sum of two key numbers in the Hebrew Bible, seven and ten, and may symbolize the concepts of holiness and perfection. Another characteristic of the number seventeen is its status as the seventh prime number—that is, a whole number that cannot be made by multiplying other whole numbers.

In conclusion, the reader must be careful in evaluating the significance of numbers in the Hebrew Bible. Both narrative and ritual texts contain numbers that bear meaning beyond their face value. It is difficult to decide in many cases whether the number maintains its quantitative value in addition to bearing a highly symbolic value.

About the Author

Elaine Adler Goodfriend holds a PhD in Near Eastern studies from the University of California, Berkeley. She writes about biblical and Jewish law.

Her recent publications include "The *Qatlanit* ('Killer Wife') in Jewish Law: A Survey of Sources," *Women in Judaism: A Multidisciplinary E-journal* 17 (2020): 1–17; and "Seven: The Biblical Number," TheTorah.com, https://thetorah.com/article/seven-the-biblical-number.

Suggestions for Further Reading

In This Book
See also chapters 10 (Tanak), 15 (apocalyptic literature), 16 (Psalms), 17 (Wisdom), 20 (genealogies), 39 (calendars), 40 (holiness), 48 (twelve tribes), 50 (magic), and 52 (covenant).

Elsewhere

Abrahams, Israel. "Numbers, Typical and Important." Encyclopedia. com. https://www.encyclopedia.com/religion/encyclopedias-almanacs -transcripts-and-maps/numbers-typical-and-important.

Friberg, Joran. "Numbers and Counting." Pages 1139–1146 in *Anchor Bible Dictionary* (volume 4). Edited by David Noel Freedman. New York: Doubleday, 1992.

Gevirtz, Stanley. "The Life Spans of Joseph and Enoch and the Parallelism šibʿatayim-šibʿim wešibʿah." *Journal of Biblical Literature* 96 (1977): 570–571.

Schimmel, Annemarie. *The Mystery of Numbers*. New York: Oxford University Press, 1993.

42

Did Giants, Nephilim, and Other Creatures Ruin the World?

Elena L. Dugan

To the first-time reader, the beginning of the book of Genesis can seem to move in fits and starts. Chapters 1–5 explore the creation of the world and the actions of its first human inhabitants and some of their isolated foibles, with enough genealogy to make some readers' eyes glaze over. But somehow, by Genesis 6:7, Yhwh has decided to wipe humans from the face of the earth, regretting making them entirely. How did things get so bad, so quickly? And is it really humanity's fault?

Sometimes, big interpretative problems come with equally big solutions. Hidden at the very beginning of Genesis 6 is one possible reason for the accelerating decay of the world's fortunes: the curious actions of beings called the "Nephilim," "sons of God," and "giants." But the solution requires a little careful reading and imagination, evidence for which we find largely outside the Bible.

In Genesis 6:2, the "sons of God" see that the "daughters of humans" are beautiful and decide to marry them. In 6:4, it is clarified that the Nephilim were on earth when the sons of God were up to their marrying business. Somebody (perhaps the Nephilim, or the sons of God) had children by the daughters of humans. And these children are described by many translations of Genesis 6:4 as "heroes of old, warriors of renown." None of this sounds so terrible; people love heroes and warriors! But in the very next verse, Genesis 6:5, it is announced, "The wickedness of humans was great on earth." What, you might wonder, just happened that triggered the cataclysmic erasure of all humans, save Noah and family, from the earth?

There are signs that something extra is going on. The Hebrew word *nephilim* can be translated literally as "fallen ones," a detail suggestive of nefarious actions. And the word rendered "heroes" is *gibborim* in Hebrew, which literally translates as "giants." In that case, there seem to have been parties *besides* run-of-the-mill humans existing on earth, somehow prompting the arrival of God's ultimate punishment. But the sequence of events in Genesis is less than crystal clear.

We have to look to another ancient account to learn what some early Jewish storytellers believed and why this circumstance was so catastrophic. This account is called Enoch (or 1 Enoch or the book of Enoch, depending on who you ask). It is not found in the traditional Roman Catholic or Protestant Bible or in the holy books of most Orthodox denominations, though it is included among the biblical books of the Ethiopian Orthodox Church.

Enoch was likely written after Genesis, though it may reflect stories that are just as old. Multiple copies were found among the Dead Sea Scrolls, so we know for certain the story was up and running by the third century BCE. Enoch's story of what happened before the flood proved tremendously popular among early Jews and Christians. It was either cited directly or known by reputation for centuries to come, spilling into the early Middle Ages. In fact, Enoch is one of the only noncanonical books cited directly in the New Testament (Jude 1:14), and the citation comes from the very section concerning fallen ones that we will now explore!

Enoch is named after the prophet to whom the story was purportedly revealed—the antediluvian (preflood) patriarch Enoch, featured in Genesis 5:21–24. Though Enoch's story gets a mere four verses in the Hebrew Bible, he really has a lot going on. First, Enoch lives for a curiously specific 365 years (the number of full days in a solar year), which may suggest some sort of special cosmic knowledge. Second, unlike all the other patriarchs mentioned in the genealogy of Genesis 5, Enoch is said to "walk with God." But the Hebrew word for "God" here is *elohim*, a word that can also refer to "angels" in the plural, especially when accompanied by the definite article "the" (*ha-*). So, when Enoch "walked with *ha-elohim*," as happens in Genesis 5:22 and 5:24, a reader could legitimately translate the phrase as "walked with God" or "walked with the angels." And if Enoch had such an unusually close acquaintance with the angels, one may wonder why and what they talked about. Third, Enoch's son, Methuselah, is the longest-lived man in the Bible, with a life span clocking in at 969 years, suggesting some great wisdom that his father had handed down. Fourth, and speaking of special treatment, Enoch is one of only two humans spared the indignity of death. The other is Elijah, taken up in a whirlwind in 2 Kings 2. Genesis 5:24 remarks that at the end of his life, Enoch "was not, for God/angels took him." In the end, Enoch somehow cavorts with angels, escapes death, and helps his son live to be nearly a millennium old.

The patriarch Enoch also shows up at a crucial place in the chronology of the book of Genesis. He is the great-grandfather of Noah—the Noah of the ark and the flood! The story of Enoch's lifetime, then, is the story of what happened in the centuries just before the flood. Enoch's father is named Jared, a name whose root means "to descend." As we are looking for something having to do with "fallen ones" (*nephilim*), perhaps you can see the outline of a story emerging.

One section of Enoch, known as the *Book of the Watchers*, turns cryptic hints from Genesis 6 into a rip-roaring story. According to Enoch, a collective of angels from atop Mount Hermon lusted after women they saw on earth below. In an action akin to a doomed movie villain's monologue, they loudly make a pact with one another to go ahead and marry some human women and take whatever punishment they get. They descend during the days of Jared, Enoch's father (recalling the "descent" pun mentioned above). Exactly why they were prohibited from being with earthly women is not entirely clear, but perhaps the underlying concern was over the mixing of heavenly and earthly beings. In any event, the text is unequivocal that these sexual relationships defile the angels. From the perspective of the writer, the outcomes for earthly beings are also disastrous. While the fallen angels are down on earth, they teach the women forbidden and magical skills, like charms and spells. One talented metallurgical angel, Azazel, teaches women how to make cosmetics (out of lead) and weapons of war. But, most dangerously of all, the women give birth to giants who are 300 cubits (450 feet) tall. The giants hungrily devour all the food on earth, move onto the flesh of humans, and finally, begin to cannibalize one another. This feels like the kind of unfixable catastrophe that might prompt God to wipe the slate clean and start over again. Indeed, the very earth cries out to God in protest!

By the end of this section of Enoch, the giants are captured, the angels are soundly punished, and the earth's fortunes are restored. The *Book of the Watchers* actually tells a story that runs parallel to the flood rather than just setting up for the canonical account. The flood basically gets sidestepped in favor of the proprietary punishments this story prefers, at least for the angels. But the story in Enoch also brings to life some of the hints found in Genesis 6:1–4. The "fallen ones" (*nephilim*) of 6:4 and the "sons of God" of 6:2 are roughly equated; they are the fallen angels who descend to earth chasing after human women. The "heroes" (*gibborim*) are to be taken darkly and literally: they are the giants, the product of these unholy marital unions, voracious for human flesh.

This salacious story does more than simply add narrative color to the terse account in Genesis. It also cleverly changes the equation of the problem of evil.

If Genesis 6 is not populated with some supernatural free radicals, the blame for the decline of humanity rests squarely on human shoulders. It is their failings that led to the flood, and we might therefore infer that there is something inherently rotten about humans. Humans experience evil outcomes because humans themselves are somehow wicked or evil. The flood was our fault.

But Enoch tells a different story. Humans are the victims of a game whose levers are far beyond our grasp. The decay of the world in the generations before Noah has to do with the lust of angels, the proliferation of illicit heavenly arts that humans never asked to learn, and the spilling of blood by creatures that should never have existed. The flood—and by extension, the very existence of widespread evil and wickedness in the earthly realm—is no longer entirely our fault.

Enoch also sketches God slightly differently than the God of Genesis. In Genesis 6, the reader gets the impression that God is an all-knowing judge who sees each iota of humanity's failings and punishes them accordingly. But in Enoch, God either doesn't know or doesn't care about what is happening on earth. When things started going downhill, "the earth brought accusation" (Enoch 7:6). Then, "as men were perishing, their cry went up to heaven" (8:4). But even though both the earth and humans cry out for aid, it is only when the archangels Michael, Sariel, Raphael, and Gabriel pick up on these cries and forward them to God that God gets prodded into action. In Enoch, God appears at the top of a managerial pyramid populated by differentiated hierarchies of angels. The biblical feeling that God is a watchful, omniscient, and scrupulous judge of human affairs recedes in favor of a distant and somewhat distractible God.

And so while it is fun to go monster hunting through the Hebrew Bible, the stakes for Genesis 6 are much higher than just a little cryptozoological curiosity. For ancient and modern readers, the need to figure out exactly what went down in this peculiar passage and exactly who (or what) was there has to do with one of the fundamental questions of human existence: Why is there evil in the world? And if the answer is "evil creatures," where does that leave God?

About the Author

Elena L. Dugan earned a doctorate in religion from Princeton University. She researches the apocalyptic literature and manuscript traditions of early Judaism, Christianity, and Islam, with a particular focus on the history of Enoch. She has published "Enochic Biography and the Manuscript History of 1 Enoch: The Codex Panopolitanus Book of the Watchers," *Journal of Biblical Literature* 140 (2021): 113–138; "On Making Manuscripts, Genre, and the Boundaries of Ancient Jewish Literature," *Metatron* 1 (2021):

1–9; and *The Apocalypse of the Birds: Enoch and the Jewish War in the First Century CE* (Edinburgh: Edinburgh University Press, 2023).

Suggestions for Further Reading

In This Book
See also chapters 5 (canons), 15 (apocalyptic literature), 34 (Dead Sea Scrolls), 43 (angels), 44 (ancestors), 50 (magic), and 51 (prophets).

Elsewhere

Nickelsburg, George W. E., and James C. VanderKam. *1 Enoch: A New Translation, Based on the Hermeneia Commentary*. Minneapolis: Fortress, 2004. (Translations of Enoch here are drawn from this volume.)

Reed, Annette Yoshiko. *Fallen Angels and the History of Judaism and Christianity: The Reception of Enochic Literature*. Cambridge: Cambridge University Press, 2005.

VanderKam, James C. *Enoch: A Man for All Generations*. Columbia: University of South Carolina Press, 1995.

43
What Does the Hebrew Bible Say about Angels and Demons?

Elisa Uusimäki

The Hebrew Bible mentions various angels and demons, but the texts in the collection derive from disparate contexts, and their writers never sought to construct systematic expositions on the topic. Yet it is clear that the Hebrew Bible reveals notions that both resemble and challenge contemporary ideas of angels and demons. While the Bible records only aspects of the ancient Israelite ideas of spiritual beings, other Jewish literature from antiquity sheds further light on such conceptions. We should also remember that there was no fixed canon in antiquity, nor is there just one Bible today. The Old Testament of the Oriental Orthodox churches of the Ethiopian and Eritrean traditions, for instance, includes books known as 1 Enoch and Jubilees, which illuminate ancient notions of angels and demons beyond what is known from the Hebrew Bible.

Angelic Beings

In the Hebrew Bible, angelic beings, typically presented as male or androgynous (Genesis 6:2–4; 18:2; 19:1–5), appear among people but are immortal and dwell in the heavenly realm. The Hebrew term for an angel is *malak*, "messenger," referring to their function as God's messengers. Angels are said to praise God (Isaiah 6:3; Psalm 148:2; Job 38:7), and the term "holy ones" (*qedoshim*) characterizes angels who do so (Psalm 89:6, 8). Other central tasks of angels include the protection of human beings (Genesis 48:16; Exodus 23:20–23; Psalm 91:11–12; Daniel 6:23; 10:13) and advocating for them before God (Zechariah 1:12; Job 33:23–24).

"Yhwh's angel" (Genesis 16:7–12; 22:11–18; Exodus 3:2; Judges 2:1–4; 1 Kings 19:5–7) and "God's angel" (Genesis 31:11; Exodus 14:19) occur several times and point to the close relationship between God and the spiritual beings governed by the deity. In fact, God and the mediatory angel figure can nearly be equated with each other (Exodus 3:2–6). Lower divine beings, in turn, are called "sons of God" (*bĕnê 'elohîm, bĕnê 'elîm*) and serve as members of the heavenly council or court (Genesis 6:2; Job 1:6; Psalms 29:1; 82:6). Similarly, biblical texts speak about the heavenly host surrounding and led by God (Joshua 5:13–15; 1 Kings 22:19).

While modern images portray angels as winged beings, wings are mentioned only occasionally in the Hebrew Bible in association with seraphs (Isaiah 6:2–4) and cherubs (Ezekiel 28:14, 16; Psalm 18:11). Such heavenly beings (not exactly angels as we conceive of them) are not humanlike. Instead, a seraph is a snake with six wings, while cherubs have four faces and four wings. Cherubs feature much more often than seraphs. They are said to guard the garden of Eden (Genesis 3:24) and to decorate sacred objects or be present in sacred spaces (Exodus 25:18–20; 1 Kings 6:23–28; Ezekiel 10:1–22; 41:17–25).

The late Second Temple era (ca. 250 BCE–70 CE) saw an increasing interest in angels. Differences in their tasks are made explicit, and notions of angels become progressively hierarchical. The book of Daniel, from the second century BCE, uses elements symbolizing God's glory (light, fire, precious metals) to describe an angel (10:5–6). It also mentions the names of two archangels, Gabriel and Michael (Daniel 9:21; 10:13), who belong to the highest category of angelic beings. Other sources from the late Second Temple era mention more proper names: some presume that there are seven archangels in total (Tobit 12:15; 1 Enoch 20:1–8), while others speak of four elevated angels (1 Enoch 9:1; 1QWar Scroll 9:15–16).

Among the Dead Sea Scrolls, the book of Jubilees describes the Angel of Presence, who mediates between God and humanity by dictating the divine revelation to Moses (Jubilees 1:27–2:1). This angel serves God in the most holy of the heavenly temple according to some of the other scrolls (1QRule of the Blessing 4:25; 1QHodayot^a 14:13).

In various Dead Sea Scrolls, angels appear as powerful beings (e.g., Shirot^e fragment 2) residing in the heavenly sphere, from where they control natural phenomena (e.g., Berakhot^a fragment 3). Liturgical texts stress mystical communication with the divine realm and its angels (e.g., 1QHodayot^a 11:21–23). According to the Daily Prayers, Berakhot, and the Songs of the Sabbath Sacrifice, humans join heavenly angels in their prayer and praise. In the latter, angels also serve as priests in the heavenly temple (Shirot^a fragment 1 i 8). Notably, cherubim and *ophannim* (literally, "wheels") are part of God's chariots in Berakhot^a (fragment 1 ii 2), which resembles their function in the later Jewish *merkabah* (chariot) mysticism.

God's troops also involve angels like the "sons of heaven" (*bĕnê šāmajim*; e.g., 1QCommunity Rule 4:22; 11:8; 1QHodayot^a 11:22) and the "angels of destruction" (*malkê hebel*) sent by God to destroy the godless (1QCommunity Rule 4:12; Damascus Document 2:6). These divine troops will take part in the war at the end of time. The *War Scroll* in particular imagines how the children of light, together with their leader and angels, will fight against evil powers. The leader of the children of light is given multiple names, including the Prince of Light, the Angel of Truth, and Melchizedek.

Evil Spirits

The Hebrew Bible also refers to evil spiritual beings. Yet there is no clear distinction between good angels and evil demons; the angels of destruction mentioned above, for example, have a close relation to God. Thus, God's troops are not necessarily benefactors. A spirit of deceit (*rûaḥ seqer*) belongs to the heavenly court (1 Kings 22:19–23), and divinely sent evil spirits (*rûaḥ ra'â*) cause friction, anxiety, and violence (Judges 9:23; 1 Samuel 16:14–23; 18:10–11; 19:9–10).

Some evil beings have special designations, most famously the *satan/* Satan, "the Adversary" (Numbers 22:22, 32; Job 1–2; Zechariah 3:1–7; 1 Chronicles 21:1). While Satan becomes an independent character only later on, he features prominently in the book of Job, where he is one of God's sons and acts with his permission. Other named evil spirits include *seirim* (Leviticus 17:7; Isaiah 34:14; 2 Chronicles 11:15) and *shedim* (Deuteronomy 32:17; Psalm 106:37), both of which are connected with idols. Isaiah 34:14 further mentions Lilith, known as a personified demon in later Jewish tradition. Finally, Azazel is mentioned in the context of the Yom Kippur ritual, which involves sacrificing a goat to this demon (Leviticus 16:8–10).

Some Hebrew terms denoting negative things may refer to either demons or demonized foreign gods, including *deber* ("Pestilence"; Psalm 91:6; Hosea 13:14; Habakkuk 3:5), *qeteb* ("Destruction"; Psalm 91:6), and *resheph* ("Plague"; Deuteronomy 32:24; Habakkuk 3:5). In the Hebrew Bible, their independent status diminishes when they become understood as being subordinate to the God of Israel (Habakkuk 3:5).

The Dead Sea Scrolls mention some evil beings not known from the Hebrew Bible, such as the leader of the demonic forces who is called Abaddon, Angel of Darkness, Azazel, Beelzebub, Belial, Melchiresha, and Shemihazah. While the Jewish group behind the scrolls thought evil spirits to be real threats, causing harm and illness, they also considered God to protect the elect and sought divine protection via ritual means such as prayer, incantation, and exorcisms (especially 4QIncantation; 4QSongs of the Sage[a–b]; 4QExorcism; 11QPsalms[a] column 19; 11QApocryphal Psalms).

The Origin of Evil

The origin of evil has puzzled people across time and place, but the Hebrew Bible never provides an answer to the question. Other early Jewish texts, however, reflect on the origins of demons and the evil caused by them. They do not speak with one voice, however, but outline two different explanations.

According to one explanation, the rebellion of heavenly beings was decisive (1 Enoch 6:1–7; Jubilees 4:15). Building on Genesis 6:1–4, 1 Enoch explains that evil emerged because the Watchers had unions with human women and produced giants as offspring. Having descended from heaven, the Watchers taught their wives illicit knowledge and skills such as metallurgy and magic (1 Enoch 6:1–8:4). The evil caused by the giants explains why God destroyed the earth by the flood (1 Enoch 9:1–11:2). Even so, the giants' souls transformed into evil spirits, which continue to vex humans on the earth (1 Enoch 15:8–16:1).

According to the other explanation, God created both good and evil spirits. This interpretation is known from the writings of the Jewish group that collected and composed some of the Dead Sea Scrolls. These documents claim that God made Belial and the spirits of darkness to be evil (1QWar Scroll 13:11; 1QCommunity Rule 3:25). This means that God is considered to have generated everything. Since the leader of the evil spirits is God's creature, he is also subordinate to him (1QHodayot[a] 12:12–13), which highlights God's omnipotence throughout time.

Conclusion

The Hebrew Bible features both angels and demons, though the distinction between good and evil beings is not clear-cut. Spiritual beings have many functions in these and other early Jewish texts: they are God's messengers and they praise the divinity, protect humans, perform tasks assigned by God, and serve in divine troops. They can also cause harm and threaten human life, but people can affect them through ritual practices. While the information derived from the Hebrew Bible remains sporadic, we have seen that notions of angels and demons developed in the late Second Temple era, with a growing number of references to spiritual beings, their names, and their functions. The texts from this period also reflect on and try to explain the origin of evil and demonic forces. It is possible that complex beliefs in supernatural beings existed earlier, but if so, they were not included in or were deliberately removed from the textual record.

About the Author

Elisa Uusimäki earned a PhD from the University of Helsinki in 2013 and a dr.theol. from Aarhus University in 2022. Her research has covered topics such as wisdom and ethics, travel and cultural interaction, the Dead Sea Scrolls, and Hellenistic Judaism. She coauthored, with Hanne von Weissenberg, "Angels and Demons: Spiritual Beings in the Bible and the Dead Sea Scrolls," pages 259–273 in *Magic in the Ancient Eastern Mediterranean: Cognitive, Historical, and Material Perspectives on the Bible and Its Contexts*, edited by Nina Nikki and Kirsi Valkama (Göttingen: Vandenhoeck & Ruprecht, 2021).

Suggestions for Further Reading

In This Book
See also chapters 34 (Dead Sea Scrolls), 42 (Nephilim), 44 (ancestors), 45 (heaven and hell), 47 (monotheism), 61 (Melchizedek), and 70 (Satan).

Elsewhere
Jones, David Albert. *Angels: A Very Short Introduction*. Oxford: Oxford University Press, 2011.

Van der Toorn, Karel, Bob Becking, and Pieter Willem van der Horst, editors. *Dictionary of Deities and Demons in the Bible*. Leiden: Brill, 1999.

Von Weissenberg, Hanne. "God(s), Angels and Demons." Pages 490–495 in *T&T Clark Companion to the Dead Sea Scrolls*. Edited by George J. Brooke and Charlotte Hempel. London: T&T Clark, 2019.

44

Why Were the Ancestors De-divinized?

Diana V. Edelman

The veneration of dead family ancestors continues as a practice in many cultures around the world today, even if it has been replaced by the veneration of saints in Christian- and Muslim-dominated cultures. One of the hallmarks advocated in early Judaism was the elimination of the family ancestral cult and its belief that selected ancestors who had joined the spiritual realm could serve as intercessors with more influential deities on behalf of their living descendants. They could bestow both blessings and curses in their own right as well.

The Hebrew Bible contains traces of the earlier beliefs and practices that eventually were abandoned as part of a debate taking place at the time the various books were composed and new beliefs were being espoused. A few texts indicate that after death, some former humans were considered to have gained a new status as members of the spiritual or divine realm. In 1 Samuel 28:13, Isaiah 8:19–20, and Numbers 25:2 together with Psalm 106:28, they are called "gods," *elohim*, the same term used to describe Yhwh in many books. Other terms also suggest belief in ongoing existence after death: "holy ones" (*qedoshim*; Psalm 16:3), ghosts (*'obot*; Isaiah 29:4), spirits of the dead (*'ittim*; Isaiah 19:3), "knowing ones" (*yidde 'onim*; Isaiah 8:19), "those who cross over" (*'oberim*; Ezekiel 39:11, 14, 15), and possibly the designation "healers" (*repha'im*; Isaiah 14:19; 26:1, 19; Job 26:5; Proverbs 2:18; 9:18; 21:16), which would refer to one of the functions attributed to ancestral spirits. Some scholars, however, prefer to translate this term as "the long dead," whose names were no longer remembered among the living.

A two-step process apparently transformed a powerless dead body into an influential ancestral spirit. The first was a physical burial in a tomb or grave. The lack of a proper burial probably was believed to condemn a dead spirit to eternal roaming of the earth or the rocky terrain of She'ol—outside the city of the dead proper, perhaps (Isaiah 14:19–20)—without care from or feeding by the living, creating an entity akin to a demon. This was the case in other ancient Near Eastern cultures. The second was a set of rites that allowed the ghost to transition to She'ol, the realm of the dead. The idiom used for this second step is "to be gathered to one's people" (Genesis 25:8), "to be gathered to one's ancestors" (literally, "fathers"; Judges 2:10; 2 Kings 22:10), or "to sleep with one's fathers/ancestors," popular in the books of Kings and Chronicles.

The rites being condemned in Isaiah 65:3–5 and 66:17 might have involved this second, transformational process. They are in a unit of the book of Isaiah that scholars call Third or Trito-Isaiah, consisting of chapters 56–66. Circumstantial evidence points to their having been written in the Persian period (538–332 BCE). They show that some of the priests serving in the rebuilt temple in Jerusalem continued to practice the household ancestral cult at that time.

Once in She'ol, it seems that some ancestors could be called upon to promote the welfare of their living family members. Specifically, they apparently used to be credited with helping secure crops (Deuteronomy 26:13–15) and controlling or helping facilitate land inheritance (Psalm 37:11, 18) before both functions were reassigned solely to Yhwh as the only divine entity. It is likely these ancestors also were thought able to help secure children, as in other ancient Near Eastern and contemporary cultures.

Ancestral spirits apparently were represented physically in the household cult by figurines referred to collectively as teraphim. They were small enough to be hidden inside a camel's saddle by Jacob's wife Rachel (Genesis 31:34) and could be positioned on a stand or on the floor beside the bed of an allegedly sick David to perform a healing ritual (1 Samuel 19:11–16) while he escaped out the back window. A body was simulated in the bed, under covers, to fool the messengers, who looked across the room, took in the scene, and reported back to King Saul that David was sick, so they could not present him in person at that time.

The physical representation of dead ancestors would have been accompanied no doubt by a similar treatment of the family's protective god or pair of gods. The latter might have taken the form of an ephod. Food and drink offerings would have been made to both types of spiritual entities, and prayers directed to them by living members of the household concerning their needs and problems in daily life. Angry ancestors could cause illness, disaster, and misfortune, while happy ones could be the source of blessing, crop and flock abundance, and good fortune, so honoring them regularly with offerings would have been considered vital.

The belief that the dead who crossed over became spirits in She'ol also resulted in the practice of necromancy. One could go and consult a "mistress of ghosts" (1 Samuel 28:1) or "a questioner of a ghost or a knowing one" (Deuteronomy 18:11). Eventually, any living person who turns to a ghost or a knowing one (Leviticus 19:31; 20:6) or seeks an oracle from the dead (Deuteronomy 18:11) is going against divine Torah teaching, and any man or woman who is found to have a ghost or a knowing one possessing him or her is to be stoned to death (Leviticus 20:27). These regulations were meant to curb earlier necromantic practices that had been acceptable, part of a larger campaign by scribes to eliminate belief in the efficacy of ancestral spirits and family gods by advocating that Israel accept Yhwh as the only form of the divine with any power.

Besides prohibiting all contact with the dead, other strategies were used in the texts of the Hebrew Bible to try to suppress former household cult beliefs and practices. One was to model what was to become "correct" belief and behavior, without pointing out that there had been other alternatives. Yhwh is credited as the sole source of all human children, which formerly appears to have been under the control of Asherah and the ancestors (e.g., Genesis 16:1; 17:16; 18:10; 20:17–18; 21:1–2; 25:21; 29:31; 30:22–24). Yhwh also becomes the sole source of healing (Exodus 15:23–26; 23:25), crop yields (Genesis 26:12; Deuteronomy 26:13–15), and land inheritance (Deuteronomy 26:13).

Polemics are employed to condemn beliefs that would be inconsistent with belief in a single divine entity within the community of Israel. Two examples can be found in Genesis. In chapter 23, Abraham's need to bury Sarah "out of his sight" and his characterization as a "mighty prince" (literally, "one brought along by God," which also can be read "a confiscator of the gods/divinized") illustrates how one is to bury the dead and not create ancestral spirits out of them. Then, in 35:1–4, Jacob's burial of the household gods under the tree at Shechem is an allusion to the teraphim Rachel stole from her father in 31:34. There is also the story of King Saul's breaking of his own prohibition against necromancers to consult the ghost of the prophet Samuel in 1 Samuel 28 and the story of Micah's house shrine in Judges 17–18. It contained teraphim and an 'ephod initially, to which was added an idol of Yhwh, all of which are against the commandment about making and worshipping images (Exodus 20:4–6; Deuteronomy 5:8–10). Both stories illustrate what *not* to do.

The identification of Yhwh as the god of the father(s) in the books of Genesis, Exodus, and Deuteronomy seems to be designed to deny that any of the forefathers became divine in their own right. Yhwh remained their god in life and in death. At the same time, it created a common set of nondivine, shared ancestral forefathers and foremothers for all members of Israel, replacing divinized family ancestors. The household cult could be eliminated altogether or redirected to the universal deity, Yhwh. Individuals could honor and pray directly to this god at home without going through their former intercessors, their ancestral spirits and family god(s). The multiple references in many different books to the people worshipping other gods or divine entities in addition to Yhwh, which eventually led Yhwh to punish both Israel and Judah with exile, is another motif meant to drive home that among those identifying as members of Israel, Yhwh was to be seen as the only form of divinity. No others were able to control or influence events in life and death.

The reversal of the status of the ancestors from divinized spiritual entities to dead and buried humans with no power was an idea that no doubt took centuries to prevail. Nevertheless, it eventually did as an important element in the collapsing of the former Judahite pantheon and the emergence of early Judaism.

About the Author

Diana V. Edelman holds a doctorate of philosophy (PhD) in biblical studies from the University of Chicago and is Professor Emerita in Hebrew Bible at the Faculty of Theology, University of Oslo. She has published "Hidden Ancestor Polemics in the Book of Genesis?," pages 35–56 in *Words, Ideas, World: Biblical Essays in Honour of Yairah Amit*, edited by Athalya Brenner and Frank Polak (Sheffield, UK: Sheffield Phoenix, 2012); "Adjusting Social Memory in the Hebrew Bible: The *Teraphim*," pages 115–142 in *Congress Volume, Stellenbosch 2016*, edited by Louis C. Jonker, Gideon R. Kotzé, and Christl M. Maier (Leiden: Brill, 2017); "Possible Rituals Involving the Dead Reflected in Isaiah 65:3–5 and 66:17," pages 96–121 in *Approaching the Dead: Studies on Mortuary Ritual in the Ancient World*, edited by Anne Katrine de Hemmer Gudme and Kirsi Valkama (Helsinki: Finnish Exegetical Society, 2020); and "Adapting Social Memory to Mold New Attitudes in the Present and Future: Examples from the Books of Deuteronomy, Judges, and Kings," pages 49–84 in *Collective Memory and Collective Identity: Deuteronomy and the Deuteronomistic History in Their Context*, edited by Johannes U. Ro and Diana V. Edelman (Berlin: De Gruyter, 2021).

Suggestions for Further Reading

In This Book

See also chapters 24 (Kings and Chronicles), 45 (heaven and hell), 46 (afterlife), 47 (monotheism), 56 (polemics), and 67 (Isaiah).

Elsewhere

Lewis, Theodore J. *Cults of the Dead in Ancient Israel and Ugarit*. Atlanta: Scholars, 1989.

Niehr, Herbert. "The Changed Status of the Dead in Yehud." Pages 136–155 in *Yahwism after the Exile: Perspectives on Israelite Religion in the Persian Era*. Edited by Rainer Albertz and Bob Becking. Assen: Van Gorcum, 2003.

Stavrakopoulou, Francesca. *Land of Our Fathers: The Roles of Ancestor Veneration in Biblical Land Claims*. New York: T&T Clark, 2010.

45
Heaven and Hell, or She'ol?

Diana V. Edelman

Surprisingly, the Hebrew Bible does not yet work with the idea that the dead will go to heaven or hell as its main understanding of the afterlife. Instead, all the living end up in the same place when they die. It is called She'ol and is located belowground, as illustrated in Numbers 16:30: "If the ground [*'adamah*] opens its mouth and swallows them up and they go down alive into She'ol, then you will know that these men have despised Yhwh."

She'ol is conceived as a city, with gates (Isaiah 38:10; Job 38:16–18), walls (Lamentations 3:6–7), and houses (Job 17:13), but also with bars that close one in forever (Jonah 2:7). It is a place where one's status in life does not carry over necessarily; "he will not be rich, nor his wealth endure, nor his possessions reach the nether world" (Job 5:29). Similarly, "Shall your wondrous works be known in the dark, and righteousness in the land where all things are forgotten" (Psalm 88:13)? Yet, like a city of the living, it appears to have more desirable areas and less desirable ones. The most extended description of She'ol, found in Isaiah 14:4–20, seems to contain a royal quarter, where former kings of the world reside together, as well as outlying, stony fringe areas, where those who do not receive proper burial end up. She'ol is a place from which the dead never return to the land of the living (Job 10:21–22).

In Psalm 88:13, She'ol is characterized as "the broad land of forgetfulness." Job 14:21 elaborates on this latter point: "His [the dead person's] sons achieve honor, but he never knows; they are disgraced, but he perceives not." Then, also, Job 21:21 asks, "What cares he for his family after him when his quota of months is spent?" Finally, the statement is made in Ecclesiastes 9:10, "There is no work or account or knowledge or wisdom in She'ol."

The entrance to She'ol is marked by two hills (Job 17:1–2), and in one text, the dead have to cross a channel of flowing water to reach it as well (Job 36:12). One exists there in perpetual darkness and gloom (Lamentations

3:6–7); Job says, "Before I go, never to return, to a land of darkness and gloom, a land of utter darkness, of gloom without order" (Job 10:21–22).

There are a number of synonyms for She'ol in the Bible. Most are found in poetic texts, where the need for parallel terms would have led to the development of a range of alternative descriptions for the netherworld. The first, not surprisingly, is "earth," which is the common term used in other ancient cultures to describe the realm of the dead. In Exodus 15:12, in describing the defeat of Pharaoh's army during the exodus event and the crossing of the Sea of Destruction, the text states, "You stretched out your right hand; the earth/underworld swallowed them." Jonah 2:7 says, "I went down to the bottoms of the mountains; the earth/underworld with her bars closed on me forever." In describing the anticipated results of the siege of Jerusalem, Isaiah 29:4 says, "Then deep from the earth/underworld you shall speak, from low in the dust your words shall come; you voice shall come from the earth/underworld like the voice of a ghost and your speech shall whisper out of the dust."

Another synonym is "the pit" (*bor*): "For She'ol cannot thank you. Those who go down to the pit cannot hope for your faithfulness" (Isaiah 38:18); "You have put me in the depths of the pit, in the regions of darkness, in depths" (Psalm 88:7); and "His soul draws near the pit, his life to the waters of death" (Job 33:22). A second term translated as "pit" is *shahat*: "You will not put me in She'ol, nor allow your devoted one to see the pit" (Psalm 16:10); "What profit is there in my blood when I go down to the pit? Shall dust praise you? Shall it declare your truth?" (Psalm 30:10); "But you, O God, shall bring them down into the pit of destruction; bloody and deceitful men shall not live out half their days; but I shall trust in you" (Psalm 55:24); "When he could have lived jubilant forever, and never seen the pit" (Psalm 49:10); and finally, "He keeps back his soul from the pit and his life from crossing the channel" (Job 33:18).

A third synonym for She'ol is "hidden place," which can reflect two different underlying Hebrew terms: *tamun* and *seter*. The first is found in Job 40:12–13: "Glance at every proud one and humble him: tread down the wicked where they stand. Bury them in the dust together, bind them in the 'hidden place.'" The second is used in Psalm 139:15: "I was made in the 'hidden place,' woven in the depths of the nether world."

A fourth synonym is "the Broad Domain," or *merhab*: "You did not incarcerate me in the hand of the enemy nor set my feet in the Broad Domain" (Psalm 31:9) and "He brought me forth from the Broad Domain; he delivered me, because he delighted in me" (Psalm 18:20). A third example is found in Job: "Have you examined the broad domain of the nether world? Tell, if you know all of it" (38:18). A fourth, colorful parallel is found in Psalm 88:13: "Are your wonders known in darkness, or your saving help in the 'broad land of forgetfulness?'"

Still another synonym for She'ol is *hamir*, or "miry depth." This is particularly interesting because in texts from the Late Bronze Age city of Ugarit (today Ras Shamra on the northern coast of Syria), the residence of Mot, the god of death, is called "Miry Deep" (*hmry*; *Ugaritic Texts* [UT] 51:VIII: 11–12). Job 17:1–2 states, "My spirit is broken, my days are spent. It is the grave for me. Indeed, the two hills are before me, and my eyes pass the night in the twin miry depths." The same reference to two hills demarcating the entrance to the netherworld is also found in the Ras Shamra texts (UT 51:VIII: 4). In Psalm 140, it is said about the enemy, "From the miry depths may they not arise." A closely related expression is "the miry bog," *tit hayyawen*, in Psalm 40:3: "He drew me up from the pit of destruction, out of the miry bog."

This latter text illustrates how She'ol is not simply the realm of the dead; it includes any situation in which life is diminished but still present, such as states of illness and misery. The concept seems to be that any diminishment of life is partial death, which involves a journey to the early stages or outer limits of She'ol. However, there is still escape from the clutches of She'ol before actual death. Other examples of this understanding and the possibility of rescue by Yhwh before death occur in Psalm 88:6 and 143:3.

Finally, the term "house," *bayit*, is used to refer to the grave and, by extension, becomes used to describe She'ol. Usage in the former sense as a grave can be seen in Isaiah 14:18, "All of them rest in glory, each in his house/tomb," and in Genesis 15:2, "Yhwh, what could you give me if I pass away childless and if the one who pours out libations on my house/ grave is Eliezer?" Usage in the latter sense of the netherworld is illustrated by Job 17:13, "If I look for She'ol as my house; if I spread my couch in the darkness," and Job 30:23, "I know you will return me to death, to the meeting house of all living."

The Hebrew texts do not dwell at length on or brood over what happens after death; they focus on living a full and fulfilling life by following the teachings revealed at Mount Sinai. Since what might or might not happen after death is unknown to the living, the lack of focus on it is not surprising. Nor is the fact that there is inconsistency over whether it is an independent realm beyond the control of Yhwh or a realm the deity controls as well. The first option is suggested by Psalm 88:6: "I have become as a man without strength; among the dead is my couch, among the slain, lying in the grave, whom you do not remember any more, but they are separated from your hand." This option is consistent with a few passages that seem to preserve a former belief that a male deity named Death (Mot) and/or a female deity named She'ol had once been recognized and that either or both had controlled the netherworld, not Yhwh (Isaiah 28:15; Jeremiah 9:20–21; 18:21; Hosea 13:14; Job 18:11–14; 28:22; Psalm 49:15). The second is expressed twice: "If I climb into heaven you are there; if I make She'ol my bed, you are there also" (Psalm 139:8) and "Ask a sign of Yhwh: Let it be as deep as She'ol or high as heaven" (Isaiah 7:11). The second option would make sense in the context of emergent monolatry that eventually becomes monotheism. Once belief in a single divine entity replaces a pantheon of deities, that entity must be assumed to play all the roles formerly associated with discrete gods (see chapter 47 in this volume).

Although the concept of the judgment of the individual immediately after death does not appear in the texts of the Hebrew Bible, there are a few possible texts dating from the Persian period (538–332 BCE) that might show the influence of the dualism of Zoroastrianism. It was this religion that introduced to the larger ancient Near Eastern world the view that two cosmic forces, good and evil, fought for control of the earth and humans and that a person's deeds were judged at death and determined whether a person would end up for eternity in paradise or in hell. Both examples that follow might but need not be seen to conflict with the older view that She'ol was the netherworld where all the dead resided, both the good and the evil: "They shall go forth and look on the dead bodies of the men who have rebelled against me; for their worm shall not die, their fire shall not be quenched, and they shall be an abhorrence to all flesh" (Isaiah 66:24). Similarly, "You put them as into a blazing furnace, at the time of your fury, O Yhwh! In his wrath he engorged them and his fire devoured them" (Psalm 21:10).

About the Author

Diana V. Edelman holds a doctorate of philosophy (PhD) in biblical studies from the University of Chicago and is Professor Emerita in Hebrew Bible at the Faculty of Theology, University of Oslo. She has published "Living with Ancestral Spirits in Judah in the Iron Age and Persian Period," pages 135–171 in *Entre dieux et hommes: Anges, démons et autres . . . Actes du colloque organisé par le Collège de France, Paris, les 19–20 mai 2014*, edited by Thomas Römer, Bernard Dufour, Fabian Pfitzmann, and Christoph Uehlinger (Fribourg: Academic Press, 2017).

Suggestions for Further Reading

In This Book
See also chapters 16 (Psalms), 17 (Wisdom), 18 (Proverbs), 19 (Job), 44 (ancestors), 46 (afterlife), 47 (monotheism), 69 (Jonah), and 70 (Satan).

Elsewhere
Bloch-Smith, Elizabeth. *Judahite Burial Practices and Beliefs about the Dead*. Sheffield, UK: JSOT, 1992.

Johnston, Philip S. *Shades of Sheol: Death and Afterlife in the Old Testament*. Downers Grove, IL: InterVarsity, 2002.

Mitchell, David C. "'God Will Redeem My Soul from Sheol': The Psalms of the Sons of Korah." *Journal for the Study of the Old Testament* 30 (2006): 365–384.

Suriano, Matthew J. *A History of Death in the Hebrew Bible*. New York: Oxford University Press, 2018.

Tromp, Nicholas J. *Primitive Conceptions of Death and the Nether World in the Old Testament*. Rome: Pontifical Biblical Institute, 1969.

46
Did the Hebrews Believe in an Afterlife?

Jan Åge Sigvartsen

Contrary to ancient Near Eastern literature and archaeological remains (Egyptian funerary texts, tombs, elaborate funeral customs), the Old Testament / Hebrew Bible displays minimal interest in the afterlife. The relevant biblical passages present death as the end of the present life rather than the beginning of another. Sheol seems to be the destiny that awaits both the righteous and the wicked (Ecclesiastes 9:1–10), a place where everyone seems to be equal (Job 3:13–19; Ezekiel 32:18–32). References to burial rites focus on mourning practices (Numbers 20:29; 2 Samuel 3:31–32; 14:2; Ecclesiastes 7:2–4), ritual pollution in the case of contact with corpses (Numbers 19:11–22), and the importance of "sleeping with one's fathers," "being buried with his fathers," or "being gathered to one's kin" (Genesis 23; 25:8; 49:29–33; 50:25–26; 1 Kings 11:43; 2 Kings 8:24)—that is, receiving a proper burial in the family tomb. The biblical writers focused on the present life, not what might happen after death.

Nevertheless, practices that tended to be frowned upon by the writers are evoked: feeding the dead (Deuteronomy 26:12, 14; Jeremiah 26:7; Hosea 9:4; Job 21:25), necromancy (Leviticus 19:31; 20:6, 27; Deuteronomy 18:11; 2 Kings 21:6; 23:24; Isaiah 8:19–20; 18:19; 19:3; 1 Chronicles 10:13; 2 Chronicles 33:6), and sacrifice to the dead (Numbers 25:2–3; Psalms 106:28). Widespread or not, these practices demonstrate a belief in a form of continuation of life after death. The most intriguing case is the story of the medium of Endor summoning Samuel from the netherworld (1 Samuel 28:7–20), an episode in which the narrator questions neither the identity of Samuel nor the possibility of bringing him up.

Contrary to Samuel, the son of the widow of Zarephath, the son of a woman at Shunem, and a dead man thrown in Elisha's tomb are merely brought back to life (1 Samuel 28:7–20; 1 Kings 17:17–24; 2 Kings 4:32–37; 13:21). Resurrection language is found in poetic and prophetic passages

(Psalms 16:8–11; 49:13–15; 71:20; Isaiah 25:8; 26:19–20; 53:10–11; Ezekiel 37:7–10; Hosea 6:1–2), but the explicit reference to resurrection to ever-lasting life in Daniel 12:2–13 is exceptional for the Hebrew Scriptures, but less so when the Apocrypha, 1 Enoch, and the book of Jubilee are considered. These works reflect the influence of Persian and Hellenistic notions.

Ideas current in the Achaemenid (559–331 BCE) and succeeding Greco-Roman Empires (fourth century BCE–sixth century CE) significantly impacted Second Temple Judaism. Increased interest in angels, the battle between good and evil, and a future bodily resurrection and judgment reflect the influence of the Zoroastrian religion of the Persians, while the belief in an immortal soul that exists separately from the physical body after the moment of death is likely due to the Hellenization of Judaism. The writers of the Second Temple period borrowed religious and philosophical concepts from Persia and Greece and amalgamated them into their own religious framework through the reinterpretation of their sacred texts. Thus, a plethora of afterlife beliefs developed and appeared in the literature of this period. The book of Daniel is a good example.

Before the sixth century BCE, however, the Hebrews seem to have understood immortality as one's legacy lasting through one's offspring. Thus, besides the lack of proper burial, the most severe punishment was to be "cut off" from the community (Leviticus 18:29; Numbers 15:30–31). The righteous could expect a peaceful death at a ripe old age surrounded by offspring and a proper burial in the family tomb (Abraham in Genesis 15:15–16; 25:7–11; Joseph in Genesis 50:24–25; Exodus 13:19; Joshua 24:32). The wicked, on the other hand, could expect a horrific death (Jezebel in 2 Kings 9:32–37). The individual was part of a household and a tribe; a group survived the death of its members when they joined their ancestors as long as enough sons were born to ensure the continuity of the family name and line.

The assimilation of the Levant into the empires that vied with one another to control its strategic positions led to the destruction of the temple in Jerusalem (587 BCE), the end of the royal line of the house of David, and the exile of local elites. These traumatic experiences fostered a greater interest in the afterlife in the Second Temple period (ca. 400 BCE–70 CE). Resurrection language became a metaphor for a future national eschatological resurrection following the destruction or metaphorical death of the nation due to the Assyrian and Babylonian exiles. The most graphic example is Ezekiel's vision regarding the valley of dry bones, in which the metaphorical death and decomposition process of the nation is completely reversed into the revival of a great army ready to serve God (Ezekiel 37:1–14).

Another significant catalyst driving the shift from communal and national thinking to include an individual aspect is the concept of "remnant." National resurrection is closely tied to the remnant motif (Deuteronomy 4:27–31; 28:62–68; 30:1–10; Isaiah 11:11–16; Jeremiah 16:14–15; Zechariah 8:6–12), covenant renewal (Jeremiah 31:31–34), and the messianic age (Isaiah 4:2–3; Jeremiah 23:5). Since a remnant is, by definition, a small part of the whole, what qualifies an individual to be counted among this specific group and, by extension, become a part of the restored people of God? Jeremiah and Ezekiel focus on the individual's covenant relationship (Jeremiah 31:29–34; Ezekiel 18:1–32), while Ezra and the Chronicler focus on the call for the exiled to return to the homeland (Ezra 9:8, 13–15; 2 Chronicles 36:15–23). Thus, individual obedience to covenantal requirements or to the call to return becomes the determining factor. When the individual aspect is introduced into the equation, the problem of theodicy has to be satisfied on both the national and individual levels.

The question of theodicy is a central theme in the Hebrew Scriptures (Genesis 18:17–32; Leviticus 16; Ecclesiastes 7:15–22; 8:9–15), but it was during the second half of the Second Temple era that the problem of theodicy came to the fore. The traditional belief that God rewards the righteous with long and prosperous lives while cutting short the lives of the wicked needed adjustment. Foreign occupations and oppressions of various kinds gave rise to the sentiment that justice had been perverted: the righteous were receiving the curses of the wicked, while the wicked enjoyed the blessings promised to the righteous. A belief in a personal afterlife could solve this acute problem. If there were an afterlife, it was argued, God could set things straight and give the righteous and the wicked their proper due. In this way, the problem of theodicy would be solved.

Biblical and postbiblical literature in the so-called Apocrypha and the Pseudepigrapha present a range of views on the afterlife and resurrection. They have two main characteristics in common: (1) how individuals live their current lives matters, as their behavior affects their destiny in the afterlife, and (2) God is ultimately just.

By the first centuries of the common era, an eschatological bodily resurrection had become the mainstream belief in rabbinic Judaism and the early Christian churches. It was a central tenet for both communities. For Christians, questioning this doctrine was equated with questioning the historicity of Jesus's resurrection, which was the guarantor of the Christian salvation hope (Romans 6:3–6; 1 Corinthians 15; 1 Peter 1:3–4). For rabbinic Judaism, questioning this faith would disqualify a person from any share in the world to come (Mishnah Sanhedrin 10:1).

About the Author

Jan Åge Sigvartsen holds a doctorate of philosophy from Andrews University. He has published *Afterlife and Resurrection Beliefs in the Apocrypha and Apocalyptic Literature*, Jewish and Christian Texts 29 (London: T&T Clark, 2019); and *Afterlife and Resurrection Beliefs in the Pseudepigrapha*, Jewish and Christian Texts 30 (London: T&T Clark, 2019).

Suggestions for Further Reading

In This Book
See also chapters 5 (canons), 15 (apocalyptic literature), 19 (Job), 20 (genealogies), 44 (ancestors), 45 (heaven and hell), 52 (covenant), 70 (Satan), and 71 (Qohelet).

Elsewhere

Brannon, M. Jeff. *The Hope of Life after Death: A Biblical Theology of Resurrection*. Essential Studies in Biblical Theology. Downers Grove, IL: IVP Academic, 2022.

Ehrman, Bart D. *Heaven and Hell: A History of the Afterlife*. London: Oneworld, 2021.

Sonia, Kerry M. *Caring for the Dead in Ancient Israel*. Archaeology and Biblical Studies 27. Atlanta: SBL, 2020.

Suriano, Matthew. *A History of Death in the Hebrew Bible*. Oxford: Oxford University Press, 2018.

47
How Did Yhwh Become One?

James S. Anderson

Belief in a single God, monotheism, is commonly considered a red thread throughout the Bible. The monotheism that eventually arose around the deity Yhwh laid the foundation for the three great monotheistic faiths: Judaism, Christianity, and Islam. However, surprisingly, in the entire Hebrew Bible, there are only some eighteen statements that can be understood to deny the existence of deities other than Yhwh, affirming today's definition of monotheism as the worship of one god that concomitantly denies the existence of other deities. They include Deuteronomy 4:35, 39; 32:39; 1 Samuel 2:2; 2 Kings 19:15, 19; and Isaiah 37:16, 20; 43:10–11, 44:6, 8; 45:5–6, 14, 18, 21; 46:9. There are many, many more examples in which the people believe in and worship other deities and spiritual entities besides Yhwh, especially Baal and Asherah.

The First Commandment is not one of them. The Hebrew text in Exodus 20:3 and Deuteronomy 5:7 says, "You shall have no other gods *before* me" (my emphasis), not "besides me," as it often is translated in English. Neither occurrence denies the existence of other gods; they both state that in the religious community that calls itself Israel, no other god is to be put in Yhwh's presence or considered higher than Yhwh.

Similarly, the statement known in Judaism as the Shema (Deuteronomy 6:4–5), which begins with the affirmation "Yhwh [is] our divinity, Yhwh [is] one," does not clearly deny the existence of other gods. It does not say "Yhwh alone." Some scholars argue that the oneness is an assertion that all known regional forms of Yhwh represent manifestations of the same god. The Bible mentions Yhwh of Hosts (e.g., 1 Samuel 1:3, 11; 4:4) and Yhwh Elohim, while inscriptional evidence mentions Yhwh of Jerusalem, Yhwh of Samaria, and Yhwh of Teman or the south. Other scholars argue that the oneness is meant to equate Yhwh with the highest concept of divinity acknowledged among the peoples, alongside gods in other nations that would have been conceived in the same way.

For these reasons, many biblical scholars prefer to label the belief system reflected in the Hebrew Bible as "monolatry" or "henotheism" instead. The former designates the worship of a single deity while not denying the existence of others, and the latter understands that certain groups worship one god, while other groups worship their respective patron deity. The inhabitants of the ancient kingdoms of Israel and Judah worshipped their god Yhwh, while their Moabite neighbors worshipped Chemosh (Numbers 21:29, Judges 11:24; 1 Kings 11:7, 33; Jeremiah 48). Milcom was the god worshipped in Ammon (2 Samuel 12:30; 2 Kings 23:13; Jeremiah 49) and Qos in Edom.

Yet both of these definitions are problematic as well. It seems, in fact, that most of these ancient kingdoms honored and worshipped a female deity conceived of as the wife of the main male god. Thus, in the world views of these kingdoms, a divine pair headed the divine realm, not a single male alone, just as a husband and wife were the norm for most households on earth. Evidence that this had been the case in Israel is supplied by an inscription that mentions Yhwh of Samaria and his Asherah found at Quntillet 'Ajrud, an ancient way station in the northeastern Sinai. A burial cave near Khirbet el-Qom, in the southwestern Judean hills, has yielded an inscription that calls for Yhwh and his Asherah to bestow blessings. It was located within the kingdom of Judah. Also, the temple dedicated to Yhwh of Hosts in Jerusalem contained symbols representing the goddess Asherah during much of its existence (1 Kings 15:13; 2 Kings 18:4; 21:3, 7; 23:4, 6, 7, 15; 2 Chronicles 15:16), and Deuteronomy 16:21 prohibits the planting of any species of tree as Asherah beside an altar of Yhwh, which suggests that this had been a formerly acceptable practice.

The crucial matter that continues to be debated is whether the different names of national deities were understood to be different designations of the same divine entity or if various gods and goddesses were believed to have populated the divine realm. Mark S. Smith (2010) refers to the first option as "translatability" and argues that as empires expanded across the ancient Near East and different cultures developed regular contact with one another, deities that functioned similarly in a given culture would have been seen to have been manifestations of the same category of divinity. In favor of the second possibility, Lowell Handy (1994) has identified the existence of a four-tiered divine pantheon in ancient kingdoms like Israel and Judah. It consisted of the head divine couple exercising the highest authority, major active gods, specialty gods, and messenger deities and spirits. Thus, a given culture would have believed in a divine realm with many forms of spiritual and divine beings. As cross-cultural contact took place, it would have been natural to equate deities known by different names that fulfilled the same functions; the Greeks and Romans did this regularly later on. Yet this equation could have taken place under both options, making it hard to know how people who lived in these ancient cultures understood the nature of divinity and the divine realm.

When and where monotheism emerged is hard to pinpoint. The various biblical books reflect a dialogue taking place concerning how Yhwh was to be conceived of and worshipped. Older views that had been prevalent during the kingdoms of Israel (ca. 1000–721 BCE) and Judah (ca. 975–587 BCE) were being challenged by newer ideas concerning a single category of universal creator divinity instead of a four-tiered pantheon. This deity simultaneously was to serve as the household deity, replacing former family gods and deified ancestors. Ideas that eventually would emerge as forms of early Judaism and develop into true monotheism would take centuries to become mainstream.

Many readers not trained as biblical scholars assume monotheism began with Moses and the revelation of the Ten Commandments at Sinai. However, we have already seen, that is not the case; the text does not advocate monotheism per se. Another common impression is that the pure form of monotheism revealed at Sinai became corrupted once the people settled in the land of Canaan and started to participate in the worship of the existing local gods alongside Yhwh. In fact, this is one of the strategies the writers of these books used to try to persuade those who continued to think and worship as their ancestors had during the monarchies that they needed to change their mindset and habits. A common rhetorical strategy used in many traditional cultures is to present new ideas as though they are old and venerable, often going back to the founding events of that group. The finding of "the scroll of the teaching" in the temple in Jerusalem during repairs (2 Kings 22:1–11), which supposedly prompted King Josiah (ca. 649–609 BCE) to undertake monotheizing religious reforms to enact its regulations, would be a good example of this strategy if it is historically accurate.

Some scholars suspect that the seeds of what would become monotheistic thought would have developed outside the homelands of Israel and Judah, where there would have been little incentive to alter the status quo, even after both kingdoms became imperial provinces. Each local form of Yhwh remained the established territorial god. It seems logical to think monotheistic ideas emerged among exiles from Judah who found themselves living among many different cultural groups. There already would have been established deities thought to control the locales where the exiles ended up, and the prevalent world view all these groups would have shared, including the newly arrived Judeans, would have led them to participate in honoring those deities to gain blessings and not suffer misfortune. It was likely a former member of the royal court, probably an educated scribe who could think for himself, who reconceptualized Yhwh, the former national god of his homeland, as both a universal god who could control events in the new, faraway setting and answer prayers by serving as his family's personal god. This new view would have collapsed the former concept of a pantheon and assigned all the roles formerly divided among discrete gods to Yhwh alone. The scribe may have persuaded some of his colleagues to think in a similar way, leading to what would develop into monolatry or henotheism and, eventually, into monotheism. These ideas gained more adherents over time, but as the books in the Hebrew Bible demonstrate, it was a process of slow growth. The ideas were resisted by other members of the educated elite and leadership, who opposed changes in tradition and presented their counterviews in the texts as well.

Other factors certainly played a role in the development of monotheism, but as we know it, monotheism finally came in full force in the Hellenistic era through interactions with Greek monotheistic philosophical thought. While the notion of a single god makes sense from a philosophical point of view, it has the disadvantage of distancing the deity from worshippers. Hence, strict monotheism soon gave birth to intermediary entities such as angels and saints in Christianity and Islam, or *sefirot* in Kabbalistic Judaism, though all agree that God manifests in different ways.

In conclusion, the monotheism begun by a group that identified itself as Israel, likely among exiles living in Babylonia in the period 587–538 BCE, took centuries to mature. In the end, monotheism gave birth to Judaism, Christianity, and Islam, so dear to millions of us today.

About the Author

James S. Anderson earned a PhD in biblical studies from the University of Sheffield. He is the author of *Monotheism and Yahweh's Appropriation of Baal* (New York: Bloomsbury T&T Clark, 2015); and "El, Yahweh and Elohim: The Evolution of God in Israel and Its Theological Implications," *Expository Times* 128 (2017): 261–267.

Suggestions for Further Reading

In This Book
See also chapters 19 (Job), 24 (Kings and Chronicles), 27 (Josiah's scroll), 28–31 (archaeology), 44 (ancestors), 51 (prophets), 56 (polemics), and 66 (Jezebel).

Elsewhere

Edelman, Diana V. "Early Forms of Judaism as a Mixture of Strategies of Cultural Heterogeneity and the Re-embedding of Local Culture in Archaic Globalization." Pages 242–292 in *Levantine Entanglements: Local Dynamics of Globalization in a Contested Region*. Edited by Terje Stordalen and Øystein LaBianca. Sheffield, UK: Equinox, 2021.

Gnuse, Robert Karl. *No Other Gods: Emergent Monotheism in Israel*. Sheffield, UK: Sheffield Academic, 1997.

Handy, Lowell. *Among the Host of Heaven*. Winona Lake, IN: Eisenbrauns, 1994.

Smith, Mark S. *God in Translation*. Grand Rapids, MI: Eerdmans, 2010.

Smith, Mark S. *The Origins of Biblical Monotheism: Israel's Polytheistic Background and the Ugaritic Texts*. Oxford: Oxford University Press, 2001.

Stahl, Michael J. "God's Best 'Frenemy': A New Perspective on YHWH and Baal in Ancient Israel and Judah." *Semitica* 63 (2021): 45–94.

48

Israel in Twelve Tribes:
Ideal or Real?

Andrew Tobolowsky

The "twelve tribes of Israel" are the centerpiece of the Hebrew Bible's vision of who Israel *is*. From twelve eponymous ancestors born to the patriarch Jacob in the book of Genesis, the tribes grow into a mighty nation in Egypt, from which, after four hundred years, they are led out by Moses—a narrative that spans the books of Exodus, Leviticus, Numbers, and Deuteronomy. From there, they conquer Canaan with Joshua, who divides the land into twelve parts and apportions it among them. They live together in the period of the "judges" and subsequently are ruled together by the famous biblical kings David and Solomon. Then, according to the biblical narrative, the kingdom of Israel splits into two kingdoms, Israel and Judah, never again to be reunited. But even so, even after Israel is conquered by Assyria in 721 BCE and Judah by Babylon in 587 BCE, the twelve tribes of Israel appear again and again. But did they ever really exist? Or is this an idealized vision of Israelite identity that developed only later on?

Today, scholars continue to debate this question, with no end in sight. The problem is a common one in the study of the ancient world; we have so little evidence to work with. In fact, this is a bigger problem in ancient Israel and Judah than in a lot of other famous ancient places. In ancient Mesopotamia, many documents were written on clay tablets that were baked in ovens, and many have survived the ravages of time, even when broken. In ancient Egypt, it is so dry that even fragile materials often survive. But we have no other texts from ancient Israel and Judah except what survives in the Hebrew Bible and precious few inscriptions. There is, therefore, not a shred of evidence outside of the Bible of any individual identifying themselves as a member of a tribe of Israel, but that might not mean anything; the absence of evidence under such circumstances need not signify evidence of absence.

So, what evidence *do* we have? Well, it depends on how you think about it. What we have to understand, first of all, is that the academic study of the Hebrew Bible developed out of the religious study of the text, so for a very long time, biblical "scholars" were those who implicitly accepted the accuracy of biblical narratives because their religious traditions suggested they should. These intellectuals also accepted the tradition that Moses himself had written the Pentateuch (Genesis, Exodus, Leviticus, Numbers, and Deuteronomy), where many of the traditions about the tribes are to be found, which led them to assume in turn that it was an eyewitness account of Israel's tribal prehistory.

In the nineteenth century, scholarship began to move away from this position and even to acknowledge the likelihood that the Pentateuchal tradition was more legendary than historical. Still, most continued to believe that even if biblical traditions were not *precisely* accurate, they likely were distorted or not-so-distorted memories of actual events and experiences.

In the twentieth century, significant differences developed between how American and European scholars tended to approach the question of what traditions did and did not preserve. American scholars continued to argue that most were basically accurate, while European approaches grew more skeptical. But even in Europe, scholars generally continued to believe that most biblical traditions about Israel's early history reflected things that had actually happened in some way and to some extent.

What this means, in a nutshell, is that many continued to believe—and still believe today—that the simple fact that the twelve tribes of Israel are so important to so many biblical writers is itself proof that they were actually important in the early history of Israel. The focus on the tribes throughout the narrative account of Israel's history spanning Genesis through Kings and in a second one that appears in the books of Chronicles *is* extraordinary, including roughly twenty-six different descriptions of tribal Israel in the form of tribal "lists," most of which occur between Genesis 29 and Judges 5 or in 1 Chronicles 1–27. The problem is that most scholars have also acknowledged since the nineteenth century that the vast majority of these descriptions were written not by early Israelite authors but by late ones, relatively speaking, and for that matter, by writers working in Judah rather than Israel.

In the Pentateuch, the writer(s) and editors scholars call the "Priestly source," presumed to have been at work sometime after the Babylonian conquest of Judah in 587 BCE, is usually considered responsible for as many as eleven of fifteen lists. There are an additional six in the equally late or later books of Chronicles and one in Ezekiel 48. If the latter is original, it would also be from the time of the Babylonian exile, but many think it was an even later addition to the original book. Either way, there is a more or less complete consensus that at least eighteen of our twenty-six lists were written after the kingdoms of Israel and Judah no longer existed, and it is likely that others were as well.

In fact, of all the tribal lists in the Hebrew Bible, only three are considered early by a majority of scholars: Genesis 49, Deuteronomy 33, and Judges 5. And of these, only Genesis 49 is *actually* a list comprising twelve tribes. Deuteronomy 33 is missing the tribe of Simeon, and Judges 5, which most regard as the earliest, not only is missing a number of the familiar tribes but is quite unusual in other ways. It mentions a group, possibly a tribe, named "Meroz" that never appears anywhere else and may well treat Machir and Gilead, which are typically presented as "subtribes" of Manasseh, as if they were individual tribes.

Returning to the question of evidence, we have a lot indicating that the twelve-tribe tradition became very popular relatively late in Judah's history but very little that it even existed in early periods, let alone that it reflects historical reality. Today, many scholars suspect that the twelve-tribe tradition was developed in Judah by Judahite writers active toward the end of the monarchy or in its successor, the province of Yehud, by Judean writers, out of an older but different Israelite tribal tradition, and various aspects of biblical tribal discourse strongly suggest as much. For one thing, Judges 5 is again likely the earliest list, and perhaps even the earliest text in the entire Hebrew Bible, which would mean that some version of the tribal tradition existed in very early periods in Israel rather than Judah. Judah, Simeon, and Levi are missing from the text, and all three are associated with Judah. Then, long before anyone suspected the twelve-tribe tradition was not early, there were those who had argued that the references to Judah and Levi in Deuteronomy 33 were later additions.

Some scholars have pointed out certain unusual aspects of the tribal list in Genesis 49 as well. This text is often referred to as the "Blessing of Jacob" because it is presented as a deathbed blessing bestowed by Jacob on his sons. In fact, however, only a handful of the blessings are actually written as if they were spoken by one person to another. So, for example, Genesis 49:3, "Reuben, you are my firstborn," is unambiguous, and so is 49:9: "Judah is a lion cub, from the prey, my son, you have gone up." But most of the blessings have nothing of "you" or "my" or "I" about them, nothing that indicates a speaker—"Issachar is a strong donkey" (49:14), "Dan will judge his people," and so on. Judah, Simeon, and Levi, along with Reuben and perhaps Joseph, are the only tribes that are clearly consistent with the testamentary framework of the "Blessing of Jacob" in its current setting.

In short, what scholars would call a "diachronic" reading of the evidence, which tries to read texts in the order they were written, straightforwardly yields the impression that an early tribal vision that looked something like Judges 5 was adopted and adapted in Judah or Yehud into the familiar twelve-tribe form. This impression is sharpened by the fact that not all biblical writers seem interested in the tribes. They are almost wholly absent, for example, from the prophetic books, which often comment on current events. Ezekiel 48 is the only complete description of the tribes of Israel in these books, but even more tellingly, the majority of tribes—that is, Reuben, Simeon, Asher, Issachar, Naphtali, Zebulun, and Manasseh—are only mentioned here and in Isaiah 9 in the entire collection. In most of the cases where a tribal name appears in the prophetic books, it can be hard to tell whether a tribe is being described, since Judah is the name of a kingdom and a region and Levi of a priesthood, and other tribal names can double as descriptions of geographic regions, including Ephraim, Manasseh, and Dan.

Then there is the fact that references to the familiar tribes can be hard to find in certain traditions that might have come from early Judah. King David himself, the Hebrew Bible's most famous Judahite, is never actually described as having a tribe. The closest the text comes is in 1 Samuel 17:12, where David is described as an "Ephrathite." While there have been efforts to explain the latter term as a "subtribe" or "clan" of Judah, there is no real evidence for such an argument. Also, while most of the Israelite judges in the book of that name are identified by their tribe, this does not hold in the case of the two Judahite judges, Ibzan of Bethlehem and Othniel, son of Kenaz. These are patterns we might expect to see if the familiar tribal tradition had not yet taken root in Judah by the time these texts were initially written, probably in Israel.

The case that the tradition of the twelve tribes of Israel was an idealized vision of Israel developed in Judah or Yehud in later periods would, therefore, seem to have more going for it than the argument that it is a reflection of early Israelite realities. If this is the case, it is likely that it was part of a monarchic Judahite or postmonarchic Judean project of redescribing themselves as Israelites by expanding a once purely Israelite tradition so that it included them. The earliest possible dating of such a development would have been after the kingdom of Israel was conquered by the Assyrians in 721 BCE and turned into the province of Samerina and Magiddu. The strategy might have helped them claim Israelite land, or prestige, or even Israelites themselves—if the Assyrians had transferred any of the Israelite population to the still surviving kingdom of Judah. It is, however, important to stress that there is little enough hard evidence for this reconstruction, and it remains reasonable to continue to debate the question. It is certainly possible that many early accounts of the twelve tribes of Israel had existed but very few survived, which would point instead toward an origin of the concept prior to 721 BCE.

Still, there is one thing we can say for certain, which often is missed even in scholarly analyses. The sheer number and variety of descriptions of tribal Israel suggest that many different writers working in the period after the Babylonian conquest of Judah found themselves utterly fascinated with this tradition, which became very important in this era and context. It is this interest that is responsible for the vision of the tribes that survives to this day, whether or not it was based on a much older twelve-tribe tradition or even a historical reality, once upon a time.

About the Author

Andrew Tobolowsky received his PhD from Brown University in 2015. His research has often focused on the history of the tradition of the twelve tribes, as in *The Sons of Jacob and the Sons of Herakles* (Tübingen: Mohr Siebeck, 2017); and *The Myth of the Twelve Tribes of Israel* (Cambridge: Cambridge University Press, 2022).

Suggestions for Further Reading

In This Book
See also chapters 11 (Pentateuch), 20 (genealogies), 24 (Kings and Chronicles), 41 (symbolic numbers), 72 (synchronic vs. diachronic), and 74 ("P").

Elsewhere

Davies, Philip R. *The Origins of Biblical Israel*. New York: T&T Clark, 2007.

Fleming, Daniel. *The Legacy of Israel in Judah's Bible*. Cambridge: Cambridge University Press, 2012.

Knauf, Ernst Axel, and Philippe Guillaume. *A History of Biblical Israel: The Fate of the Tribes and Kingdoms from Merenptah to Bar Kochba*. Sheffield, UK: Equinox, 2016.

Na'aman, Nadav. "The Jacob Story and the Formation of Biblical Israel." *Tel Aviv* 4 (2014): 95–125.

Weingart, Kristin. "'All These Are the Twelve Tribes of Israel': The Origins of Israel's Kinship Identity." *Near Eastern Archaeology* 82 (2019): 24–31.

49
Is "Torah" Law or Teaching?

Megan Turton

When we speak of "law" in the Hebrew Scriptures, what are we talking about? We could point to the three major "law codes" of the Pentateuch, also known as the Torah in Jewish tradition. The collections of laws are often called the "Covenant Code" (Exodus 20:22–23:19), the "Deuteronomic Code" (Deuteronomy 12–26), and the "Holiness Code" (Leviticus 17–26).

Almost immediately, however, we run into questions of categorization. The biblical laws are not presented in the same way as modern law codes or statutes. They are embedded within the wider narrative of the scriptural text of the Torah, where they are introduced as divine revelation, mediated to the Israelite people by the prophet Moses at Mount Sinai (Exodus 20:22; Leviticus 17:1) or on the plains of Moab, before the Israelites enter the promised land (Deuteronomy 12:1). Critical scholarship has convincingly argued that despite the narrative framing, the collections represent a variety of traditions and discourses that do not always cohere. This is because they likely originated in different sources, historical periods, and social contexts. These are contested, but traditionally, the Covenant Code was assigned to the presettlement period (1200–1000 BCE) or early monarchical period (1000–700 BCE), Deuteronomy to the seventh century, and the Holiness Code to the period of the exile or afterward (587 BCE onward). In any case, the legal texts, as we have inherited them, are presented as revelation and expressions of the divine will. They form the content of a covenant or covenants with the Israelite God, Yhwh (Exodus 24:7; Leviticus 26:16; Deuteronomy 29:1). In addition to purporting to constitute a political and social community, the laws have a fundamentally religious and theological dimension.

Accordingly, the legal corpora are made up of components that many modern peoples do not easily recognize as "law." Certainly, there are rules for adjudicating civil matters, including restitution for theft (Exodus 21:6–11), and criminal laws, like those that deal with homicide (Exodus 21:12–14; Deuteronomy 19:4–13). There are, however, also general moral and ethical admonitions to not wrong or oppress the foreigner, widow, and orphan (Exodus 22:21–24); proscriptions on sexual relationships (Leviticus 18; 20); festival calendars (Exodus 23:14–19; Leviticus 23; Deuteronomy 16:1–17); and stories about legal processes (Leviticus 24:10–23). Outside the law codes, extensive priestly instructions predominate Exodus 25–31, 35–40; Leviticus 1–16, 27; and Numbers 1–10. Do they constitute law even though they are mostly limited to cultic rules for building the tabernacle, conducting the sacrificial system, and maintaining purity? What about the Ten Commandments, which appear in at least three different forms (Exodus 20:1–17; 34:11–26; Deuteronomy 5:6–21)? Some of the commandments appear impossible to enforce, including the prohibition against coveting a neighbor's wife, house, and property (Exodus 20:17; Deuteronomy 5:21). Should the narratives within the Pentateuch, which describe the creation of new legal rulings, be considered law (e.g., Numbers 9:1–14; 15:32–36; 27:1–11)? What about the revelations given to the prophet Ezekiel concerning "statutes" and "laws" for the future temple (Ezekiel 40–46)?

"Law" is a familiar concept and institution for peoples who live within the political reality of modern nation-states. The state claims jurisdiction over a select territory and creates and upholds laws through various governmental and legal institutions: the executive, legislature, courts, and a police or military force. It is easy for us to think of familiar instruments of law—constitutions, law codes, statutes, judicial decisions—and assume that we know what law *is* and *how it works*. Nevertheless, isolating exactly what makes "law" and explaining what is distinctive about why we are obligated or "ought to" comply with its directives has proven notoriously difficult. This is because the directives of law are only one of many "norms." A norm is something that is or serves as a standard to guide someone's conduct, belief, or emotion. The normative universe contains many different "oughts" outside of legislation and even law: parental advice; company policies; rules for organizations; military orders; religious, moral, and ethical duties; and cultural narratives. Is there anything, then, that makes law unique?

One line of thinking contends that law is imposed by a sovereign, like the legislator, with the power to compel obedience through the threat of sanction. When it comes to biblical laws, Yhwh is the sovereign power; however, evidence of the enforcement of written law in ancient Israel and Judah is scanty, especially before the exile. In judicial commissions and instructions, judges and officials are instructed not to directly apply written law to resolve disputes but to impose the divine will or general principles of justice, fairness, and impartiality (Exodus 18:15–21; Deuteronomy 1:16–17). The explicit appeal to written law is largely absent in the arguments and rendering of legal decisions described in narrative and historical texts (e.g., 2 Samuel 14:1–24; 1 Kings 3:16–28). Arguments and decisions are generally based on principles of justice, wisdom, and the oracular consultation of the deity. Even after the inception of legal writing, it is probable that oral and customary law continued to inform legal practice in ancient Israel.

The complex concept of torah, which predates any of our own modern assumptions about law, exemplifies how legal norms are often intimately interconnected with other sorts of norms. The Hebrew noun has a multiplicity of meanings within the biblical text. It can denote an individual legal precept (Exodus 12:49) or a collection of them in the plural (Genesis 26:5). In these instances, the meaning of torah is analogous to the words for "law," "legal decision," "commandment," and "statute" (e.g., Exodus 16:28; Leviticus 26:46). Nevertheless, torah can also indicate divine revelation or the "word of Yhwh" in whatever form that took, including the oracles of priests (Deuteronomy 17:11–12; Haggai 2:11) and words of the prophets (Isaiah 1:10; 8:16). Within the wisdom literature, torah is associated with the teaching of the wise or parents (Proverbs 13:14; 1:8) and so presents more broadly as a "guide to life." Thus, the broadest meaning of torah appears to be "instruction, teaching, education."

Torah can indicate a major literary work. Deuteronomy refers to itself as "this book of Torah" (Deuteronomy 28:61). By the postexilic period, the idea of torah is expanded to include all teachings and instructions associated with Moses (Ezra 7:6; Nehemiah 8:1; 2 Chronicles 30:16). Yet, even leading into the Common Era, the Torah of Moses was a dynamic entity. The biblical manuscripts reveal that both legal and narrative texts continued to change in textual transmission. Furthermore, the Mosaic Torah likely encompassed editions and copies that are quite different from what later became Jewish and Christian canon, including the Qumran compositions of the Reworked Pentateuch, the *Temple Scroll*, and the book of Jubilees. Eventually, "Torah" became synonymous with the first five books of canonized Scripture, but those books continue to be dialogical, preserving diverse perspectives and literary genres: law, narrative, poetry, genealogy, priestly instruction, and so on.

At the level of the narrative, it is clear that the Torah as a whole and the commandments, statutes, cases, and instructions within it were supposed to provide a didactic function. Moses is expected to teach the people all the laws (Exodus 18:20; Deuteronomy 5:31), as are the priests (Leviticus 10:11). In Deuteronomy, the king, under the oversight of the Levitical priests, is directed to study the Torah (17:18–20). Households are instructed to keep the commanded words in their hearts, recite them to their children, and speak them daily (6:6–9).

Similarly, the forms of biblical law suggest a pedagogic function. Some laws are formulated in the "apodictic" style: an unconditional, categorical demand on behavior: "You shall not kill" (Exodus 20:13). Others, however, are composed in the conditional, "casuistic" style. They describe a particular situation (protasis), introduced by "if," followed by the resolution that restores balance (apodosis), "then": "*If* an owner knocks out a tooth of a male or female slave, *then* the slave shall be let go, a free person, to compensate for the tooth" (Exodus 21:27; my emphasis). The conditional laws show a very close affinity to older case laws produced by the surrounding cultures of ancient Western Asia. We can, therefore, deduce that some provisions were exemplar cases, formulated and transmitted by scribes to teach correct principles and legal reasoning, so that each individual judgment could be logically extended to other situations through analogy.

Some biblical laws employ rhetorical features designed to influence the audience's thoughts and beliefs and persuade them to alter their behavior. Legal "motive clauses" provide explanatory, ethical, religious, and historical comments that appeal to the conscience of the people and pedagogically aid and motivate them to observe the law. For example, precepts on the humanitarian treatment of the foreigner or slave often urge compliance by reminding the Israelite people that they themselves were once foreigners and slaves in Egypt (Exodus 23:9; Deuteronomy 15:12–15).

How do we summarize the character of "torah"? Evidently, torah is not just one thing. Torah applies to not only a range of individual normative traditions but also their combination. Torah is teaching and instruction, but it is also law: statute, judicial decision, commandment. It is the integration of law and narrative. It is divine revelation, political constitution, and human interpretation.

About the Author

Megan Turton holds a doctorate of philosophy (PhD) in biblical studies from the University of Sydney. Her research interests include the character and functions of biblical law. She is the author of *Law and Narrative: Textual Fluidity in Exodus 19–24*, FAT I (Tübingen: Mohr Siebeck, forthcoming).

Suggestions for Further Reading

In This Book

Elsewhere

Bartor, Assnat. "Legal Texts." Pages 160–181 in *The Hebrew Bible: A Critical Companion*. Edited by John Barton. Princeton, NJ: Princeton University Press, 2016.

Burnside, Jonathan. *God, Justice and Society: Aspects of Law and Legality in the Bible*. New York: Oxford University Press, 2011.

Morrow, William S. *An Introduction to Biblical Law*. Grand Rapids, MI: Eerdmans, 2017.

Vroom, Jonathan. *The Authority of Law in the Hebrew Bible and Early Judaism: Tracing the Origins of Legal Obligation from Ezra to Qumran*. JSJSup 187. Leiden: Brill, 2018.

50
Where Is the Magic?

Shawna Dolansky

The central drama of the book of Exodus commences when the God of Israel faces off against the gods of Egypt. Yhwh states an intention to "multiply signs and wonders in the land of Egypt" through the agency of Moses and Aaron so that "the Egyptians will know that I am Yhwh" (Exodus 7:3, 5; my translation). Israel's god initiates the showdown by having Aaron cast down his rod in Pharaoh's presence, whereupon the rod becomes a snake. Pharaoh's *ḥakammim* (wise men) and *mekaššepim* (sorcerers), collectively referred to as *ḥartummim* (magicians), respond by throwing down their rods, which also become snakes (Exodus 7:11). Although Aaron's snake devours its Egyptian counterparts, the fact that Pharaoh's magicians are said to be able to replicate Yhwh's own "signs and wonders" here and elsewhere in the plague narratives begs some important questions. Are Moses and Aaron also magicians? Didn't biblical religion forbid the practice of magic? How did the biblical authors and original audiences of these stories understand magic?

Our English word "magic" derives from the ancient Greek *mageia*, a term that technically referred to the religion of Persian Zoroastrian priests known as magi. In common usage, however, it was applied to any ritual that seemed alien and foreign to Greek (and later Roman) customs. In fact, it was mostly employed as a way of casting suspicion upon or denigrating the practices of Others, because Greek and Roman rituals and beliefs shared in the same general world view. According to this understanding of how the world functioned, certain actions, individuals, rituals, and objects imparted qualities of or were able to communicate with a supernatural realm. An outsider to this world view is hard-pressed to differentiate between what scholars today might call "magic" and what we regularly term "religion." Yet it seems that in the classical world, these terms functioned more as political or social designations (or accusations) and depended entirely on the standpoint of the term's user.

Similarly, modern biblical scholarship began in the nineteenth century with a focus on the supposedly inherent differences between the higher "religion" of ancient Israel and the lower "superstitions" and magical practices of non-Israelite cultures. Such premises built on anthropological frameworks that saw non-Christian cultures as inferior heathens and compared them with the nations that the Hebrew Bible claimed had been displaced by God to make way for the people of Israel. In the twentieth and twenty-first centuries, however, biblical scholars tend more often to eschew this Christian-centric anthropology and to understand the religion of the Hebrew Bible as much more complex and nuanced, arising out of the larger ancient Near Eastern environment rather than standing against it. Although there is little consensus about precisely how to define "magic" for the ancient world from which the Hebrew Bible emerged, it is generally agreed that what we call magic is an activity related to the human ability to access and/or wield power from a supernatural realm. As such, based on what we know from both the biblical and archaeological records, the ancient Israelite world view was rife with beliefs in magic.

And yet, there are clear condemnations of magical practices in the biblical law codes. For example, Leviticus 20 forbids a variety of practices using categories relating to divination, sorcery, necromancy, and magic; we can translate these words based on cognate terms from other ancient Near Eastern cultures. Similarly, Deuteronomy 18 prohibits the existence of practitioners of these arts in Israel, explaining that such mantic practices are foreign to Israel and had formerly led to Yhwh's dispossession of other nations from the land. These means of accessing the divine are, therefore, forbidden to Israelites, for whom prophecy is the designated way in which Israel is to receive communications from the divine.

Leviticus is even more strict in limiting access to practitioners of magic. Prophecy is not mentioned here as a legal alternative to necromancy, divination, or magic. Rather, only priestly ritual activities designed to propitiate or communicate with the divine are legitimate, and the techniques by which nonpriests might access the supernatural (sorcery, necromancy, divination, and the like) are punishable by their practitioners being "cut off" or even stoned to death. Such reprisals are usually reserved for socially dangerous and reprehensible acts.

However, neither legal prescription categorically condemns the performance of supernatural activities or the acquisition of information from metaphysical realms. Rather, they are solely concerned with limiting supernatural access to those deemed qualified within the Israelite community—in Deuteronomy, this means prophets, while Leviticus favors priests. Magic in and of itself, whether we define it broadly or narrowly, is not anywhere condemned in the Hebrew Bible.

Prohibitions of magical activities are purely social and political in nature. Further, there is no question that the ancient Israelites believed in the effectiveness of these practices, whether conducted by sanctioned personnel or performed outside the strictures of the prescriptions.

For example, in 1 Samuel 5–6, the Philistines are plagued by mice and hemorrhoids as punishment for capturing the ark of Yhwh. Their priests and sorcerers recommend an act of sympathetic magic to alleviate the plagues: gold models of the mice and the hemorrhoids are sent back to Israel along with the ark, and the plagues end. Similarly, in 1 Samuel 28, when Yhwh refuses to communicate with King Saul by the usual priestly and prophetic means, Saul finds a "woman-master of the pit" (ba'alat 'ob) who can raise the dead prophet Samuel for him and facilitate supernatural communication. The irony is that Saul had banished such necromancers from his realm; yet clearly, some remained, and their methods were believed to be effective. The narrative relates not only that the dead prophet Samuel was raised to prophesy to Saul but also that the prophecy came true. Nowhere do the biblical authors express doubt that these mantic acts work. Rather, they condemn the acts when they are performed by Israelites as a way of circumventing prophetic or priestly authority.

Many biblical heroes are credited with magical abilities that both demonstrate and reinforce their divine authority and extraordinary standing in Israel's history. Samson's uncut hair affords him superhuman strength (Judges 16:17). Joshua is able to stop the motion of the sun and moon in the sky (10:13), part the Jordan River (Joshua 3), and bring down the walls of Jericho with trumpet blasts (Joshua 6). In Genesis 30, Jacob performs some sort of fertility magic to ensure that he inherits the strongest animals from the flocks of his father-in-law, Laban. His son Joseph rises to power in Genesis 39–41 by experiencing and interpreting the dreams of others as an oneiromancer. Daniel is also a successful interpreter of prophetic dreams and performs magical feats (Daniel 6:18–24).

Similarly, men who are described as "men of God" or prophets demonstrate incredible abilities to manipulate reality in ways that can only be described as magical. The feats of Elijah and Elisha include the multiplication of food and the resurrection of a child (1 Kings 17; 2 Kings 4), both "miracles" that will later be credited to Jesus in the New Testament. Elisha also removes toxicity from water in 2 Kings 2, removes poison from food in 2 Kings 4, and removes leprosy from a man named Naaman in 2 Kings 5. Elijah brings rain to end a drought in 1 Kings 18. The prophet

Isaiah heals King Hezekiah in 2 Kings 20 and Isaiah 38. Not all of their magical actions bring positive effects, however: in 2 Kings 2, Elisha causes bears to appear and tear apart forty-two children who are taunting him for being bald, and Elijah rains fire down on scores of soldiers attempting to apprehend him in 2 Kings 1. This seems to suggest that although the power derives from Yhwh, the "men of God" are able to wield it as they see fit.

This differentiates the power such figures have from the abilities of ordinary priests to commune with the divine in the Hebrew Bible. Though both priests and prophets have access to the divine supernatural, prophets and the men of God among their ranks not only seem to be chosen by God somewhat at random, but once they receive their power, they need not necessarily use it only according to Yhwh's instructions. Priests, on the other hand, are born into a lineage that establishes their ability to connect with the divine in prescribed manners via rituals such as blessings, prayers, and sacrifices. While we may prefer to think that such rituals pertain to "religion" rather than to "magic," the ancient biblical authors did not make this distinction, as is evident in a variety of priestly objects, activities, and rituals described throughout the text.

Priestly acts of divination include the casting of lots (1 Chronicles 24–26; Nehemiah 10:35), sacred dice known as Urim and Thummim (Numbers 27; 1 Samuel 14), and the use of an object called the ephod (1 Samuel 23; 30).

We also have descriptions of priestly rituals that effect results that have no physical, causal connection with the initiating actions of the participants—in other words, rituals that we might indeed refer to as involving magic. Two that stand out in this regard include the "trial" of the suspected adulteress described in Numbers 5 and the physical transference of sin pollution to a scapegoat in Leviticus 16. In the case of the suspected adulteress, the priest administers an oath and "waters of bitterness" to the woman and pronounces a curse. The curse will take effect only if the woman is guilty of an act for which there was no eyewitness or physical evidence. The scapegoat ritual was an annual ceremony during which the sins of the people were magically transferred by the high priest to the head of a goat, and as the goat was sent out to the uninhabited wilderness, the pollution that threatened the ability of the people to remain in the promised land was removed from the community.

As magic and religion are virtually indistinguishable in the Israelite world view, ordinary people also had limited abilities to affect reality in supernatural ways. For example, pronouncing blessings and curses was a magical way for people to attempt to bring about desired outcomes in the world. In Genesis 27, the blessing of Esau is understood by Isaac as a way of easing the burden that his earlier accidental blessing of Jacob, which cannot be undone (Genesis 27:33), unintentionally placed on his eldest son. In Deuteronomy 28, Moses lays out blessings and curses for the Israelite people as they are on the brink of entering the promised land: If they keep the terms of the covenant, they will be rewarded with an abundance of desired outcomes. However, if they disobey Yhwh's stipulations, a long list of horrible consequences will ensue. Similarly, prayer is understood as having protective and salvific effects that operate according to the same world view. Prayers could also be worn as protective devices: variations on the Priestly Benediction in Numbers 6 were discovered by archaeologists in a seventh-century BCE context in an area of Jerusalem called Ketef Hinnom. They were etched on silver, rolled up, and worn as amulets to ward off evil. This further exemplifies the ways in which our modern conception of magic as distinct from religious activity and belief does not apply to the ancient world.

Belief in magic pervades the Israelite world view. It is an intrinsic aspect of the way in which they understood the universe to operate. The relationship between humans and the divine was mediated by magic, and the correspondence between human actions and their divinely dispatched consequences is a magical one. Whether one defines magic broadly as a ritualized activity designed to communicate with the supernatural (e.g., to learn something from it, as in the case of divination, necromancy, or even prophecy) or to effect change in the world (e.g., turning rods into snakes, multiplying food, purifying what has been polluted, or pronouncing blessings and curses), what we think of as "magic" in the Hebrew Bible is fully encompassed by our concept of religion.

About the Author

Shawna Dolansky holds a doctorate of history (PhD) from the University of California, San Diego. Her research interests include ancient Israelite religion and historiography, with a focus on understanding constructions of gender and portrayals of women in the ancient world. She has published *Now You See It, Now You Don't: Biblical Perspectives on the Relationship Between Religion and Magic* (Winona Lake, IN: Eisenbrauns, 2008), in addition to numerous articles and essays in print and online.

Suggestions for Further Reading

In This Book

See also chapters 1 (scholarly perspective), 2 (religion), 3 (religious in a scientific world), 42 (Nephilim), 43 (angels), 51 (prophets), 52 (covenant), 62 (Joseph), and 63 (Moses).

Elsewhere

Hamori, Esther J. *Women's Divination in Biblical Literature: Prophecy, Necromancy, and Other Arts of Knowledge.* Anchor Yale Bible Reference Library. New Haven, CT: Yale University Press, 2015.

Nikki, Nina, and Kirsi Valkama, editors. *Magic in the Ancient Eastern Mediterranean: Cognitive, Historical, and Material Perspectives on the Bible and Its Contexts.* Göttingen: Vandenhoeck & Ruprecht, 2021.

Schmidt, Brian B. *The Materiality of Power: Explorations in the Social History of Early Israelite Magic.* Tübingen: Mohr Siebeck, 2016.

Smoak, Jeremy D. *The Priestly Blessing in Inscription and Scripture: The Early History of Numbers 6:24–26.* New York: Oxford University Press, 2015.

51
Were the Biblical Prophets Diviners?

Philippe Guillaume

The ancient world was rife with figures associated with oracular utterances from the gods. They are best known from Babylonian sources that mention the *raggimu* (shouter, proclaimer), *šabrû* (seer), *mahhû* (ecstatic), *lallaru* (wailer), and *zabbu* (frenzied), among many others. Neo-Assyrian rulers (ninth to seventh centuries BCE) took the messages of these often peripheral figures seriously enough to have them recorded and classified on clay tablets, to be reused later to legitimize a royal decision by quoting inspired words previously uttered in another context or, quite simply, "out of the blue."

The Hebrew Bible mentions such figures too. They are sometimes designated "men of God" (1 Samuel 2:27; 9; 1 Kings 12:22; 13; 17:24; 20:28; 2 Kings 1; 4–8). Elijah is the most famous one. In the New Testament, the Christian Messiah is introduced by John the Baptist, an Elijah-like figure who roamed the wilderness, performed miracles (most of them repeated by Jesus of Nazareth), and pronounced fiery condemnations of the rulers of his days (1 Kings 13:1–5; 16:1; 21:17–24; 2 Chronicles 19:1; Matthew 14).

In contrast, Elisha, presented as Elijah's successor, is a member of the elite who moves freely in court circles (2 Kings 4:8; 5:1). The son of a family wealthy enough to put twelve pairs of yoked oxen simultaneously to plow a field (1 Kings 19:19), Elisha is involved in local (2 Kings 6:32) and international politics (2 Kings 3:11–14; 6–9; 13). He also seems to lead some sort of college of sons of the prophets (2 Kings 2:15; 4:1; 4:38; 5:22; 6:1).

Besides Elijah, a number of specialists who determined the divine will in the kingdom of Judah and likely also in Israel have been lumped together in the Hebrew Bible under the heading of the most influential type, or the most useful type for the purposes of the scribes who composed the prophetic books. This is the *nābî'*, the one who enters an ecstatic trance—induced, for instance, by music (2 Kings 3:15)—to receive a divine vision, audition, or both simultaneously. This would have been in response to a question they had been asked by their client, with the answer being an oracle. Closely related professions included the *rōeh* (seer) and *ḥōzeh* (visionary). We no longer can determine how they differed.

Then there was a group of professionals who interpreted omens seen to portend the future or express the divine will in natural phenomena: the actions of birds, movement of trees, patterns in clouds or smoke (*mᵉʿōnēn*), and movements of the planets or eclipses. Other related forms involved the interpretation of patterns after pouring oil into water (Genesis 44:5) and the observation of the shape and color of the liver or possibly other internal organs of a sacrificed animal or perhaps the smoke patterns from the animal parts burned on the altar after a sacrifice (*bōqer*; Psalm 5:4).

Additionally, references are found to casting lots (e.g., Numbers 26:55; Joshua 18:6–10; 1 Samuel 10:19–21) and using the Urim and Thummim. The latter were likely two different colored stones or throw sticks placed inside a cloth pocket. After asking a yes-no question before the deity, the priest reached in and pulled one out, and whichever one it was, representing yes or no, gave the divine reply (1 Samuel 14:19, 36–42; 23:2–4, 9–13).

Finally, it was believed that dreams could reveal the divine will. A person could go to a temple to undergo dream incubation (1 Kings 3:5) when wanting an answer to a specific issue troubling them. After fasting, and possibly with the aid of a hallucinogenic drug, they would fall asleep and experience a dream, which was then interpreted by a professional on-site the next morning. Others might receive a divine communication directly via a dream at home, without having sought such a communication. They then would have to go find a professional dream interpreter to tell them what it meant (1 Samuel 28:6).

Biblical scholars have always been reluctant to lump the prophets of the Bible together with the somewhat wild figures known from neighboring cultures, and legitimately so. To account for the critiques of the manipulations of prophecy (Deuteronomy 13:1–6; 18:10–22; Jeremiah 28; Isaiah 9:15–16) and of the venality of some prophets (Micah 3:5, 11; Zechariah 13:2–6), in the Bible, seers, visionaries, ecstatics, and perhaps other related determiners of the divine have been tamed and "booked." The utterers of divine words are now fixed in writing and collected into books or, in fact, scrolls associated with individuals. While prophecy survived as a functioning practice well into the Persian period, it lost favor, probably in power struggles associated with the rebuilt temple. It is condemned in Zechariah 13:1–6. Ecstatic utterances were not always predictable, and the move toward the Torah becoming the main source of divine teaching rather than ongoing, new revelations went hand in hand with the creation of prophetic books, a uniquely biblical genre produced by the scribes of the kingdom of Judah or its successor, the province of Yehud.

The Bible's prophetic books contained past divine revelations culled from a much larger collection of such pronouncements and supplemented with additional "predictions" to suit the ideology of those in power. The result was a completed revelation that could be controlled. The episode of the transmission of the prophetic office from Elijah to Elisha provides a graphic description of the transformation. The reluctance of Elijah to let Elisha inherit a double share of his spirit (2 Kings 2:9) illustrates the transformation of traditional prophecy into a literary phenomenon. It is only as he manages to seize the mantle that fell off Elijah's shoulders when he was ravished by a chariot of fire that Elisha can succeed Elijah. Yet, prophetic power is now embodied in the mantle rather than in any human prophet. Once rolled up like a scroll, the mantle is able to split the Jordan again, thus serving as a prophet like Moses, who split open the Reed Sea (Exodus 14:21–22; 2 Kings 2:8–15).

Once divided into scrolls, the Bible's prophetic books could be introduced with a title designating them as the records of the words of a particular figure—a bookish figure that we tend to erroneously view as the "author" of the scroll. In fact, Isaiah, Jeremiah, Amos, and the others served as the colophon for each scroll—that is, a small piece of writing dangling from the scroll that allowed the identification of each scroll in the pigeonholes in which they were stored, just as the classification numbers and codes glued on the spines of our books in a library help us find the volume we are looking for, saving us from having to open each one. It is only recently that scholars have realized that the colophon is not the author and that the dates indicated in the introductions of many of the prophetic books of the Bible do not necessarily date the utterance of the oracles contained in that scroll.

Taming the prophets into scrolls did not prevent them from being used as oracular devices in a type of divination called bibliomancy. Usually frowned upon by religious authorities, mantic practices were nevertheless tolerated when, instead of using crystal balls, senet boards, tea leaves, or coffee grounds remaining in a cup, words of God in the form of directions from God to take important decisions were obtained randomly by using a wheel, a needle, dice, and other devices to point to a verse selected from a prophetic scroll, the Torah (1 Maccabees 3:38; 2 Maccabees 8:23), and eventually, from an entire Bible. Such practices are well attested in all ages, including our own. Though they may smack of mere superstition, they reflect a legitimate desire to place one's life in conformity with the divine will and to invoke God's help before making decisions whose consequences will influence the rest of one's life. In any case, bibliomancy requires as much interpretation as scholarly exegesis does, since the "answers" provided by any biblical verse never address the actual situation and issue over which the oracle is consulted. Hence, several tries are usually necessary to clarify or confirm whatever message is drawn from the various biblical verses.

While the biblical prophets were the product of scrolls that recorded oracles from different sources and times, it is the practical needs of flesh-and-blood individuals who turn to a biblical passage for guidance that make the bookish prophet a precious guiding tool.

About the Author

Philippe Guillaume holds a doctorate of theology from the University of Geneva and a habilitation from the University of Berne. Among others, he has published "Miracles Miraculously Repeated," *Biblische Notizen* 98 (1999): 21–23; and "Aaron and the Amazing Mantic Coat," pages 101–117 in *Studies in Magic and Divination in the Biblical World*, edited by Helen R. Jacobus, Anne Katrine de Hemmer Gudme, and Philippe Guillaume (Piscataway, NJ: Gorgias, 2013).

Suggestions for Further Reading

In This Book
See also chapters 5 (canons), 10 (Tanak), 13 (genres), 33 (Septuagint), 47 (monotheism), 49 (Torah), 50 (magic), 62 (Joseph), 67 (Isaiah), 68 (Jeremiah), 69 (Jonah), and 83 (reception criticism).

Elsewhere

Ben Zvi, Ehud. "Matters of Authorship, Authority, and Power from the Perspective of a Historian of the World of Yehudite/Judean Literati." Pages 93–114 in *Authorship and the Hebrew Bible*. Edited by Sonja Amman, Katharina Pyschny, and Julia Rhyder. Tübingen: Mohr Siebeck, 2022.

Edelman, Diana V. "From Prophets to Prophetic Books: The Fixing of the Divine Word." Pages 29–54 in *The Production of Prophecy: Constructing Prophecy and Prophets in Yehud*. Edited by Diana V. Edelman and Ehud Ben Zvi. London: Equinox, 2009.

Ghantous, Hadi. "From Mantle to Scroll: The Wane of the Flesh and Blood Prophet in the Elisha Cycle." Pages 119–134 in *Studies in Magic and Divination in the Biblical World*. Edited by Helen R. Jacobus, Anne Katrine de Hemmer Gudme, and Philippe Guillaume. Piscataway, NJ: Gorgias, 2013.

Knauf, Ernst Axel. "Prophets That Never Were." Pages 451–456 in *Gott und Mensch im Dialog: Festschrift für Otto Kaiser zum 80. Geburtstag*. Edited by Markus Witte. Berlin: De Gruyter, 2004.

Nissinen, Martti. *References to Prophecy in Neo-Assyrian Sources*. State Archives of Assyria 7. Helsinki: Neo-Assyrian Text Corpus Project, 1988.

52
What Is a Covenant?

Diana V. Edelman

"Covenant" is an old-fashioned word that most encounter only in English Bibles and in legal contexts. In both, it involves a solemn promise made by one party to another to do or to refrain from doing something. A covenant sets forth the conditions of an agreement, which can be a contract or pact between two private individuals of equal or unequal status (e.g., Genesis 26:28; 31:44; 1 Samuel 18:3; 20:8; 23:18), a treaty or pact between two rulers or parties of equal or unequal status (e.g., Genesis 14:13; 21:27, 32; 26:28; Exodus 23:32; 34:15; Deuteronomy 7:2; 1 Samuel 11:1; 2 Samuel 3:12–13, 21; 5:3; 1 Kings 5:12; 15:19; 20:34; Ezekiel 17:13), or a formal agreement made between a people and its god, as in the Hebrew Bible. The latter clearly involves unequal status and is a central theme in the canonical collection.

Two Hebrew terms designate such a formal agreement that was sealed by an oath: the most frequent is *berit*, which creates a "bond" between the contracting parties, but *'edut* also is used. It is thought that most formal agreements in the wider ancient Near East, including Judah and Israel, consisted of two elements: a document spelling out the obligations of one or both parties and a sworn oath uttered by one or both parties before witnesses, which could include the invoking of curses upon those who broke the agreement. In early Akkadian, the terms *rikiltu* (or *rikistu* or *riksu*) *u māmitu*, "bond and oath," designated such a formal pact, where the first element designated the written terms and the second the oath. In Neo-Assyrian, the preferred phrasing became (*tuppu* = tablet) *adê māmitu/ tāmīti*. Similarly, in the Hittite sphere, such agreements were known as *išḫiul* and *lengai*, "bond" and "oath," respectively. In both spheres, it was possible to use the first element only, "bond," as a shorthand to refer to the official document and oath.

In the covenant made on the plains of Moab, the people are said to have sworn an oath (*'alah*) after having heard the terms of the covenant relayed orally (Deuteronomy 29:14, 19–21; 13, 18–20 in Hebrew). Earlier in the book, three terms describe the contents of the obligations: 'edot (often rendered "decrees" but more accurately "obligations"), *huqqim* (customary practices/statutes), and *mishpatim* (judgments) (4:45; 6:17–20). In Exodus, the Sinai covenant includes Moses telling the people all the words of Yhwh and his judgments, which they agree orally to perform in solemn declaration, and then he writes them in the scroll of the covenant that is read to the people, who once again proclaim they will follow. This is essentially a sworn declaration, even if the verb "to swear" or the noun "oath" does not appear. So, we can assume the same two elements were part of the *berit* covenant tradition in Israel and Judah as well.

A review of the occurrences of 'edut (singular) and 'edôt (irregular plural) demonstrates that the term tends to signify, collectively, the written terms or stipulations of a formal agreement more than the end result (*berit*; e.g., Exodus 31:18; 32:15; 34:29; Number 17:4, 10; Psalm 78:5). The plural, on the other hand, refers to individual elements within the collective whole (e.g., Deuteronomy 4:45; 6:17; 2 Kings 17:15; 2 Kings 23:3; Psalm 25:10; 78:58; 99:7; 119:24, 31, 46). The same applies to the singular and plural use of the term "Torah," where the singular typically designates a collection of teachings but can also refer to one item in that collection, while the plural always designates more than one individual teaching within a larger group.

The chest that contained the tablets inscribed with the Ten Commandments representing the contractual obligations of the people of Israel is more frequently called the ark of the 'edut than the ark of the *berit*. This is probably because it housed the physical documents recording the obligations or conditions, which were to be protected during the wilderness wanderings by being placed inside a special tent called "the tent of the ['edut]" (e.g., Numbers 9:15; 10:11; 17:4, 7–8). In contrast, when the phrase "the ark of the [*berit*]" is used, it emphasizes the abstract concept of a formal agreement sealed by an oath entered into between Israel and Yhwh by referencing the preservation of the written terms for posterity in a chest (e.g., Deuteronomy 10:8; 31:9, 25; Joshua 3:3, 6, 8, 11; 4:18; 6:6, 8; 8:33; 1 Samuel 4:3–5; 2 Samuel 15:24; 1 Kings 6:19; 8:1, 6, 21; 1 Chronicles 15:25). The first focuses exclusively on the written testimony and obligations, while the latter uses them rather than the sworn oath to symbolize the completed covenant; there is a slight difference. Both phrases, however, view the ark and its contents as holy relics.

God makes a series of covenants in the various books of the Hebrew Bible, beginning with Noah (Genesis 6:18; 9:9–17) on behalf of all living creatures on earth in primeval times and then with Abraham (Genesis 15:8; 17; Leviticus 26:42; Nehemiah 9:8) concerning his direct offspring through Isaac (Genesis 17:21, 26:2–5; Leviticus 26:42) and Jacob (Genesis 28:13–15; Exodus 2:24; Leviticus 24:8; 26:42) in the patriarchal era. The most famous covenant is probably the one mediated by Moses between Yhwh and the people of Israel at Mount Sinai/Horeb (Exodus 19:5; 24:7–8; 31:6, 18; 32:15; 34:10, 27, 29; Deuteronomy 4:13, 23; 5:2; 9:9, 11, 15) and expanded or updated on the plains of Moab in the book of Deuteronomy (29:1), with new conditions that are to apply once Israel crosses the Jordan River to dispossess the Canaanites living west of the river in Cisjordan. Both take place during the wilderness wanderings. This covenant is renewed, commemorated, or completed after the successful occupation of Cisjordan at a ceremony led by Joshua conducted outside of Shechem (Joshua 24), in the era of the conquest and occupation of the promised land. Further covenants are entered into by Yhwh with Aaron and his direct descendants (Numbers 18:19; Nehemiah 13:29), especially his grandson Phinehas (Numbers 25:10–13); and with Levi (Deuteronomy 10:8; 33:9 implicitly; Malachi 2:4, 8; Psalm 50:5, Nehemiah 13:29) during the wilderness wanderings; and with David and his dynasty (2 Samuel 7:4–17; 23:5; Jeremiah 33:21; Psalm 89:3, 28, 34; 132:4; 2 Chronicles 13:5) during the period of the united monarchy. Finally, the prophet Jeremiah announces the idea of a new covenant with the houses of Israel and Judah in which the Torah will be inscribed directly on their hearts (31:31–33) in the era of the divided monarchy or the exile. The prominence of the concept of covenant, which spans most of the biblical periodization of the past, has made it a central focus in Old Testament theology.

The discovery of copies of political treaties between the Hittites and other world powers led biblical scholars from the 1950s until today to conceive of the covenants at Mount Sinai/Horeb and in the plains of Moab as a form of political vassal treaty, with Israel the lesser party and Yhwh the overlord. Within the last decade, however, this view has been challenged. Examples of oath-bound agreements from the Hittite and Neo-Assyrian spheres have established that formal agreements were used in the royal sphere to bind servants to loyal service to the crown. A group of texts dubbed "Hittite Royal Instructions" and Esarhaddon's Neo-Assyrian loyalty oath documents illustrate this category, as do, possibly, the formal agreements entered into between the Judahite kings Joash (2 Kings 11:4–20) and Josiah (2 Kings 23:1–3) with the people. It is now being proposed that the covenant at Sinai/Horeb and/or the plains of Moab might be an example of this form of agreement rather than a political treaty. In both alternatives, the people of Israel become formally bound to the deity Yhwh.

About the Author

Diana V. Edelman holds a doctorate of philosophy (PhD) in biblical studies from the University of Chicago and is Professor Emerita in Hebrew Bible at the Faculty of Theology, University of Oslo. She has published "The Role of Covenant in the Book of Deuteronomy," in *Deuteronomy: Outside the Box*, edited by D. Edelman and P. Guillaume (Sheffield, UK: Equinox, forthcoming); and "Deuteronomy as the Instructions of Moses and Yhwh vs. a Framed Legal Code," pages 25–75 in *Deuteronomy in the Making: Studies in the Production of Debarim*, edited by D. Edelman, B. Rossi, K. Berge, and P. Guillaume (Berlin: De Gruyter, 2021).

Suggestions for Further Reading

In This Book

See also chapters 13 (genres), 16 (Psalms), 22 (periodization), 27 (Josiah's scroll), 36 (Old Testament theology), 48 (twelve tribes), 49 (Torah), 60 (Abraham), 63 (Moses), 65 (King David), and 68 (Jeremiah).

Elsewhere

Lauinger, Jacob. "The Neo-Assyrian *adê*: Treaty, Oath or Something Else?" *Zeitschrift für altorientalische und biblische Rechtsgeschichte* 19 (2013): 99–115.

McCarthy, Dennis J. *Treaty and Covenant: A Study in Form in the Ancient Oriental Documents and in the Old Testament*. Rome: Pontifical Biblical Institute, 1981.

Miller, Jared. *Royal Hittite Instructions and Related Administrative Texts*. Atlanta: SBL, 2013.

Tagger-Cohen, Ada. "The Hebrew Biblical Bérit in Light of Ancient Near Eastern Covenants and Texts." *Canon and Culture* 14 (2020): 5–50.

Issues

53

Can Religious Texts Serve as Legitimate Explanations of the Origin of the Universe and Terrestrial Life in a Scientific World?

Fabien Revol

Can the story of the origins of the universe in the first two chapters of the Hebrew Bible still have any meaning in the Western world, where a nontheological, scientific culture dominates? To read Genesis 1–2 literally as though it were a scientific treatise is ill-advised. It never was and still isn't. It cannot inform a nontheological theory of the origins of the universe and life on earth that is based on physical evidence and logical reasoning. One could certainly conclude it has no relevance to a modern understanding of how the universe and terrestrial life came to exist. There is no inconvertible proof that God exists or that such an entity instigated or initiated the process that has resulted in the universe and life on earth. Those who do not believe in the existence of a supreme being are likely to take this stance. But should those who believe in God similarly reject all the contents of Genesis 1–2 as irrelevant to understanding the origins of the universe and life?

Before answering both questions from the opening paragraph, we need to understand why Genesis 1 and 2 were written and how they likely functioned. These two chapters of the book of Genesis narrate things in the opposite order. Genesis 1 goes from the creation of the natural elements to the first human pair and the Sabbath. Genesis 2 goes from the creation of Adam to that of the surrounding universe. These chapters were not necessarily written at the same time, and they belong to different literary genres. Genesis 1 reads like a liturgical text, while Genesis 2 is a mythical text. This means that factual consistency was not the primary goal of the scribe who set these two chapters side by side.

As some sort of liturgy, Genesis 1 was not meant to be a scientific treatise. Nonetheless, this text evokes the cosmological knowledge available at the time of writing as a backdrop for a critical outlook toward polytheistic thought in surrounding cultures. For instance, light and darkness alternate regularly and can be used to mark the passage of time. The sun, the moon, the stars, and the planets are also useful for reckoning longer periods of time and marking festivals and seasons, but they are not god symbols, as they were in Babylonian thought and astronomy.

The biblical version of creation omits the myths of the creation of the gods and the battle for kingship over the divine realm; in the Babylonian liturgical text, *Enuma Elish*, these precede the splitting of the defeated watery deity Tiamat by the new divine king (Marduk in Babylonia, Assur in Assyria) to create heaven and earth. Instead, Genesis 1 narrates its story from when God began to create heaven and earth, with the sole deity splitting a de-divinized watery chaos as a first act of the creation of the heavens, earth, and terrestrial life. It has no interest in presenting the origin of the various gods, probably because the scribe who included it conceived of a single god. The fact that the Hebrew text of Genesis 1:1 begins "In a beginning" and was rendered into Greek indefinitely as well likely was an intentional hint. Discerning members of the ancient audience who were familiar with the ideas expressed in the *Enuma Elish* would have understood that the Israelite myth was deliberately omitting other "chapters" that preceded this one in the Babylonian liturgy celebrated at the Akitu festival. Erudite scribes could have learned about the contents of the *Enuma Elish* when the Babylonians were the rulers of much of the ancient Near East (626–539 BCE) or as exiles in Babylonia (598–ca. 450 BCE). Thus, Genesis 1–2 probably is polemical to some degree, in addition to its being a liturgical, mythical text, not an ancient or modern scientific account explicating the ancient understanding of how the universe, the earth, and terrestrial forms of life came to exist.

The Hebrew text clearly states that creation is an act of splitting chaos, *tohu wa-bohu*, and ordering it. Chaos already exists in the story world. We are not told how it came into being, because that was not the focus of liturgical interest; recounting acts that prove that Yhwh Elohim is the only creator god is. In ancient Hebrew thought, chaos and created order are opposites; when the latter is interrupted or undone, chaos takes over again.

The Greek translator rendered the Hebrew compound phrase *tohu wa-bohu* as "in-visible" (*a-oratos*) and "unprepared, raw, uncut" (*a-kataskeuastos*). He thus preserved the basic understanding that this was an existing entity prior to creation. But in the subsequent Hellenistic climate (200s BCE–100s CE), this preexistent chaos came to be understood instead as "nonexistence" (2 Maccabees 7:28; Romans 4:17), a notion that was perpetuated in Latin as ex nihilo, "[creation] out of nothing." Many church fathers understood the passage to indicate that chaos was created from nothing and so could not oppose God's creative omnipotence.

It can be noted, however, that Genesis 1 is not totally inconsistent with the evolutionary setting of the biological sciences. Contrary to antique philosophies that envisioned an eternal world, Genesis claims that the universe has a beginning. This is in accord with present-day scientific, cosmological theories that date the origins of the physical universe from a singularity—a point of infinite density and temperature—some thirteen to fifteen billion years ago. The so-called big bang hypothesis was revolutionary, and the scientific world resisted it until the 1960s because it sounded too religious with its origin in a single, uncreated source.

Additional beginnings also are envisioned after the initial separation of heaven and earth in Genesis 1. Each of the first six days in the Greek translation and seven days in the older Hebrew text marks the beginning of one or more particular life-forms in its absolute novelty. Yet, while God is frequently said to act directly (Genesis 1:7, 16–17, 21, 25, 27) to fulfill the previously divinely voiced word during the first week of ongoing creation, in other instances, the command is accomplished by self-organization (1:3, 9) or by a process of existing matter generating new biodiversity (1:12). The latter two forms of generation fit within the parameters of nondirected Darwinian evolution. As David Bartholomew (2008, 174) argues, chance is the best means of the creation of new entities over time.

For those today who believe in a supreme being who played both a direct and indirect role in the creation of the universe, chance is not opposed to divine providence; it serves as the means of accomplishing creation in partnership rather than in a deterministic program, be it divine or random. In Genesis 1, God sometimes delegates creative powers to earthly creations. The deity communicates the needed information to the creatures so that they can produce new entities over time in processes involving relationships between natural beings that sustain ecosystems. It is in the midst of natural and ecological relationships that biological novelty appears.

Should it matter to believers that these few overlaps between biblical understanding and contemporary scientific understanding exist? Only if one is working under two misconceptions: that Genesis 1–2 is somehow an intentionally factual account and that the ancient Israelite or Hebrew world view should prevail in contemporary Western societies. Otherwise, what meaning can both religious and secular individuals today derive from the opening two chapters of Genesis?

Focusing on the mythic nature of Genesis 2 and the mytho-liturgical nature of Genesis 1 allows us to understand that the scribe intended to convey what he considered to be a theological truth: there is one supreme entity, Yhwh Elohim, who is the creator deity and ultimate life-giving source and maintainer of order versus chaos, even if the latter responsibility can be delegated to humanity. Armed with that knowledge, an individual needs to decide if he or she shares that same belief.

In addition, the story suggests that being in the image of God (Genesis 1:26) implies no superiority, since, according to Genesis 2:7, we are made of the same material as other creatures. But being in the image of God also means, as man and woman, representing God in creation by taking the place of the statues that had represented the divinity in the old pagan cults. While the king was thought to represent the divinity for his people, humans represent the unique God for all sentient and nonsentient creatures. In Genesis, it is each one of us, not merely rulers and governments, who are called to preserve creation from reverting to chaos.

Notions of rule and dominion are implied in Genesis 1:26–28. Genesis 2:15 defines this dominion as service to making the garden of creation flourish: "to till" and "to serve" are the same verb in Hebrew. Understanding how the ancient Israelite scribe conceived of humanity's role within creation as part of his larger world view can prompt us to consider if we would endorse that same conception as making sense within our current world view(s). What part of the message might we consider to transcend cultural boundaries and still apply today? Do we still want to consider it our vocation to be good wardens or stewards of the earth, whether or not we see ourselves as unequal partners in the creative process alongside God, where we are creative by delegation?

About the Author

Fabien Revol holds a DPhil from the Catholic University of Lyon and a sacred theology doctorate from the Jesuit Faculties of Centre Sèvres. He is the director of the Hélène and Jean Bastaire Center for Integral Ecology. His research includes creation in dialogue with science and religion and integral ecology. He has published "Theology of Continuous Creation," *Theology and Science* 19(3) (2021): 287–299; "The Concept of Continuous Creation Part I: History and Contemporary Use," *Zygon* 55 (2020): 229–250; and "The Concept of Continuous Creation Part II: Continuous Creation; Toward a Renewed and Actualized Concept," *Zygon* 55 (2020): 251–274.

Suggestions for Further Reading

In This Book

See also chapters 1 (scholarly perspective), 2 (religion), 3 (religious in a scientific world), 13 (genres), 15 (apocalyptic literature), 22 (periodization), 39 (calendars), 40 (holiness), 47 (monotheism), and 58 (ecology).

Elsewhere

Bartholomew, David. *God, Chance and Purpose: Can God Have It Both Ways?* Cambridge: Cambridge University Press, 2008.

Fretheim, Terence E. *God and the World in the Old Testament: A Relational Theology of Creation.* Nashville: Abingdon, 2005.

Haught, John F. *God after Darwin: A Theology of Evolution.* Boulder, CO: Westview, 2008.

Peacocke, Arthur. *Evolution, the Disguised Friend of Faith: Selected Essays.* Philadelphia: Templeton Foundation, 2004.

Peters, Ted, and Martinez Hewlett. *Evolution from Creation to New Creation: Conflict, Conversation, and Convergence.* Nashville: Abingdon, 2003.

Russel, Robert John. "Theological Debates around Evolution." Pages 645–663 in *Biological Evolution: Facts and Theories; A Critical Appraisal 150 Years after "The Origin of Species."* Edited by Gennaro Auletta, Marc Leclerc, and Rafael A. Martinez. Rome: Gregorian and Biblical Press, 2011.

54
Does the Hebrew Bible Endorse Genocide?

James S. Anderson

War is a constant phenomenon in human past and present, whereas genocide is a recent concept developed in the wake of larger-than-ever massacres of civilian populations in the twentieth century—in particular, Armenians in the Ottoman Empire and modern Turkey, Jews in Europe, and Tutsis in Rwanda. The 1948 United Nations Convention on the Prevention and Punishment of the Crime of Genocide defines it as war crimes motivated by an intentional attempt "to destroy, in whole or in part, a national, ethnical, racial or religious group." The definition of genocide can apply in war as well as in peaceful times and extends beyond killing. It includes serious physical bodily or mental harm, preventing births, and the forceful transfer of children.

Yhwh's command to utterly destroy the Canaanites fits the definition of genocide, as the stated aim is the total elimination of the population of the promised land designated as Canaanites as well as Hittites, Hivites, Perizzites, Girgashites, Amorites, and Jebusites. The social realities behind these terms are not always clear. The Hittites, for instance, were a bygone empire centered in modern-day Turkey; the Perizzites were the inhabitants of villages, while "Jebusites" seems to refer to the Canaanite population of Jerusalem.

The book of Exodus ascribes driving out the Canaanites to Yhwh himself, while Numbers 21:1–3 mentions a first destruction at the hands of Israel as a result of a vow to destroy the cities of the king of Arad in the Negev. Deuteronomy 7 and 20 explain that the divine promise to clear away the inhabitants of the promised land is to be fulfilled by Israel. The need to "utterly destroy" them is to avoid any political alliance and intermarriage with these groups presented not only as mightier than Israel but also as practitioners of abhorrent rituals that Israel would be unable not to imitate, in which case, Yhwh would have no other choice than to destroy his own people; a Canaanized Israel would be equally abhorrent. As is the case with most wars and genocides, the need to destroy is presented as a survival strategy.

In the Bible, the duty to eliminate the Canaanites falls to Moses's successor. Though historically, Canaanite practices probably differed little from Israel's—there is a debate over the existence and significance of child sacrifice—wars are always justified by a process of "othering" that dehumanizes the enemy in order to ease the conscience of the killers. This is the underlying principle of any "just" or "holy" war theory, defended already circa 400 CE by Augustine of Hippo in his *Questions on Joshua*.

If reality sometimes extends beyond fiction, the book of Joshua relates a succession of defeats and half victories, whose result is far from the required genocide. Even before entering Canaan, the spies make an agreement to spare Rahab and her entire family (Joshua 2:14). The slaughter of the population of Ai is more thorough (Joshua 7–8), but the inhabitants of Gibeon save their skins with a simple trick (Joshua 9). The sequel of the conquest focuses on the execution of kings and of the population of a number of towns. Yet, the success reported in the summary of Joshua 11:16–23 is dampened when 13:1 states that although Joshua is old, "very much of the land still remains to be possessed," giving the lie to the notion of a thorough elimination of the Canaanites and thus of a genocide.

Finally, Judges 1 admits that the destruction was not complete and that the Israelites remained confined in the hills due to a lack of iron chariots to vanquish the Canaanites. Exodus 23:29–31 anticipates the incomplete elimination of the Canaanites by attributing it to a divine plan of gradual population replacement to avoid the proliferation of wild beasts in case the land was to remain underpopulated while the Israelite population was too sparse. In another attempt to deal with the failure, the Canaanites are recycled into divinely endorsed thorns in the side of Israel and their gods a snare for Israel (Judges 2:1–3; 2 Kings 12:3; 13:5–6; 14:4; 15:35; 17:9–18; 18:4; 21:2–9, 14–15).

That the Bible itself admits that Israel failed to obey the divine command is hardly sufficient to assuage the qualms of its modern readers. Scholars have responded to the serious ethical problem raised by divinely ordained genocide in a variety of ways, depending on their personal beliefs, faith, or secularity. For the third group, the biblical accounts of divine commands to commit genocide remain troubling, but they do not impinge on a nonexistent religiosity. For a very small minority in this group who might once have believed in God, such texts that portray a bloodthirsty deity might have led them to conclude that such a deity is not worthy of worship. Practicing Jewish and Christian biblical scholars, on the other hand, have more at stake. Some choose not to engage with the issue, but among those who do, some coping strategies are discernible.

As part of a strategy to mitigate the problematic command of violence by Yhwh, Catholics often appeal to the different senses of Scripture to suggest that today, only the spiritual sense holds weight and is worthy of discussion. Thus, these texts serve as a metaphor revealing that just as the Israelites were to eradicate all in the land so the Israelites would not be corrupted, humans today are to utterly eradicate all sin in them. The story of the Israelites shows what happens when a person does not obey God and fails to utterly destroy that which keeps him or her from God. Such spiritualizing readings avoid the historical quagmire that makes it difficult to reconcile a loving God with these texts.

Among Protestant Christians who find these texts troubling, it is common to disconnect God from this violence in some way. For example, some appeal to archaeological data to deny the historicity of the events involving the Canaanites, arguing that the composition of these texts dates to a time period long after the Canaanites had already disappeared from history. Thus, it did not really happen, even if the divine command stands.

Others suggest that Jericho and Ai, Canaanite cities Joshua suppos-edly thoroughly destroyed, were only inhabited by military personnel, so no civilians were slaughtered. Another approach appeals to the mention of giants in Canaan (Anakim, Rephaim, Nephilim; see Numbers 13:32–33; Joshua 14:12–15). The victims of Joshua's troops are seen not to have been humans exactly but the fruit of the sinful copulation of such mythical crea-tures with fair human daughters (Genesis 6:2). In the first case, only those who opposed Israel were killed. In the second case, they weren't humans.

Finally, some argue that God never commanded Israel to utterly destroy the Canaanites. For example, Eric Seibert (2009) argues that the Israelites either misunderstood what God wanted them to do or willfully chose to act other than what he intended. Blame Israel, not God!

The divinely commanded genocide also has been read in light of other ancient Near Eastern war reports that are full of bravado, depicting total devastation to cover up a less glorious reality. A variation of this compara-tive, contextual strategy tries to reduce Israel's guilt by arguing, in light of the Mesha stele, that whatever massacres were committed in Joshua's days were no different from what Moab claimed to do to the Israelite population of the Transjordanian town of Nebo. On that stele, King Mesha states,

Chemosh [a deity] said to me, "Go, take Nebo from Israel." I went in the night and I fought against it from the break of day till noon, and

I took it. I killed in all seven thousand men . . . women and maidens,
for I devoted them [*herem*] to Ashtar-Chemosh; and I took from it
the vessels of Yhwh, and offered them before Chemosh.

The term *herem* (חרם) means "to set aside from profane use; dedicate
something to a god." In the Bible, it is commonly rendered as "to destroy
utterly." Hence, Israel was only following the mores of the day, which consisted of claiming that war was commanded by one's own god, that there
was no option but to comply, and that dedicating persons and animals via
herem was an act of worship.

As is the case in Deuteronomy, the inhabitants are killed in order to
clear the city so it can be resettled by a new group. Here, however, the Moabite king devotes the lives of the Israelites to his gods, while in the Hebrew
Bible, the deity Yhwh commands that the Canaanites be killed.

Finally, a more radical approach is to argue that being sovereign, God
is fully entitled to decree the destruction of any creatures to make room
for others. It is not for humans to dispute the justice of divine decisions.

Significantly, in Exodus 22:20, Israelite idolaters who had worshipped
a god other than Yhwh were also subject to *herem*. The same idea is
repeated in Deuteronomy 13:16. Although *herem* is not mentioned explicitly, the death penalty is.

Exodus 22:20 seems to have been the basis for the subsequent rabbinic
use of *herem* in the Jewish Mishnah, compiled circa 200 CE, to refer to
excommunication from the Jewish community. This punishment was
imposed by a rabbinical court on someone found guilty of disobeying the
Torah or the authorities. The length of time involved in the banishment
could vary depending on the level of remorse.

While the rabbis tended to accept that *herem* against the populations
living in Canaan was a legitimate command of God, they tried to soften
its import in creative ways. Some suggested Joshua treated the locals as
though they lived outside Canaan (Deuteronomy 20:10–14) and offered
them peace and permission to remain in the land if they gave up their
idolatry. Maimonides included three options: flight, peace, or war. Others
proposed that the divine command concerning holy war only was applicable during the Israelite conquest of Canaan and was not to become a
general practice through time, as it did subsequently with the spread of
Islam, the Crusades, and subsequent massacres of civilian populations
justified by appeals to the biblical command to wipe out the Canaanites.

For any reader who does not agree with these different attempts to
cope with the genocide of the Canaanites ordered by God, the laments in
the book of Psalms provide a model for struggling with God and contesting

the divine management of the world: one can lament not only life circumstances but also the memory of God's past actions.

About the Author

James S. Anderson earned a PhD in biblical studies from the University of Sheffield. He is the author of *Monotheism and Yahweh's Appropriation of Baal* (New York: Bloomsbury T&T Clark, 2015); and "El, Yahweh and Elohim: The Evolution of God in Israel and Its Theological Implications," *Expository Times* 128 (2017): 261–267.

Suggestions for Further Reading

In This Book
See also chapters 22 (periodization), 26 (conquest of Canaan), 28–31 (archaeology), 36 (Old Testament theology), 37 (rabbinic interpretation), 42 (Nephilim), 49 (Torah), 63 (Moses), and 66 (Jezebel).

Elsewhere
Cogan, Mordechai. "Deuteronomy's Herem Law: Protecting Israel at the Cost of Its Humanity." TheTorah.com. https://www.thetorah.com/article/deuteronomys-herem-law-protecting-israel-at-the-cost-of-its-humanity.

Hawk, L. Daniel. *The Violence of the Biblical God: Canonical Narrative and Christian Faith*. Grand Rapids, MI: Eerdmans, 2019.

Seibert, Eric. *Disturbing Divine Behavior: Troubling Old Testament Images of God*. Minneapolis: Fortress, 2009.

Trimm, Charlie. *The Destruction of the Canaanites: God, Genocide, and Biblical Interpretation*. Grand Rapids, MI: Eerdmans, 2022.

Webb, William J., and Gordon K. Oeste. *Bloody, Brutal, and Barbaric: Wrestling with Troubling War Texts*. Downers Grove, IL: IVP Academic, 2019.

55
Is the Hebrew Bible Patriarchal?

Philippe Guillaume

In the wake of feminist studies that legitimately denounce the many cases of abuse against women justified by appeals to the Bible, the Latin expressions paterfamilias (family father) and patria potestas (paternal power) have become pet designations for fathers in the Bible and in ancient Israel. On the basis of how fathers in imperial Rome were imagined, biblical fathers are conceived as little dictators with rights of life and death over all the members of their household. In the words of Julye Bidmead (2014, 404), men in the ancient Near East "had exclusive financial, sexual, and legal jurisdiction over their wives and over their daughters."

In 2006, however, Steven Thompson had already warned that the actual powers Roman law granted to the paterfamilias over his wives and children were more limited than generally presumed. Nevertheless, the paterfamilias remains a favorite target of feminist and womanist biblical exegetes, despite Simone Paganini's warning in 2010 that the biblical paterfamilias is used as an overly convenient straw man. Four years later, Carol Meyers (2014) argued that archaeology reveals a world in which women were indispensable and were often the chief executives of essential areas and life-sustaining tasks.

The acrostic poem of Proverbs 31:10–31 gives a vivid portrait of such a chief executive who runs her home and a cottage industry in clothing, imports food from afar, gets wasteland cleared to plant a vineyard, and gives alms to the poor, all for the benefit of her husband, who trusts her (verse 11) so he can sit at the gate with the other grandees to deal with local politics. His influence is commensurate with his wife's repute as a wise businesswoman, and the final verse advises her fortunate husband to make sure to let her have a share of the profit.

Such a portrayal of an elite woman is certainly not a reflection of the actual condition of ordinary women in biblical times, even though it is far from idealistic. The poem makes no secret about the price this woman of great worth pays for her achievements. Ahead of everyone else, she is up before dawn (verse 15) and is still busy after sundown (verse 18). She is no fat cow of Bashan wallowing on an ivory bed and waiting for her husband to bring more drink, as Amos (4:1; 6:4–6) describes the elite women of Samaria.

The life of the ordinary wife has to be discerned between the prophet's male chauvinistic slur and the poetic embellishment of Proverbs. In the Bible as in many parts of the world today, men and women are not equals. Men certainly had exclusive financial, sexual, and legal jurisdiction over their slaves—when they were rich enough to afford slaves—but they had no exclusive sexual and legal rights over their wives and daughters.

It made no more economic sense for a father to have sex with his daughter than for a slave owner to beat and starve his slaves, who represented a major investment that was lost when slaves ran away or died from mistreatment. Virginity is difficult to prove (see Deuteronomy 22:13–19), but pregnancy is not. An unmarried pregnant daughter covered her parents with shame, a disaster in terms of reputation and social capital for the entire family (see Sirach 22:4–5).

A father's sexual jurisdiction over his daughter was limited to the choice of her husband, though a young enterprising girl could overrule parental veto by eloping with her lover, at least according to Deuteronomy 22:28–29. Biblical laws, though not exact descriptions of the reality of family relations, do not support the view of women as the powerless victims of patriarchs.

The silence over daughters in the list of forbidden sexual partners (Leviticus 18:6–23) ought not be read as a license for fathers to use their own daughters sexually. Such things certainly happened as they do today, but this does not mean they were condoned.

What about wives? Did husbands have exclusive financial, sexual, and legal jurisdiction over their wives? Recently, Sandra Jacobs (2018, 346) wrote that marriage made the wife's personhood "an object of her husband's property." A year earlier, however, Tracy Lemos (2017, 77) warned that referring to women as property is inaccurate and confusing. Much of the confusion stems from the term "bride-price," which designates the dowry fathers paid to the bride's family.

"Bride-price" suggests that the husband bought a wife, who thus became his property in the same way that slaves he bought on the slave market or who were born in his own household did. In fact, what a man disbursed to obtain a wife were presents for her father, presents in exchange for the dowry the father disbursed to his daughter as her share of his estate, paid in advance upon her marriage, contrary to her brothers, who had to wait until their father's death to enjoy their share. Being her share of her paternal estate, the wife remained the exclusive owner of her dowry, even when her husband invested it. Upon divorce, he had to return the dowry. So much for the exclusive financial jurisdiction of the husband.

The exclusive jurisdiction of husbands over their wives was mostly limited to the sexual realm. Wives could not say no, and the notion of marital rape was as unknown as it still is in most parts of the world. Procreation was so crucial to the survival of the group that wives had little incentive to say no. The main status changer for a woman was motherhood. Whereas sterility justified repudiation or forced the acceptance of a second wife, bearing a viable son secured for the mother an almost unassailable position in the household.

We should beware of approaching biblical texts with views tainted by modern concerns like equality. Equal status between men and women was not an issue for the biblical writers. Genesis 1:28 mentions en passant the creation of men and women together, while Genesis 2 delays the creation of Eve until after the animals. Genesis has certainly been used to argue that women are inherently inferior to men. Such arguments ignore both Genesis 1, which considers men and women integral parts of humanity, and Genesis 2, which elevates Eve as the crown of creation.

Besides the excess in prophetic texts, later writings such as Sirach (7:23–25; 26:10; 42:9–14) and the New Testament (1 Corinthians 11:3–9; 14:33–35; 1 Timothy 2:9–15; Ephesians 5:22–30; Colossians 3:18–19) expressed anxious views regarding women and daughters. Such views reflected the urban settings of the Hellenistic era, which provided more freedom to mingle among members of the other sex thanks to the anonymity afforded by large cities. In villages, the strict confinement of daughters was irrelevant; everyone lived under the gaze of everyone else. Song of Songs 3 depicts the challenge of finding privacy, while the labor of unmarried girls was needed outside during times of intense activities like the harvest and for collecting water and firewood, for which they were sent out in groups.

What may appear today as patriarchal in the Hebrew Bible results from adaptation to the material conditions of a premechanized agricultural mode of production, low demography, and high mother and child mortality. In such contexts, the division of labor between men and women is essential to survival. Paradoxically, it ascribes a greater value to women than is the case in industrial and postindustrial societies, where gender differences are suppressed, forcing women to combine careers with motherhood in the name of women's liberation. At the same time, the latter types of societies expect women to remain attractive sexual partners even though marriage is optional.

In the ancient Near Eastern world, marriage was not an option. The Bible has no word for spinsters. Independent women came from two sources. They were either divorcées who often had experienced sterility in their previous marriages, annihilating their chance to establish another one, or widows who had lost much value on the marriage market.

The Bible designates a woman who has to take care of herself as a *zonah*, a term erroneously translated as "prostitute," although making both ends meet by providing sexual services was not considered shameful as such. Like divorcées and widows, the only threat these women represented was to the budget of their male clients (a mere loaf of bread according to Proverbs 6:26!), whereas an adulteress exposed the adulterer to life-threatening retaliations (Proverbs 6:26–35). The warnings against prostitutes in Proverbs 7 are addressed to a young and probably unmarried man who might be tempted to dilapidate his revenues instead of becoming a father and a responsible head of household.

About the Author

Philippe Guillaume earned a ThD from the University of Geneva and a habilitation from the University of Berne. His research includes "Deuteronomic Parenting," in *Deuteronomy: Outside the Box*, edited by Diana V. Edelman and Philippe Guillaume (Sheffield, UK: Equinox, online 2022).

Suggestions for Further Reading

In This Book
See also chapters 10 (Tanak), 16 (Psalms), 17 (Wisdom), 18 (Proverbs), 49 (Torah), 53 (creation), 64 (Ruth), and 81 (gender studies).

Elsewhere
Ackerman, Susan. *Women and the Religion of Ancient Israel.* New Haven, CT: Yale University Press, 2022. https://doi.org/10.2307/j.ctv29pg509.

Bidmead, Julye, Lauren Caldwell, Robert N. Stegmann, Judith Hauptman, and David M. Reis. "Legal Status." Pages 402–424 in *The Oxford Encyclopedia of the Bible and Gender Studies* (volume 1). Edited by Julia M. O'Brien. Oxford: Oxford University Press, 2014.

Ebeling, Jennie R. *Women's Lives in Biblical Times.* London: T&T Clark, 2010.

Jacobs, Sandra. "The Disposable Wife as Property in the Hebrew Bible." Pages 337–356 in *Gender and Methodology in the Ancient Near East.* Edited by Stephanie L. Budin, Megan Cifarelli, Agnès Garcia-Ventura, and Adelina Millet Albà. Barcelona: Edicions de la Universitat de Barcelona, 2018.

Lemos, Tracy. *Violence and Personhood in Ancient Israel and Comparative Contexts*. Oxford: Oxford University Press, 2017.

Meyers, Carol L. *Rediscovering Eve: Ancient Israelite Women in Context*. New York: Oxford University Press, 2013.

Meyers, Carol L. "Was Ancient Israel a Patriarchal Society?" *Journal of Biblical Literature* 133 (2014): 8–27.

Paganini, Simone. "Gesetze für, gegen bzw. über Frauen im Buch Deuteronomium." *Protokol zur Bibel* 19 (2010): 21–34.

Pressler, Carolyn. "Wives and Daughters, Bond and Free: View of Women in the Slave Laws of Exodus 21.2–11." Pages 147–172 in *Gender and Law in the Bible and the Ancient Near East*, JSOTSup 262. Edited by Victor H. Matthews, Tikva Frymer-Kenski, and Bernard M. Levinson. Sheffield, UK: Sheffield Academic, 1998.

Scholz, Susanne, editor. *The Oxford Handbook of Feminist Approaches to the Hebrew Bible*. New York: Oxford University Press, 2021.

Stol, Marten. *Women in the Ancient Near East*. Berlin: De Gruyter, 2016.

Thompson, Steven. "Was Ancient Rome a Dead Wives Society? What Did the Roman Paterfamilias Get Away With?" *Journal of Family History* 31 (2006): 3–27.

56

Are There Polemics (Even) in the Hebrew Bible?

Diana V. Edelman

The Old Testament / Hebrew Bible is not as homogenous as many might assume, given its nature as religious literature. In fact, it is a hotbed of competing views on various contested issues, or, in other words, polemics. Today we might expect the predominant view on an issue to prevail as though it were a consensus and the minority view(s) to be erased or silenced in the literature of an authoritative majority. However, it seems the biblical writers were sensitive to the complexity of reality and the possibility that the dominant view could shift over time and were willing to express that complexity and shifting hierarchal status by including a range of viewpoints. In addition, those writing and reading the books that currently comprise the Old Testament / Hebrew Bible primarily would have been a small group of educated scribes who considered each other peers, so professional respect might have led to the acknowledgment of differing views held within the group instead of a hierarchical approach in which those in charge censured differing views.

Some polemics are easy to spot, like the purpose of the story of the wandering of the ark of Yhwh among the Philistines in 1 Samuel 5:1–6:12: Yhwh is the God of Israel and is superior to other gods—in this case, those of the Philistines. The subject is mentioned explicitly, as is the stance taken. This is an explicit or open polemic. Some polemics, however, are implicit, where the subject will be explicit, but the stance taken will only be expressed by indirect means. An example is the binding of Isaac in Genesis 22, which explicitly deals with child sacrifice (22:2), but whose stance depends on the recognition as the story develops that the divine command to Abraham to sacrifice Isaac is a test and that the appearance of the ram in the thicket means that animals from the flock or the herd are to be acceptable sacrificial offerings, not humans.

Other polemics are hidden, which usually means they deal with a particularly sensitive topic or, in some cases, perhaps, that the biblical writer held a minority view he was not willing to voice openly but would allude to in other ways. His stance is made clear, however. Four criteria have been highlighted for identifying the presence of a hidden polemic: (1) the subject is not mentioned explicitly; (2) other biblical materials confirm the existence of the controversial nature of the implied topic; (3) the writer has embedded sufficient signs in the narrative that point the reader to the polemical subject that it will be uncovered, even though it has not explicitly been announced; and (4) the exegetical tradition of the text in question has previously noted the likely presence of the hidden polemical subject. The third criterion carries the primary burden of proof; the second and fourth serve as controls to show that such a controversy was topical among the biblical writers and that a proposed polemic is not the result of an idiosyncratic scholarly imagination. The first is a working assumption. Hidden polemics rely on indirect means of persuasion that avoid the initial resistance by a reader who would hold an opposing viewpoint and so not knowingly listen to competing views. It also can be a means of avoiding outright "censorship" as a minority view by going underground.

An example of a hidden polemic can be found in the narrative in Judges 17–18 about Micah's shrine, the Danites' stealing of its cultic statues and Levitical priest, and their founding of the cultic center in the town of Dan using this priest and the images. It appears alongside both direct and indirect polemics. The hidden polemic in this story is about the cultic status of Bethel, which is not mentioned directly in the text (criterion 1). Bethel is viewed both positively (e.g., Genesis 12:8; 28:10–22; 31:13; 35:1–6; Hosea 12:5) and negatively (e.g., Hosea 4:15; 5:8; 10:5; Amos 3:14; 4:4; 5:5; Jeremiah 48:9; 1 Kings 10:29; 12:28–33; 13; 2 Kings 23:4, 15, 19) in various biblical texts (criterion 2).

A series of six signs allude to Bethel as the topic of a polemic. The first is the unusual use of the regional name, the hill country of Ephraim, rather than an actual place name to mark the location of Micah's shrine (17:1, 8; 18:2, 13), in contrast to the giving of such information for the origin of the Levite from Bethlehem in Judah (17:7, 8, 9) and the dwelling place of the Danites at Mahane-Dan near Kiriath-Jearim (18:12) before they migrate north, passing Micah's "house" or "shrine," to Laish, which they conquer and rename Dan. The second sign is the use of the synonymous regional name Mount Ephraim. Both the hill country of Ephraim and Mount Ephraim occur in this story about the Danites as well as in Jeremiah 4:15, where Dan is referred to as a wicked city. The geographical terms are meant to evoke in the minds of readers the other infamous "wicked city" located in Mount Ephraim: Bethel (Hosea 4:15; 5:8; 10:5, 8; Amos 5:5).

Third, the phrase in Judges 17:5 "house of God / God's house," without the use of the definite article ("*the* house of God"), only appears two other times in biblical narratives. Both are in the story in Genesis 28:17, 22 about Jacob's theophany at Bethel, the site of a future "house of God." This results in the creation of a sense in the narrative that arriving at Micah's "house" was the same as arriving at "God's house" in Bethel.

Fourth, Bethel and Dan are closely linked by having been established as the sites of royal temples containing statues of golden calves made by King Jeroboam I in 1 Kings 12:26–33 and are again mentioned together in 2 Kings 10:29. Related to that, fifthly, Micah's "molten"—or more likely, foil-wrapped—image over a carved wooden core (*pesel umasseka*), when viewed in combination with the other references to either a *pesel* or being "foil-wrapped" (*masseka*; Judges 18:17, 18, 20, 30, 31), recalls more specifically calf images made to represent Yhwh. The first is the *'egel masseka*, "foil-wrapped calf," the Israelites and Aaron make in Exodus 32:4, 8 while Moses is on Mount Sinai for forty days (other references to this incident are found in Psalm 106:19 and Hosea 13:2). The second consists of the two foil-wrapped calves King Jeroboam I makes and places in cultic centers at Dan and Bethel in 2 Kings 17:16.

As the sixth and final sign, there is an ideological and linguistic connection between the description of Micah's appointment of priests who are not from the tribe of Levi, which they should be as God's chosen hereditary intermediaries (e.g., Deuteronomy 10:8–9; 21:5), and the priests King Jeroboam I appointed to serve in Dan and Bethel (1 Kings 13:33). In both cases, the priests were appointed at the will of the individual without ensuring a Levitical pedigree, and the act of their placing in service is described by the idiom *lemala' yad*, "to fill the hand" (Judges 17:12; 1 Kings 13:33), meeting criterion 3.

Within Jewish midrashic tradition, Micah was specifically connected to Bethel in Mount Ephraim. In modern biblical scholarship, the same has been done by various commentators in spite of the lack of an explicit reference to the location. Thus, criterion 4 also is fulfilled.

This hidden polemic allowed the ongoing cult at Bethel to be condemned indirectly by someone who felt that only Jerusalem was a legitimate cult center. Eventually, the Samaritan temple on Mount Gerizim was identified as Bethel, so it could become the new object of indirect attack via this hidden polemic.

Judges 17–18 also takes an explicit stance on the subject of monarchy as a form of positive polemic while conveying a negative polemic indirectly or implicitly against the two cultic centers that Micah and the Danites set up for themselves, which contain illicit cultic objects and a priest with a Levitical pedigree who has no problem with the objectionable items. It is very clear that a situation where there is no centralized, stable leadership in the form of a king is problematic, as exemplified by the actions of Micah, the Levite, and the tribe of Dan when "there was no king in Israel." Micah's shrine is explicitly condemned (17:6); his appointment of the Levite in place of his son as a priest in his shrine, where the foil-covered idol and family gods continue in use, is partially condemned (18:1). Dan's conquest of Laish and the transfer of Micah's priest and the cultic images is implicitly condemned through plot and character development; there is anarchy throughout, and all the characters in both chapters are negative.

A fourth type is the seemingly hidden polemic, which shares with the hidden polemic the failure to mention the topic, but the verb expresses a clear stance on it using direct or indirect means. It provides such a clear-cut sign or signs, however, that the reader cannot miss the implied subject and does not have to search for textual hints that will lead to it. The Joseph story in Genesis 37–50 contains such a seemingly hidden polemic on exile and views it as something not to be feared. Even if it is traumatic and prolonged, one can live a good life in a new location while preserving their national identity and the hope of a return to the homeland. Joseph and his brothers experience provisional exile in Egypt, prosper while there, but maintain a desire to return to Canaan, which they do eventually.

Another example of a seemingly hidden polemic, this time against the worship of the goddess Asherah, is found in the book of Genesis in the stories of the barren matriarchs, Sarah (15:2–4; 16:1–2; 17:16–21; 18:10–15; 21:1–6), Rebekah (25:21), and Rachel (29:31; 30:1–3, 22–24). There is a very strong emphasis on how Yhwh and Yhwh alone can open and close human wombs in each case, providing or withholding children. Asherah is never mentioned by name in any example; nevertheless, she is the implicit, unspoken target of this explicit, repetitive emphasis. In monarchic-era Yahwism, Yhwh's wife, Asherah, would have been in charge of human fertility. Secondarily, the divinized family ancestors and household god(s), who would have functioned as intercessors between the individual and Asherah, are also being rejected. While the stories of all three matriarchs use the folktale motif of a future prominent person being born to a once barren woman, they also clearly advocate an emergent view in which the pantheon has collapsed and Yhwh, the only god in Israel, takes over all the roles formerly associated with his wife and lesser deities and divine entities. One might prefer to characterize this example as a polemical theme or motif, since it recurs across a number of narratives.

About the Author

Diana V. Edelman holds a doctorate of philosophy (PhD) in biblical studies from the University of Chicago and is Professor Emerita in Hebrew Bible at the Faculty of Theology, University of Oslo. She has published "Hidden Ancestor Polemics in the Book of Genesis?," pages 35–56 in *Words, Ideas, World: Biblical Essays in Honour of Yairah Amit*, edited by Athalya Brenner and Frank H. Polak (Sheffield, UK: Sheffield Phoenix, 2012); and "Adapting Social Memory to Mold New Attitudes in the Present and Future: Examples from the Books of Deuteronomy, Judges, and Kings," pages 49–84 in *Collective Memory and Collective Identity: Deuteronomy and the Deuteronomistic History in Their Context*, edited by Johnnes U. Ro and Diana V. Edelman (Berlin: De Gruyter, 2021).

Suggestions for Further Reading

In This Book
See also chapters 24 (Kings and Chronicles), 37 (rabbinic interpretation), 44 (ancestors), 47 (monotheism), 50 (magic), 51 (prophets), and 62 (Joseph).

Elsewhere
Amit, Yairah. *Hidden Polemics in Biblical Narrative*. Boston: Brill, 2000.

Amit, Yairah. "The Joseph Story: Between a Family and a Polemical Story." Pages 69–92 in *The Hunt for Ancient Israel: Essays in Honour of Diana V. Edelman*. Edited by Cynthia Shafer-Elliott, Kristin Joachimsen, Ehud Ben Zvi, and Pauline A. Viviano. Sheffield, UK: Equinox, 2022.

57
Is the Hebrew Bible "Pro-Choice" or "Pro-Life"?

Athalya Brenner-Idan

That women should have control over their sex life and, especially, fertility seems obvious. That women have always cared about that control cannot be disputed. That they were always looking for ways to enhance fertility as well as to curb it, as the situation may be, is also logical. Women could always have control in this regard. However, it cannot be disputed that religion and religious texts have always diminished women's agency and judgment in such matters. And the Hebrew Bible is no exception. And yet, the basic women's right for self-regulated fertility—not to mention independent sexual activity—is still questioned and limited, as men still control women and limit them, ostensibly in the name of religion and, in Judaism and Christianity specifically, in the name of the Bible.

Fertility, the command to "be fruitful and multiply" (Genesis 1:28), is the first command given to the first human couple created as male and female. We assume here that they are married, man and wife, since Adam and Eve have sex and multiply after the garden (Genesis 4). Indeed, fertility seems to be paramount. On the other hand, recreational, consensual hetero-sex is not frowned upon for males and females, unless the female is "owned" by a husband or father or another male family member and her virginity is at stake (see the love lyrics of the Song of Songs). But recreational sex may have a price for the female: an unwanted pregnancy may require either contraception before or an abortion after. Thus, there is a permanent tension between the divine commandment, undoubtedly a reflection of social needs and ideologies, and life's reality.

There are scant references to female contraception and abortions in the biblical texts, so we have to tease out that information. On the one hand, we find no knowledge of abortions but perhaps of miscarriages (the *sôṭâh* ritual in Numbers 5) or a damaged fetus (Exodus 20:22). On the other hand, we find much fertility propaganda concerning women, who are often presented as infertile and always wishing for sons (Sarah in Genesis 11:30; 16:1–2; 17:17, 19, 21; 18:11–14, Rebecca in Genesis 25:21, Rachel in Genesis 29:31; 30:1–2, 22, Samson's mother in Judges 13:2–24, and Hannah in 1 Samuel 1:1–11). No male is presented as infertile or sterile; women are. Midwives are always female (Shiphrah and Puah in Exodus 1). Females know nothing about birth prevention, but males do (Onan in Genesis 38). Song of Songs 4:12–15 displays a list of aromatics and perfumes used as aphrodisiacs and possibly contraceptives, and postbiblical literature (*Bereshit Rabbah* 23:2 for Genesis 4:23) mentions a drink of oral contraception Lamech prepares ahead for his two wives. Ultimately, the Hebrew god is the giver and carer of successful female pregnancy.

The point is that if humans had knowledge about fertility drugs like the mandrake root used by Rachel and Leah (Genesis 30:14–18), they also were likely to have known about inducing infertility. Anyone knowledgeable about birth probably knew how to prevent it, thus interfering with God's control over female fertility.

Now, fertility is one thing, but the emphasis on sons in the Hebrew Bible shows societal rather than biological motivation; the number of baby girls is far more crucial to a community's survival than the number of baby boys. Moreover, life expectancy for females was much lower than for males because of frequent pregnancies not always brought to fruition and maternal death during delivery (Genesis 35:18); hence, the need for propaganda for females to comply with the motherhood ideal.

And yet, it is clear from looking at other cultures in the southern Levant (Egypt, Mesopotamia, and Greece) and later rabbinic literature that both contraception—usually of vegetal or mechanical origin—and abortion, not to mention natural miscarriage, were well known in the ancient world, albeit presented as known mainly by male practitioners. This is certainly a distorted picture: male practitioners are presented as knowing all about the birth procedure (Ezekiel 16), while females are vilified as witches, apparently for similar life-giving work (Ezekiel 13). According to the Hebrew Bible, women had no access to self-help and medicinal plants, the two sides of the ob-gyn coin, but traces of their former existence and practice or use have been given above.

Centuries of biblical exegesis and interpretation have complied with biblical propaganda by idealizing the figure of the mother. Many feminist critics of the Hebrew Bible have acquiesced and even appropriated this idealized picture of the biblical desire for motherhood as their own—after all, the ability to conceive and give birth is uniquely female/feminine.

Let us point out the facts, easily obscured by pro-motherhood propaganda: (1) so-called pro-life policies might have meant early death for its ancient female adherents and (2) female birth control, although almost completely "overlooked" or treated as nonexistent by the male writers of the books of the Hebrew Bible, perhaps in the interest of group survival, must have been practiced in ancient Israel, as it was in several other ancient cultures of the southern Levant. It defies logic to think that contraception and other antifertility measures were known and practiced all around ancient Israel and in early Judaism but were totally unknown in ancient Israel itself. The knowledge, part of which was certainly women's knowledge, was available but never explicitly disclosed in the biblical literature.

An accidental omission of such data from the Bible is possible but not plausible in the light of biblical procreation ideologies. Contraception and antifertility are generally discussed not for their own sake but as incidental to other superordinate concerns. Finally, the association of antifertility as well as fertility-advancing knowledge with women might have contributed to its neglect (at best) or suppression (at worst). It could have been expected that if biblical writers/compilers knew about female contraception but objected to it in principle, they would have prohibited it explicitly by formulating laws against it.

In other words, are we here faced with authorly ignorance, disinterest, indifference, or suppression? Ignorance can be ruled out. So can disinterest and indifference, as evidenced by procreation ideologies. It is perhaps relevant to emphasize once more that most of the biblical materials were authored, compiled, preserved, transmitted, and later studied by males and for males, the true members of the community construct. Female voices were largely edited out or muted—only traces of those can be laboriously and uncertainly reconstructed. If birth control was felt, as it was in other cultures in general, including later Judaic sources, to fall primarily within the province of women's interest and praxis, then the silence about it fits with other silences concerning women's lives. At any rate, only traces of birth control practices can be found. It remained for postbiblical Judaic sources, highly preoccupied with women's fertility while no less preoccupied with procreation than biblical literature—and perhaps even more so— to acknowledge female (and male) contraceptive measures incidentally when discussing other concerns.

Men tend to deny women the right to regulate their productivity, anchoring that denial in the sacred. The women who suffer most are the devout and the poor; they are firmly placed in an inferior, even deadly, personal place.

Finally, let us state the obvious once more. Medical research and knowledge are gendered and have always been so, from the viewpoints of the researchers, of the practitioners, and of the ones helped or left by the wayside. Knowledge is power; the withholding of knowledge, as well as the withholding of available practice, is a matter of social dominance or strife. It is not by chance that birth control is medically available to women but then socially denied to them because of religious claims. It is not by chance that birth control for males lags behind. This is a social, not a divine matter. Ultimately, the Hebrew Bible knows about contraception but pretends not to. "Pro-choice" seems not to exist as an option or concept. "Pro-life" is not an issue; fertility problems are. A lesson to us all? Go somewhere else for your "pro" ideology, whatever it is.

About the Author

Athalya Brenner-Idan holds a doctorate of philosophy (PhD) from the University of Manchester and an honorary PhD from the University of Bonn. She is the chief editor of A Feminist Companion to the Hebrew Bible series (20 volumes, 1993–2015) and Texts@Contexts (8 volumes, 2011–2024). She has published widely on feminist readings, including "Aromatics and Perfumes in the Song of Songs," *Journal for the Study of the Old Testament* 25 (1983): 75–81; *The Intercourse of Knowledge: On Gendering Desire and "Sexuality" in the Hebrew Bible* (Leiden: Brill 2016); and "Women Regulate Their Fertility: Proactive and Reactive Aspects," pages 165–176 in *The Woman in the Pith Helmet: A Tribute to Archaeologist Norma Franklin*, edited by Jennie Ebeling and Philippe Guillaume (Atlanta: Lockwood, 2020).

Suggestions for Further Reading

In This Book
See also chapters 3 (religious in a scientific world), 20 (genealogies), 50 (magic), 53 (creation), 55 (patriarchalism), 56 (polemics), and 81 (gender studies).

Elsewhere
Meyers, Carol. *Exodus: New Cambridge Bible Commentary*. Cambridge: Cambridge University Press, 2005.

Riddle, John M. *Eve's Herbs: A History of Contraception and Abortion in the West*. Cambridge, MA: Harvard University Press, 1999.

Rosen-Zvi, Ishay. *The Mishnaic Sotah Ritual: Temple, Gender and Midrash*. Leiden: Brill, 2012.

Teubal, Savina J. *Hagar the Egyptian: The Lost Tradition of the Matriarchs*. San Francisco: HarperSanFrancisco, 1990.

Teubal, Savina J. *Sarah the Priestess: The First Matriarch of Genesis*. Athens, OH: Swallow, 1984.

58
How Does the Hebrew Bible Deal with Ecological Issues?

Jonathan K. Kavusa

In May 1966, Iranian Islamic scholar Seyyed Hossein Nasr presented a series of lectures at the University of Chicago focusing on the spiritual dimensions of the environmental crisis. On December 26 of the same year, medieval historian Lynn Townsend White Jr. (1967) gave a lecture entitled "The Historical Roots of Our Ecologic Crisis" at the American Association for the Advancement of Science. It was published a year later in *Science*.

These lectures reflected the growing awareness that, as White (1967, 1204) noted, "no creature other than man has ever managed to foul its nest in such short order." The impact of the modern Industrial Revolution has been so devastating on the natural environment that the word "ecology," which first appeared in the English language in 1873, changed in meaning. It went from the study of the relationships of living organisms to their physical environment to the denunciation of the degradation of the planet's ecosystems and the struggle in favor of environmental politics and natural resources management.

Both scholars noted that the root of the present ecological crisis lies in the way Western Christians have read the Old Testament, in particular the first creation narrative in Genesis. Because Genesis 1:26–27 distinguishes between a humanity formed in God's image and the rest of creation and charges humanity with the task of dominating (Hebrew *kabash*) the animals, the entire physical world has been viewed as created to serve humankind's purposes. This has fed a trend of anthropocentrism that, over time, has eroded the primary view of nature as a symbolic system through which God speaks to humans—that is, the ant is a sermon to sluggards (Proverbs 6:6–9). By the late eighteenth century, God had become irrelevant to scientific research. Though many Christians would be flattered to realize that "modern Western science was cast in a matrix of Christian theology," White (1967, 1206) has concluded that "Christianity bears a huge burden of guilt" now that science and technology have joined forces "to give mankind powers which, to judge by many of the ecologic effects, are out of control."

The critiques by Nasr and White are particularly relevant for Old Testament theologians, who tend to read the biblical creation accounts in the framework of the history of salvation, which establishes a dualism between humanity and nature. As a result, many insist it is God's will that human beings exploit nature for their own ends, leading to a rejection of ecological readings of the Bible. Fundamentalist Christians also tend to reject ecological readings of the Bible but use a different line of scripturally based reasoning. They begin by citing the warnings about a forthcoming cosmic destruction that will occur on the day of God's judgment in Revelation 13. They then combine that with 1 John 2:15, where the love of the world and the love of God are opposed, to argue that any human effort to preserve the earth implies working against God's plans. Instead, the elect look forward to a new heaven and a new earth and hope to be rescued from a hostile earth.

Readers who are aware that meaning does not reside in a text but is created by an individual's life experiences in interaction with a text recognize that there inevitably will be different kinds of ecological readings of the Bible. One approach has tried to rescue the Bible from the charge of espousing an anthropocentric vision that legitimizes utilitarian attitudes toward the natural world. Its advocates argue that the unrestrained exploitation of creation is not an intrinsic feature of Genesis 1:26–28. Rather, it emerged secondarily when the text was read through the lens of nonbiblical Greek thoughts and gained currency in the context of the Renaissance philosophy of human strength and progress. They argue that Genesis, in fact, provides a model of stewardship rather than of dominion. The Green Bible series intentionally selects texts that can be interpreted to show how God intimately interacts with all of creation. Attention is paid to the way the elements of creation are interdependent, how nature responds to God, and the way humans are appointed to care for all of God's creation.

Esias E. Meyer (2011) notes, however, that the Old Testament has very little (if anything) to say on ecological and conservation matters. Indeed, biblical texts were written in a premodern society that could have known nothing about our present-day ecological crises. Any eagerness to justify the eco-friendliness of the Bible runs the risk of finding what we want or need to find in the Bible, though it is not really there (eisegesis).

To avoid a similar critique, a second approach championed by the Earth Bible series resists the biblical narratives in the hope to retrieve the voice of the earth that has been suppressed by anthropocentric bible readings. Genesis 1 shows that nature existed before humans; thus, human beings are not a necessary element for solving Earth's problems. The Earth Bible series has adopted a strategy of resistance toward biblical texts deemed ecologically gray because they devalue the earth and its members. The audience is encouraged to adopt a reading stance in which they do not reflect *about* Earth in the text but rather reflect *with and within* Earth, to see things from the perspective of Earth.

This geocentric approach gives prominence to the contemporary ecological crisis to condemn or justify readings on the basis of eco-justice principles that function as canonical ecological lenses. They include the following:

Earth and all its components have intrinsic worth/value.

Earth is a community of interconnected living things that are mutually dependent on one another for life and survival.

Earth is a subject capable of raising its voice in celebration and against injustice.

Earth and all its components are part of a dynamic cosmic design within which each piece has a place in the overall goal of that design.

Earth is a balanced and diverse domain where responsible custodians can function as partners, not rulers, to sustain a balanced and diverse community.

Earth and its components not only suffer from injustices at the hands of humans but actively resist them in the struggle for justice.

To go beyond common greening strategies and contribute positively to ecological issues, however minimal that contribution may be, Hebrew Bible scholars should begin by setting the record straight. The anthropocentrism rightly identified by Nasr and White stems from Psalm 8:5–6 (verses 6–7 in Hebrew) more than from Genesis 1:26–27. The former verses celebrate man's (*'enosh*) near equality to the gods, the crowning of the son (masculine noun) of Adam with glory and honor, and the granting to him of dominion over the works of God's hands, putting them under his feet. Reading Genesis 1 in light of Psalm 8, the Alexandrian translators of the LXX chopped off an entire day from the week of creation to have Elohim complete creation in *six* days, even though the Hebrew text of Genesis 2:3 has it accomplished in *seven* days. With this sleight of hand, they shifted the crown of creation from the holy Sabbath to man and woman.

Yet, even in this truncated version of the original week, man and woman are created on the same day as land animals. This is a more promising avenue than the feeble attempts to downplay the violence of the verb "dominate" (*kabash*) in Genesis 1 and elsewhere. Genesis was produced in a natural environment in which human settlements were surrounded by large expenses of "wild-erness" teeming with predators large and small that threatened humans, their livestock, and their crops. The Hebrew text of Genesis is akin to the graphic Neo-Assyrian representations of lion hunts meant to demonstrate the faithfulness of the king in accomplishing his divine commission as protector of the realm and bulwark against an ever-threatening chaos. In such ecological conditions, the sustainability of human life was linked to the number of lionlike enemies the king managed to slaughter.

The present ecological crisis, whose gravity should in no way be minimized, is less the consequence of the divine order to subdue creation than our remarkable obedience to the first God-given commands recorded in the Hebrew Bible: "multiply, fill the land, subdue it, and dominate the animals" (Gen 1:28). The unprecedented size of the human population today has turned sustainability requirements upside down. Our survival now depends on the protection of natural biotopes and of near extinct species, lions and myriad others. Whatever the actual contribution of the Bible to population growth, an exponential demographic explosion has occurred due to the destruction of primeval environments, their transformation into agricultural land, and the extinction of large numbers of wild species.

The relevance of the first creation account in Genesis relies on several features: gender equality, our intrinsic equality with nonhuman animals, and the fundamental goodness of creation. Gender equality means that women are not unfinished males. Since humankind was created male and female at the same time (against Genesis 2), females are equal mirrors of divinity.

Our intrinsic equality with nonhuman animals resonates with anti-speciesism. Humanity is one segment of the animal world, and the animality of humankind is to be celebrated and practiced. Does this imply that animals should not be killed and eaten? Any regular supply of healthy food depends on the effective control of pests that cause damage. To do so, ecological agriculture replaces chemical means with mechanical solutions as much as possible. The reduction of meat consumption in the affluent West has begun, but the effects of veganism on the health of its practitioners and on the environment are not all positive. Humankind was created as an omnivorous species, like, for instance, the despised pig and dog. The food chain is a hard fact. Life means eating before being eaten. There is no escape from our humanity and animality.

Finally, the fundamental goodness of creation is an antidote to eco-anxiety. Despite our resistance to change and counterecological disasters, the complexity and resilience of ecosystems are far beyond our most advanced scientific understanding. However much we have managed to foul our nest, the first creation account of Genesis is a radical move away from the anthropocentrism denounced by Nasr and White. Simply put, creation does not depend on humankind to function. If the next great extinction involves the extinction of humankind alongside many other species, creation will survive us. The sun will continue to rise and set, and the moon will continue to wax and wane, whether we are there to marvel at their cycles or not (Genesis 8:22). The contribution of biblical scholarship to the great challenge ecological crises pose today is small, but it is not insignificant.

About the Author

Jonathan K. Kavusa holds a PhD from the University of South Africa. He currently serves as an associate researcher with the University of Pretoria and also is the president and legal representative of the Baptist Church in Central Africa (www.cbca-kanisa.org). His publications include "Ecological Hermeneutics and the Interpretation of Biblical Texts Yesterday, Today and Onwards: Critical Reflection and Assessment," *Old Testament Essays* 32 (2019): 229–255, https://ote-journal.otwsa-otssa.org.za/index.php/journal/article/view/272; *Water and Water-Related Phenomena in the Old Testament Wisdom Literature: An Eco-theological Investigation* (London: Bloomsbury, 2020); and "Creation as a Cosmic Temple: Reading Genesis 1:1–2:4a in Light of Willie van Heerden's Ecological Insights," *Journal for Semitics* 30 (2021): 1–23, https://doi.org/10.25159/2663-6573/8761.

Suggestions for Further Reading

In This Book

See also chapters 1 (scholarly perspective), 3 (religious in a scientific world), 6 (biblical exegesis), 9 (audiences), 33 (Septuagint), 36 (Old Testament theology), 77 (literary and form criticism), 81 (gender studies), and 82 (postcolonial studies).

Elsewhere

Bauckham, Richard J. *Living with Other Creatures: Green Exegesis and Theology*. Waco: Baylor University Press, 2011.

Habel, Norman C. *The Birth, the Curse and the Greening of Earth: An Ecological Reading of Genesis 1–11*. Sheffield, UK: Sheffield Phoenix, 2011.

Horrell, David G. *The Bible and the Environment: Towards a Critical Ecological Biblical Theology*. London: Equinox, 2010.

LeVasseur, Todd, and Anna Peterson. "Religion and the Ecological Crisis: The 'Lynn White Thesis' at Fifty." *Journal for the Study of Religion Nature and Culture* 13 (2019): 101–107.

Meyer, Esias E. "Respect for Animal Life in the Book of Leviticus: How Green Were the Priestly Authors?" *Old Testament Essays* 24 (2011): 142–158.

Simkins, Ronald A. "Attitudes to Nature in the Hebrew Bible and the Ancient Near East." Pages 269–283 in *The Oxford Handbook of the Bible and Ecology*. Edited by Hilary Marlow and Mark Harris. Oxford: Oxford University Press, 2022.

Van Dyk, Peet J. "Eco-theology: In and Out of the Wilderness." *Old Testament Essays* 30 (2017): 835–851.

White, Lynn Townsend, Jr. "The Historical Roots of Our Ecologic Crisis." *Science* 155 (1967): 1203–1207.

59
Does (or How Does) the Old Testament Deal with LGBTQIA Issues?

Rhiannon Graybill

Contemporary debates over LGBTQIA issues are peppered with appeals to the Bible—often to justify repressive, homophobic, or transphobic ideas and policies, but sometimes in defense of LGBTQIA rights. Both sides seem to believe that the Hebrew Bible is on their side. But what about the texts themselves?

Discussions of LGBTQIA identities and the Bible have traditionally focused on homosexuality. Here, a handful of passages known colloquially as the "clobber texts" (because they are used to "clobber" LGBTQIA people) attract significant attention. Just three of the seven clobber texts are found in the Hebrew Bible: Genesis 19, Leviticus 18:22, and Leviticus 20:13. The remaining texts (Romans 1:24–27, 1 Corinthians 6:9–10, 1 Timothy 1:9–10, Jude 7) occur in the New Testament. Genesis 19 is the story of Sodom and Gomorrah. In it, God sends messengers to visit the city of Sodom, which has already been judged as wicked. Abraham's nephew Lot welcomes the messengers into his home; however, the "men of the city, a deprived lot" quickly pound on the doors and demand to "know" (i.e., have sexual intercourse with) the visitors. Lot protests and offers his virgin daughters instead; they are, however, spared. The messengers assist Lot, his wife, and his daughters in fleeing; shortly after, the cities are destroyed by fire and brimstone. Lot's wife looks back and is transformed into a pillar of salt.

This story is often interpreted as a divine judgment on homosexuality: the men of Sodom are assumed to be homosexual (as shown by their desire for homosexual intercourse with the male messengers) and the city's destruction is a judgment on homosexuality. Another common interpretation suggests that the "sin of Sodom" was not homosexuality but rather bad hospitality: the Sodomites do not treat strangers appropriately. This reading gains some support from an appeal to Judges 19, the account of the Levite's concubine, which offers a similar story of bad hospitality, but this time paired with heterosexual rape. Still other interpreters have suggested the problem in Sodom was rape or threatened rape (in general) rather than homosexual rape (in particular). And while scattered references to Sodom and Gomorrah occur elsewhere in the biblical texts, mostly in the Prophets, the cities appear simply as symbols of desolation and divine judgment without further clarity about what is being judged. In short, while "Sodom" and "sodomy" are often used against contemporary LGBTQIA people, it is not at all clear that this is the focus of the original story at all.

The other two passages seemingly addressing homosexuality are legal texts. The typical translation of Leviticus 18:22 reads, "You shall not lie with a male as with a woman; it is an abomination," while Leviticus 20:13 offers a slight variation: "If a man lies with a male as with a woman, both of them have committed an abomination; they shall be put to death; their blood is upon them." Both of these laws are frequently interpreted to prohibit male-male anal intercourse; sometimes this is assumed to imply a broader condemnation of homosexuality, though, as noted above, the biblical text is focused on specific acts rather than identity. "Sexual orientation" is itself a contemporary invention. On closer examination, however, the text becomes less clear: more literally, each verse prohibits a male from "lying with a male the beds of a woman." What "the beds of a woman" refers to, or what it would mean to perform this act with a man, is not necessarily straightforward.

There are no biblical laws prohibiting sex between women; neither are there any explicit references to lesbians. This may reflect the texts' general lack of interest in women beyond their relationships with or utility to men; nevertheless, from an antihomophobic perspective, it is heartening. The Bible also includes positive representations of intimacy and love between women, most notably Ruth and Naomi. Indeed, the pair has a lengthy history of lesbian interpretation. Ruth is also sometimes lifted up as a biblical example of bisexuality, given her relationships with both Naomi and Boaz.

Another candidate for biblical bisexuality is David, who has close relationships with both women (Michal, Bathsheba, Abigail, etc.) and men (Saul, Jonathan). David's bond with Jonathan—which he himself describes as "surpassing the love of women" (2 Samuel 1:26)—is also sometimes interpreted as romantic and/or sexual. David's intimacies with men are never criticized by the text, and he can be read as a positive example of homoeroticism, homosexuality, or bisexuality.

The Hebrew Bible has even less to say about gender identities (transgender, cisgender, nonbinary) than it does about homosexuality. This is not really surprising: gender identity is itself a contemporary category, at least in the way we generally understand it. Still, there are a few passages worth considering. One verse that is sometimes identified as a transgender "clobber text" or "text of terror" is Deuteronomy 22:5, which reads, "A woman shall not wear a man's apparel, nor shall a man put on a woman's garment; for whoever does such things is abhorrent to the Lord your God." While this passage is focused on attire rather than identity, it is sometimes used to suggest that the Bible condemns transgender identities. Other anti-trans interpreters have suggested that the statement in Genesis 1:27 that "male and female he created them" indicates that gender and sex are identical (that is, gender identity must match the sex assigned at birth) and that to assume otherwise is to go against God's will. This represents the repackaging of an older homophobic argument in a new transphobic guise.

Not all readings concerned with transgender issues are transphobic, however. Biblical interpreters have also raised the possibility of reading various biblical characters as transgender. Jael (Judges 4 and 5) is an especially frequent example because her gender performance is nonnormative in multiple ways. Also, perhaps tellingly, Sisera refers to Jael using a second-person masculine form in Judges 4:20, which also destabilizes Jael's gender. Jezebel has also been interpreted as a trans character, in part because of her highly staged performance of her gender before her death at Jehu's hands.

Nonbinary identities are an increasingly visible part of our contemporary landscape of gender identities. In the Hebrew Bible, this is not really the case, although Jael in particular has been offered as an example of a biblical nonbinary subject. Of course, "binary" gender identity is also foreign to the Hebrew Bible: this is a modern way of categorizing identities and bodies and asserting a relationship between sex and gender.

"Queer," once a slur, has been embraced as an identity. Queer is generally understood to be more a flexible and capacious term than "lesbian," "gay," or "bisexual." It generally describes sexual orientation but can sometimes extend to gender identity as well (as with "genderqueer"). Queer celebrates same-sex eroticism but is not limited to it; nonnormative heterosexual sex (such as kink, BDSM, or sometimes sex work) is often described as queer as well. In its broadest sense, queer names an adversarial relationship to norms, sexual and otherwise. It is also important to remember that this definition has been critiqued for being too broad and evacuated of specificity.

While interpreters sometimes describe specific biblical characters as queer, this approach runs the risk of assuming that sexualities are stable, transhistorical, and accurately represented by texts—all assumptions that many queer interpreters resist. It is more common for queer biblical interpretation to turn to the tools offered by the academic discipline of queer theory.

Queer interpretations often seek to "queer" the text through playful and imaginative readings. A queer reading might find queer ways of reading the creation story, the bodies of prophets, or even the character of God. Contemporary LGBTQIA readers often find queer readings exciting in their rejection of timidity and refusal to repeat the same old homophobic readings. Some readers, however, find queer readings too speculative, too self-interested, or simply not historical (critiques that also are levied against many contemporary approaches, including feminist, critical race, and postcolonial criticism).

The letter "I," for "intersex," sits a bit uneasily in the LGBTQIA acronym. Unlike the other letters, which refer primarily to identities, "intersex" describes bodies that "do not fit typical binary notions of male or female bodies," the definition from the UN High Commissioner for Human Rights. Sex as "male" or "female" is determined by a mix of chromosomes, gonads, and genitals; these do not always align or agree. Such bodies are intersex.

Intersex biblical interpretation remains quite limited. In part, this is because the Bible does not reflect our own contemporary scientific understandings of sexual difference. There are no explicit biblical characters who are positively identified as intersex, just as there are no laws that directly comment on intersex people or their bodies. Sometimes, Adam in Genesis 2 is interpreted as an androgyne (with both male and female characteristics) prior to the creation of the woman. This holds the possibility for an intersex interpretation. A major concern of many intersex activists is resisting medical intervention on the bodies of intersex children, which often seeks to "fix" ambiguous genitals or sex. Such surgeries can have serious physical and psychological consequences and are typically performed without the child's consent. From this perspective, the biblical laws preventing men with mutilated genitals from entering God's assembly (Deuteronomy 23:1) may be relevant. Other biblical laws about preserving bodily integrity may offer space for possible intersex textual engagement.

The final letter, "A," denotes "asexual" (often shortened to "ace"). Asexuality refers to a lack of sexual attraction; it is often understood as a sexual orientation. Asexuality is not the same as celibacy or abstaining from sex. Like intersex, the Bible has little to say about asexuality. It is possible that a character such as Boaz, who spends a long time unmarried and then marries Ruth, a woman with other significant attachments, is an example of biblical asexuality. However, this remains speculative.

About the Author

Rhiannon Graybill holds a PhD in Near Eastern studies from the University of California, Berkeley. Her research interests include feminist, queer, and literary approaches to biblical texts. She is the author of *Are We Not Men? Unstable Masculinity in the Hebrew Prophets* (Oxford: Oxford University Press, 2016); and coeditor with Lynn R. Huber of *The Bible, Gender, and Sexuality: Critical Readings* (London: T&T Clark, 2020) and the *Ruth* volume in the new series Themes and Issues in Biblical Studies (Sheffield, UK: Equinox, forthcoming).

Suggestions for Further Reading

In This Book
See also chapters 36 (Old Testament theology), 49 (Torah), 55 (patriarchalism), 64 (Ruth), 65 (King David), 81 (gender studies), and 83 (reception criticism).

Elsewhere
Goss, Robert E., and Mona West, editors. *The Queer Bible Commentary* (2nd edition). London: SCM Press, 2022.

Goss, Robert E., and Mona West. *Take Back the Word: A Queer Reading of the Bible*. Cleveland: Pilgrim Press, 2000.

Graybill, Rhiannon, and Lynn R. Huber. "Introduction." Pages 1–13 in *The Bible, Gender, and Sexuality: Critical Readings*. Edited by Rhiannon Graybill and Lynn R. Huber. London: T&T Clark, 2020.

Hornsby, Teresa J., and Deryn Guest. *Transgender, Intersex, and Biblical Interpretation*. Semeia Studies. Atlanta: SBL, 2016.

Selected Biblical Figures

60

Is Abraham/Ibrahim an Ecumenical Figure?

Carol Bakhos

Songs, stories, and tales about Abraham abound, but we know nothing of the real Abraham—who he was or where and when he might have lived. No mention of him is made in any of the hundreds of thousands of ancient Mesopotamian, Egyptian, and Syro-Palestinian documents in our possession. And yet, he is considered the first monotheist and a major figure in Judaism, Christianity, and Islam, where he plays different roles.

It is in Genesis 12 that we first meet Abraham. God summons Abraham to leave his family, his home, and his homeland, Ur of the Chaldeans, and journey to an unknown destination that God will show him. Thus, at the age of seventy-five, Abraham (then still called Abram); along with his wife, Sarai, who becomes Sarah in chapter 17; and his nephew Lot leave all that is familiar and venture into the unknown. While Abraham is sojourning in Canaan, God appears to him and informs him that his seed is to inherit the land of Canaan. This inheritance is reiterated in later chapters and is what is often referred to as the Abrahamic covenant. The promise God makes to Abraham is of great significance, especially in Judaism and Christianity. For Jews and Christians, that promise is maintained through Abraham's son Isaac with Sarah, and not with Ishmael, his firstborn son with Hagar, Sarah's maidservant.

The Jews trace their theological, national, and genealogical lineage back to Abraham, whom God singled out among all the inhabitants of the world. Whether Jews identify religiously or ethnically, Abraham is considered the forebear of the Jewish people, of 'am Yisrael. His encounter with God, who makes a covenant with him and his descendants, sets the Jewish people apart from the nations of the world.

Even though God announces to Abraham that he will be a father of many nations (Genesis 17:4), the covenant that promises the inheritance of the land of Canaan to him and his seed is through his second son,

Isaac (Genesis 15:18; 17:4–8, 19–21); Ishmael is blessed separately and is to become the father of a great nation and twelve princes (17:20; 21:18), while the six sons he has after Sarah's death with Keturah (Genesis 25:1–2) become the forefathers of tribal nations east of Canaan, like Ishmael. The chosen status of Isaac and his descendants as heirs of the covenant is quite explicit: "And God said, 'Sarah your wife shall bear you a son, and you shall call his name Isaac, and I will establish my covenant with him for an everlasting covenant with his offspring to come'" (Genesis 17:19). While early Jewish literature—in fact, even rabbinic literature—acknowledges that Abraham is the father of a multitude of nations, the Jewish metanarrative emphasizes his role as the father of the Israelites and, by extension, the Jewish people.

Christianity highlights Abraham's role as both the father of the Israelites with whom God makes a covenant and the father of a multitude of peoples. It also envisions Abraham as a model of faith.

The story of Abraham and his family as narrated in the book of Genesis provides the basis for his depiction in the New Testament. Here, mention is made of Abraham, and in many instances, it is assumed that the reader is aware of aspects of his biography detailed elsewhere. The New Testament opens with the genealogy of "Jesus Christ, the son of David, the son of Abraham," one of seven mentions of Abraham in the Gospel of Matthew. The significance of linking Jesus and Abraham cannot be overstated. Jesus Christ, seen by Christians as the fulfillment of God's promise of salvation for humankind, is understood here as the fulfillment of the covenantal promise, the seed of Abraham through whom all nations will be blessed. That the first pages of the New Testament proclaim this ancestry is noteworthy in light of the relationship between the Old and New Testaments.

Paul's writing, especially the Epistle to the Romans, is central to the history of Christian thought. The Apostle Paul depicts Abraham as a model of faith, most famously in Romans 4. And how is Abraham a model of faith, according to Paul? What did Abraham believe? To begin with, Abraham believed in the God "who gives life to the dead and calls into existence the things that do not exist" (Romans 4:17). Furthermore, despite the promise of descendants at an advanced age, and despite Sarah's barrenness, Abraham did not falter in his faith (Romans 4:19). He was given credit for his faith. So, too, all those who believe in the God "who raised Jesus our Lord from the dead" (Romans 4:24) are considered righteous in the eyes of God.

The inclusion of Gentiles and Jews in God's salvific purposes is taken up again in Romans 9–11. Although Romans portrays Abraham as a man of faith whose descendants are believers, children of the promise, he is also the father of Jews. According to Paul, God has not abandoned unbelieving Jews: "As regards the gospel, they are enemies of God for your sake; but as regards election they are beloved, for the sake of their ancestors; for the gifts and the calling of God are irrevocable" (Romans 11:28–30). In other words, even though they oppose the gospel message, the election of the Jews is immutable.

In the book of Hebrews, Abraham serves as a paragon of persistent faithfulness but is also a type for the Levitical priests. Melchizedek, a type of Christ, is greater than Abraham and hence greater than the priesthood, for it is Abraham who pays the tithe to Melchizedek. James 2:20–24 also depicts Abraham in terms of modeling what it means to be a person of faith.

The Christian exegetical tradition takes up this image of Abraham as the man of faith but gradually jettisons his role as the forebear of the Jewish people. Some early authors like Marcion relinquished Abraham to the Jews, whereas others—among them Barnabas, Ignatius, and Clement of Alexandria—Christianized him. The use of Abraham in early Christian polemics against Jews takes on many forms, in genres ranging from letters and commentary to apology and treatise, and is given different expressions, but over time, the most persistent image of Abraham in the Christian tradition is that of a man obedient to God and in whose faith in God all believers partake and are blessed.

Abraham plays a major role in the theological history of Islam. Second only to Moses, he figures prominently in the Qur'an, with more than 245 verses referring to him throughout several chapters (suras). He is depicted as the model of virtue, obedient to God and a true monotheist, and is described as a "Friend of God" (*khalīl Allāh*), "upright" or "pure of faith" (*ḥanīf*), and "truthful" (*ṣiddīq*). According to the Qur'an, Abraham is neither a Jew nor a Christian but rather the paradigmatic monotheist, the quintessential Muslim.

The most prevalent Qur'anic image of Abraham, developed in early ancient Jewish literature, is that of the defiant son who ardently battles against his father's idolatry (see Genesis 11:27–30, where the name "Terah" evokes the Hebrew word *yeraḥ*, "moon") and the rampant idolatry of those around him (Qur'an 2:127–132). Abraham is vindicated against Nimrod (see Genesis 10:8–9), who is threatened by him and tries to kill him and thus defeat God, only to face his own demise. Abraham is the father of a line of prophets, and with his son Ishmael, he builds the Kaaba in Mecca.

Abraham is the believer in God par excellence, and because of his unflinching conviction, he incurs the wrath of his own people. Often told in the Qur'an and with great detail, the story depicts Abraham as the valiant defender of God. Here and elsewhere in the Qur'an, Abraham is the precursor of the prophet Muhammad, and like Moses, Abraham serves as a model for Muhammad, who confronts not only the unbelievers in Mecca but also the Jews and Christians who do not accept his revelation.

Muslims commemorate the near sacrifice of Ishmael on the great feast, Eid al-Adha, that marks the end of the hajj period. Both father and son are exemplars of complete submission to the will of God in the Qur'anic narrative.

Abraham is the father of the faithful in Islam; Muslims who follow the religion of Abraham and all his descendants in the Qur'an are righteous believers in the one true God. In Qur'an 2:124, God makes Abraham a leader of humankind. When Abraham inquires as to the fate of his descendants, God responds, "My covenant does not apply to the evil doers." Whereas in Judaism, biological descent from Abraham bestows membership, in Islam, one must follow the path set out by the prophets, and membership is available to all who do so, not just to Abraham's descendants.

As terse as the Bible is in rendering details of Abraham's early years, tales of his special birth, precociousness, recognition of the one true God, and fearless revolt against Nimrod gained popularity throughout the centuries and took on a variety of forms in Jewish, Christian, and Islamic sources. Many readers of the Bible are surprised to discover that the story of Abraham's rejection of idol worship is not biblical. Indeed, this popular portrayal of Abraham, prominent in the Qur'an, is found in sources such as Jubilees, the *Apocalypse of Abraham*, and the midrash *Genesis Rabbah*.

About the Author

Carol Bakhos holds a doctorate of rabbinics from the Jewish Theological Seminary. Her research interests include ancient Judaism, comparative scriptural interpretation, and the reception of the biblical tradition from past to present. She has published *The Family of Abraham: Jewish, Christian and Muslim Interpretations* (Cambridge, MA: Harvard University Press, 2014) and is the editor of *Emerging Judaism*, Posen Anthology of Jewish Civilization 2 (New Haven, CT: Yale University Press, forthcoming).

Suggestions for Further Reading

In This Book
See also chapters 20 (genealogies), 21 (dates), 37 (rabbinic interpretation), 44 (ancestors), 52 (covenant), 53 (creation), 55 (patriarchalism), 61 (Melchizedek), and 74 ("P").

Elsewhere

Firestone, Reuven. *Journeys in Holy Lands: The Evolution of the Abraham-Ishmael Legends in Islamic Exegesis.* Albany: State University of New York Press, 1990.

Kugel, James. *How to Read the Bible: A Guide to Scripture Then and Now.* New York: Free Press, 2007.

Levenson, Jon D. *Inheriting Abraham: The Legacy of the Patriarch in Judaism, Christianity, and Islam.* Princeton, NJ: Princeton University Press, 2012.

Lowin, Shari. *The Making of a Forefather: Abraham in Islamic and Jewish Exegetical Narratives.* Leiden: Brill, 2006.

61
Why Is Melchizedek So Mysterious?

Panagiotis L. Kampouris

In the Hebrew Bible, Melchizedek appears suddenly at the end of Genesis 14, only to reappear once in Psalm 110:4. The Dead Sea Scrolls are hardly more eloquent about this mysterious figure. By contrast, the New Testament dedicates a long development to Melchizedek. On the basis of the mention of an "order of Melchizedek" in Psalm 110, Hebrews 5:6–10; 6:20–7:17 contrasts this priestly order with the Old Testament priesthood of Aaron and Levi, presenting Jesus as a member of this eternal, high priestly order.

Genesis 14 is unique in its portrayal of Abram (whose name has not yet been changed to Abraham) as a warlord who intervenes in the rebellion of local kings against Chedorlaomer. Called for help by the kings of Sodom and Gomorrah, Abram leads three hundred of his own men to free his nephew Lot, who had migrated with him from Ur before falling captive to Chedorlaomer and his allies.

On his victorious return, Abram is met by the king of Sodom and by Melchizedek, king of Salem and priest of God the Most High (*ʾel ʿelyon*). Melchizedek "takes out bread and wine" and blesses Abram in the name of the God who created the heavens and the land and delivered Abram from his enemies (Genesis 14:18–20). In recognition of Melchizedek's special status, Abram "gives him a tenth of everything." Melchizedek disappears from the scene, and the chapter closes with some sort of haggling between Abram and the king of Sodom over the division of the spoil.

El-Elyon (Greek *theos hypsistos*) is a common divine name (Numbers 24:16; Deuteronomy 32:8; 2 Kings 22:14; Psalms 58:3; 77:35, 56; 96:9; Isaiah 14:13–14). As creator, it represented the highest entity in the Canaanite pantheon, whereas, according to the older text of Deuteronomy 32:8 preserved in the Greek versions, Yhwh was one of the younger gods. "Salem" is often equated with Jerusalem on the basis of Ur-Salim, "City of Salem," the

Akkadian name of the city in the Tell el-Amarna tablets (fourteenth century BCE). In Genesis 14, "Salem" is often taken as a reference to Jerusalem. If so, it is the sole reference to Jerusalem in the entire Pentateuch, albeit a veiled one.

The combination of priestly and royal status in the person of Melchizedek was common in the ancient Near East and is attested in Phoenician, Egyptian, Babylonian, and Arabic sources. More surprising is the single mention of Melchizedek's name in the Hebrew text, which can be read as "kings of righteousness" (*malkê-ṣedeq*) or "my king [is] righteousness" (*malkî ṣedeq*). It is through the Greek rendering that the form "Melchizedek" has become the standard designation in modern languages.

One of the many puzzles in this strange passage is the meaning of the bread and wine Melchizedek takes to Abram. Is it a ritual act, a gesture of hospitality, or part of an act of covenant making? The text is too terse to provide a firm answer. The same ambiguity pertains to the tithe Abram hands over to Melchizedek, if that is indeed what happens. The Hebrew text only states, "He gave him a tithe from all," leaving open who exactly gave what to whom. The traditional view is that Abram deducted the tithe from the booty and offered it to Melchizedek, either in return for peace between the two parties or as tribute.

The rest of the episode underlines Abram's generosity and his care not to enrich himself from the spoil taken during the campaign. The oath Abram swears before the king of Sodom combines Yhwh and El-Elyon into a single entity to indicate Yhwh's gradual appropriation of other divine names and functions. This in itself is enough to explain the episode of Abram's interference in the affairs of local kings, though it can function without any reference to Melchizedek. Therefore, verses 18–20 are often viewed together as an interpolation in chapter 14, because these verses are not essential to the flow of the story that continues smoothly from verse 17 to verse 21 without the interruption of Melchizedek. A version of Abram's victory without any mention of Melchizedek is found in the nonbiblical book of Jubilees (13:22–28).

Despite the brief appearance of Melchizedek in Genesis 14, he was not forgotten. Psalm 110 (109 in Greek and some English Bibles) introduces the notion of an eternal priesthood (*kohen le'olam*; Psalm 110:4) granted by Yhwh to his anointed one, whom he sits at his right hand (Psalm 110:1). Verse 4 also mentions some kind of "order" (Hebrew *dibrati*; Greek *taxis*) of Melchizedek. This order gave rise to the notion of the Messiah as an eternal figure combining high priestly and royal offices, which is consistent with Melchizedek's portrayal in Genesis 14.

The combination of priestly and royal functions is also mentioned in Jeremiah 40:14–22 and in Zechariah 3–6. First Maccabees (10:20; 14:41) indicates that it became a major political issue in the time of the Seleucid rule over the southern Levant (ca. 200–130 BCE). These times of political turmoil gave rise to a hope in the advent of a royal priesthood mentioned in the Testament of Levi. A fragmentary manuscript found in cave 11 at the Dead Sea site of Qumran names Melchizedek as the leader of God's angels to wage war against the angels of darkness (11Q13 or 11QMelch).

It is in the context of the fierce competition between Judaism and nascent Christianity that the royal priestly Melchizedek, an alternative to the high priestly line of Aaron, was recruited as a precursor to the Christian Messiah. To this end, Hebrews 7:3 interprets the lack of a genealogy for Melchizedek in Genesis 14 to mean that he is "without father, without mother, without genealogy, having neither beginning of days nor end of life," traditional attributes of the Egyptian creator god Ptah. Conversely, in rabbinic literature, Melchizedek is identified with Shem, one of Noah's three sons (Genesis Rabbah 46:7). 11QMelch identifies him with the Angel of Light or the archangel Michael, while in the "Rise of Melchizedek" (2 Enoch 69–73), he is the son of Nereus, Noah's brother.

In conclusion, the enigmatic Melchizedek is a significant example of the successful trajectory of a figure that, on the basis of a couple of verses, evolves into either a human figure (Pseudo-Eupolemus; Genesis Apocryphon; Philo of Alexandria in *Allegorical Interpretation* 3:79–82 and in *On the Life of Abraham* 235:4–5; Flavius Josephus in *Jewish War* 6 and in *Jewish Antiquities* 1:179–181; Jubilees), an Old Testament prophet (Ignatius, *To the Philadelphians* 4:4), or an angelic personality (4QShirShab[b]; 4QAmram[b]; 1QapGen).

About the Author

Panagiotis L. Kampouris holds a PhD in theology from the National and Kapodistrian University of Athens. His research interests include Old Testament, Jewish and Christian apocalypticism and mysticism, and the ancient Near East. He is the author of "The Priesthood of Melchizedek in Biblical and Extra-biblical Sources and Its Relevance to the Ancient Near Eastern Divine Kingship," *Studies in Theology of the School of Humanities, Hellenic Open University* 11 (2020): 123–144; "Heavenly Ascents in the Jewish Apocalyptic: The Examples of Enoch (1 Enoch 17–36; 2 Enoch 3–22) and Abraham (Testament of Abraham 10–15)," *Nea Sion* 95 (2018): 193–216; and "*Voces magicae*: The Importance of the Invocations of Divine Names in the Prayer of Jacob," *Studies in Theology of the School of Humanities, Hellenic Open University* 9 (2018): 197–217.

Suggestions for Further Reading

In This Book
See also chapters 11 (Pentateuch), 16 (Psalms), 34 (Dead Sea Scrolls), 37 (rabbinic interpretation), 44 (ancestors), 47 (monotheism), 52 (covenant), 60 (Abraham), and 73 (source criticism).

Elsewhere
Fitzmyer, A. Joseph. "Melchizedek in the MT, LXX, and the NT." *Biblica* 81 (2000): 63–69.

Florentino, García Martínez. "The Traditions about Melchizedek in the Dead Sea Scrolls." Translated by W. G. E. Watson. Pages 95–108 in *Qumranica Minora* (volume 2), STDJ 64. Edited by Eibert J. C. Tigchelaar. Leiden: Brill, 2007. Originally published as "Las tradiciones sobre Melquisedec en los manuscritos de Qumrán," *Biblica* 81 (2000): 70–80.

Granerød, Gard. *Abraham and Melchizedek: Scribal Activity of Second Temple Times in Genesis 14 and Psalm 110*. Berlin: De Gruyter, 2010.

McNamara, Martin. "Melchizedek: Gen 14, 17–20 in the Targums, in Rabbinic and Early Christian Literature." *Biblica* 81 (2000): 1–31.

Rooke, W. Deborah. "Jesus as Royal Priest: Reflections on the Interpretation of the Melchizedek Tradition in Heb 7." *Biblica* 81 (2000): 81–94.

62
Joseph: Does His Ability to Interpret Dreams Represent Actual Divinatory Practice?

Scott B. Noegel

Few other biblical figures are associated with dreams and their interpretations more than Joseph—so much so that they provide a thematic structure to the entire cycle of narratives that feature him. The story depicts Joseph's dreams and expertise in decoding them as both sources of consternation for his family and invaluable resources that enable his upward social mobility among Egypt's elite. Thus, he first dreams of sheaves of grain that bow down to him and then of the sun, moon, and eleven stars that prostrate before him, which his brothers understand as suggesting Joseph's intention to rule over them (Genesis 37:8–10). Later, while in an Egyptian prison, Joseph shows his skill at decrypting the enigmatic dreams of two fellow inmates (the king's cupbearer and baker), which earns him a reputation and a chance to divine two strange dreams disturbing the pharaoh (Genesis 40–41). Dreams that occur in pairs are an ancient indicator of their divine import. The dreams provide Joseph with an opportunity for initiative and personal advancement. His success in interpreting them impresses the king so much that he appoints Joseph to manage the grain supply during a fourteen-year famine. Consequently, when his brothers visit Egypt to obtain food during the drought, they find him ruling over them (Genesis 42–43).

Despite the story's setting in Egypt and many references to Egyptian customs, beliefs, and realia, evidence there for the practice of omen interpretation is much scanter and of a later date than in Mesopotamia. While there exist a few omen fragments that concern the overhearing of chance remarks or the listing of lucky and unlucky days (ca. 1825 BCE), the earliest dream omen text is a single manuscript from the twelfth century BCE. Thereafter, no dream manual appears until the fifth–fourth centuries BCE. Nevertheless, the practice of interpreting dreams appears in literary form on a stela of Tanutamani (reigned 664–657 BCE).

Our evidence for dream omen manuals in Mesopotamia goes back to the eighteenth century BCE, though literary references to dream interpretation are attested already in the twenty-second century BCE. Nevertheless, dream manuals occur in more complete collections in the library of Assurbanipal (ca. seventh century BCE) all the way through to the time of the Seleucid kings (ca. fourth–first centuries BCE). It is uncertain whether the Egyptians developed the practice of dream interpretation independently, but since there is no documentation for the custom prior to the single manuscript, and since the format and organization of dreams in that text are very similar, many see the imprint of Mesopotamia upon the Egyptian tradition as likely. Perhaps future discoveries will shed light on this thorny historical issue.

While dreaming is a human universal, the methods by which people interpret dreams are culturally specific. Therefore, it also is of great interest that the commonest method employed in the Egyptian dream manuals and stela is the same as that used by earlier Mesopotamian ritual professionals to interpret omens of all kinds, including dreams. In particular, narratives connect dreams to their interpretations by way of polysemes, homonyms, or words that share a similarity in sound. So for example, in the Mesopotamian dream manuals, we find the following:

1. If a man dreams that he is eating a raven (*arbu*); he will have income (*irbu*).
2. [If] one gives him the head (SAG) of a pick-axe; his head (SAG.DU) [will be cut off].
3. If a man dreams that he is traveling to Idran (*ID-ra-an*); he will free himself from a crime (*aran*).

In the first dream, the word *arbu*, "raven," suggests the interpretation *irbu*, "income," by way of paronomasia. The second example exploits the Sumerian sign SAG (= Akkadian *rēšu*, "head") in two different senses. The third case demonstrates how a cuneiform sign (in this case, ID) can be employed for its multiple values (here as Á), thereby suggesting an altogether different word—namely, *arnu*, "crime." The last interpretation illustrates the emphasis that Mesopotamian ritual professionals placed on the erudite knowledge of cuneiform signs and the centrality of writing in the interpretive process. Similar exegetical strategies inform the Egyptian manuals as well as Mesopotamian and Egyptian literary texts that report the interpretations of dreams.

It is this method that we also find on display in all biblical illustrations of dream divination. Thus, in the case of Joseph, the chief baker explains his dream: "Three (šelošâ) baskets of white-stuff (ḥorî) were upon my head ('al-r'ošî). In the uppermost (hā-'elyōn) basket there were all sorts of baked ('ōpê) food (ma'ăkal) for Pharaoh, but the birds were eating it out of the basket that was on my head (mē'al-r'ošî)" (Genesis 40:16–17). Joseph's rendering molds the baker's words into a new frame: "The three (šelošet) baskets are three (šelošet) days; within three (šelošet) days Pharaoh will lift up your head (r'oš)—from (mē'al) you!—and hang you on a pole, and the birds will eat the flesh from you" (Genesis 40:18–19). In addition, the "white stuff" (ḥorî) in the dream of the baker ('ōpê) suggests the "heated anger" (ḥorî 'ap) of Pharaoh (see Exodus 11:8; 1 Samuel 20:34). Moreover, the term "food" (ma'ăkal) appears elsewhere in reference to human corpses devoured by vultures (e.g., Deuteronomy 28:26; Jeremiah 7:33, 16:4; Psalms 79:2). In essence, the words used to describe the dream become the raw materials from which Joseph constructs his interpretation, just as one finds in the Mesopotamian and later Egyptian dream manuals and literary texts.

It is worth emphasizing that the Bible nowhere labels the practice of dream interpretation "magic" (however defined) or connects it to other illicit means of divination (see Leviticus 19:31; Deuteronomy 18:10–11). Likely, this is because dreams were widely accepted as divine omens far beyond the circles of priests and prophets. This also was the case in Mesopotamia and Egypt, where one could invoke certain gods in an effort to receive dreams. Nevertheless, biblical accounts differ from their Near Eastern analogs by lacking any ritual component to ward off the evil of bad dreams and by attributing the power to decipher dreams to Yhwh rather than to learned mantic experts (Genesis 41:16, 38–39). While in Mesopotamia and Egypt, gods could inspire dreams and drive away their inauspicious consequences, there is no evidence that gods informed their interpretations. Compare this with Joseph's query to his cellmates, "Do not interpretations belong to God?" (Genesis 40:8). This theological perspective finds polemical support in the consistent characterization of Israelite heroes (e.g., Joseph and Daniel) as solely capable of interpreting dreams, even when foreigners do the dreaming and are surrounded by diviners renowned for their wisdom and interpretative abilities. The literary theme of an Israelite nonprofessional besting the courtier mantics would provide a productive model for later Jewish writers.

Genesis 44:2–5 also mentions a silver goblet that Joseph used for drinking and divination. According to the story, he had his steward plant it in a bag belonging to one of his brothers as a ruse to accuse them of theft and bring them back to the Egyptian court. While there is limited evidence for the use of vessel (and water or oil) divination in later demotic texts, it did not play a major role in the ritual life of the Egyptians (unlike the Mesopotamians) until the Hellenistic period and later. Joseph's actions and speech also subtly distance him from the practice by devaluing the vessel enough for him to send it away in an ordinary sack and by having him rhetorically ask, "Do you not know that one such as I can practice divination?" (Genesis 44:15). The operative phrase here is "one such as I" (literally, "a man like me")—that is, not me specifically but an Egyptian man ordinarily in my position. Furthermore, the text does not attach the goblet to Joseph's oneirocritic abilities but, instead, references its silver construction so as to explain why the brothers might have stolen it. On the other hand, the narrator does not condemn the use of the divining goblet or Joseph's ownership of it. So perhaps the vessel was considered an acceptable form of accessing the divine along with dreams, the casting of lots, and the use of the Urim and Thummim (Leviticus 16:7–10; Numbers 27:21).

The careful way in which the story distances Joseph from the divination vessel again underscores that one cannot divorce the depictions of Joseph's extraordinary talents from the literary and polemical contexts in which they occur. Each of the accounts sets the stage for an ironic flourish while validating Joseph's abilities at the expense of the Egyptian religious establishment. Therefore, though the narratives legitimize dreams as sources of divine oracles, as one finds elsewhere in the Near East, and evince a knowledge of the methods by which Mesopotamian and Egyptian ritual professionals interpreted them, they relate Joseph's interpretative talents and authority from an Israelite theological perspective that attributes all divine knowledge and power to Yhwh.

About the Author

Scott B. Noegel received his PhD in 1995 from Cornell University. He is a professor at the University of Washington. He has authored more than a hundred publications on diverse topics related to the ancient world, including *Nocturnal Ciphers: The Allusive Language of Dreams in the Ancient Near East* (New Haven, CT: American Oriental Society, 2007); *"Wordplay" in Ancient Near Eastern Texts* (Atlanta: SBL, 2021), https://faculty.washington.edu/snoegel/; *Nocturnal Ciphers: The Allusive Language of Dreams in the Ancient Near East* (New Haven, CT: AOS, 2007); and with Kasia Szpakowska, "'Word Play' in the Ramesside Dream Manual," *Studien zur altägyptischen Kultur* 35 (2007): 193–212.

Suggestions for Further Reading

In This Book
See also chapters 11 (Pentateuch), 13 (genres), 17 (Wisdom), 35 (Philo), 50 (magic), 51 (prophets), and 56 (polemics).

Elsewhere

Butler, S. A. L. *Mesopotamian Conceptions of Dreams and Dream Rituals*. Münster: Ugarit-Verlag, 1998.

Gnuse, Robert. "The Jewish Dream Interpreter in a Foreign Court: The Recurring Use of a Theme in Jewish Literature." *Journal for the Study of the Pseudepigrapha* 7 (1990): 29–53.

Grossman, Jonathan. "Different Dreams: Two Models of Interpretation for Three Pairs of Dreams (Genesis 37–50)." *Journal of Biblical Literature* 135 (2016): 717–732.

Quack, Joachim F. "Postulated and Real Efficacy in Late Antique Divination Rituals." *Journal of Ritual Studies* 24 (2010): 45–60.

Shupak, Nili. "A Fresh Look at the Dreams of the Officials and of Pharaoh in the Story of Joseph (Genesis 40–41) in the Light of Egyptian Dreams." *Journal of Ancient Near Eastern Studies* 30 (2006): 103–138.

Szpakowska, Kasia. *Behind Closed Eyes: Dreams and Nightmares in Ancient Egypt*. Swansea: Classical Press of Wales, 2003.

63
Moses: How Many Faces?

Benedetta Rossi

Who is Moses? Perhaps the best-known figure in the Hebrew Bible besides Abraham and David, it is curious that his name is not Hebrew in origin but Egyptian. "Moses" derives from the Egyptian root *msj*, meaning "give birth" or "beget," a typical element of other Egyptian names constructed as sentences. An example is Rameses, "Ra has given birth to / begotten him," or basically, "son of Ra." In its present form, "Moses" only maintains the verb but not the deity who was considered his father. The biblical writer has suggested a native Hebrew etymology for the name "to draw out [of the water]" from the root *mšh* (Exodus 2:10), perhaps to try to make this national figure more "native" and less foreign-sounding. In the narrative world, the Egyptian princess is not a Hebrew speaker, so it makes little sense for her to give him a Hebrew name.

From its very first lines, the story of Moses is interwoven with the destiny of an Israel he will lead out of Egypt to the threshold of the promised land. Following the biblical account of his life, which extends from Exodus 2 to Deuteronomy 34, Moses is born during Israel's enslavement and persecution in Egypt. Contravening the order to kill every firstborn male child, his mother abandons him in a basket in the river, and Pharaoh's daughter retrieves the basket and baby and raises him as her son. He is educated in the royal court but flees to the land of Midian, modern Saudi Arabia, after killing an Egyptian who was beating a Hebrew.

In Midian, Moses marries Zipporah, daughter of the Midianite priest Reuel, by whom he has a son, Gershon. While grazing his father-in-law's herd, he receives a revelation from Yhwh, who speaks to him from a burning bush and orders him to return to Egypt to free the Israelites from slavery and lead them to the promised land.

With his brother Aaron, Moses is the main character in the events leading up to the exodus from Egypt. Ten plagues strike the Egyptians until the night of deliverance, when the Israelites flee, having stripped the Egyptians of goods. After crossing the Sea of Reeds parted by a divine wind, Moses leads the Israelites to Mount Sinai (Mount Horeb in Deuteronomy), where they receive two stone tablets with the Decalogue. Before receiving the tablets, Moses stays on the mountain for forty days in conversation with Yhwh. In his absence, the people make a golden calf; this image provokes Yhwh's wrath, which Moses appeases by supplication. Alarmed by the report of spies Moses sent to reconnoiter Canaan, the Israelites refuse to enter the land and wander in the desert for forty years. During this time, they repeatedly rebel against Moses, even wishing to return to Egypt.

Moses and Aaron cause water to spring from a rock to quench a rebellion caused by thirst. For some reason, they are blamed, and like the entire generation that escaped Egypt (except for Caleb and Joshua), both die prior to entering the promised land. Before being buried directly by Yhwh, Moses is granted a glimpse of the land from Mount Nebo in today's Jordan. So ends the current Pentateuchal version of the life and career of Moses, which contains 647 of the 766 references to this figure in the Hebrew Bible. According to another tradition transmitted by Hecataeus of Abdera, a Hellenistic historiographer who wrote at the end of the fourth century BCE, however, Moses led the Israelites into Canaan and founded Jerusalem, promulgated laws, and introduced the worship of a god without images.

Scholars have noted how the story of Moses parallels that of three other historical figures to some degree. The first is an official with a Semitic name, Beya, who was in the service of Pharaoh Siptah (1193–1189 BCE). Following an attempt to seize power at the expense of Pharaoh Sethnakht (1186–1184 BCE), Beya fled from Egypt at the head of a group of *hapiru*, possibly an antecedent to the term "Hebrew," having stolen gold and silver from the Egyptians. Yet, he was tried and executed in Egypt during the reign of Siptah, which was not the fate of Moses, so any proposed identification of Moses with Beya is partial at best.

Others have noted how the account of Moses's birth in Exodus 2:1–10 closely recalls the legend of the birth of King Sargon of Akkad. Sargon is the son of a priestess; Moses's mother is a descendant of Levi, an ancestor of the priestly tribe. Both babies are born in secret, placed in a basket of reeds daubed with pitch, and consigned to the waters of a river. Although an illegitimate son, Sargon will become king thanks to the love of the goddess Ishtar. Moses, the son of a Hebrew woman, will be brought up as a prince in the Egyptian court and exhibits many royal traits as the leader of Israel.

The composition of the legend of the birth of Sargon of Akkad goes back to the reign of Sargon II (722–705 BCE) in the eighth century BCE, when the kingdom of Israel was subjected to the Neo-Assyrian Empire.

If one assumes the biblical writer knew the legend of Sargon's birth, the tradition of Moses's birth would date, at the earliest, during or shortly after the reign of Sargon II. In this case, Moses could have been presented by a scribe living in the kingdom of Israel as an antitype to the Neo-Assyrian sovereign, and his story could have served as a counterhistory to that of the Assyrian ruler.

The legend of Moses's origins could also have arisen in the Persian era, however. It shares similarities with the legend of the birth of King Cyrus handed down in Herodotus's *Histories* (I, 107–122). Astyages, king of the Medes, orders Cyrus, the son of his daughter Mandane and the Persian king, Cambyses, to be killed immediately after he is born. The newborn is given to a herdsman to abandon to certain death in the mountains. The herdsman and his wife, however, spare Cyrus's life by swapping him with their own baby son, whom they dress in Cyrus's royal robes and expose to the elements and wild animals instead. Cyrus is then raised by this shepherd family and eventually becomes king. The birth narratives of Moses, Sargon, and Cyrus share a recurring motif of ancient tales: that of the hero's birth, abandonment to death, and rescue.

The biblical portrayal of Moses reflects many features typical of ancient Near Eastern sovereigns. Three are especially prominent: an architect and patron of the sanctuary, a lawgiver, and an intercessor for his people. In Exodus 25–40, Yhwh passes on to Moses detailed instructions for the construction of the mobile desert sanctuary, which serves as the archetype for the future, permanent temples in Jerusalem and on Gerizim.

The presentation of Moses as a lawgiver is complex, since, besides the two slightly different versions of the Decalogue, or Ten Commandments, in Exodus 20:1–17 and Deuteronomy 5:6–21, the Pentateuch transmits three other collections of "laws": the so-called Covenant Code (Exodus 20:22–23:33), the Holiness Code (Leviticus 17–26), and the so-called Deuteronomic Code (Deuteronomy 12–26). Though these lists are often understood to be proper functioning legal codes, it is far from certain that they had that status. It is more likely that what we have here are fictional laws derived from the development of scribal exercises dealing with legal matters and questions of law.

Finally, Moses is repeatedly characterized as an intercessor and mediator between God and Israel. Ancient Near Eastern kings were typically deemed servants of their national god and shepherds of the people. Whenever Yhwh is enraged by Israel's behavior, Moses intervenes to ensure the continuation of the covenant relationship.

The figure of Moses assumes particular features in the book of Deuteronomy. There, Moses is presented as the first and greatest of the prophets of Israel. Deuteronomy 18:9–22 presents prophecy as a mode of divine revelation; contrasted with other forms of divination found in Canaan, it is the only one described as legitimate for Israel. The text presents Moses as a model and point of reference for every prophet to come in the future. The Deuteronomic Moses speaks as a prophet when he foretells the people's disobedience, destruction, and exile (31:16–18).

Mosaic prophecy becomes an unsurpassable model in Deuteronomy 34:10–12, which records a tradition contrasting with that found earlier in 18:9–22. At the conclusion of the book, prophecy is limited to Moses and is destined to end with him: no prophet will arise after him. After the death of Moses, the greatest prophet, the Torah of Moses is to be the only path of access to divine revelation.

Moses is also presented as a teacher who instructs Israel by repeating to them the whole of Deuteronomy in a single day. According to the programmatic declaration of Deuteronomy 1:5, the subjects of Moses's speeches are the prescriptions Yhwh gave to the people on Sinai. Moses thus fulfills the command to teach the people what he had received from Yhwh in Exodus 24:12, which had not yet been implemented in the narrative dynamic of the preceding books in the Pentateuch.

Moses's teaching (torah) is presented in different forms in Deuteronomy: the retrospective narrative of the journey Israel has taken from Horeb to the threshold of the land of Canaan, beyond the Jordan (1–3), is followed by a long section giving strong encouragement (6–11), where the people are repeatedly instructed to keep faith with the covenant and the teaching that Moses is giving. Rather than a code of laws, Deuteronomy 12–26 is shaped as alternating prescriptions and exhortations. Before his death (34), Moses pronounces blessings and curses on Israel (28), composes and delivers a song in poetic form to be committed to memory (32), and like Jacob before his death (Genesis 49), blesses the people according to their different tribes (33).

Closely connected with the portrait of Moses as a teacher in Deuteronomy is his depiction as the first scribe in Israel. All the teaching imparted orally in Moab, together with the song in chapter 32, is put into writing by Moses in the scroll of the Torah (*sefer hattorah*; 31:9), which is then entrusted to the elders and the Levitical priests. The latter have to read the content of the scroll once every seven years to all the people gathered for the feast of Sukkot (Deuteronomy 31:11–13).

Deuteronomy is shaped as the testament of a scribe who bequeaths to the Levitical priests the scroll of the Torah and the instructions for its transmission in the future. The book of the Torah is Moses's legacy to the Levitical priests. A close look at the content of the scroll—which can be identified with Deuteronomy 1:6–30:20; 32—confirms this. The characteristics typical of the scribe, which include interpretation and teaching of the people in addition to writing and recording, are set out in the four discourses uttered by Moses before his death (1:6–4:40; 4:44–28:68; 28:69–32:52; and 33:1–34:12). More importantly, the *sefer hattorah* displays a collection of literary patterns typically taught in the curriculum of ancient scribes from Mesopotamia and Egypt. The sequence of patterns and genres scribes learned to master is then further framed as Moses's farewell speech. In this way, the curriculum is given a fictional story setting in which, on the eve of his death, Moses personally bequeaths its content to a scribal elite, the Levitical priests, thus legitimizing them as his professional "successors." Thus, another, less recognized characteristic of Moses's character is portrayed in Deuteronomy. Moses is depicted as a master scribe and the forefather of a scribal guild, the Levitical priests. The latter are responsible for portraying Moses as their ancestor, legitimizing their authority, and creating a background for their social ascent.

About the Author

Benedetta Rossi holds a doctorate in biblical science from the Biblical Pontifical Institute in Rome. Her research includes Jeremiah, Deuteronomy, and relations between the Pentateuch and prophetic literature. She has published "Master Scribe and Forefather of a Scribal Guild: Moses in Deuteronomy," in *Deuteronomy: Outside the Box*, edited by Diana V. Edelman and Philippe Guillaume (Sheffield, UK: Equinox, forthcoming); "Reshaping Jeremiah: Scribal Strategies and the Prophet like Moses," *Journal for the Study of the Old Testament* 44 (2020): 575–593; and "Basis for a Relaunch or Epic Failure? Contrasting Receptions of Exodus in the Prophets," pages 96–114 in *The Reception of Exodus Motifs in Jewish and Christian Literature*, edited by Beate Kowalski and Susan E. Docherty (Leiden: Brill, 2022).

Suggestions for Further Reading

In This Book
See also chapters 7 (who wrote the Bible?), 11 (Pentateuch), 13 (genres), 20 (genealogies), 21 (dates), 35 (Philo), 38 (Samaritans), 48 (twelve tribes), 49 (Torah), 51 (prophets), 52 (covenant), 60 (Abraham), 65 (King David), 72 (synchronic vs. diachronic), and 78 (ideological criticism).

Elsewhere

Assmann, Jan. *Moses the Egyptian: The Memory of Egypt in Western Monotheism.* Cambridge, MA: Harvard University Press, 1997.

Carr, David M. "The Moses Story: Literary-Historical Reflections." *Hebrew Bible and Ancient Israel* 1(1) (2012): 7–36.

Otto, Eckart. "Moses." Pages 568–571 in *Religion Past and Present* (volume 8). Edited by Hans Dieter Betz, Don Browning, Bernd Janowski, and Eberhard Jüngel. Leiden: Brill, 2010.

Römer, Thomas. "Moses, the Royal Lawgiver." Pages 81–94 in *Remembering Biblical Figures in the Late Persian and Early Hellenistic Periods: Social Memory and Imagination.* Edited by Diana V. Edelman and Ehud Ben Zvi. Oxford: Oxford University Press, 2013.

64
Ruth: Whore or Matriarch?

Philippe Guillaume

The book of Ruth is an all-time biblical favorite. It is short (four chapters), with a clear plot that builds narrative tension heightened with sexual innuendos, and it ends well. The tale begins with the plight of three women. Naomi, the widow of Elimelech, a Judahite from Bethlehem who had immigrated to Moab to escape a drought, finds herself left with her two widowed daughters-in-law, Orpah and Ruth. Naomi decides to return to Bethlehem, having heard that the situation had improved in Judah. Orpah vanishes as soon as she agrees to return to her mother's home, whereas Ruth, who decided to cling to Naomi, eventually gives birth to a baby boy listed as the grandfather of King David.

Ruth's words to Naomi are memorable: "Wherever you go I shall go . . . your people will be my people, your god will be my god, wherever you die I will die" (Ruth 1:16–17). These are touching words of loyalty and selflessness, long read as a parade example of religious conversion.

Boaz, a wealthy, influential man of Bethlehem, is the main male character. Though he is not the closest relative to Elimelech, Boaz convinces the closer relative to give up his preemptive right to Elimelech's estate by, it seems, presenting Ruth as an encumbrance.

As Elimelech's widow, Naomi holds a certain right to Elimelech's estate, often misunderstood as a field. In fact, the "portion of field" in 4:3 (*ḥelqat ha-sadeh*; חלקת השדה) refers to a share in the pool of arable land cultivated by the local village community. Naomi's right of use of this share remains valid despite a ten-year absence from Bethlehem (Ruth 1:4). This is confirmed by ethnographic studies, which show that in the absence of shareholders, their shares return to the pool of communal arable land until their return. Periodic distributions occur whenever the number of shareholders changes due to death, departure, return, or the coming-of-age of sons.

The return of Naomi is strategically timed during the harvest (1:22), when everyone's stores are at the fullest, which is six months before the next plowing season. This gives Naomi enough time to obtain the land she is entitled to. In the meantime, she needs to find food for herself and for Ruth, whose right to her late husband's share is left in limbo. Though her late husband was Elimelech's son and thus a Judahite too, the fact that Ruth is a Moabite is a complication.

The notion of moving to Moab to escape a drought in Judah (Ruth 1:1) is weird, since the rain levels in Judah are necessarily greater than those in Moab. To survive a severe drought, Judahites and Israelites moved south to Egypt, not east to Moab. Hence, the choice of Moab for Ruth's origins may have been motivated by a desire to placate the repudiations of foreign wives narrated in Ezra 10 and Nehemiah 13. This may be why the Hebrew canon places Ruth among the Writings, like Ezra and Nehemiah, while the Greek canon places Ruth in chronological order, between the book of Judges (see Ruth 1:1) and the books of Samuel, hence before the birth of David (see Ruth 4:17–22). Yet, the mention of the "days of the judges" in the introduction and the final Davidic genealogy could well be late additions, as they are found in the first and last verses of the booklet, where additions were easiest to introduce. In this case, an earlier tale may have had little to do with the judges and David. Still, Moabite or not, the arrival of two empty-handed widows causes a great commotion in Bethlehem. Who is going to feed them during the next twelve months until the next harvest?

While sending Ruth off to glean behind the harvesters to provide for their immediate needs, Naomi searches for more permanent solutions. Ruth is to seduce Boaz and convince him to marry her, which would save deciding whether she is entitled to a share of communal land, as Naomi is. This long-term solution is impossible for Naomi, who is too old to marry (Ruth 1:11). Instead, she offers to rent her share of land, implicitly against a share of its annual yield or in exchange for her upkeep. No price is mentioned for the transaction, indicating it was not an outright sale, which was not possible when communal land was involved.

Eventually, Boaz takes the entire package. He marries Ruth, fathers a son, and acquires Elimelech's land share from Naomi. For this, Boaz has long been understood as the selfless redeemer of Ruth the Moabite, a foreign woman whose ancestors are mocked as the descendants of a drunken man who slept with his own daughter (Genesis 19:30–37) and of those who hindered Israel's passage and whose well-being Israel should thus never seek (Deuteronomy 23:4–7). The redeemer theme resonates deeply among Christians, for whom it prefigures Christ's ministry on the cross.

Among scholars interested in legalities, the story has been read in light of the laws of the Jubilee (Leviticus 25) and of the levirate (Deuteronomy 25:5–10), though doubts have been raised against such readings due to inconsistencies in details. For instance, the narrator's mention of a sandal ritual in Ruth 4:7–8 hardly fits the way it is prescribed by the Deuteronomic text. The narrator is clearly less concerned about legalities than in telling a good story that could challenge common practices or invite its readers to go beyond the call of duty.

After centuries of idyllic readings, recent studies of the book are more suspicious. Is Ruth another victim of a patriarchal society that left her no option other than selling herself to an old rich man to survive? Gerald West and Beverley Haddad, for example, see a parallel with a modern practice some women engage in. On the other hand, on the basis of the lack of expressions of affection in the dialogues between Ruth and Boaz, Brett Krutzsch suggests that Boaz had no desire for women.

Encouraged by the suggestiveness of the midnight scene on the threshing floor, much ink has been spilled over what exactly took place when Ruth uncovered Boaz's feet, though this may have been a foil to distract attention from the actual denouement. Sound methodology requires privileging the parameters supplied by the text over filling in the blanks. The bare facts are a menopaused widow, Naomi (1:11); a younger but possibly infertile Ruth (who is childless despite a previous marriage); an outraged Bethlehem at their return; a wealthy Boaz (2:1); and a less affluent, closer relative (4:6).

From this data, future advances in Ruth scholarship are likely to come from recent evaluations of Ruth, Boaz, and Naomi as resourceful agents smartly navigating social constraints to obtain what they need. Naomi certainly uses Ruth and Boaz to obtain for herself an heir for her late husband: the moment Ruth gives birth, the son is declared Naomi's, not Boaz's or Ruth's (4:16–17); Ruth uses Boaz to secure food and lodging that come with marital rights; and Boaz secures a leonine deal consisting of *three* shares of communal land in exchange of the upkeep of *two* women (4:9). This is not the deal offered to the close redeemer. Instead of using Ruth as an encumbrance, Boaz asserts her right to a share of land, like Naomi, but he adds for himself the share of Orpah's late husband to the deal, though she never turned up in Bethlehem and thus does not represent any burden. Nevertheless, no elder dares to challenge Boaz, as it saved them from feeding two unexpected mouths for an entire year before their own land shares would supply their needs.

All in all, the crux is whether self-care is a matter of selfishness. The protagonists put their resources, however few they might be, at the disposal of others who could benefit from them. Does this make Naomi a pimp, Ruth a seductress, and Boaz a profiteering, dirty old man? Naomi's stratagem, Ruth's seduction, and Boaz's ruse result in mutual care. They are certainly not equal partners in the relationships they establish. The women are subordinated to the men, but they are not powerless victims. Boaz the patriarch is the wealthy party, which is why he is sought out; he is the most powerful man in Bethlehem and ends up even more powerful. Yet, what is a clear case of mutual exploitation occurs within the formation of secure and beneficial relationships for all parties concerned, including Israel. It is helpful to put on hold moral evaluations to perceive the message of the story before rushing to laud or condemn.

About the Author

Philippe Guillaume earned a ThD from the University of Geneva and a habilitation from the University of Berne. His present research focuses on economics in the Hebrew Bible. He published *The Economy of Deuteronomy's Core* (Sheffield, UK: Equinox, 2022); and "Basic Toolbox to Figure Out the Economy of Deuteronomy 12–26," in *Deuteronomy: Outside the Box*, edited by Diana V. Edelman and Philippe Guillaume (Sheffield, UK: Equinox, online 2022). With coeditor Rhiannon Graybill, he prepares the *Ruth* volume for the Themes and Issues in Biblical Studies series at Equinox.

Suggestions for Further Reading

In This Book
See also chapters 17 (Wisdom), 20 (genealogies), 24 (Kings and Chronicles), 44 (ancestors), 49 (Torah), 55 (patriarchalism), and 81 (gender studies).

Elsewhere
Johnson Williams, Jennifer. "Contracts and Care of Oneself in the Book of Ruth." *Horizons in Biblical Theology* 42 (2020): 14–46.

Krisel, William. "The Place of Ruth in the Hebrew Canon: A New Hypothesis." *Estudios bíblicos* 79 (2021): 63–76.

Niggemann, Andrew J. "Matriarch of Israel or Misnomer? Israelite Self-Identification in Ancient Israelite Law Code and the Implication for Ruth." *Journal for the Study of the Old Testament* 41(3) (2017): 355–377.

Weiss, Shira. "Biblical Seductresses." *Biblical Interpretation* 30 (2022): 171–196.

West, Gerald O., and Beverley Haddad. "Boaz as 'Sugar Daddy': Re-reading Ruth in the Context of HIV." *Journal of Theology for Southern Africa* 155 (2016): 137–156.

65
King David: Famous or Infamous?

Baruch Halpern

After God and Moses, King David casts the longest shadow in the Hebrew Bible. As the Tel Dan and Mesha stele (ca. 800 BCE) acknowledge, he founded a state. To "belong" in Judah was to belong to the house of David. He owes an endless celebrity in stone, paper, canvas, and celluloid to a cinematic characterization from 1 Samuel 16 to 1 Kings 2. This portrait, which some think was sketched within decades of his death, layers dimension on dimension. Later traditions reduce David to the iconic numen, emblem, and role model of a dynasty. He enjoys a silhouetted afterlife in his figuration of the apocalyptic messiah in Judaism and Christianity.

The books of Samuel periodize the biographical portrait: David and Saul (1 Samuel 16–26); David as a Philistine captain (1 Samuel 27–2 Samuel 1); his coronation in Judah, then Israel; his new capital, dynastic charter, and martial prizes (2 Samuel 2–8); and the revolt engineered by his own son, Absalom (2 Samuel 9–20). After appendices on Saul's descendants, David's heroes, and his acquisition of legal title to the ark's future precinct, an enfeebled David charges Solomon, his heir, to balance the moral universe.

Because the biography serves state purposes, its historical value varies. It licenses us to discount his combat with Goliath as a notional tribute to his valor by assigning the giant's defeat to a Davidic subordinate in a later list (2 Samuel 21:19). We may also doubt David's encounters with Samuel or Saul, which legitimize his legend. We might dismiss David's repeated unconventionality—bringing a sling to hand-to-hand combat with Goliath (1 Samuel 17), sparing or mourning opponents (1 Samuel 24; 26; 2 Samuel 17:37), jettisoning the ark and diviners to flee Absalom (2 Samuel 15:24–29). The story almost invites us to question David's "Ephrathite" roots (1 Samuel 17:12) among settlers in the central hill country. Upstart David's genealogy reaches back one generation versus Samuel's or Saul's five (1 Samuel 1:1; 9:1; 10:21).

Second Samuel 8 summarizes David's conquests: he annexed the territory of Edom, fought with some Philistines and Moabites somewhere, and in Transjordan, defeated Aramean armies and conquered Ammon. The actual achievements are framed with far-reaching campaigns as far as the Euphrates, a universal practice. Evocative rhetoric flattered courtiers at the same time as it eulogized the king.

The biography also shields David from contemporary accusations: his alibis for the wholesale slaughter of the rival royal leadership include blissful ignorance (2 Samuel 3:26), absence from the scene (2 Samuel 4:5–8), poetic mourning displays (2 Samuel 1:17–27), and executing killers who report to him (2 Samuel 1:15–16; 4:9–12); he executes Saul's surviving sons and distaff grandsons (2 Samuel 21:1–9).

These elements, like the complex personal and blood loyalties and relations in 2 Samuel, appear to speak to concerns from David's time. David's version of events becomes the official one. But around 2 Samuel 7 and 9–20, the voice changes; the narrative points toward Solomon's succession. A few scholars impute these chapters to Bathsheba, Solomon's mother.

The most impressive, sustained narrative is Absalom's revolt in 2 Samuel 9; 13–19, a family drama with nations as extras. David is silent when his eldest son rapes and dismisses his brother Absalom's sister. Absalom murders the rapist and takes refuge abroad with his mother's family. Joab arranges for his repatriation and eventual release from house arrest. Then Absalom politicks with ethnic Israelites, and the general population march with him to rid themselves of David. David's personnel and Transjordanian forces meet the people's army, Joab executes Absalom in the field, and Judah and Israel restore an emotionally devastated David as king. Rumors swirl; upheaval multiplies and spins into a second, minor uprising. The outcome is another conquest for Joab, this time of the Aramaean city-state Abel, at the base of the Beqaa Valley west of Dan.

The narrative leaves no doubt that the upheaval can be traced to an incident during David's royal expedition to Ammon. That conquest is related in tactical detail as background to a murder plot resulting in Solomon's birth. David impregnates Bathsheba, the wife of a senior officer, and secretly arranges the soldier's death. Yhwh's curse, delivered by Nathan, Solomon's prophetic supporter, is unending conflict in David's house (2 Samuel 11–12). The curse works itself out in the Absalom revolt and in another son's attempt to preempt the succession when Solomon stages his palace coup.

As archaeological resolution does not yet distinguish Davidic phases from others, what we can know must be won from critical reading informed by a general cultural and material background. Historically, David was one instance of a widespread contemporary phenomenon. As the Egyptian Empire choked off its support for Canaan's city-states in the twelfth century BCE, bands of former transients began establishing themselves on arable lands in significant numbers. Over the succeeding decades, rural regional webs, rooted in rustic landscapes, developed wider regional webs. It is to the endpoint of that development that Samuel's world belongs, with Canaan divided into competing ethnicities: Ammonites, Amorites, Philistines, Hivites, Hittites, Canaanites, Amalekites, and Israelites. These populate Samuel's landscape, still, in a way that fits a time of new political and ethnic formations across the Levant, before circa 900 BCE. Most of these "territorial" identities, including Aramaeans and Neo-Hittites in Syria, developed dynastic monarchies through the activity of strongmen like Saul and David.

On Samuel's canvas, Saul was still prosecuting "the wars of Canaan" or "of Yhwh" against competing identities, each waving the flag of its god. David, however, having won the civil war, bested Philistines near Jerusalem, and based the ark there, achieves "rest from about." David completes the conquest of Israel's territory.

In reality, David did so by incorporating the populations Saul had persecuted. The Hivite population represented by the towns allied with Gibeon were, like the inland Philistine towns, locked in a struggle with Saul, whose program involved uprooting other ethnic communities. The books of Samuel document David's collaboration with Gibeon, Ammon, and Philistines. They claim he imposed Israelite governance from Dan to Beersheba and dominated the southern Beqaa Valley and Damascus, but questions like the local penetration of royal authority, zone by zone, remain unanswerable. They claim credibly that he had to flee Jerusalem but won his way back to power and reelection as king, though victorious armies have a way of influencing elections.

Most of all, David's story exposes the culture of its audience, in Jerusalem. Various royal apologies, starting with eighteenth-century BCE Hittite annals, indicate that scribes resolved catastrophic conflicts among the ruling elite. Official literature generally colors the roles of kings in a courtly, official light. The writer of Samuel delves more deftly into personal relations and ideations and dwells less on dignity siphoned from institutions. As in the old Hittite annals, which share the same level of detail, the storytelling reflects a consciousness that institutions and social locations are still developing. The Absalom revolt followed by the coup on the brink of David's death develop the conflict motif and prepare readers for Solomon's solution to comparable chaos.

In such tentative, incipient stages, honor and social status dominate the action. The stage is tiny and packed with individual characters. The characters and lists of ministers, officials, and officers in the books of

Samuel suggest that senior administrative staff numbered in the dozens. These officeholders are named because they are important, and they are important because they are named. The intimacy of the power sphere is shared with the text's audience. So, for example, combat is regulated by an etiquette developed by a community of "knights." Divination, regular until the civil war, is a public show, incidental within the social fabric of the early monarchic "squirearchy." Religion is simple. Most insights into providential workings, densest in the Absalom account, spill out unwittingly from characters' mouths. A few, like Absalom's hanging between heaven and earth, stem from the narrator, but not as authoritative pronouncements.

Foregrounded action in the narrative world assumes a culture of shame less marked by institutional status and motivations than later, more formalized, royal propaganda. In David's shifting world, the relation of the state to other groups plays in the background. And yet, the text masks some relations pertinent to historical analysis: many scholars infer from hints that Bathsheba's grandfather was Absalom's chief advisor; Solomon may have been Uriah's son. In other cases, the war with Saul's son, Ishbaal, invokes personal relationships frequently, some across political lines. The focus is on complex social and political location, and the text assumes audience immersion in the knightly culture to explain them, as with David's hatchet man Joab, whose solicitude sometimes embroils his royal cousin in moral misfortune. The story, starting even before David's appearance, justifies Davidic ascendancy over the house of Saul while denying David's role in decimating it. It reduces Absalom's uprising to family fracture rebalancing the cosmos: it welcomes those former rebels whom Solomon needed to institutionalize Jerusalem's monarchy.

The political bias sheds doubt on particular claims: Which factions in "Judah" and "Israel" elect David before and after Absalom? How real are David's alibis for deaths from which he benefits? Was Uriah Solomon's real father? Did David arrange the undetectable murder of Bathsheba's Hittite husband or, rather, take a chief advisor's daughter into his harem as a hostage? Did David enforce Solomon's succession? Did he instruct Solomon to remove his personal loyalists? Did Jonathan's son expect to be restored as the king of Israel?

Saul's house claimed to represent Israel without establishing authority in the south or Galilee. Even in its heartland, enclaves resisting assimilation into the new Israelite identity, however it was defined within Saul's community, survived his onslaughts. When military collapse undercut the ideological fervor behind this crusade, David was positioned to take power: he had been serving, ably, a premier Philistine power center and recruited advocates from and engineered a community among settled communities in the territory, Judah. Elected Judah's king while commanding a Philistine army from Gath, he reached out to the Gibeonite towns Saul had targeted in Benjamin, which had offered an easy route to Gath, and took up residence in Jerusalem, whether by conquest or by the invitation of a local party. He befriended the king of Ammon, whom Saul is said to have defeated, and recruited allies in Transjordan by removing threats from both Ammon and Aram to populations hitherto unaffiliated with them. He allied by marriage with an Aramean king in northern Transjordan and established relations to contain Aramaeans in the Beqaa Valley. Eventually, he allegedly cemented relations with Tyre, of which Solomon later availed himself, not least to dispose of the territory identified with Asher. David enjoyed secure relations—that is, with power establishments on every side of Saul's Israel—and it would be surprising were the same not to have held for the lowland fortresses of the Jezreel Valley. He hemmed Israel in and swallowed it while constructing a new monarchic administration that was no longer ethnically purist Saulide. But it remained governed by a shame culture in which affronts among the elite were questions of honor in personal dealings before its transition to presenting itself as a ritual-bound mountain theocracy, under Davidic supervision, in an Assyrian imperial world.

About the Author

Baruch Halpern holds a doctorate of philosophy from Harvard University in Near Eastern languages and civilizations. His research includes ancient historiography and continuity and rupture in social and cultural history. Among his publications are *The Constitution of the Monarchy in Israel* (Chico, CA: Scholars, 1981); *The First Historians: The Hebrew Bible and History* (1988; repr., University Park: Pennsylvania State University Press, 1996); *David's Secret Demons: Messiah, Murderer, Traitor, King* (Grand Rapids, MI: Eerdmans, 2003); and "The United Monarchy: David between Saul and Solomon," pages 337–362 in *The Old Testament in Archaeology and History*, edited by Jennie Ebeling, J. Edward Wright, Mark Elliot, and Paul V. M. Flesher (Waco: Baylor University Press, 2017).

Suggestions for Further Reading

In This Book

See also chapters 1 (scholarly perspective), 9 (audiences), 20 (genealogies), 21 (dates), 24 (Kings and Chronicles), 28–30 (archaeology), 44 (ancestors), 48 (twelve tribes), 72 (synchronic vs. diachronic), 75 (historical criticism), and 77 (literary and form criticism).

Elsewhere

Knapp, Andrew. "The Succession Narrative in Twenty-First-Century Research." *Currents in Biblical Research* 19 (2021): 211–234.

Sergi, Omer. "Narrative, Story, and History in the Biblical Traditions about the Formation of the Israelite Monarchy (1 Samuel 9–2 Samuel 5)." Pages 13–45 in *Prophecy and Gender in the Hebrew Bible*. Edited by L. Juliana Claassens and Irmtraud Fischer. Atlanta: SBL, 2021.

Steussy, Marti J. *David: Biblical Portraits of Power*. Columbia: University of South Carolina Press, 1999.

Thomas, Zachary. "On the Archaeology of 10th Century BCE Israel and the Idea of the 'State.'" *Palestine Exploration Quarterly* 153(3) (2021): 244–257, https://doi.org/10.1080/00310328.2021.1886488.

66
Jezebel: Does She Deserve Her Bad Reputation?

Kristin Joachimsen

The story about Jezebel is scattered between 1 Kings 16:31 and 2 Kings 9, within a larger discussion of Israel defining itself in relation to surrounding nations. Her story is embedded in intrigues related to royal succession, mixed marriages, and the worship of deities other than Yhwh. Jezebel is associated with her husband, King Ahab of Israel, Yhwh's prophet Elijah, the vine grower Naboth, eunuchs, and King Jehu of Israel. She is presented as the daughter of King Ethbaal of Sidon, in modern-day Lebanon. Her murderer, King Jehu of Israel, stresses that she should be buried as a king's daughter (2 Kings 9:34). Her husband, King Ahab of Israel, is the son of King Omri. Ahab and Jezebel are the parents of Jehoram, king of Israel. Jezebel is never referred to by the title queen in the Hebrew Bible and is only deemed queen mother to her underaged son posthumously and anonymously (2 Kings 10:13).

Jezebel is first mentioned as part of the indictment of her husband, King Ahab, for doing evil in the eyes of Yhwh by building a Baal temple in Samaria, worshipping Baal, and making an Asherah to worship (1 Kings 16:31–33). The storyline seems to suggest that Ahab's marriage to Jezebel prompts his practice of worshipping deities other than Yhwh, illustrating the threat some foreign women might pose, like Solomon's wives in 1 Kings 11:1–8. In other cases, relationships between Israelites and foreigners of the opposite gender do not receive any particular attention. An example is Hiram, the craftsman in charge of building the temple in Jerusalem, who has an Israelite mother and a father from Tyre (1 Kings 7:13–14).

In 1 Kings 18–19, Jezebel issues a death sentence to the prophet Elijah, who has murdered 450 prophets of Baal and 400 prophets of Asherah "who were eating at Jezebel's table" (18:19). Jezebel becomes a symbol of a political and religious difference that threatens the identity of Israel, including its affiliation with Yhwh. Such a fierce polemic against other gods reveals the existence of a variety of practices within the Israelite religion, shared with Israel's immediate neighbors, that some circles came to perceive as a threat to Israel's distinctive identity due to what was viewed as assimilation to "foreign" cults.

Then Jezebel plots against Naboth, who cultivates a vineyard that Ahab wants as a vegetable garden. As Naboth refuses to part with the inheritance of his ancestors, Jezebel seals letters with the royal seal and devises a scheme to get Naboth executed, and Ahab receives the land. The moment Ahab takes possession of the coveted vineyard, the prophet Elijah steps in and accuses Ahab, not Jezebel, of the murder of Naboth. However, in an aside, the narrator states that Jezebel urged Ahab to become Israel's most evil monarch (1 Kings 21:25). Elijah proclaims that the entire royal house of Ahab shall be eradicated, and dogs will lick up the blood of the royal dynasty (1 Kings 21:19–24; 22:38). When Ahab hears the prophetic announcement, he repents, and the annihilation of his line is postponed to the succeeding generation (1 Kings 21:27–29). Ahab's main offense is not his abuse of Naboth, however, but his having done what was evil in the eyes of Yhwh by endorsing the cults of Jezebel's gods.

Finally, in 2 Kings 9–10, Jezebel's death is narrated within the larger context of a coup to control the kingdom of Israel; Jehu overthrows the Omride dynasty with the support of Elisha, Elijah's successor as Yhwh's prophet. On this occasion, Jehu describes Jezebel as a woman who continues to act as a harlot with other deities; sexual promiscuity is a common metaphor for infidelity toward Yhwh (2 Kings 9:22). In her death scene, Jezebel is vividly depicted painting her eyes and adorning her hair to encounter Jehu before being thrown out the window, trampled by horses, and eaten by dogs (9:32–33), just as Elijah had predicted to Ahab (1 Kings 21:23) and the prophet disciple of Elisha (2 Kings 9:7–10). When Jezebel's eunuchs throw her to her death, they contribute to a transition of power from the dynastic rule of the house of Omri, represented by Jezebel, to the new dynasty Jehu hopes to establish (2 Kings 9:30–37).

Jehu orders the burial of "this cursed woman, for she is a king's daughter" (2 Kings 9:34). Here, Jezebel's foreignness is emphasized; her royal status comes from her father, the king of Sidon, not her Israelite husband, Ahab. In the perception of the Israelite usurper, she remains an "outsider" in spite of her marriage to the king of Israel, producing the future heir to the throne. When the entire house of Ahab is annihilated, evil is reflected in their walking after other deities.

Nevertheless, Jehu gets no credit for the elimination of the Omrides. Being a king of Israel rather than Judah, he follows Jeroboam's example, turning to the golden calves at Bethel and Dan (2 Kings 10:28–29). Jehu is even blamed for the blood he shed in Jezreel in the initial chapter of the collection of Minor Prophets (Hosea 1:4).

The portrayal of Jezebel in 1–2 Kings reflects the aims of those who produced and interpreted her story. It is a product of a Judean discourse about the former kingdom of Israel and its kings, prophets, and deities. Remembering Jezebel reinforced for audiences in Judah and Jerusalem memories of the rival kingdom of Israel as hopelessly evil. While in 1–2 Kings, all the kings from Israel are presented as bad, the picture is more mixed for those from Judah, among whom Hezekiah (2 Kings 18:3–6) and Josiah (2 Kings 22–23) stand out as particularly good.

In the story of the kings and queens of Israel and Judah, it is interesting to compare the portrayals of Jezebel and her daughter Athaliah, born to King Ahab (2 Kings 10:13). Though viewed as a foreigner because she belongs to the kingdom of Israel, not because of her Sidonian mother, Athaliah becomes the queen in Judah due to a diplomatic marriage contracted to ally the two kingdoms. Athaliah rules Judah for six years (2 Kings 11:1–15), and during her reign, Baal worship is allowed (see 2 Kings 11:3, 18), just as Jezebel had promoted Baal worship in Israel. Both queens lead their husbands astray (1 Kings 16:31–32; 2 Kings 8:18). Jezebel eliminates the prophets of Yhwh (1 Kings 18:4), and Athaliah erases the royal seed of Judah (2 Kings 11:1). Both queens face a shameful death: Jezebel's body ultimately is deprived of burial and remembrance because there is not enough left to bury (1 Kings 9:36–37); Athaliah disappears before any mention of her death and burial. Like her outsider Sidonian mother Jezebel, Athaliah is viewed as a foreigner when she marries into the royal house of Judah and is portrayed as an equally dangerous and corrupting influence.

Jezebel exemplifies the trope of the dangerous foreign woman, who can lead native-born men astray to assimilate into her "foreign" cults. The entire house of Ahab is annihilated due to their walking after other deities, which are, in fact, Jezebel's. At the same time, she illustrates the fuzziness or permeability of identity boundaries. She dies because she is considered an "insider" member of the royal dynasty of Ahab; yet even after becoming queen, she continues to be perceived as a "Sidonian," exposing the inability of foreigners to be allowed to shed former ethnic labels completely under new circumstances. She is both an outsider and an insider simultaneously. She also serves as an example of why women should not become monarchs. But, like all the kings of Israel and most of the kings of Judah, she lacks fidelity and loyalty to Yhwh and acts unscrupulously and violently to get what she wants, making her a typical royal in spite of her gender.

About the Author

Kristin Joachimsen holds a doctorate in Hebrew Bible from the University of Oslo. Her research includes studies on the historiography of ancient Israel; prophetic and poetic literature (especially the book of Isaiah); the books of Ezra, Nehemiah, and Esther; identity constructions related to religion and ethnicity; and the construction of "the other." She also applies perspectives taken from postcolonial and gender studies. She has published "Jezebel as Voiced by Others in 1 and 2 Kings," *Die Welt des Orients* 50(2) (2020): 216–233; and "Esther in Shusan: Narrative Constructions of Otherness Related to Gender, Ethnicity, and Social Status within the Persian Empire," pages 204–223 in *Foreign Women—Women in Foreign Lands Studies on Foreignness and Gender in the Hebrew Bible and the Ancient Near East in the First Millennium BCE*, edited by Angelika Berlejung and Marianne Grohmann (Tübingen: Mohr Siebeck, 2019).

Suggestions for Further Reading

In This Book
See also chapters 24 (Kings and Chronicles), 25 (Deuteronomistic History), 38 (Samaritans), 47 (monotheism), 48 (twelve tribes), 51 (prophets), 55 (patriarchalism), 56 (polemics), 64 (Ruth), and 79 (memory studies).

Elsewhere
Brownsmith, Esther. "To Serve Woman: Jezebel, Anat, and the Metaphor of Women as Food." Pages 29–52 in *Researching Metaphor in the Ancient Near East*. Edited by Marta Pallavidini and Ludovico Portuese. Wiesbaden: Harrassowitz, 2020.

Crowell, Bradley L. "Good Girl, Bad Girl: Foreign Women of the Deuteronomistic History in Postcolonial Perspective." *Biblical Interpretation* 21 (2013): 1–18.

Walsh, Carey. "Why Remember Jezebel?" Pages 311–331 in *Remembering Biblical Figures in the Late Persian and Early Hellenistic Periods: Social Memory and Imagination*. Edited by Diana V. Edelman and Ehud Ben Zvi. Oxford: Oxford University Press, 2013.

67
How Many Isaiahs?

Ehud Ben Zvi

How many Isaiahs were or are there? Biblical scholars have identified three
distinctive sections in the book associated with this name (chapters 1–39,
40–55, and 56–66) and use the shorthand First Isaiah, Second Isaiah, and
Third Isaiah to refer to each, respectively. Differing concerns; styles of
writing, or "voices"; and explicit references to Cyrus (Isaiah 44:28; 45:1)
lead them to these subdivisions. Yet there remains the sticky situation
that Isaiah can designate both a prophet and a book, and this raises the
question, Did the historical prophet Isaiah author the entire book of Isaiah, or might he have been a prophet others remembered and with whom
they associated the prophetic book they wrote and edited over a long
time? When people read the scroll of Isaiah toward the end of the Persian
period (538–332 BCE) and in the early Hellenistic era (332–64 BCE),
they had only one scroll containing all the material that subsequently was
divided into 66 chapters with numbered verses, not three separate scrolls
containing, respectively, the contents of what is now chapters 1–39, 40–55,
and 56–66.

Is an emphasis on the actual or "historical" author appropriate when
dealing with biblical books? Did ancient readers care about authorship—in
our sense of the term—or care more about the prophetic persona with
whom a particular case of divine "word" or "vision" was associated? Scholars recognize that all biblical books, including Isaiah, have been edited by
subsequent redactors who have added, deleted, or rewritten verses and
sections and who also could have shifted beginnings and endings. If what
unifies a prophetic book is not historical, single authorship but the single
personage of the prophet with whom the divine words or visions reported
in the book are associated, then a prophetic book cannot really have more
than one central prophetic figure.

All these questions and issues have been engaged by biblical scholars
implicitly or explicitly and are interwoven in the current scholarly debate
over whether the role of the critical reader is to read a book, to reconstruct

the "historical" prophet, or to reconstruct how the prophet was portrayed in prophetic texts produced in ancient Judah.

There can be no doubt that traditionally, readers of the book of Isaiah assumed "Isaiah" referred to a very important prophet who lived during the days of Uzziah, Jotham, Ahaz, and Hezekiah, kings of Judah (Isaiah 1:1). According to these readers, either he wrote down his sayings himself or they were recorded and compiled by one or more contemporary scribes to form the book of Isaiah. This prophet Isaiah almost always was seen as primary and the book secondary, serving as a tool that let generation after generation be guided by the light of the prophet Isaiah rather than the other way around (see Sirach 48:22–25).

The association of the great prophet with "his" book was not strongly debated for centuries. Although Ibn Ezra, who lived in the twelfth century, seems to have suggested that the author/prophet of Isaiah 1–39 was not that of Isaiah 40–66, it was only in the late eighteenth century, with the beginning of the critical study of biblical texts, that substantial voices maintaining that the author/prophet of Isaiah 40–66 was not the eighth-century prophet began to gain acceptance. As this view became more and more accepted in the nineteenth and early twentieth centuries, a standard version of the triad of Isaiahs emerged: Isaiah (1–39), Deutero- or Second Isaiah (40–55), and Trito- or Third Isaiah (56–66). That said, the division of texts within the mentioned triad and their respective authors was never clear-cut. This is particularly true for Isaiah 1–39. For instance, some scholars maintained that sections of Isaiah 1–39 were written by Deutero-Isaiah (e.g., chapters 13–14; 34–35) or that Isaiah 1–39 was substantially edited by Deutero-Isaiah. In addition, some scholars argued that Isaiah 40–66 constituted Deutero-Isaiah, denying the existence of a Trito-Isaiah. Beyond these general trends, many scholars have proposed that various chapters were written by diverse authors over the centuries.

Although these debates are extremely helpful for identifying the best options for the historical authorship of the various chapters in Isaiah, each with their strengths and weaknesses, they do not address the questions of how the character of Isaiah is portrayed in the book and how he has been imagined and remembered by the readership of Isaiah 1–66 (i.e., the entire book of Isaiah) since the time this book emerged, most likely in the late Persian or early Hellenistic period.

The original audience read the book and imagined a single prophet, Isaiah. The persona of this prophet was associated with and brought together multiple crucial memories, images, characters, and events that figured prominently within the memory of this community. The prophet became so memorable precisely because all of the above were embodied and evoked by him. Like other central characters within the world of memory of the community, especially Moses and David, the figure of Isaiah served as a magnet that attracted voices, images, narratives, and ideological issues central to the community, which became integrated into one persona. A continuous feedback process that continued well after the Persian period resulted in the ongoing growth of Isaiah as a figure of memory. For instance, his words/prophecies concerning the virgin birth (see Matthew 1:22–23 and Isaiah 7:14, especially in the Greek version) and the image of the Suffering Servant (see Isaiah 53) were configured and associated with Jesus in early Christian communities. Such an association would have been unthinkable from the perspective of cross-cultural memory if Isaiah had not already been a very memorable character of the past. At the same time, no one would doubt that Jesus was the most central site of memory in the early Christian community or that associating him with Isaiah's words drew increased attention to the figure of Isaiah and his prophecies and to the community's understanding of them.

In Yehud, the province that succeeded the kingdom of Judah, those reading the book in the late Persian or early Hellenistic period saw Isaiah as a unique prophetic character whose voice, which also conveyed Yhwh's voice, evoked and addressed the entire era from the Assyrian to the (early) Persian period and onward, to the future empire of Yhwh. Isaiah evoked images of the salvation of Jerusalem due to the piety of its leadership, from the siege of the Assyrian King Sennacherib in 701 BCE, to the eventual fall of Jerusalem and the Temple, and to exile in 587 BCE. Isaiah 39 directly leads into Isaiah 40 and a second exodus, this time leading not just to the land but to Jerusalem, the place of the unique temple of Yhwh. In addition, remembering this Isaiah triggered the remembering of two opposite pairs: King Hezekiah and Isaiah, on the one hand, and King Zedekiah and Jeremiah, on the eve of the destruction of Jerusalem, on the other. When the king listened to the prophet, Jerusalem was saved; when the king did not listen to the prophet, Jerusalem was destroyed.

Remembering Isaiah also meant remembering foreign kings. Readers were prompted to recall that one foreign king was about to destroy Jerusalem and Yhwh's temple (Sennacherib), another succeeded in destroying them (Nebuchadnezzar), but a third (Cyrus), unlike Pharaoh, willingly authorized a second exodus and initiated the process of restoration that eventually, it was hoped, would lead to a utopian future. Thus, remembering Isaiah was intertwined with memories of both local and foreign kings and, above all, was a narrative that moves toward the hope of a utopian future while rooted in the remembering of a difficult past. This narrative of the prophet Isaiah covers Israel's past and future, but it also is Yhwh's narrative, since Yhwh is the agent of both destruction and salvation.

The second exodus encoded in Isaiah's prophecies (Isaiah 42:14–16; 43:1–7; 16–21) is depicted as glorious, but Isaiah is still not Moses. Returning to the land may be wonderful, but the renewed community not only is far from utopian but, in many ways, sinful (Isaiah 55–66). Reading Isaiah evoked a sense that Israel needs a superhuman Davidic king (see Isaiah 11), but also, that there is no need for a king at all, since Yhwh is its king (see Isaiah 33:17–24) and the covenant with David has shifted to the people (Isaiah 55:3–5). Not only does the figure of Isaiah the prophet bring multiple crucial narratives and characters in Israel's memory together in multiple ways, but it also integrates multiple voices standing in tension, balancing and informing one another, into a single prophetic individual.

Certainly, a personage of memory and imagination who can do all that is a most memorable figure! It is not by chance that this figure was able to continue to impact communities of readers and their memories centuries after it emerged. It was able to do that because this Isaiah of memory was rooted in and evoked by Isaiah 1–66. This means that in a world in which this Isaiah is a key site of memory, there is no room for a Deutero- or Trito-Isaiah. The latter becomes meaningful when we are seeking to identify the best options for the historical authorship of the various chapters in Isaiah and for reconstructing the various editorial processes that led eventually to the book of Isaiah.

About the Author

Ehud Ben Zvi holds a doctorate (PhD) from Emory University. His research investigates ancient Israelite history and historiography, social memory in ancient Israel, the latter's intellectual history, and the prophetic and historiographical books that eventually became part of the Hebrew Bible. He has published "Isaiah, a Memorable Prophet: Why Was Isaiah So Memorable in the Late Persian/Early Hellenistic Periods? Some Observations," pages 365–383 in *Remembering Biblical Figures in the Late Persian and Early Hellenistic Periods: Social Memory and Imagination*, edited by Diana V. Edelman and Ehud Ben Zvi (Oxford: Oxford University Press, 2013); *Social Memory among the Literati of Yehud* (Berlin: De Gruyter, 2019); and "From 'Historical' Prophets to Prophetic Books," pages 5–16 in *The Oxford Handbook of the Minor Prophets*, edited by Julia M. O'Brien (Oxford: Oxford University Press, 2021).

Suggestions for Further Reading

In This Book
See also chapters 8 (anonymity), 9 (audiences), 13 (genres), 33 (Septuagint), 51 (prophets), 52 (covenant), 68 (Jeremiah), 72 (synchronic vs. diachronic), and 79 (memory studies).

Elsewhere
Hays, Christopher B. "The Book of Isaiah in Contemporary Research." *Religion Compass* 5(10) (2011): 549–566.

Sawyer, John F. A. "Isaiah, Book Of." Pages 549–555 in *Dictionary of Biblical Interpretation* (volume 1). Edited by John H. Hayes. Nashville: Abingdon, 1999.

Sawyer, John F. A. *Isaiah through the Centuries*. Hoboken, NY: John Wiley & Sons, 2020.

68
Jeremiah: Why Is He So Well Remembered?

Benedetta Rossi

The book of Jeremiah, the longest in the Hebrew Bible, is bound up with the events that led to the end of the kingdom of Judah and the conquest of Jerusalem by the army of Nebuchadnezzar, king of Babylon, in 587 BCE. The book's opening (1:1–3) encloses the words and deeds of Jeremiah in a symbolic temporal span of forty years, from the thirteenth year of King Josiah's reign (627 BCE) to the eleventh year of King Zedekiah (587 BCE).

Historically, these forty years were marked by the decline of the Neo-Assyrian power, ending with the destruction of Nineveh in 612 BCE by the Neo-Babylonians. This new imperial power was responsible for the end of the kingdom of Judah and the destruction of Jerusalem. Five kings sat on the throne of Judah in these turbulent years. Josiah died in 609 at Megiddo and was succeeded by Jehoahaz (a.k.a. Shallum in Jeremiah 22:11), who remained on David's throne for only three months. During the reign of his successor, Jehoiakim (609–597 BCE), the Babylonian king Nebuchadnezzar appeared on the international stage. Jehoiakim's revolt against Babylon led to a deportation of Judahites to Babylon in 597. Jehoiachin succeeded Jehoiakim, and then the Babylonians replaced him with Zedekiah, who was to be the last sovereign in Judah. In July 587 BCE, the Babylonian army entered Jerusalem; the following month, they burned the city, the palace, and part of the temple. The Jerusalemite elite were deported to Babylon.

The book of Jeremiah, however, continues beyond 587 to include the assassination of Gedaliah, the governor (or king) the Babylonians established in Mizpah, north of Jerusalem. The crime provoked Babylonian retaliation, followed by a further deportation in 582. These events led the leaders of the revolt against Babylon to flee to Egypt, taking Jeremiah with them, against his will. There he uttered his last prophecies against the immigrants from Judah who had settled in Tahpanhes (Jeremiah 43).

The rise of the Neo-Babylonian imperial power in the ancient Near East and the fate of Judah, which rebelled unsuccessfully against it, form the context in which the prophecies attributed to Jeremiah are set. They consist of oracles, primarily in chapters 1–25, and narrate significant events in his life, mostly in chapters 26–52. Jeremiah's prophecy is characterized by announcements of judgment and disaster, though chapters 29–33 announce consolation too. Jeremiah was a prophet of priestly pedigree (Jeremiah 1:1), connected by descent not to the priesthood of Jerusalem but to the lineage of Abiathar, priest who had been exiled to Anathoth, 2.25 miles northeast of Jerusalem, by Solomon (1 Kings 2:26–27).

The book's elevated degree of literary elaboration makes it difficult to employ this text as a source for reconstructing the historical figure of the prophet, even though it assembles a structured and detailed portrait of the prophet so distinctive as to be emblematic. No other prophetic book devotes so much space to the figure of the prophet. As is the case in Isaiah 6, Ezekiel 2–3, or Amos 7, Jeremiah 1:4–19 is devoted to the prophet's calling. But the second part of the book is largely given over to the account of the events surrounding Jeremiah's ministry: his conflict with the authorities over his announcement of the destruction of the temple. Jeremiah is arrested and tried in the presence of all the people (chapter 26). Contrary to the other prophets who foretell peace and prosperity (e.g., 14:13; 23:9–40), Jeremiah proclaims the imminent end of Jerusalem, starting with the royal house (Jeremiah 22:1–23:7) and including the temple cult and sacrifices (Jeremiah 7:1–8:3).

Jeremiah is a lone voice, a prophet persecuted by the political and religious establishments. The torture inflicted by the priest Pashhur (20:1–6) and the clash with the prophet Hananiah (chapter 28) are emblematic of the hostility of the ruling class. The destruction of the scroll containing the prophet's words by King Jehoiakim (chapter 36) targets Jeremiah's subversive message. Yet, a new scroll is written (36:32), displaying the superiority of prophecy over political powers.

Jeremiah equally experiences rejection on the part of his fellow citizens. They are more inclined to welcome the announcement of peace and prosperity from the other prophets than his call to abandon idolatry in order to turn to Yhwh. Jeremiah thus appears as a prophet opposed by the political and religious authorities and isolated from the community.

Against this background, the book of Jeremiah devotes considerable space to the detailed treatment of the interior life and psychology of the prophet in a series of texts known as *Confessions* (Jeremiah 11:18–12:6; 15:10–21; 17:14–18; 18:18–23; 20:7–18). Speaking in the first person, Jeremiah expresses the profound crisis he experiences in relation to his community, to his mission, and even to Yhwh. These texts are unique in prophetic literature; they are akin to the psalms of individual lamentation, rendering the figure of Jeremiah as close to that of Job and Isaiah's picture of the Suffering Servant.

To whom is the book addressed? The audience in the narrative world is the people of Jerusalem in the final years of the kingdom of Judah. The last sovereigns, Jehoiakim and especially Zedekiah, are recipients of oracles, together with other figures, whether opponents or collaborators of the prophet, like Hananiah the prophet; Pashhur, priest of the temple; and the faithful scribe Baruch. According to 1:5, the prophet is appointed "prophet for the nations." This expression underlines the universal scope of Jeremiah's announcement, and as already noted, Jeremiah addresses his final oracles to the Egyptian diaspora in Egypt (44:1) at Tahpanhes (43:8). He also sends a letter of consolation to Judean exiles in Babylon (chapter 29). In addition, Egypt, the Philistines, Moab, Ammon, Edom, Damascus, Kedar, Hazor, Elam, and Babylon are the subjects of the series of oracles against the nations of chapters 46–51. The text also contains traces of pronouncements destined for Israel (e.g., Jeremiah 2:1–37; 3:6–4:2).

Within the narrative sections or in the titles, the narrative voice, which sometimes coincides with the prophet (e.g., Jeremiah 32), is addressed to recipients both internal and external to the world of the narrative. Who are the external addressees? The scribes at work in the book of Jeremiah make use of older biblical traditions (e.g., Hosea) and texts of the Torah, especially Deuteronomy but also those from the Priestly tradition. These traditions are transformed and combined, with the intention of transmitting an innovative message. This is the case, for example, with the arrangements concerning divorce in Deuteronomy 24:1–4, to which Jeremiah 3:1 refers, rereading it in a creative way. The external addressees have the capacity and competence to grasp the references and, at the same time, appreciate the innovations. Very probably, the earliest external addressees should be sought among the scribes responsible for the production of the text itself.

The book of Jeremiah is the product of a complex history of composition, apparent from the coexistence of different writing styles, where poetic prophetic oracles alternate with prose narratives, and from the many "doublets," or repeated sayings. For example, the speech at the gates of the Jerusalemite temple reported in 7:1–15 returns in chapter 26, and sometimes identical verses or passages are repeated (i.e., 8:10–12 = 6:12–15). The chronology of the book is not linear: the references to sovereigns, regnal years, and events provide anticipations and inconsistencies. The events of chapter 21 are placed during the reign of Zedekiah, but then 26:1 returns to the beginning of the reign of Jehoiakim, Zedekiah's predecessor.

Even the order of chapters and the length of the book differ in the Greek translation (Septuagint; LXX), which is shorter than the Hebrew version by about a sixth and presents the series of oracles against the nations after 25:13, while the Hebrew text places them in chapters 46–51, immediately before the conclusion to the book in chapter 52. In the Greek text, these oracles precede the announcement of Yhwh's judgment on all the nations, described in the form of a cup of wine the nations have to drink, a metaphor for Yhwh's anger and judgment (Jeremiah 32LXX).

Many interpreters attribute the differences between the LXX and the Masoretic Text (MT) to the presence of a shorter version of Jeremiah available to the translator. Even if divergences can be ascribed to translation choices in some cases, however, the differences in quantity and arrangement of the material between the LXX and the MT indicate that the Jeremiah scroll was still evolving in the last centuries of the common era and represented much more than a record of the words uttered by the prophet Jeremiah. The complex history of the development of the text as well as the references to other biblical books and the differences between the LXX and MT lead to the reasonable hypothesis of a date in the Persian period (538–332 BCE) or even later for the initial composition of the book.

The words or passages that may be ascribed to the historical figure of the prophet of Anathoth are not easily identified. Thanks to titles and frames, however, the reader can ascribe the words that follow as those uttered by the prophet of Anathoth. Even if it is difficult to trace the successive stages of the development of the text with precision, it is possible to identify the interests underlying the different traditions, interests that can be ascribed to groups in the Second Temple period. Thus, the book of Jeremiah is to be understood as a literary product of tradition, to be investigated on the basis of its literary characteristics.

About the Author

Benedetta Rossi holds a doctorate in biblical science from the Biblical Pontifical Institute in Rome. Her research includes Jeremiah, Deuteronomy, and relations between the Pentateuch and prophetic literature. She has published "Jeremiah," pages 875–940 in *The Jerome Biblical Commentary for the Twenty-First Century*, edited by John J. Collins, Gina Hens-Piazza, Barbara Reid, and Donald Senior (London: Bloomsbury T&T Clark, 2022); and "Lost in Translation: LXX-Jeremiah through the Lens of Pragmatics," pages 157–182 in *New Avenues in Biblical Exegesis in Light of the Septuagint*, edited by Leonardo Pessoa da Silva Pinto and Daniela Scialabba (Turnhout: Brepols, 2022).

Suggestions for Further Reading

In This Book

See also chapters 4 (sacred books), 9 (audiences), 10 (Tanak), 11 (Pentateuch), 19 (Job), 21 (dates), 27 (Josiah's scroll), 28 (archaeological proofs), 33 (Septuagint), 34 (Dead Sea Scrolls), 41 (symbolic numbers), 51 (prophets), 65 (King David), 67 (Isaiah), 74 ("P"), 75 (historical criticism), 76 (redaction and text criticism), and 77 (literary and form criticism).

Elsewhere

Fischer, Georg. "Jeremiah (Book and Person): Hebrew Bible/Old Testament." Pages 908–918 in *Encyclopedia of the Bible and Its Reception* (volume 13). Edited by Constance M. Furey, Joel Marcus LeMon, Brian Matz, Thomas Römer, Jens Schröter, Barry Dov Walfish, and Eric Ziolkowski. Berlin: De Gruyter, 2016.

Mills, Mary E. *Jeremiah: Prophecy in a Time of Crisis; An Introduction and Study Guide*. London: Bloomsbury T&T Clark, 2017.

Najman, Hindy, and Konrad Schmid, editors. *Jeremiah's Scriptures: Production, Reception, Interaction, and Transformation*. Leiden: Brill, 2016.

Weis, Richard D. "Textual History of Jeremiah." Pages 495–513 in *Textual History of the Bible: Pentateuch, Former and Latter Prophets* (volume 1B). Edited by Armin Lange and Emanuel Tov. Leiden: Brill, 2017.

69
Jonah: How to Survive in the Belly of Hell?

Philippe Guillaume

Everything in the Jonah booklet (only four chapters) is big: the city of Nineveh, its wickedness, the storm that rocked the boat, the sailors' fear when the sea abated, the fish that swallowed Jonah, Jonah's anger at God's decision not to destroy Nineveh after all, Jonah's joy over the plant God grew to shade him, and Nineveh's population.

At first sight, this booklet delivers simple moral lessons. In fact, Jonah is a brilliant faux-naïve narrative. The magic of a free ride in the whale fascinates children until they are old enough to ask how to sing psalms while swimming in gastric juices for three days and three nights. At this point, they are then ready to appropriate precious lessons when life sucks them into a whirlwind and they are swallowed by deep waters.

A first lesson for readers is to resist being put in a box. Bible canonizers put Jonah among the so-called minor prophets, even though he is a total misfit there. Only Jonah's namesake in 2 Kings 14:25 is deemed a prophet. The Jonah of the book of Jonah is at best an offbeat prophet: he flees from the job (Jonah 1:3); sings bits and pieces of Psalms (2:1–9); delivers the shortest possible "sermon" (3:4); reproaches God for being gracious, slow to anger, and versatile (4:2); and pities the loss of a plant that grew by itself (4:9) but insists on the destruction of Nineveh and would rather die than see it spared (4:1). The writer apparently intended readers to challenge their understanding of prophecy.

Most readings view Jonah's decision to flee to Tarshish as disobedience, though God never shows any displeasure toward Jonah. He saves him from drowning, from sunstroke, and from depression. Jonah is no Prodigal Son who needs to repent. Jonah simply refused to obey a life-threatening and senseless order. Why warn Nineveh if its sin was so great that it had reached God? Exegetes tell us that God wanted to give it a chance to repent, though all Jonah proclaims is its impending destruction

(3:4). As every student of ancient history knows, Nineveh was indeed destroyed in 612 BCE, something every Bible reader knows too, since the first chapter of Nahum gloats over the fall of Nineveh. What good would it do to send a Hebrew to Nineveh? Weren't there prophets in Nineveh?

One may object that it was worth sending Jonah, since the Ninevites proved to be highly receptive to his message, even more so than the sailors who feared the Lord when the storm was stilled (1:16). The moment they heard Jonah's five-word oracle, all the Ninevites repented, fasting in ashes and sackcloth from the king to the lambs (3:6–8). Jonah is not impressed. He takes exaggerated behavior for what it is. The sailors and the Ninevites are mere foils, useful stereotypes to contrast with Jonah, but they are exactly the kind of figures that support the common but wrongly assumed view bemoaned by J. H. Gottcent (1986, xxvi)—namely, that biblical characters are all "straitlaced, tedious saints whose stories demonstrate a steadfast—and boring—piety." If Nineveh's sin was that great (1:2), great sinners can put up great shows of piety, another crucial life lesson. If so, Jonah's incongruous psalm (2:1–9) may fall in the same category, unless it conveys another great lesson.

Singing praises (rather than "crying out") in the belly of Sheol, the biblical precursor to heaven and hell where all the dead go, tames the mighty Leviathan, the destructive powers of chaos, whose head Jonah's God crushed (Psalm 74:14). Accordingly, in Psalm 106:26, Leviathan morphed into God's plaything, a benevolent servant appointed to save Jonah (1:17) and ship him toward Nineveh. The "God of the heavens who created the sea and the dry land" is in control. There are no more dark forces opposing him. Hence, even in the belly of Sheol, Jonah has no reason to despair. His "psalm" is incongruous until it is understood as the expression of a steadfast hope that in the thick of life's struggles, deliverance is not far off. In the belly of the tamed Leviathan-Sheol, resourceful Jonah is making plans for the future and vows to offer a sacrifice to his Deliverer (2:10).

Back on firm land, Jonah tackles another theological issue. Having dispatched the endless struggle between God and evil forces, Jonah attacks the matter of divine fickleness head-on. He burns with anger (4:1) at the narrator's hint that God had a change of heart about the evil to be passed on Nineveh (3:10). In other words, how could a truly sovereign God be moved by a show of fasting bipeds and quadrupeds in sackcloth? Jonah is not challenging the idea that God is essentially merciful, slow to anger, and abounding in steadfast love (4:2). This is a fact (Exodus 34:6–7; Numbers 14:18–19; Psalm 103:8–11; 145:8; Joel 2:13). Such a God should not, however, turn into a soft-hearted divine Daddy moved by shows of superficial piety. Were prayers, vows, and sacrifices able to manipulate God, the world would sink back into chaos. Jonah would rather die than live in such a world. He rejects, therefore, God's attempts to soothe him with shade and coax him with a heat wave (4:3–9). Yet, angry as he is with God's supposed change of mind over Nineveh, Jonah is not embittered to the point of being incapable of enjoying the shade of the God-given plant (4:6; see Colossians 3:15–17).

Still, at times, anger is superior to pity, and throughout, Jonah ben Amittai (1:1) "son of truth" or something similar, remains true to himself. He flees when he sees no need to obey. He expresses anger when he is angry. He does not play the hero. He identifies with a fragile, fast-growing, and fast-shriveling plant and asks for death rather than commit suicide when conditions become overwhelming (4:8).

While most readers consider that Jonah does everything wrong, in the end, he is vindicated by God. As in any truly good story, everything clinches at the very end. The king's "who knows" (3:9) is placated by the last verse that many translators render as a rhetorical question when nothing in the Hebrew or in the Greek indicates that it is a question. "But I will not show pity over Nineveh the great city" (4:11) means that despite the huge size of its population, Nineveh shall be destroyed, and God will do nothing to save it from the Babylonians or save Jerusalem from the same Babylonians in 587 BCE (Jeremiah 52).

Indeed, God commissions storms, fish, plants, worms, heat waves, and messengers at will, but he lets corrupt regimes meet their fate in due course. The moral is that there is no automatic retribution for individuals. As Malachi (3:15) complains, the wicked often prosper (see also Jeremiah 12:1–2; Psalm 10). Even when Jonah's behavior seems offensive, God never seeks his loss. But for Nineveh as much as for Samaria, Jerusalem, and eventually Babylon and even Rome, on the day of reckoning, each fell, irrespective of its greatness in its heyday.

From a scholarly point of view, Jonah is a rare biblical book; early reader responses to it are provided in the Bible itself. Whereas the Greek translation of the Minor Prophets places Nahum immediately after Jonah in order to underline that Nineveh was destroyed immediately after God's final words in Jonah 4, in Hebrew Bibles, the seven chapters of Micah separate Jonah and Nahum to delay the destruction. This delay corresponds to the forty days Jonah mentions in his sermon (3:4). The Greek text, however, has only three days, which reflects the Jonah-Nahum sequence of the Greek canon.

The fate of Nineveh is also mentioned in the book of Tobit, which closes by recalling "the word of God that Nahum spoke about Nineveh" (14:4). Knowing that all the words of the prophets come true, Tobit orders his son and grandsons to hurry off to Babylonia before Nineveh's destruction. Jonah is ignored, a clue that he was already misunderstood as a dubious if not a false prophet.

The *Life of the Prophets*, a Hellenistic compilation of legends about the biblical prophets written around the turn of the era (first century BCE or CE)—remembers Jonah as the prophet whose prophecy was not performed. The New Testament Gospels, however, are more sympathetic to the message of the book of Jonah. Jonah is a sign of the resurrection (Matthew 16:4; Luke 11:29) as well as a model of trust in God. Hence, Jesus is asleep in the boat during a storm and only stills the wind after his disciples wake him up (Matthew 8:24; Mark 4:38; Luke 8:23). Jonah saves the sailors by willingly asking them to throw him overboard (1:12); Jesus accepts the bitter cup (Matthew 26) and dies to save humanity.

In the Qur'an, sura 37:139–148 recalls Jonah's full story. He is called Yunus (Arabic for Jonah), "Him of the Fish" (sura 21:87; 68:48), and an apostle of Allah (4:163; 6:86).

Western literature recalls Jonah in the adventures of Pinocchio, where he represents those who stray from God. Herman Melville's *Moby Dick* (1851) features a truly repentant Jonah who does not clamor for pardon but is grateful for punishment (chapter 83). And of course, Jonah in the whale is a favorite figure in children's Bibles, as the notion that God cared enough for little sheep is comforting. For adults, however, the nonrhetorical end of Jonah holds serious implications for the survival of political regimes, independently of their manipulation of religion.

About the Author

Philippe Guillaume holds a doctorate of theology from the University of Geneva. His research interests include rhetorical questions in the Bible. He has published "The End of Jonah Is the Beginning of Wisdom," *Biblica* 87 (2006): 243–250; and "The Unlikely Malachi-Jonah Sequence (4QXIIa)," *Journal of Hebrew Scriptures* 7 (2007), https://doi.org/10.5508/jhs.

Suggestions for Further Reading

In This Book

Elsewhere

Bolin, Thomas M. *Freedom beyond Forgiveness: The Book of Jonah Reexamined.* Sheffield, UK: Sheffield Academic, 1997.

Collodi, Carlo. *The Adventures of Pinocchio: Story of a Puppet*. 1883. Reprint, Berkeley: University of California Press, 1991.

Gottcent, J. H. *The Bible: A Literary Study*. Boston: Twayne, 1986.

Pyper, Hugh S. "Swallowed by a Song: Jonah and the Jonah-Psalm through the Looking-Glass." Pages 337–358 in *Reflection and Refraction*. Edited by Robert Rezetko, Timothy H. Lim, and W. Brian Aucker. Leiden: Brill, 2007.

70

Is Satan in the Hebrew Scriptures?

E. Macarena García García

Who has not heard of Satan? The prince of evil, the lord of demons and spirits, the ultimate cause of human disgrace. Today, we perceive the figure of Satan as a superhuman being characterized by acting beyond God's established and desired order, opposing Yhwh and the people of Israel. However, the term "satan" was not always identified with this evil force. At first, a or the *satan* appears in the Old Testament / Hebrew Bible as a common noun with the meaning of "enemy" or "adversary," especially in a military context (i.e., 1 Samuel 29:4; 2 Samuel 19:23; 1 Kings 5:18; 11:14, 23, 25), as well as "accuser" in the judicial sphere (i.e., Psalm 109:6). The characterization of Satan as a supernatural entity opposing God and humanity is not, therefore, original but secondary. It gradually took shape during the Second Temple period, beginning with some references dating to the Persian period (537–332 BCE).

Initially, the satan is not an independent figure, as the episode of Balaam's encounter with the angel shows. To oppose Balaam, "the angel of the Lord took his stand in the road as his adversary" (Numbers 22:22). Here and in verse 32, the words "as his adversary" (in Hebrew, לשטן; *leśāṭān*) simply describes the angel's mission to oppose Balaam.

In Zechariah 3:1–2, however, the satan and an angel of Yhwh are two separate entities: the satan is accusing the high priest Joshua. Though the New Revised Standard Version of the Bible removes the definite article ("the") before the noun "satan" in the Hebrew text and translates "Satan," in both cases, the figure in question functions as a prosecutor in the divine court that supervises world affairs (see Psalms 109:6–7). It is his job to accuse Joshua, and the divine rebuke does not mean that the satan has overstepped the bounds of his function.

This is also how the first two chapters of the book of Job portray the satan. As an angelic entity of the heavenly court, he acts as the accuser of pious Job. It is with God's permission that the accuser destroys Job's possessions, his offspring, and eventually, his health. Job rightly reproaches God rather than the satan for the injustice of his plight. It is significant that the satan does not reappear in the final chapters of the book. The accuser is not needed anymore, as God assumes full responsibility for the evils he allowed the satan to visit on Job.

Later theologies of retribution will side with Job's friends to shift the blame onto Job, while theodicy will use the satan as a ploy to shield God from any inklings of unfairness toward Job. Though evil is an undeniable element in human life, a satan acting without full divine approval inevitably reduces divine sovereignty by granting the accuser a quasi-divine status. The conclusion of the book of Job resists this tendency.

Yet, the temptation to explain misfortunes and blame someone for it is hard to resist. The first verse of 1 Chronicles 21 is the only place in the Hebrew Bible where Satan appears without an article and could be considered a proper name. In the corresponding passage in the book of Samuel, it is the "anger of Yhwh" that incites David to order a census, because Yhwh was angry with Israel (2 Samuel 24:1–9). What motivated the divine anger against the people need not be specified, because the presupposition is that all evils come ultimately from God. In this framework, the extermination meted out by the angel of Yhwh is justified. Though David claims to be solely responsible for the census, the epidemic strikes the people from Dan to Beer-sheba, sparing David and Jerusalem. The aim of the story is to explain the origins of the altar that will justify the erection of a temple of Yhwh in Jerusalem (2 Samuel 24:10–25).

Logical as it is, the story of the census is liable to uncomfortable readings due to the fact that it fails to name a specific fault that justifies God's wrath. The infinite goodness of the divinity could be called into question if the "anger of Yhwh" was not fully justified and the ensuing massacre was, as is the case in Job, simply a fact of life. For some reason (the rising popularity of Persian dualism?), the Chronicler ignores "the anger of Yhwh" at the beginning of the story: "Satan stood up against Israel, and incited David to count the people of Israel" (1 Chronicles 21:1). Set at the beginning of the verse, "Satan" requires a capital "S," though in Hebrew, *waya'amod sātān* (וַיַּעֲמֹד שָׂטָן) can equally be translated as "An accuser stood up" against Israel. As in the case of Job, what motivates the epidemic is unstated, but we readers are like Job's friends. We are prone to look for sin to explain misfortune and picture God as the righteous punisher of sins rather than incapable of protecting us from the inevitable mishaps that punctuate life.

Therefore, 1 Chronicles 24 isolates the accuser's stance against Israel from any direct command of God. The brevity of the reference can give the impression that the accuser is not content to accuse but enjoys greater freedom of action to incite David to sin. Again, it is the angel of Yhwh that executes the punishment but stops immediately when God (Elohim) has pity on Jerusalem and orders the end of the calamity (1 Chronicles 21:14–15).

Has this satan been upgraded to benefit from greater freedom to initiate evil actions, or is it still the obedient accuser of the books of Zechariah and Job? Is the Chronicler's satan different from the angel of the Lord and less subordinated to God than the exterminator? No definite answer can be given to these questions because key information in the text is lacking. Nonetheless, the ambiguity of 1 Chronicles 24 contributed to the evolution of the character of Satan.

Outside the Hebrew Scriptures, Jewish works from the Greco-Roman period (third century BCE–second century CE) crystalized the character of Satan as no longer satisfied with accusing humans; now the figure actively opposes God. In the *Ethiopic Book of Enoch* (or 1 Enoch), a group of Watchers—a kind of angel—rebels against God's created order and abandons the heavens to come down to earth and mingle with beautiful women, causing evil throughout the world.

The action of some celestial beings is less and less linked to God's will in the book of Jubilees, where Mastema appears either as an accuser and punisher of human sins by Yhwh's command (Jubilees 10:7–13) or as a supernatural being whose actions against humankind go beyond divine designs, acting freely as an oppressor for no apparent reason, to justify his indiscriminate attack (Jubilees 11:5).

Around the turn of the millennia, the satanic figure is definitely identified with a rebellious celestial power acting independently. The book of Wisdom—not included in the Hebrew Bible but part of the canonical books of the Orthodox and Catholic churches—explains that despite the fact that "God created us for incorruption and made us in the image of his own eternity," we nevertheless die due to the devil's envy (Wisdom 2:23–24). This brief reference can be linked to other Judeo-Christian works such as the *Slavonic Book of Enoch* (or 2 Enoch), the *Greek Apocalypse of Baruch* (3 Baruch), the *Apocalypse of Abraham*, and the *Life of Adam and Eve*, where the satanic figure appears under different names (the devil, Satan, Samael, Azazel) and is hidden behind the serpent in the garden of Eden.

Although Genesis 3 simply characterizes the serpent as the most intelligent creature and thus spurs Eve to gain knowledge, readers at the beginning of the Common Era came to blame the devil for Adam and Eve's disobedience. Instead of assuming the cost of access to wisdom (a burdensome enterprise according to Qohelet 12:12), Adam becomes the victim of Eve's fickleness and inability to resist the devil's temptation, a most convenient logic that justified the subordination of women to men.

In conclusion, the popular view of the devil is the result of a fairly clear evolution of the theological understanding of the figure of a or the satan over the centuries. The term "satan" evolved toward a common noun designating the specific function of a key figure of the divine court: the accuser in charge of reporting evildoers and ensuring their punishment to prevent injustice from producing havoc in the world. But there are evils that do not seem to respond to a punishment of the Lord for a committed fault, and the temptation to blame others for our own errors is hard to resist. As time goes on, we can find Judeo-Christian works where Satan appears as an autonomous entity whose actions deliberately seek to cause evil in the world. Nevertheless, according to the aforementioned passages of the Old Testament / Hebrew Bible, the evils we experience are neither imputable to the machinations of the devil nor reductive of God's sovereignty.

About the Author

E. Macarena García García holds a PhD in religious studies from Complutense University. Her research includes Jewish apocalyptic literature, focusing on the problem of evil and its protagonists. She has published "Who Tempted the Woman? Variations of the Edenic Episode in Jewish Apocalyptic Literature," *Collectanea Christiana Orientalia* 18 (2021): 75–94.

Suggestions for Further Reading

In This Book
See also chapters 15 (apocalyptic literature), 19 (Job), 42 (Nephilim), 43 (angels), 45 (heaven and hell), 47 (monotheism), 53 (creation), 55 (patriarchalism), and 71 (Qohelet).

Elsewhere
Kelly, Henry Ansgar. *Satan: A Biography*. Cambridge: Cambridge University Press, 2006.

Oldridge, Darren. *The Devil: A Very Short Introduction*. Oxford: Oxford University Press, 2012.

Russell, Burton. *The Devil: Perceptions of Evil from Antiquity to Primitive Christianity*. Ithaca, NY: Cornell University Press, 1977.

71

Was Qohelet Fighting Depression?

Steinar A. Skarpnes

How can one cope with life's uncertainties and absurdities under the sun? The book of Ecclesiastes, called Qohelet in Hebrew, opens and closes with "Vanity of vanities. All is vanity" (Qohelet 1:2; 12:7). The "Teacher," as the (feminine) Hebrew noun *qohelet* may be rendered, realizes that everything sooner or later becomes a puff of smoke that fades away. Eventually, every sense of satisfaction becomes insufficient, be it accomplishments, wealth, sensual pleasures, or even wisdom. In the end, death levels out everything and turns it into nothing. Readers have long been puzzled by this book's ambiguous message: Is Qohelet arguing that the glass is half full or that it is half empty? And what are these pessimistic chapters doing among the authoritative texts of the Hebrew Bible?

A helpful starting point for understanding the book's message is to emphasize how the main character's search for coherence and significance addresses issues about the meaning or value of human life and activity in this world. Philosophical perspectives thus provide an appropriate tool to discern whether Qohelet's core concern is epistemological or existential in nature, dealing with the meaning of life, or attempts to evaluate the merit of existence, as in the question "Is life a worthwhile experience?"

More specifically, the book's skeptical rhetoric can evoke today's nihilistic philosophy, which adds a psychological dimension to his message. God might not be dead, but by conceiving of an impersonal and distant God beyond our reach, Qohelet sounds like an agnostic voice in the Hebrew Bible. His evaluation of the bottom line of human existence leads him close to the edge, where he faces the void of depression.

Still, even though Qohelet observes the incongruent and senseless aspects of human existence, it does not necessarily mean that life is an utterly "meaningless" or "worthless" experience to have. Using the distinction between *passive* and *active* nihilism can help explain Qohelet's development of coping strategies to endure his existential distress. For the *passive* nihilist, everything eventually loses value because there is a lack of motivation to transcend a life-negating, cynical outlook. In contrast, the *active* nihilist manages to generate a life-affirming value system despite the absurdities of existence.

Ecclesiastes is considered part of the wisdom tradition of the Hebrew Bible, together with Proverbs and the book of Job. A characteristic of this literature is that it draws on everyday experiences to convince us to acknowledge the laws and causalities of the world and divine providence. Ecclesiastes, however, disapproves of the confidence in the human capacity to reach such insights found in the book of Proverbs (Qohelet 7:23–29). Therefore, some interpreters view Ecclesiastes and Job as representative of a critical strand of wisdom literature, in contrast to the didactic wisdom in Proverbs.

The designation of Qohelet as "son of David, king in Jerusalem" (Qohelet 1:1) suggests that the writer is King Solomon, something that contributed to securing the book's status as authoritative Scripture among traditional interpreters. Today, scholars generally exclude the possibility of Solomonic authorship, in particular on the basis of linguistic evidence. The Hebrew language in Qohelet is clearly late and dates Ecclesiastes no earlier than the fifth century BCE.

The text displays a variety of literary genres, including poems on the concept of time (1:4–11; 3:1–8; 12:1–7); autobiography (1:12–2:26); proverbs (7:1–12) and instructions (9:7–10). Furthermore, the text alternates between first and third person; the speaker is sometimes "the king" (1:12), sometimes "the Teacher" (7:27), and sometimes an anonymous advisor of rulers concerning wise conduct (8:2–5; 10:4–7). The mixture of styles and personifications obscures the book's overall position and gives the impression that Ecclesiastes is merely a combination of ambiguous or contradictory considerations held together by sheer repetition.

Nevertheless, the book consists of a frame and a main body. The frame has a third-person voice that introduces "the Teacher" and his leitmotif (1:1–2) and evaluates his teachings in a closing epilogue (12:8–14). In contrast, an autobiographical "I, the Teacher" (see 1:12) guides the reader through the text's main body (1:3–12:7). Initially, this "I" is a "king over Israel in Jerusalem" who accomplishes impressive building projects (1:12–2:11). However, this guise of king becomes less significant as the main character conducts an inner dialogue in his mind (cf. 1:13, 16, 17, 2:1, 15) to process his experiences in the exterior world. The repetitive and erratic nature of the internal dialogue might explain the book's puzzling literary disposition; it might be meant to resemble the dynamics of a thinking process that reaches new insights.

The initial section (1:3–6:9) lays out Qohelet's project to discover what individuals gain from all their efforts in life (1:3). He examines various rewards achieved through hard work, pleasure (2:1–2), accomplishments, status (2:4–11), wisdom (2:3; 2:12–16), and wealth (4:8; 5:9–10). All are vanity (*hevel*)—that is, "breath," "vapor," something insubstantial or of fleeting significance (1:14; 2:11, 17, 26; 4:4, 16; 6:9)—which leads Qohelet to low points of despair (2:17–23; 6:1–6). In this first half, Ecclesiastes displays the coping mechanism of a *passive* nihilist who sinks into grief and apathy.

In the second half (6:10–12:7), Qohelet accepts the reality of emptiness; as his temporary apathy dissipates, he is able to move forward to build new meaning. Unable to gain much insight into the workings of the universe, he accepts that a human is incapable of "knowing" or "finding" (8:7, 17; 9:2, 12); nevertheless, he provides advice on how to handle life's uncertainty and ambiguity (7:14, 16–22; 8:2–3, 9:7–10; 11:1–10). In particular, enjoyment (2:24–26; 3:12–13, 22; 5:17–19; 8:15) is presented as a consolation for the many "vanities" of life in the first half. By accepting the fleeting nature of life, Qohelet teaches the significance of staying present in the here and now to enjoy mundane gifts such as eating and drinking (9:7–10). In the despair and frustrations that first drove him to introversion, Qohelet discovers resilience and the life-affirming perspective of the *active* nihilist.

The epilogue (12:9–14) provides an initial interpretation of the book's teachings, both commending (12:8–10) and criticizing Qohelet's work (12:12) before urging, "Fear God, and keep his commandments!" This reference to God's commandments seems out of character for Qohelet. It is, therefore, commonly credited to a later hand that directed the reading of Ecclesiastes toward a more pious application. The final statements in 12:12–14 harmonize Qoheleth's radical message with other biblical traditions. By reminding the reader to stay anchored in the teachings of the Torah instead of drifting away in introspection, the epilogue ensured Qohelet's inclusion in the biblical canon while accepting the validity of its teaching.

As much as the implied attribution to Solomon in 1:1, the ambiguous epilogue of 12:8–14 reveals how Ecclesiastes continued to touch a nerve among the religious readership. Jewish and Christian interpreters of the Middle Ages were frustrated by how literal readings of Ecclesiastes created internal contradictions and challenged many tenets of faith; for example, it promoted an agnostic view concerning belief in an afterlife (3:19) and contradicted Moses's admonition of self-restraint (Numbers 15:39) with its "hedonistic" call to enjoyment (11:9).

Yet, for monastic interpreters, Qohelet's experiences of vanity became an encouragement to renounce the material world. An allegorical reading understood Qohelet's call to enjoyment as an invitation to participate in the Eucharist. Jews, on the other hand, read Qohelet during the autumn feast of Sukkot, a favorable season for reflecting on the fruits of one's labors. The huts of Sukkot symbolize a temporary residence evocative of life's vanities. Living under the sun during Sukkot can be conducive to the contemplation of the transitory and absurd experience of living. Thus, Qohelet's sober words remind us of life's gloomy sides so that we can truly appreciate festive and merry moments. While there are inevitably times to weep and to mourn, there should also be times to laugh and to dance.

The book's invitation to contemplate the meaning and value of everyday human experiences makes it available to a broader audience across time, regardless of religious or secular convictions. In today's societies, where many feel alienated and separated from themselves and the world, self-help literature sells abundantly by providing people with quick-fix solutions to cope with the pace of modern industrial life. Ecclesiastes represents an ancient and pragmatic alternative to discovering how to live the "good life." Qohelet's message that human toil for wealth and knowledge as an effort to get the upper hand and gain control over life recognizes the existential ambition of modern humans to achieve more as a means to prevail over their anxiety and denial about death. By aspiring to be like Qohelet the king (1:12–2:26), people today involve themselves in an unrelenting chase after more profit and truth in their pursuit of happiness and fulfillment. However, Qohelet exposes the human tendency to seek escape in illusions by emphasizing how an insatiable hunger for more gain entails only the realizations of lack and loss ("vanity"), consequently nurturing a cynical, nihilistic view of life as a meaningless or unworthy experience. Instead, Qohelet solemnly commends realism and a willingness to accept the passing nature ("vanity") of existence by embracing and enjoying the mundane gifts received here and now. Using philosophical and psychological perspectives to read Ecclesiastes demonstrates how its teachings provide a timeless consolation for filling human existential distress with meaning and significance.

About the Author

Steinar A. Skarpnes is completing a PhD at MF Norwegian School of Theology, Religion and Society on Hezekiah: "The Making of a Leadership Ideal in Judean Memory." His master's thesis at the University of Oslo dealt with the "vanity-complex" in Qohelet.

Suggestions for Further Reading

In This Book
See also chapters 9 (audiences), 13 (genres), 17 (Wisdom), 18 (Proverbs), 19 (Job), 65 (King David), and 69 (Jonah).

Elsewhere
Fox, Michael V. *A Time to Tear Down and a Time to Build Up: A Rereading of Ecclesiastes*. Grand Rapids, MI: Eerdmans, 1999.

Keefer, Arthur. "The Meaning of Life in Ecclesiastes: Coherence, Purpose, and Significance from a Psychological Perspective." *Harvard Theological Review* 112(4) (2019): 447–466.

Peterson, Jesse M. "Is Coming into Existence Always a Harm? Qoheleth in Dialogue with David Benatar." *Harvard Theological Review* 112(1) (2019): 33–54.

Provan, Iain. "Fresh Perspectives on Ecclesiastes: Qohelet for Today." Pages 401–416 in *The Words of the Wise Are like Goads: Engaging Qohelet in the 21st Century*. Edited by Mark J. Boda, Tremper Longman III, and Cristian G. Rata. Winona Lake, IN: Eisenbrauns, 2013.

Methods and Approaches

72
Synchronic versus Diachronic Readings: Why Choose?

Diana V. Edelman

In biblical studies, there are two ways to read a text; each has different underlying presuppositions concerning how the text was produced. The most prevalent approach is to read diachronically, or "through time," focusing on perceived inconsistencies and possible indications of additions made to the text over time to "update" it and keep it relevant to the communities reading and rereading it. There is an assumption that the current form of the text is not the "original one" due to secondary scribal glosses, errors, and deliberate alterations. If those can be identified and removed, it is thought, it might be possible to get back to an earlier, original form of the text and its contents. The other way is to read synchronically, or "at one time," as though the text in its current form came from the hand of its original composer. This approach tries to make sense of the received text as a piece of literature and to seek explanations of perceived inconsistencies, first in terms of literary devices and rhetorical strategy and secondarily, if the first approach does not yield logical results, in terms of textual expansion.

Both approaches agree that the texts comprising the Hebrew Bible were written anonymously and have been altered over time. A comparison of the manuscripts we have of various books of the Bible, beginning with the Dead Sea Scrolls and continuing through medieval exemplars in a range of languages, demonstrates clearly that there is no "final form" of any biblical book. There are hundreds of minor variations among the manuscripts and, from time to time, substantive differences in wording. Even in Jewish tradition, the standardized Masoretic Text used to create all torah scrolls preserves evidence of variant readings in its system that identifies problematic wordings and suggests how one is to read (*qere'*) the received written strings of unvocalized consonants (*ketiv*). Translations of the Hebrew Bible into modern languages tend to rely heavily on one selected manuscript but rarely follow it alone; they often adopt some of the variant readings found in other manuscripts.

A synchronic versus diachronic approach tends to assume that the text of a given book was produced by a master scribe, who often drew on written and oral source material but freely composed the book in question. The scribe used skill and imagination to create a piece of literature employing a range of literary devices to convey the message. Something like 90 percent of the current text can be attributed to his hand, with the remaining 10 percent being secondary changes due to scribal errors in copying, scribal glosses, and deliberate alterations, usually done for theological purposes.

By contrast, a diachronic approach tends to assume that a scribe edited and combined written and oral sources to produce a given book, with almost no independent contribution of his own. It is hard to estimate what percentage of the current text is typically to be assigned to him. Scholars who use this approach often try to identify various underlying source materials more than the "first edition" of the text before subsequent additions and changes. Unlike in a synchronic reading, this approach assumes that a number of systematic redactions of a single book or a number of books collectively took place in ancient times. These altered the "original book" more substantially than in the assumed case of the master scribe so that perhaps only 50 to 75 percent of the current text would have been original.

The diachronic approach has dominated biblical studies for more than a century and continues to be used. The synchronic approach was adopted by a minority of scholars beginning in the 1980s after a theory known as reader-response criticism became popular in literary studies in the late 1960s. This theory proposes that a text takes on an independent life of its own after it is composed and has no meaning inherent in it. Readers assign meaning to the words they encounter based on their own life experiences and cultural presuppositions. According to this theory, all meanings constructed by readers are legitimate; actual audiences are not merely passive receivers or consumers of an author's intended meaning.

Biblical scholars do not have the luxury of interviewing the original scribes to confirm what meanings they had hoped their readers would assign to their creations versus what actual readers have construed. At most, scholars can analyze the literary techniques and rhetorical strategy embedded in the text in order to propose what the implied author might have intended to convey to his audience. Clearly, a real person created the first version of the text, but we can only really speak about this writer in terms of what we can deduce or infer from the text itself—hence, the "implied author," although the term "author" is somewhat inappropriate because the writer is anonymous in addition to being implied. This latter approach, which is based on a hypothetical "final form" synchronic close reading, accepts that meaning is constructed by the reader; however, it also predicates that there is an intended authorial meaning embedded in the text, even if we cannot confirm what it was or whether any reader has constructed it as the author intended. It assumes the writer was trying to communicate a particular viewpoint or understanding to his audience. A "final form" close reading concentrates on the text more than the reader.

It is important to recognize that we cannot automatically assume that all the same literary devices or genres we are familiar with in our current cultures were shared by ancient writers. We might miss points that members of an ancient audience would have understood because we are not familiar with certain ancient conventions, or we might read something into the text based on what we assume is a familiar pattern or device that was not part of the repertoire of the Hebrew master scribes. Thus, when literary criticism is applied to biblical texts, one can read through modern lenses and construe a meaning that one finds satisfactory. If one is interested in situating the book in its ancient context, however, and trying to read it as a member of its target ancient audience, then it is likely that adjustments will need to be made. They should take into account the world view of the master scribes, their own identified genres, and literary devices that are evident within the wider collection and, preferably, also utilized in surrounding ancient cultures as well. In the absence of a manual that describes literary devices and techniques, the latter can establish the likelihood that we have deduced a legitimate practice with a higher degree of probability.

Many different questions can be asked of the biblical texts, and the methods used in analysis will vary depending on the ultimate goal. Those who are interested in diachronic questions need to begin with the equivalent of a "final form" synchronic reading (using literary criticism) in order to construct meaning before suggesting which elements of the text might be secondary and why. From there, hypothetical underlying sources, redactions, and stages of growth can be proposed, employing source criticism, form criticism, redaction criticism, and tradition-historical criticism. While text criticism might be used initially to establish the wording that will comprise the "final form," it can also be reconsidered in light of the results of the synchronic literary-critical reading. For those interested in a synchronic reading, text criticism will establish the "final form" and literary criticism the literary devices and rhetoric embedded in the text. This can be a goal in itself, in which case, diachronic questions will not be pursued.

About the Author

Diana V. Edelman holds a doctorate of philosophy (PhD) in biblical studies from the University of Chicago and is Professor Emerita in Hebrew Bible at the Faculty of Theology, University of Oslo. She has published *King Saul in the Historiography of Israel* (Sheffield, UK: Sheffield Academic, 1991).

Suggestions for Further Reading

In This Book

See also chapters 1 (scholarly perspective), 8 (anonymity), 13 (genres), 21 (dates), 73 (source criticism), 76 (redaction and text criticism), 77 (literary and form criticism), and 78 (ideological criticism).

Elsewhere

Iser, Wolfgang. *The Act of Reading: A Theory of Aesthetic Response*. Baltimore, MD: Johns Hopkins University Press, 1976.

Iser, Wolfgang. *The Implied Reader: Patterns of Communication in Prose Fiction from Bunyan to Beckett*. Baltimore, MD: Johns Hopkins University Press, 1974.

Hong, Koog P. "Synchrony and Diachrony in Contemporary Biblical Interpretation." *Catholic Biblical Quarterly* 75(3) (2013): 521–539.

Noble, Paul R. "Synchronic and Diachronic Approaches to Biblical Interpretation." *Literature and Theology* 7(2) (1993): 130–148.

73
What Is Source Criticism?

Kåre Berge

Why criticize the sources of the biblical text? Isn't the Bible inspired and the inspiration of major world civilizations? Indeed, source criticism is no challenge to the value of the Bible. Usually called *Literarkritik* in German, which literally translates as "literary criticism," it is a methodology searching for the origin and history of the biblical texts by identifying hypothetical earlier written sources behind the texts preserved in the final form of the biblical books.

The essence of the method is the division of the biblical text into different literary sources, which were supposedly integrated to produce the present text. Originally, source criticism was developed as an analysis of the literary growth of the Pentateuch, but it was also applied to other books in the Bible.

The juxtaposition of what appears as two different creation narratives in Genesis 1 and 2 had long been taken as a clue that the biblical text was somewhat composite. Because the creator is named Elohim in chapter 1 and Yhwh Elohim in chapter 2, it was logical to infer that one source or document used Yhwh for the deity from the time of creation (Genesis 2), while another source delayed the revelation of the divine name until Moses (see Exodus 6:2–3). However, in Genesis 4:26, humans are said to have called on the name of Yhwh already in the time of Seth and his son Enosh, and then in Genesis 28:13–16, the deity presents himself to Jacob as Yhwh. As Jacob realizes after his dream at Bethel that Yhwh "is in this place but [he] did not know it," he knows the divine name well before Moses, to whom it was supposedly first revealed. The assumed parallel between Exodus 6:2–3 and chapter 3:14–15 was explained by postulating another source that also delayed the divine name until Moses.

The number of animals to be taken into the ark (compare Genesis 6:19–20 and 7:2–9) is another case of contradiction that led to the idea that more than two different sources must have been used in these two chapters. That it is Yhwh rather than Elohim or Yhwh Elohim who decrees the flood in Genesis 6 fits the scenario of neither Genesis 1 nor 2. That chapter 7 has the same Yhwh change the previous order to include extra pairs of animals needs to be explained away to avoid the otherwise inescapable conclusion that God's commands are somewhat unstable.

This led early biblical scholars to suggest that different sources underlay more than just the initial chapters of the Bible and that logically, extended sources covering much of the same storyline had been woven together and combined, leaving variants intact. Whereas modern authors are expected to avoid flagrant plot incoherence, their colleagues in antiquity followed different rules and had other aims. Instead of altering the narrative logic of venerable sources and traditions they had been entrusted with, they might have sought to preserve them by setting them intact in broader narrative frameworks, irrelevant of the internal tensions generated by such a process. Simply downplaying these internal tensions would not do. Biblical literature had to be taken on its own account, and source criticism was one way to do so.

Although he was not the initiator of source criticism, the method is tied to the name of Julius Wellhausen, who in the years 1876–1878 undertook a detailed source division of the entire Pentateuch and of the succeeding books to argue that the sources reflected a progressive development of the religion of ancient Israel. The basic assumption was that the books of Genesis to Deuteronomy are an amalgam of four different literary sources or documents: the Yahwistic, the Elohistic, the Deuteronomic, and the Priestly sources. This is referred to as the "four-source hypothesis," or the Documentary Hypothesis. Influenced by his own biography—Wellhausen imagined the Priestly source in the garb of the influential Lutheran clergy of his days—Wellhausen reversed the relative dates of the sources current in earlier scholarship and deemed the Priestly source as the latest of the four and also inferior to the Yahwistic source and prophetic literature that, for him, represented the apex of Israelite religion. A small school of Jewish-Israeli biblical scholars fought with little success for the primacy of the Priestly source.

Therefore, until the 1980s, the oldest document or source was considered to be the Yahwist, dated to the time of Solomon (tenth century BCE). An underlying assumption was that the earlier source was closer to the original version, a gem unadulterated by the work of subsequent redactors that either were clumsy or had ulterior motives.

The Elohistic source was always difficult to identify and date because the only clear "evidence" for it was found in Genesis 20, 21, and 22 in addition to scattered elements, primarily in Exodus 3. It was characterized by the consistent use of "Elohim" to designate God. Classical source criticism thus regarded Exodus 3 as one of the clearest instances of source conflation, as Exodus 3:1, 4b, and 6 are consistent with Exodus 6:2–3 in referring to Elohim; Exodus 3:2, 4a, and 7 know the name Yhwh already. The conclusion that the chapter is a conflation of two sources gained support from the repetition of verse 7 in verse 9. Recent scholarship, however, is less inclined to draw source-critical conclusions from such variations.

The Deuteronomic source originally was limited to the narrative segments that form the present frame of Deuteronomy (approximately chapters 1–11 and 27–34). The "D" source is now mostly regarded as a redaction covering the whole Pentateuch as well as the subsequent books of Joshua, Judges, Samuel, and Kings. This redaction is recognizable through set formulas and terms found in Deuteronomy and taken up in the other books to form the Deuteronomistic History, another hypothesis now being challenged too.

Source criticism is a mixed method that combines text-internal criteria to divide verses into constituent sources on the basis of the comprehensive hypothesis about these sources delineated above. Accordingly, there is a clear circularity in the method. For this reason, the Documentary Hypothesis did not remain unchallenged. Instead of a combination of four sources, other scholars argued that many smaller units, both written and oral, were combined and supplemented over time, leading to inconsistencies in the texts. The multiplication of small fragments of texts that once supposedly belonged to a coherent narrative became unmanageable, however.

Having run its course and resulted in the uncontrollable fragmentation of the biblical text, source criticism as Wellhausen's successors practiced it is now obsolete. What had been considered inconsistencies—for example, the use of different divine names, different versions of the same episode, the relation between Ishmael and Isaac (Genesis 16 and 21), and repetitions of a single motif, like the so-called endangered ancestress (Genesis 12:10–20; 20:1–18; and again in 26:1–11)—are now more commonly viewed as "midrash," or elaborations of the same motif made to fit their present context.

A decisive argument against the Documentary Hypothesis is the observation that the Genesis and Exodus narratives were originally separate and independent stories until the Persian period, when they were combined for the first time either in the Priestly source or during a (Deuteronomistic) redaction. Either current understanding precludes any hypothesis of pre-Priestly sources covering the concept of a "Pentateuch."

Today, the existence of the Elohistic source has been given up, and the few scholars (like John van Seters) who hold on to the idea of a writer

376 THE OLD TESTAMENT HEBREW SCRIPTURES IN FIVE MINUTES

dubbed "the Yahwist" who produced the so-called Yahwistic source shift its date to the time of the Babylonian exile or later. The majority of scholars, however, dissolve the Yahwistic source into some sort of redaction, primarily connected with the Deuteronomist.

The influence and status of the source-critical method have been significantly reduced, and one should thus be wary today to even use the terms "Yahwist" and "Elohist" despite their popularity in the twentieth century. References to the Yahwist and Elohist today ignore the growing prestige of redaction criticism as well as the results of close reading in literary criticism, in which repetitions and contradictions are viewed as stylistic features that do not necessarily reflect different writers, theological schools, or the time of writing.

Nevertheless, some doublets, contradictions, and changes in terminology remain valid indicators of the growth of the text through time. Recent scholarship, especially in Germany, is working to refine the criteria of diachronic growth through a combined source-critical and text-critical study, which also involves ancient manuscripts such as the Dead Sea Scrolls.

About the Author

Kåre Berge holds a doctorate of theology (ThD) from the University of Oslo. His research includes studies in the Yahwist source in Genesis. For instance, Kåre published *Die Zeit des Jahwisten* (Berlin: De Gruyter, 1990); and *Reading Sources in a Text* (St. Ottilien: EOS Verlag, 1997).

Suggestions for Further Reading

In This Book
See also chapters 1 (scholarly perspective), 8 (anonymity), 21 (dates), 25 (Deuteronomistic History), 72 (synchronic vs. diachronic), and 74 ("P").

Elsewhere
Barton, John. "Source Criticism." Pages 162–165 in *Anchor Yale Dictionary* (volume 4). Edited by David N. Freedman. New York: Doubleday, 1992.

Blenkinsopp, Joseph. *The Pentateuch: An Introduction to the First Five Books of the Bible*. New York: Doubleday, 1992.

Boorer, Suzanne. "Source and Redaction Criticism." Pages 95–130 in *Methods for Exodus*. Edited by Thomas B. Dozeman. Cambridge: Cambridge University Press, 2010.

Childs, Brevard. *Exodus*. London: SCM Press, 1971.

Wellhausen, Julius. *Prolegomena to the History of Ancient Israel, with a Reprint of the Article "Israel" from the Encyclopaedia Britannica*. Gloucester, MA: Peter Smith, 1973.

74

What Is "P"—Source or Editor?

Philippe Guillaume

Studies in the first five books of the Bible often mention "P," a siglum standing for "Priestly." As it is difficult to accept that Moses wrote about his own death in Deuteronomy 34, the idea that Moses did not write the entire Torah imposed itself and led to the search for different "hands" involved in the production of the anonymous biblical texts.

The most pervasive system used the letters "JEDP" to distinguish four different writers, layers, documents, sources, redactors, or theological schools. The first two refer to the divine names: "J" for "Yhwh" (in German) and "E" for "Elohim," which some Bible translations such as the New Revised Standard Version render as "the Lord" and "God," respectively. "D" stands for "Deuteronomistic" to denote similarities in style and theology with the book of Deuteronomy. Matters pertaining to the cult and priests are attributed to "P." P was considered the earliest of the four until Julius Wellhausen (1844–1918) argued that it is, in fact, the latest. Instead of writings of the very beginnings of Israel, P was understood as the product of scribes associated with the temple before its destruction or, later, with the restoration of the cult attributed to Ezra, a scribe skilled in the "Torah of Moses" (Ezra 7:6). Ezra would have combined J, E, and D with P to complete the five books of Moses.

The shift of the date of P from the premonarchic era to the Persian era represents over a half millennium between the events narrated in the Pentateuch and their writing, a temporal gap implying a major loss of historical reliability, since it is unlikely that events were remembered and recorded exactly after such a long time.

Ideological biases are at work in the different dates of P. Wellhausen, for whom the prophet Elijah was the pinnacle of biblical religion, viewed P as a significant decline from the ethical outlook of the prophets. P reflected a theocracy that reminded Wellhausen of the Lutheranism in which he was raised. Naturally, the so-called Kaufmann school of Jewish and Israeli scholars rejected this notion and argued (with modest success) in favor of a return to the premonarchic date of P.

In Europe, the JEDP system broke down in the 1980s but still enjoys some popularity elsewhere for convenience, since no comprehensive alternative has emerged. Instead, subsequent research fragmented P and identified pre-P and post-P strands—and even P passages couched in Deuteronomistic language. It became virtually impossible to ascribe a clear context to any priestly material apart from rivalries between priestly families claiming privileges for themselves on the basis of Aaronic ancestry. In this case, P designates unrelated material found mostly in Exodus, Leviticus, and Numbers.

Other scholars relied on P to move beyond the breakdown of the JEDP system by ascribing to P some of the material that used to be ascribed to J and E. As the first creation account was and continues to be ascribed to P, the identification of P's end became a contested issue. If P begins with Genesis 1, where does it end? Much depends on the nature of P. Is it a collection of fragments or does it represent a continuous narrative? If it is fragments collected from various sources, neither a beginning nor an end is necessary. If, on the contrary, P designates the basic narrative thread other traditions were strung onto, it is crucial to find out where it ends, since a coherent narrative needs a beginning and a conclusion that marks the resolution of the crisis that provides the narrative tension for the whole. If so, P is designated as the "Priestly Document" or *Priesterschrift* or "Pg" for *Priesterschrift Grundschicht* in German. Then material relative to priestly and ritual matters deemed secondary additions are designated "Ps" for *Priesterschrift Supplement*.

The additions to Pg may be either older oral or written traditions or later literary creations. The difference could theoretically be distinguished on the basis of the historical evolution of the Hebrew language, though it is always possible that a new creation was penned in imitation of antiquated forms, as when today, someone uses the old English pronoun "thou."

So far, several options are available for the extent of the Priestly Document: a mini Pg ending somewhere in Exodus, at Sinai or with the completion of the mobile sanctuary Moses built in the wilderness; a medium Pg going as far as Deuteronomy; or a maxi Pg extending beyond Deuteronomy with a conclusion in Joshua.

As with any scholarly hypothesis, there are pros and cons for each of these understandings of Pg. A mini Pg sets the revelation of the law as the apex of biblical religion and implies that the wilderness is the place of revelation and a fitting conclusion of the liberation from Egypt. Israel is left wandering endlessly without ever entering the land promised to Abraham already in Genesis 12:7.

In favor of a medium Pg is its compliance with the well-established division between the Torah (Genesis–Deuteronomy) and the prophets or historical books that begin with the book of Joshua. The figure of Moses is key, and his death in the last chapter of Deuteronomy marks the end of the initial block of the biblical scenario. Like the mini Pg, a medium Pg leaves Israel at the doorstep of the promised land. By contrast, a maxi P closes with the completion of the conquest of Canaan and the fulfillment of the promises given to Abraham, Isaac, and Jacob. A conclusion in Joshua overrides the closure of the Torah in Deuteronomy 34 and shifts the focus away from the law and the lawgiver onto the possession of the land.

The rare verb *kabash*, usually rendered as "to subdue" in Genesis 1:28 and in Joshua 18:1, forms a neat inclusion in favor of a maxi Pg. In Genesis 1, humanity receives the mission of subduing creation, a mission accomplished in Joshua 18 when the Israelites, the last landless people in the list of Genesis 10, take possession of their God-given land allotment. Such an ending provides a satisfying closure for Pg, while the wanderings of the patriarchs and of Israel out of Mesopotamia and in and out of Egypt are episodes begging for such a resolution of the narrative tension. In this case, Pg is a full-fledged narrative that fits the prerequisites of ancient literary techniques, though its theological profile remains undetermined. Is it nonviolent? Is it in favor of a temple? What is its stance on sacrifices?

Ultimately, the choice between these different Pgs revolves around the choice between land or law as the main focus of the Pentateuch. The decision tends to be made on the basis of theological preferences, as textual evidence can be interpreted in different ways. Exegetes can reject or downplay the significance of elements at odds with their favored hypothesis by considering them later additions, scribal mistakes, or modern misunderstandings of the original meaning.

Whatever version of P is favored, Bible readers are confronted with an overabundant narrative and are forced to choose between favoring one alternative at the cost of ignoring the other or admitting the existence of competing presentations of Israel's past.

Alternative views are simply juxtaposed, which makes them easier to recognize, or interwoven, which represents additional challenges to separate the different strands. Creation out of a watery chaos is followed by a creation out of dry land in Genesis 2. P's justification of the flood as caused by violence (Genesis 6:11–13) follows the mention of the union of fair human daughters with sons of God (Genesis 6:1–4). The order to enter a pair of animals in the ark is followed by the order to take *seven* pairs of clean animals fit for sacrifice (Genesis 6 and 7). The covenant with Abraham in Genesis 15 is picked up again in chapter 17 with a different emphasis, and so is the expulsion of Hagar (Genesis 18 and 21). More or less contradicting versions of the same events continue in the other books of the Pentateuch: Sinai or Horeb for the place of revelation in Exodus, two accounts of the revelation of the divine name (Exodus 3 and 6), two slightly different versions of the Ten Commandments (Exodus 20 and Deuteronomy 5). The differences do not necessarily indicate different dates and hands, though this can be the case for Israel's refusal to enter the promised land, as the difference in the two explanations is flagrant. The Israelites either balked at the sight of giants (Numbers 13:28) or were afraid of an inhospitable and empty land that devoured its inhabitants (Numbers 13:32). The two contradictory notions are simply juxtaposed: the land is either already settled by unconquerable inhabitants or so hostile that it is empty. In both cases, the people's fear is justified, but the difference has implications for the occupation of Canaan. Was the land empty when the Israelites crossed the Jordan and celebrated the first Passover with wild grain (so Joshua 5:10–12) or did they have to conquer Jericho and eliminate the Canaanites (so Joshua 6; 8–12)? If Canaan was conquered, the figure of Joshua as Moses's successor is necessary. If the land was empty, priests led the procession into Canaan (Joshua 3–4). The conquest of Jericho combines the two concepts by granting the breaking of the city wall to the priests and the slaughter of the population to the army led by Joshua.

The beauty of the Bible resides in the constant debate between alternative views for which P constitutes a parade example in Pentateuch scholarship.

About the Author

Philippe Guillaume holds a doctorate of theology (ThD) from the University of Geneva and a habilitation from the University of Berne. He published *Land and Calendar: The Priestly Document from Genesis 1 to Joshua 18* (New York: T&T Clark, 2009); and "Non-violent Re-readings of Israel's Foundational Traditions in the Persian Period (the Calendar System in P)," pages 57–71 in *Religion in the Achaemenid Persian Empire*, edited by Diana V. Edelman, Anne Fitzpatrick-McKinley, and Philippe Guillaume (Tübingen: Mohr Siebeck, 2016).

Suggestions for Further Reading

In This Book

Elsewhere

Blenkinsopp, John. "The Structure of P." *Catholic Biblical Quarterly* 38 (1976): 276–292.

Fretheim, Terence E. "The Priestly Document: Anti-temple?" *Vetus Testamentum* 18 (1969): 312–329.

Kaufmann, Yehezkel. *The Religion of Israel: From Its Beginnings to the Babylonian Exile*. Translated and abridged by Moshe Greenberg. Chicago: University of Chicago Press, 1960.

Knight, Douglas A., editor. *Julius Wellhausen and His Prolegomena to the History of Israel*. Chico, CA: Scholars, 1983.

Lohfink, Norbert. "The Priestly Narrative and History." Pages 136–172 in *Theology of the Old Testament*. Edited by Norbert Lohfink. Minneapolis: Fortress, 1994.

75
What Is Historical Criticism?

Michael C. Legaspi

What does it mean for something to be old? A thing can be old because it belongs to a time that has passed. The conditions in which it once flourished, functioned, and mattered no longer exist. It may seem odd or interesting, but it no longer answers to the moment. Yet a thing can also be old in a different, less disjunctive sense. It is old because it belongs to an earlier phase of a situation that is still ongoing. Its advanced age does not mean that it no longer matters; it means that it has mattered for longer. To call a person "old" is dismissive; to mark someone as an "elder" is to include them in the present.

The Bible is old; indeed, it has been old for a very long time. Biblical writings were even considered old when Jewish and Christian communities began collecting, copying, and canonizing them in the early centuries of the Common Era. What it *means* for the Bible to be old, however, has been construed in a variety of ways. One option is to see the Bible as continuous with the present by virtue of cultural and religious traditions that mediate across time ways of life understood to be, in some sense, bound up with realities to which the Bible bears literary witness. Therefore, Jewish and Christian communities who regard the Bible as old in this sense may be called "traditional."

Though it has always been possible to question traditional perspectives on the Bible, doubts concerning the intellectual coherence and moral soundness of these perspectives were not articulated, published, and widely circulated before the age of the printing press. It was thus in the early modern period of Western culture (sixteenth and seventeenth centuries) that the ancientness of the Bible came into public view in a new way. While the impact of Gutenberg's first printed Bible cannot be underestimated, other developments caused people to question a range of traditional perspectives. These include, for example, the Protestant Reformation, the Scientific Revolution heralded by Copernicus and Galileo, the exploration of the "New World" by western Europeans, and the rise of liberal political movements. The questioning was not limited to the Bible but also took place in the domains of history, philosophy, politics, education, art, and theology.

Historical criticism, then, emerged in the early modern period as a way to make sense of the Bible without the aid of traditional perspectives. Figures often seen, in retrospect, as early exemplars of historical criticism took as their starting point the recognition that the Bible was not only old but culturally distant. It was a book belonging to distant peoples in bygone times. Although this was not by itself a revolutionary insight, the idea that this distance is the chief obstacle to understanding the Bible correctly was. It makes sense that historical criticism surfaced in the incipient phases of modern culture, since it assumes, as moderns do, that the present is fundamentally different from the past. That was then; this is now.

As the name suggests, historical critics turned to historical inquiry to assess the gap between the old world of the biblical authors and the world in which they lived. Perhaps the most famous example of an influential, early historical critic is the Jewish philosopher Baruch Spinoza (1632–1677). In 1670, a work authored by Spinoza, *Tractatus Theologico-politicus*, was published anonymously in Amsterdam. In it, Spinoza, who believed in the strict separation of political and ecclesial authorities, argued that religious leaders should not have a say in matters of state. Since ministers based their prescriptions and policies on the Bible, Spinoza turned to biblical interpretation to support his argument.

The philosopher explained that a correct understanding of the Bible, a set of texts written by humans long ago in ancient Hebrew (a language very different from modern European ones), requires knowledge of what the texts meant when they were originally composed. Linguistic and historical investigation guided only by reason and a desire to understand what the biblical authors intended to communicate yields an understanding of the Bible very different from that of traditional theologians. Spinoza aimed to show that when compared to his rational explanation of what biblical laws meant and what biblical prophets were really like, inherited interpretations of the Bible used by churchmen to regulate society are exposed as theological fabrications perniciously designed to augment the political power of churches.

For Spinoza, then, the oldness of the Bible (among other qualities) disqualified it as a resource for politics and philosophy. Though published anonymously, the *Tractatus* was traced to Spinoza, and he was branded a radical and freethinker. Yet despite being a highly controversial figure, Spinoza's mode of historical criticism endured after his death. Just a few decades after the publication of the *Tractatus*, German Protestant scholars began to adopt critical postures toward many of the same traditional perspectives targeted by Spinoza. Lutheran Pietists like Gottfried Arnold (1666–1714) claimed on the basis of impartial historical investigation that the traditional view of the Christian churches as faithful stewards of biblical teaching was inverted: the so-called heretics were right, and the orthodox were wrong. To rescue "true Christianity" from the distortions of tradition, church history had to be rewritten. Working in a similar vein, renowned biblical scholar Johann Salomo Semler (1725–1791) used critical analysis to show that New Testament writings were not a unified corpus of divine revelation; he showed instead that the Christian movement was a human enterprise, beset by conflict, in a historical situation very different from our own.

In the nineteenth century, biblical scholars (especially German ones) built on the legacy of Arnold, Semler, and others in developing modes of analysis oriented toward the history of biblical texts and the ancient contexts of the people who wrote and edited them. Drawing on new fields like comparative philology, textual criticism, source criticism, form criticism, and scientific archaeology, scholars demonstrated that the narrative of "sacred history" (or "salvation history") gleaned from the Bible was not so much an accurate retelling of the past as it was a conglomeration of myth, legend, and tradition assembled to serve the interests of religious leaders and scribal elites responding to the cultural and political challenges of their time. It was a momentous period in the history of biblical scholarship. Work began and continued into the twentieth century. Scholarly research clarified linguistic obscurities and generated critical editions of biblical texts based on painstaking examinations of newly discovered manuscripts. Scholars made illuminating comparisons between the Bible and materials from neighboring ancient civilizations: Egypt, Assyria, Babylon, and Persia. In this way, historical criticism began to uncover the lost world of ancient Israel.

The period spanning the nineteenth and early twentieth centuries marked the heyday of historical criticism. At this time, historical criticism and biblical studies were virtually synonymous. By virtue of rigorous research and historical analysis of the Bible's ancient contexts, biblical studies became a recognized academic discipline. Impressed by these successes, German Protestant theologians like F. D. E. Schleiermacher (1768–1834), Ernst Troeltsch (1865–1923), and Gerhard Ebeling (1912–2001) argued that historical criticism, in clearing away the false assurances of tradition, creates new possibilities for faith—not only a modern faith fully cognizant of new perspectives on science and history but also a liberated faith unencumbered by what Schleiermacher called "dead" tradition.

Since that time, however, the dominance of historical criticism has lessened. The World Wars shattered confidence in the inherent meaningfulness of history. Theologians like Karl Barth (1886–1968) expressed dissatisfaction with a Christian theology that terminates in historical description and insulates the Bible from a contemporary world in need of redemption. With the rise of critical theory in the decades following World War II, philosophers began to question whether historical objectivity was even an attainable goal. Postmodern perspectives on knowledge and the production of knowledge emphasized the roles of power and politics in what was once thought to be neutral scientific research. Biblical studies expanded accordingly to include the perspectives of readers and communities beyond the old, white, male-dominated guild of historical critics. Additionally, traditional Jewish and Christian biblical interpretation, though previously vilified, has become the object of historical study in its own right. Even so, historical criticism in various forms still represents the mainstream of biblical studies. What has changed in the last fifty years is that it now exists alongside newer, nonhistoricistic understandings of what it means for an old book like the Bible to be read, studied, and believed.

About the Author

Michael C. Legaspi holds a PhD from Harvard University. His research includes the history of biblical scholarship and the concept of wisdom in ancient thought. He has published *The Death of Scripture and the Rise of Biblical Studies* (Oxford: Oxford University Press, 2010); and *Wisdom in Classical and Biblical Tradition* (Oxford: Oxford University Press, 2018).

Suggestions for Further Reading

In This Book
See also chapters 1 (scholarly perspective), 5 (canons), 28–30 (archaeology), 73 (source criticism), 76 (redaction and text criticism), and 77 (literary and form criticism).

Elsewhere
Collins, John J. "Historical-Critical Methods." Pages 129–146 in *The Cambridge Companion to the Hebrew Bible / Old Testament*. Edited by Steven B. Chapman and Marvin A. Sweeney. Cambridge: Cambridge University Press, 2016.

Frei, Hans. *The Eclipse of Biblical Narrative: A Study in Eighteenth and Nineteenth Century Hermeneutics.* New Haven, CT: Yale University Press, 1974.

Law, David R. *The Historical Critical Method: A Guide for the Perplexed.* London: Continuum, 2012.

Levenson, Jon D. *The Hebrew Bible, Old Testament, and Historical Criticism: Jews and Christians in Biblical Studies.* Louisville, KY: Westminster John Knox, 1995.

76

What Are Redaction and Text Criticism?

Kåre Berge

How did the texts of the Hebrew Bible get their present shape and formulate their theological message? Academic biblical scholarship continues to consider most biblical texts as the product of a complex process of expansion, revision, and reshaping spanning centuries. Redaction critics ascribe this process to successive writers called redactors (preferred German term) or editors (English equivalent) instead of authors because they assume the scribes involved "edited" preexisting sources.

Redaction criticism works from the assumption that the reconstruction of the editorial process is possible, though to what extent is debatable. While redaction critics claim to be able to discern the hands of the successive redactors, our ability to reconstruct the stages of editing and explore the intent of each level of redaction has been challenged.

Nevertheless, an interest in the theological profiles of these postulated redactors/editors represents a significant advance over the delineation of four postulated sources, the so-called Yahwist (or *Jahwist* in German), Elohist, Deuteronomist, and Priestly writer, which was the primary approach toward understanding the growth of the first five books, Genesis–Deuteronomy, in the heydays of the Documentary Hypothesis. Back then, the redactors were conceived as editors/redactors who combined these preexisting sources into a patchwork of interwoven compositions without interfering much with their shape.

A major shift in approach was initiated by German scholar Martin Noth, who identified the books of Deuteronomy to 2 Kings to have comprised a Deuteronomistic History. Noth argued that the original Deuteronomistic History was thoroughly composed by a single redactor—indeed, an *author*—who brought together narratives and lists to deliver the single message that the destruction of Jerusalem did not prove Yhwh inferior to the Babylonian gods. In Noth's view, no sources lay behind this work telling an extensive story like the alleged Pentateuchal sources. Instead of focusing on the individual pieces brought together by the Deuteronomistic redactor, Noth's interest was in the meaning of the new product he perceived as a history.

The lasting popularity of the Deuteronomistic History hypothesis is largely due to the interest in redaction criticism in large compositional units—that is, entire books or sequences of books—which eclipses the previous interest in the individual, preexisting units of oral and sometimes written traditions. This shift in focus opened up the possibility of exploring the motivations of individual scribes who could well be understood as authors rather than mere editors.

Problems abound, however. Some of the postulated redactors did not necessarily want their work to be recognizable and thus covered their tracks, which makes it virtually impossible to prove that a biblical text is at all composite. Redaction critics tend to dismiss the possibility that a single writer could present divergent or seemingly contradictory views, which is not necessarily the case. For instance, is the epilogue of the book of Job (42:7–17) a later addition that soothes Job's harsh critique of divine injustice, or is it the necessary closure that vindicates Job? In other places, the presence of secondary reworkings is easier to demonstrate, in particular when new material—a few words or entire paragraphs—is placed at the beginning and at the end of a particular passage or book, or when textual "bridges" and "hinges" seem to hold together elements that would have been previously independent or establish a transition to a newer part that corrects an older one. This could be the case in Ruth 1:1 and 4:17–21 with the mention of the days of the judges and King David, added to justify the placement of the book of Ruth between Judges and Samuel in the Greek Bible. That the Hebrew canon places Ruth after Proverbs is another clue in support of the presence of secondary material in Ruth 1:1; 4:17–21, though the possibility that the entire book was produced with these verses cannot be ruled out. Ultimately, the question is, What difference does it make to our understanding of Ruth?

In the Pentateuch, the reference in Exodus 3:6 and 15–16 to Yhwh as the "god of your father(s), the god of Abraham, the god of Isaac, and the god of Jacob" is likely to be a literary connector meant to tie together the Genesis stories with the exodus, which they now introduce. Similarly, the promise to carry Joseph's bones to the promised land (Genesis 50:24) reinforces the link to the theme of the exodus from Egypt. Finally, Deuteronomy 34:4 connects with Genesis 12:7; 50:24; and Exodus 33:1 to form the canonical Pentateuch, or Torah. Combined with a hypothesis of textual growth through editorial practice, these passages can be regarded as redactional additions to a preexisting text by a Deuteronomistic editor or, in Deuteronomy 34:4, by the final "canonical" editor.

Obviously, the ability of redaction critics to piece together the history of the text would be seriously impaired if the redactors altered the shape of individual pieces or even deleted parts that did not fit their agenda. Since arguing from silence is an unacceptable scholarly procedure, redaction critics work from the premise that the ancient redactors had too great a respect for the venerable texts they received to alter them and only allowed themselves to give them a new spin by adding transitions, hinges, and bridges.

The present popularity of synchronic readings is, in part, a reaction to the excesses of redaction criticism based on the belief that the details of textual growth are hidden in the darkness of the past. As a result, only some comprehensive redactions can be identified.

Redaction criticism is limited to a focus on the *literary* development of the texts, not their possible oral prehistory, the so-called oral *traditions*. The oral prehistory of a biblical text is beyond the scope of redaction criticism because the method works from the premise that the literary production is *in any case* a meaning production of its own, regardless of its possible oral background. It is much more than the codification and reproduction of oral traditions. On the other hand, when put into writing, redaction criticism insists that the text's later additions and reworkings have altered and modified the original shape and meaning of a text. These changes are usually designated as *reception* and *interpretation*, although scholars more often reserve the term "reception history" to denote their "postcanonical" use and interpretation.

Because the postulated reworkings would reflect the social and religious background of the redactors, redaction criticism has some bearing on the history of the religion of ancient Israel. The theological profile of the successive editors would represent different stages in the intellectual evolution of ancient Israel. The latter assumption overlooks the possibility, however, that some ancient edits of the text were done by contemporaries who had competing theological philosophies and were trying to persuade the other side to adopt their views.

In some biblical texts, redaction history joins hands with textual criticism, as the study of the different families of ancient manuscripts represents a continuum with the identification of the work of redactors. The differences evinced by certain manuscripts and early translations into Greek, Aramaic, Coptic, and so on appear as intentional theological changes in the original Hebrew text in the same way as the postulated redactions. Yet, the major difference between redaction and textual criticism is that textual critics reconstruct hypothetical earlier versions on the basis of variant readings attested by actual manuscripts.

Though textual criticism is barely regarded as a "method" of biblical study, it is in fact a crucial step that provides the physical basis for the study of any biblical text insofar as we do not have any "original" biblical manuscript—if there ever was something like an "original." While scholarly Hebrew Bible editions, the old *Biblia Hebraica Kittel*, the current *Biblia Hebraica Stuttgartensia* (*BHS*), and the more recent *Biblia Hebraica Quinta* (*BHQ*) are adaptations of the Codex Leningradensis (from 1008 CE), textual criticism compares it with the older available Hebrew manuscripts and translations into ancient languages such as the thousands of fragments found in caves near the site of Qumran and elsewhere. Hence, all suggestions are based on actual physical evidence or "witnesses"—that is, ancient manuscripts or a family of manuscripts that bear the same textual variant. The criteria are thus far more reliable than is the case with the editors imagined by redaction critics.

As with any other scientific method, textual criticism has its limits too. Some textual variants are clearly the result of copying mistakes that textual critics designate, for instance, as *dittography* for the accidental repetition of a word or phrase, *haplography* for the accidental deletion of a word or phrase, and *homoioarcton* (same beginning) for the accidental omission of a word or passage when the scribe skipped from one sequence of letters at the beginning of a word to a similar sequence down the page and its inverse error of *homoioteleuton* (same ending) for a similar omission due to similar letter sequences at the end of a word. Textual criticism uses a range of such technical terms abbreviated in the textual apparatus of the three *Biblia* editions mentioned above, such as "ditt," "hapl," "homarc," and "homtel" for the four common scribal mistakes mentioned above. Those terms and their abbreviations are daunting for anyone beginning in the scholarly study of the Old Testament / Hebrew Bible. Yet, the effort necessary to navigate the critical apparatus of the *BHS* and *BHQ* is rewarding because the decisions of the editors as to which variant is preferable are not always devoid of a theoretical perspective or standpoint. The basic principle to decide which of two variant readings is likely to be older is to prefer the *lectio difficilior*, "the more difficult reading." It is assumed that a text that is hard to understand would have been changed to make better sense, yielding the *lectio facilior*, "the easier reading," so that the more obscure reading of the two is probably older.

For instance, is the mention of Mount Ebal in Deuteronomy 27:4 as the site upon which the Israelites are to set up the stones inscribed with the words of the Torah preferable to the location at Mount Gerizim attested by the Samaritan Pentateuch? That an earlier version had neither Ebal nor Gerizim and that Judean scribes later added Ebal while Samaritans added Gerizim, each to bolster the legitimacy of their own sanctuary as the only one chosen by Yhwh, cannot be ruled out. Yet, the ability to decide with a fair amount of certainty between Ebal and Gerizim (or neither of them) would make a huge difference in determining the origin of Deuteronomy and pinpointing one stage in the formation of the Pentateuch/Torah. New light is now thrown over this issue by textual studies arguing that the Deuteronomic verbal form "he will choose," which designates Yhwh's future choice of the location of the central sanctuary—long thought to be older and preferable to the variant "he has chosen" in the Samaritan Pentateuch—may in fact represent a late correction by Judahite scribes eager to challenge the Samaritan claim that Mount Gerizim is the sole location of Yhwh's resting place.

Such minute textual changes may appear quite irrelevant, but they cannot be brushed aside. While it is crucial to remember that no scientific method can deliver eternal truths and no critical method will ever recover the actual words penned by, say, Jeremiah or his scribe Baruch (Jeremiah 32), faithfulness to the biblical text requires taking the results of these methods seriously.

About the Author

Kåre Berge holds a doctorate of theology (ThD) from the University of Oslo. His research includes studies in the Yahwist source in Genesis. For instance, he published *Die Zeit des Jahwisten* (Berlin: De Gruyter, 1990); and *Reading Sources in a Text* (St. Ottilien: EOS Verlag, 1997).

Suggestions for Further Reading

In This Book
See also chapters 1 (scholarly perspective), 3 (religious in a scientific world), 5 (canons), 25 (Deuteronomistic History), 34 (Dead Sea Scrolls), 72 (synchronic vs. diachronic), 74 ("P"), 75 (historical criticism), 77 (literary and form criticism), and 78 (ideological criticism).

Elsewhere
Boorer, Suzanne. "Source and Redaction Criticism." Pages 95–130 in *Methods for Exodus*. Edited by Thomas B. Dozeman. Cambridge: Cambridge University Press, 2010.

Carr, David M. "Rethinking the Materiality of Biblical Texts." *Zeitschrift für die Alttestamentliche Wissenschaft* 132 (2020): 594–621.

McCarthy, Carmel. "Textual Criticism and Biblical Translation." Pages 532–551 in *The Hebrew Bible: A Critical Companion*. Edited by John Barton. Princeton, NJ: Princeton University Press, 2016.

77
What Are Literary and Form Criticism?

Kåre Berge

How do biblical texts achieve their meaning? This is the central focus of the method of literary criticism in the Hebrew Bible. Also central to this kind of criticism is the idea that biblical literature has artistic or aesthetic qualities. The subject matter of literary criticism is the textuality of a given piece of writing; this method does not search for the historical background or historical development of the text. Even when historical realities from the time of the text's origin may play a role, literary criticism is interested in the "poetics," or building blocks, and the rules used to assemble them into a given text. The "world" that interests the literary critic is the imaginative world created by the text, not the world in which the writer lived.

It is difficult to summarize what literary criticism is about because it has resulted in many approaches, interests, and "methods" of studying biblical texts. The following will, accordingly, provide a brief overview and survey.

Literary criticism receives its strongest impetus from focusing on the techniques and modes of design, also called the literary devices or poetics, in biblical narratives. It borrows from linguistic studies but pays attention to the communicative strategies in a text. The literary-critical study of biblical narratives investigates how the stories get their persuasive power, how they convince readers. Sometimes it is called the method of "close reading" because it is attentive to how the text creates narrators, characters, plots, motifs, and the beginning and endings of a narrative. Where source and redaction critics identify discontinuities, breaks, and repetitions as clues of different authors, literary criticism investigates them for their poetic and aesthetic value. Learning from Russian formalism, literary critics take strange and erratic features in a text as signals meant to attract the reader's attention. This is also why the method is labeled synchronic; it ignores the possible diachronic explanations of such features.

The *characters* in a text are a primary focus of literary criticism. They are either "round," meaning well-developed and exhibiting growth over time, or "flat," meaning mere secondary figures required by the plot. Characterization may occur by having the narrator describe the person's physical appearance or moral character traits (e.g., righteous, wicked, wise, or foolish) or via the character's own actions or words. In biblical narratives, the characters' inner states, emotions, and attitudes usually are conveyed indirectly in their actions or their speeches. Poetic effect is frequently achieved through contrasting figures.

Narrative *plot* is important to literary criticism, either as a meaningful chain of interconnected events in time, or by building the story around a conflict between or among the primary and secondary characters or the internal conflict of a single character. The difficult aspect for beginners to handle is often the narrator's point of view, which governs the narrative and steers the reader's involvement in the story toward sympathy or antipathy.

Literary criticism regards biblical texts as imaginative literature; they imitate reality but make no claims to reflect or describe reality. Everything in the text describes an alternative reality, which is *analogous* to the real world and real people. In this sense, it is altogether metaphorical. One consequence is that the conflicting voices in a text do not signal different authorship—as is the case in source and redaction criticism—but are the result of the split voice of the author, without which the poetic power of the text would be tamed. Another approach that takes the conflicting voices in a text seriously analyzes these conflicts as subconscious processes in the (imagined) character in the text.

To literary critics, determining meaning in a narrative is primarily a process that requires continual revision. One may talk about meanings, not meaning. This ambiguity or indeterminacy of meaning appears through a combined set of literary devices and the inferences readers are led to draw from the artistic composition of the piece. The position of the reader becomes an important issue, also triggered by general literary studies of the role of the reader. From there, it is only a short step toward the interaction between text and reader. The shift from texts alone to texts *and* readers came to the fore in a direction called "cultural studies," which situates the readers and their presuppositions in different cultures—for example, African, Hispanic, Asian, or Native American. What we see is a shift from an interest in the literary *devices* in a biblical text to a hermeneutical interest in the ideology of reading. Seminal to this change was feminist criticism, followed by various kinds of liberation criticism, postcolonial criticism, and the comprehensive deconstruction criticism. At this point, biblical scholarship has moved away from interpretation and become a critique of biblical texts. The standpoint of these approaches is not in the texts but *before* them or above them, with a human reader judging the value of the text and laying bare its ideology and the function set forth or assumed by the text.

This cursory tour, from the textuality of texts to texts and readers, reveals that biblical texts—even when looked upon as poetic and imaginative—hold political and social force. Texts are relational; they have historical, social, or political resonance.

The ancestor of literary criticism was form criticism, sometimes also referred to as "genre criticism." The subject matter of form criticism is just what the term says—the *form* of the text, its beginning, end, space in between, and components. The form may also be seen as its structure.

Form criticism originated in Germany as *Formgeschichte*, or "history of genres," because its interest focused on literary genres rather than on the origins and development of a text. Accordingly, there is little specific interest in the poetics of the texts. Genre criticism was originally a diachronic program introduced by German scholar Hermann Gunkel in his most accessible work, his 1901 Genesis commentary. Gunkel's main objective was not the text but the religious life reflected in it. His main entry into the religious life of the ancient Israelites was biblical folklore, which he was able to identify through the common forms (genres) of the individual texts. Thus, texts led him to oral traditions, from which, in his view, one could reach the deep roots of folk religion.

The crucial idea was that biblical narrative texts originated in oral short stories. Their combination into larger literary units was the work of authors or editors, who were of almost no interest to Gunkel. Thus, the original method was not really constructed to comprehend larger literary units. Its "next of kin" was tradition history and modern folklore studies of the Bible.

Soon after the form-critical study of the individual stories in Genesis, the method was applied to the Psalms and to prophetic oracles. Today, it remains hardly possible to study the Psalms without returning to Gunkel's idea of their genres. The study of "form," subsequently, was broadened to include larger narrative "traditions" in the Pentateuch—like those behind the Sinai pericope, the exodus narrative, and the Genesis patriarchs—in order to locate the cultic sites that produced these traditions in ancient Israel. An entire series of commentaries was devoted to the forms of Old Testament literature—for instance, one by Marvin A. Sweeney (1996) on Isaiah 1–39 and one by George W. Coats (1999) on Exodus 1–18. The concept of these commentaries follows the traditional interests of form and genre criticism: structure, genre, setting, and intention, where "setting" stands for the common historical-critical questions about the text's origin and its redaction history. Today, form criticism tends to leave aside pretextual interests and focuses on the text itself—its form, structure, and possible genres. This makes it an approach that for literary critics is limited to the surface of the text and fails to take into account its poetic quality.

About the Author

Kåre Berge holds a doctorate of theology (ThD) from the University of Oslo. He has published "Divine and Human Wisdom in the Book of Hosea: A Pedagogical Perspective," pages 19–36 in *Poets, Prophets, and Texts in Play: Studies in Biblical Poetry and Prophecy in Honour of Francis Landy*, edited by Ehud Ben Zvi, Claudia V. Camp, David M. Gunn, and Aaron W. Hughes (London: Bloomsbury T&T Clark, 2015).

Suggestions for Further Reading

In This Book
See also chapters 1 (scholarly perspective), 3 (religious in a scientific world), 5 (canons), 13 (genres), 16 (Psalms), 34 (Dead Sea Scrolls), 67 (Isaiah), 72 (synchronic vs. diachronic), 75 (historical criticism), 77 (literary and form criticism), and 78 (ideological criticism).

Elsewhere
LITERARY CRITICISM

Amit, Yairah. *Reading Biblical Narratives: Literary Criticism and the Hebrew Bible*. Minneapolis: Fortress, 2001.

Bar-Efrat, Shimon. *Narrative Art in the Bible*. Sheffield, UK: Almond, 1989.

Berlin, Adele. *Poetics and Interpretation of Biblical Narrative*. Sheffield, UK: Almond, 1983.

Clines, David J. A., and J. Cheryl Exum. "The New Literary Criticism." Pages 11–25 in *The New Literary Criticism and the Hebrew Bible*. Edited by J. Cheryl Exum and David J. A. Clines. Sheffield, UK: JSOT, 1993.

Jasper, David. "'The Bible as Literature': From R. G. Moulton to T. R. Henn." Pages 455–480 in *The Hebrew Bible: A Critical Companion*. Edited by John Barton. Princeton, NJ: Princeton University Press, 2016.

Robertson, David. *The Old Testament and the Literary Critic*. Philadelphia: Fortress, 1977.

FORM CRITICISM

Coats, George W. *Exodus 1–18*. Grand Rapids, MI: Eerdmans, 1999.

Gunkel, Hermann. *Genesis*. Translated by Mark E. Biddle. Macon, GA: Mercer University Press, 1997.

Hayes, John H., and Carl R. Holladay. "Form Criticism: The Genre and Life Setting of the Text." Pages 115–127 in *Biblical Exegesis: A Beginner's Handbook* (4th edition). Louisville, KY: Westminster John Knox, 2022.

Lohfink, Gerhard. *The Bible: Now I Get It! A Form-Criticism Handbook*. New York: Doubleday, 1979.

Sparks, Kenton L. "The Methodology of Genre Criticism." Pages 55–94 in *Methods for Exodus*. Edited by Thomas B. Dozeman. Cambridge: Cambridge University Press, 2010.

Sweeney, Marvin A. *Isaiah 1–39*. Grand Rapids, MI: Eerdmans, 1996.

Tucker, Gene M. *Form Criticism of the Old Testament*. Philadelphia: Fortress, 1971.

78
What Is Ideological Criticism of the Hebrew Bible?

Patton Taylor

The term "ideology" denotes the world view of a given group, class, or community—not just any set of ideas but an action-oriented system, most often in connection with issues of politics and power. In the Bible, this might be a royal or a temple ideology. The term can be used in a specifically positive sense to denote a set of beliefs that cohere and inspire a laudable cause. More often, "ideology" is used pejoratively to imply "false consciousness," partisanship, an oversimplified body of ideas, or rigid dogma. In biblical studies, the term is often used in a critical sense—for example, the claim that Old Testament texts encode the political ideology of an intellectual elite.

The ideological standpoint of any individual is to some degree unconsciously predetermined by inherited factors, such as social class, gender, nationality, and religion, as mediated by life experience. None of us can completely dispossess ourselves of the consciousness derived from our social location.

Ancient texts were not produced for mere antiquarian or aesthetic purposes. The aim of a text was to advocate or challenge a prevailing ideology (or theology)—often to reinforce, or sometimes to undermine, the vested interests of those in power. As the production of texts and books is costly, the ideological critic must ask, Who in the ancient context had the leisure and the means to produce and/or read texts? Who could afford to sponsor authors, editors, or compilers? Who controlled the processes by which books were written, copied, and circulated? Whom were they seeking to persuade and for what purpose?

Bible readers typically find themselves succumbing to the ideology of the text, finding it obvious and commonsensical. Critics have tended to confine themselves to mere understanding and explanation, screening out questions of value. For ideological critics, however, understanding a text is not the final goal of interpretation. There is an essential further step of evaluation.

In biblical studies, ideological criticism flourished in the 1990s, largely inspired by the rise of Marxist theories of literary criticism, particularly as articulated by Terry Eagleton and Frederic Jameson. Unlike traditional critical methodologies, Marxist criticism did not lay claim to objectivity; it sought to critique literary texts from its own value base.

Eagleton (1976) explains that critical analysis must begin with the economic and political conditions under which a text was produced. For Jameson (1981), all literary texts have a "political" dimension. The "world of meaning" in a text is inevitably correlated with the ideology under which the text was produced and with the ideological lens through which it is interpreted, *even if neither the author nor the reader is consciously aware of this*. Therefore, all literary products, including biblical texts, have what Jameson calls a "political unconscious," which it is the task of the ideological critic to elucidate.

Jameson further maintains that a text may also encode a "utopian vision," or an idea of what a perfect society might be like. This applies particularly to texts of resistance, which challenge those in power, holding out hope for a better world. But even a text of oppression will encode the utopian vision of the oppressed group to some degree. Jameson thus argues that a text can simultaneously be both ideological and utopian. The ideological critic may therefore be able to extrapolate a utopian vision even from an oppressive text. For instance, even those readers who deplore the patriarchal or oppressive nature of biblical texts may nonetheless be able to elaborate from the text a counterideology that delineates a utopian vision of a nonpatriarchal society.

Unsurprisingly, many biblical scholars had a knee-jerk reaction against a Marxist methodology. Some turned to other models, such as Paul Ricœur's (1986) more nuanced understanding of ideological criticism. Ricœur designed a critique that promotes constructive evaluation as opposed to the deconstructive tendency of Marxist ideological criticism.

For the ideological critic, no literary text should be taken at face value. Texts take sides in debates. They seek not only to inform but also to persuade. The author achieves this by a selective presentation of the material, deflecting the reader's attention from alternative perspectives. Therefore, the critic must take careful note of what the text does not say, as this may be even more significant than what is actually stated. A text may be factually true but functionally false because of a selective or slanted presentation. The critic must be on the watch for clues of the opposing argument, reading between the lines and against the grain of the text.

The critic searches for cracks and fissures in the text, revealed by weaknesses in the argument, inconsistencies, and contradictions. These can pinpoint glimpses of a silenced counterideology, or, in the case of the Hebrew Bible, they may indicate later additions to the text that reflect a counterideology to the original. Attention must also be given to voices relegated to the margins of the text, or even those that are totally silenced—for example, women's voices. In other words, ideological critics adopt a hermeneutic of suspicion, seeking to grasp new connections between old facts and to disentangle recognition from misrecognition.

These principles and methods have also supplied a theoretical undergirding for subtypes of ideological-critical approaches such as feminist, liberationist, and postcolonial criticisms. Furthermore, an awareness of ideological factors has gained traction generally in the world of biblical interpretation. As much as a text is never neutral, scholars have come to realize the need to incorporate moral value judgments within critical scholarship, bringing to bear their own personal ideological convictions on their critique of a biblical text.

Ideological criticism, therefore, not only is concerned with the ideology of the text itself and its interpretative tradition but equally involves a critique of the ideology of contemporary interpreters, commentators, and the scholarly guild at large. Critics are encouraged to declare up front their own ideological position. Ultimately, ideological criticism seeks to be action oriented, which means applied to real situations in the world within which biblical texts are read and interpreted.

The fact that many biblical scholars find themselves in significant disagreement with Marxism as a political philosophy does not mean that we have nothing to learn from Marxist insights. Marxist critics have rightly alerted us to the political and economic undergirding of biblical texts. They have bequeathed to us useful critical tools that are broader than any one philosophical base. They have made us aware of the need to subject a text to ideological critique based on our own ideological holdings.

Whereas faith-based interpretations were once condescendingly dismissed in the academy as necessarily biased and unacademic, it is now time for academic exegetes to acknowledge up front their own conscious and unconscious ideological holdings and to develop a form of criticism that breaks the bonds of the academic ivory tower. Ideological criticism should also be action oriented, applauding justice and opposing oppression. Traditional historical criticism will never change the world. With ideological criticism, there is at least the possibility of actualizing a utopian vision.

About the Author

Patton Taylor holds a doctorate (PhD) from the University of Sheffield. He has published *Knowing God's Ways: A User's Guide to the Old Testament* (Bletchley, UK: Scripture Union, 1991); and "Esther, Ideological Criticism, and the Theology of Liberation," *Irish Biblical Studies* 29 (2011): 100–115.

Suggestions for Further Reading

In This Book
See also chapters 1 (scholarly perspective), 9 (audiences), 55 (patriarchalism), 56 (polemics), 57 (pro-choice), 75 (historical criticism), 80 (social anthropology), 81 (gender studies), 82 (postcolonial studies), and 83 (reception criticism).

Elsewhere
Barr, James. *History and Ideology in the Old Testament: Biblical Studies at the End of a Millennium*. Oxford: Oxford University Press, 2000.

Boer, Roland. *Marxist Criticism of the Hebrew Bible*. London: T&T Clark, 2015.

Clines, David. *Interested Parties: The Ideology of Writers and Readers of the Hebrew Bible*. Sheffield, UK: Sheffield Academic, 1995.

Dyck, Jonathan. "A Map of Ideology for Biblical Critics." Pages 108–128 in *Rethinking Contexts, Rereading Texts: Contributions from the Social Sciences to Biblical Interpretation*. Edited by M. Daniel Carroll R. Sheffield, UK: Sheffield Academic, 2000.

Eagleton, Terry. *Criticism and Ideology*. London: New Left Books, 1976.

Jameson, Frederic. *The Political Unconscious*. Ithaca, NY: Cornell University Press, 1981.

Jobling, David, and Tina Pippin, editors. *Ideological Criticism of Biblical Texts*. Atlanta: Scholars, 1992.

Ricœur, Paul. *Lectures on Ideology and Utopia*. New York: Columbia University Press, 1986.

79
How Are Memory Studies Applied to the Study of the Hebrew Bible?

Ehud Ben Zvi

All historical social groups share memories that are key for their social maintenance and continuity. Memories about past events as imagined and remembered by a group provide it with a sense of a shared past. This past is not static; shaping and reshaping are constantly intertwined with ongoing processes of forming the relevant group's understanding of itself. The past is never a "thing" to be retrieved; instead, it is always construed and experienced in the present. Thus, the past changes over time, and images of the past may even change within a particular period, depending on the context in which they are evoked. Similarly, individuals tell stories about themselves differently in different situations.

When a group shapes its memory of the past, it not only must construe important characters and crucial events in a particular space and time but also must project an image of the general cultural knowledge, social institutions, and ways of thinking (and feeling) that shaped the world of the characters and in which their actions, thoughts, feelings made some sense. Without that comprehensive image of their cultural system, their motivations and actions are neither intelligible nor memorable.

Although that eco-cultural system and its social institutions must be associated with the past of the remembering group and the personages of old, it must also relate to and be meaningful in the present of the remembering group. For instance, neither Moses, David, nor the Jerusalemite temple could have been considered relevant only for past generations. No important figure or site of memory within a group's collective memory can be relevant only for a limited time in the past. The exodus and Yhwh's torah conveyed by the hand of Moses are not just some trivial pieces of information for the intended readers of the biblical books; they are crucial foundational events, texts, or notions for those remembering them. Ongoing generations of readers will maintain them as crucial memories for their identity and will modify them to suit their current needs and collective self-understanding.

We all know that remembering is not just an intellectual exercise. It involves and shapes emotions. When people read a text that teaches them about their own past, they encounter their heroes; villains; missed opportunities; instances in which, against all expectations, a dreadful future failed to come about; and foundational and traumatic events. In all these cases, they learn to "hear" what these characters say and how they talk to each other and their inner thoughts. They also encounter horrific as well as wonderful events via these characters. They see what the remembered individuals see—and even more, because unlike the characters they recall, they have knowledge of what will happen to them and why. When engaged in recalling and thus vicariously experiencing great joyful events, like the inauguration of the temple in Jerusalem and its service (e.g., 1 Kings 8), readers and anyone within the group sharing the past portrayed in the Hebrew Bible vicariously delight. Yet, they cannot but lament when "experiencing" its destruction along with the city more generally. Likewise, they "feel" the hope conveyed by some prophecies (e.g., Isaiah 2:2–4; 54:9–10) and the terror that other texts inspire (e.g., Deuteronomy 28:15–68; Amos 9:1–4; Micah 3; Lamentations). Remembering is a socially affective act. It brings up emotions, and sometimes in certain societies, it even engages in what we may call socially shared "chosen" (or selected) traumas that keep impacting every generation of the remembering community. The exile and the destruction of Jerusalem and its temple play the role of "chosen" traumas for the postmonarchic communities in which most of the texts of the Hebrew Bible emerged and for subsequent generations of Jewish groups as well.

The readers of these past-shaping and past-evoking texts identify with the human personages who represent "Israel." That said, the "real" future of the personages of old is the readers' past. Since the former were described in texts written by scribes who knew "the future" of the personages, at times, the most crucial among them were imagined as (prophetically) foreseeing the ("real") future. For instance, Moses "knew" of the future exile (see, e.g., Deuteronomy 31:16–21), and David and his community even asked Yhwh to "gather and rescue us from among the nations" when they were celebrating the successful transfer of the ark to the city of David at the height of David's rule (1 Chronicles 16:35). Isaiah even knew about Cyrus and the return of the exiles (e.g., Isaiah 40–55). The majority, however, were not remembered as having foreseen the future.

A foreseen future is different from a past. Unlike the personages of the past who populate the texts, the readers know well what will happen

to them, and in fact, they have already vicariously (through acts of imagination) "experienced" what they will end up experiencing. In some ways,
they are like the narrator of a story, who most often "knows" far more than
its characters.

In addition, remembering the past and imagining the future involve
what scholars have called "mental time travel." Memory facilitates the
imagination of situations and deeds in the future and vice versa. The group
shares "memories" of the future when they imagine the future and empa-
thetically identify with the hopes of personages populating that future and
vicariously experience their new environment (e.g., Isaiah 11; Jeremiah
31:30–33; Ezekiel 40–48). Memories shared by any group require human
agents shaping, modifying, and transmitting them.

Since the Hebrew Bible is a collection of books that shapes and communicates memories of the past, it is most appropriate to use approaches
informed by social memory studies to examine it. These approaches provide socioanthropological comparative data and generate helpful questions for research.

Even if only imagined and remembered by a social group, key sites of
memory like places, events, or figures tend to contribute much to the periodization of the group's past. In the case of the past evoked by the Hebrew
Bible, Moses communicates a periodization defined by internal factors
within the Pentateuch, the books of Genesis to Deuteronomy, and the
larger collection known as the Enneateuch, which extends from Genesis to
2 Kings. He draws attention to the foundational period of Israel, defined
by the key events of the deliverance from Egypt and the giving of torah at
Mount Sinai/Horeb, found in the books of Exodus to Deuteronomy. The
pre-Mosaic period is related in Genesis in the stories of the patriarchs
Abraham, Isaac, Jacob, and the twelve sons who serve as the founders of
the twelve tribes. The story of the fulfillment of Moses's prophecies is then
found in the books of Joshua to 2 Kings.

At times, memories serve to recall the passing of time. Genealogies
create a sense of temporal distance that is balanced with kinship. It is linear
time that is both biological and social. Other memories evoke a sense of
temporal trajectories that form helical or spiral cycles, which often draw
attention to matters of both continuity and discontinuity. In the Hebrew
Bible, we find a trajectory that moves from the first to the second temple
and, eventually, to the utopian temple described in Ezekiel 40–48. All these
temples are conceptually associated and distinctive. The same may be said
of the exodus from Egypt that leads to the land and the return of the exiles
from Babylon to Jerusalem and Judah. Another example is the original
David and the future David. One may also add trajectories from David to

Cyrus that combine both linear and somewhat circular time. In all these cases, memories and trajectories serve to explore key notions of the group and to teach it via "concrete" examples.

Social memory approaches also help us look comparatively at images of founding figures, last rulers, heroes and villains, and golden periods, seeing similarities and differences. For instance, contrary to expectations, in the cases of Moses, Abraham, and Joshua, images of warrior heroism are downplayed. Moreover, despite substantial narratives about the conquest of the land, it is called not "the land that Joshua conquered" but "the land that Yhwh promised to the patriarchs," who never possessed it. Military conquest is thus de-emphasized. Further, in Chronicles and Psalms, even the image of David as a warrior, which is so prominent in Samuel and Kings, is downplayed in favor of the exemplary pious king, singer of songs. Why is this tendency present in the Hebrew Bible?

Important sites of memory serve as nodes to which multiple key stories and concepts are attached. Moses is associated with torah, with the exodus, with the establishment of priesthood, and with prophecy. David is associated with Jerusalem, the temple, kingship, monarchy, and godly songs and the proper service at the temple. Social memory studies have shown that memory nodes are a common feature.

Scholars also have observed a general tendency toward oneness that occurs by narrowing the number of main sites of memory associated with particular events. This trend is found, for example, in the case of the Assyrian siege of Jerusalem in 701 BCE, which is remembered via the prophetic figure of Isaiah. Yet there are two main sites of memory associated with the calamity of the capture of Jerusalem and the destruction of the temple in 587 BCE, which include what immediately preceded and followed the event as well as what will occur in the future. They are the prophetic figures of Jeremiah and Ezekiel. Such a divergence from expectation prompts the reading community to reflect on different possible understandings of a core traumatic experience for the remembering community. It raises questions about the need for these multiple understandings and their association not only with remembered pasts but also with imagined and remembered futures.

In various cultures, important sites of memory tend to be associated with various traditions and serve important roles in social cohesion by facilitating the integration of various memories and concepts that seem to be in tension. For instance, Moses was remembered as stating things that seem to contradict one another (e.g., Exodus 12:9 and Deuteronomy 16:7). At the general conceptual level, the Moses of Exodus–Numbers is remembered differently from the Moses of Deuteronomy; he is thus remembered as having spoken with more than one style of speech and as expressing and authoritatively communicating different concepts in each of these styles. Hosea was remembered as prophesying not only about an ideal future in which a Davidic king would rule over Israel but also about a future in which there would be no Davidic king. Readers of Joshua are to learn and remember that the entirety of the land was conquered and also that it was not (see Joshua 11:23; 18:1; 22:43; cf. 10:41–42 and then, in contradiction, Joshua 13:1–6; 15:63; 16:10; see Judges 1). Readers of Chronicles are to remember that certain kings removed and did not remove the cultic "high places" (2 Chronicles 14:2, 4 vs. 15:17; 17:6 vs. 20:33). In the Hebrew Bible, key sites of memory tend to be multivocal—one may say even "fuzzy."

All in all, memories of the past and future are evocative and bring about mental worlds, but they are not constrained by narrowly defined "logic." Memories serve to teach multiple lessons and explore social notions. Unlike in classical Greece, in ancient Israel and the wider ancient Near East, ideas were not discussed in abstract terms. The pros and cons of different political organizations like monarchy, charismatic leadership, nondynastic "monarchy," a priestly led polity, and theocracy were not debated as we might do today. Instead, various concrete examples were set forth as options or possibilities.

The selected examples presented above show the potential of studies informed by social-anthropological memory studies for research in the Hebrew Bible. This is a relatively new way of approaching the biblical texts, but it holds exceptional promise.

About the Author

Ehud Ben Zvi holds a PhD from Emory University. His research investigates ancient Israelite history and historiography, social memory in ancient Israel, the latter's intellectual history, and the prophetic and historiographical books that eventually became part of the Hebrew Bible. He has published *Social Memory among the Literati of Yehud* (Berlin: De Gruyter, 2019); "Leadership in the World of Memories Evoked by Chronicles in the Context of the Late Persian / Early Hellenistic Period," pages 185–200 in *Transforming Authority: Concepts of Leadership in Prophetic and Chronistic Literature*, edited by Katharina Pyschny and Sarah Schulz (Berlin: De Gruyter, 2021); "Memories of Female (and Male) Sages in Late Persian / Early Hellenistic Yehud: Considerations Informed by Social Memory and Current Cross- and Trans-disciplinary Trends in the Study of Wisdom," pages 119–147 in *Representing the Wise: A Gendered Approach; Proceedings of the 1st Melammu Workshop, Lille, 4–5 April 2016,* edited by Stéphanie Anthonioz and Sebastian Fink (Münster: Zaphon, 2019); and "Memories of Kings of Israel and Judah within the Mnemonic Landscape of the Literati of the Late Persian / Early Hellenistic Period: Exploratory Considerations," *Scandinavian Journal of the Old Testament* 33 (2019): 1–14.

Suggestions for Further Reading

In This Book
See also chapters 9 (audiences), 20 (genealogies), 22 (periodization), 51 (prophets), 60 (Abraham), 63 (Moses), 65 (King David), 68 (Jeremiah), 75 (historical criticism), and 83 (reception criticism).

Elsewhere
Edelman, Diana V. "Introduction." Pages xi–xxiv in *Remembering Biblical Figures in the Late Persian and Early Hellenistic Periods: Social Memory and Imagination*. Edited by Diana V. Edelman and Ehud Ben Zvi. Oxford: Oxford University Press, 2013.

Fine, Gary Alan. *Difficult Reputations: Collective Memories of the Evil, Inept, and Controversial*. Chicago: University of Chicago Press, 2001.

Zerubavel, Eviatar. *Social Mindscapes: An Invitation to Cognitive Sociology*. Cambridge, MA: Harvard University Press, 1997.

Zerubavel, Eviatar. *Time Maps: Collective Memory and the Social Shape of the Past*. Chicago: University of Chicago Press, 2003.

80
How Is Social Anthropology Used to Understand the Hebrew Bible?

Emanuel Pfoh

In the late nineteenth century, social (or cultural) anthropology produced observations about "primitive" societies that were in some way related to the Hebrew Bible. For instance, William Robertson Smith (1885) studied rituals and religions of ancient and modern Semitic populations, and James G. Frazer (1918) examined the mythic qualities of some biblical stories. The twentieth century saw a new focus on the cultural legacy of the Hebrew Bible in Western civilization. In both cases, the key factor was to consider the biblical text as a cultural artifact like any other, an artifact to be tested against other cultural human expressions in history.

In a seminal article, George E. Mendenhall (1962) used modern ethnographic insights to explain the rise of early Israel in the Iron Age I (ca. 1150–1000 BCE) as an indigenous process rather than the result of a foreign conquest, as the Bible presents it. Norman K. Gottwald (1979) added a peasant revolt to Mendenhall's indigenous process, and Niels Peter Lemche (1985) deployed a wealth of ethnographic data from the Middle East to understand Israelite society. Among others, John W. Rogerson (1978) and Bernhard Lang (1985) revealed, for instance, the relevance of segmentary lineage in African contexts for interpreting biblical stories and understanding the process of ethnogenesis and state formation in ancient Israel.

Today, the idea that ancient Israel did not arise simply as the result of the conquest of Canaan by tribes fleeing out of Egypt is accepted by the scholarly guild. The proposed alternative notion of a peasant revolt, however, is more than questionable, because the Marxist construct of the urban proletariat that it evokes may be quite irrelevant to agrarian societies such as those of the southern Levant.

While these studies strove to transcend the mere commentaries on the biblical text that were the norm, they found it hard to free the research agenda from the uncritical acceptance of the basic biblical scheme of progression in Israelite history (settlement → tribal formation → state formation → state fragmentation → deportation → exile) as an accurate background for the social processes at work in the first millennium before the Common Era. Nevertheless, the approaches to the biblical texts commonly designated as "social scientific" introduced the classical topics of anthropological research into biblical research—for example, politics and social organization, economics, honor and shame, family and kinship, gender, myth and narrative, religion and rituals, folklore, violence, friendship, and dress and clothing.

A key issue of social anthropology is its emphasis on detecting cultural diversity. The recognition of cultural diversity reveals the process of othering at work in the Bible. Not only is Israel presented as having to be entirely other than Canaan, but the Israel of the Bible also ignores many of the social components that constituted the actual Israel within which the Bible arose.

Another key issue of social anthropology proper, when applied to the Hebrew Bible, is that as an ancient source, it needs to be translated culturally and not simply linguistically. A cultural translation of the biblical data, as a methodological principle, requires putting the usual tendency to rapidly historicize the biblical narrative on hold. Instead of presenting a realistic historical account, the primary goal of social-scientific approaches is to deal with cultural issues by distinguishing between *emic* and *etic* perspectives.

The *emic* perspective aims at grasping the "indigenous discourse" of a particular culture, group, or society—namely, the internal logic that produces and explains a certain reality according to the particular cultural traits of the members of that culture, group, or society. The *etic* perspective, on the contrary, is constructed from outside the culture under study. As Marvin Harris (1968) described, it is precisely an interpretative discourse that integrates and explains the *emic* perspective through concrete analytical categories. In this sense, we may distinguish between the *emic* perspective found in biblical narratives or related to them and the *etic* perspective. The *emic* perspective includes, for example, mythic depictions, literary tropes and motifs, and biblical periodizations, while the *etic* perspective deals not only with the production of the biblical texts and the formation of the biblical narrative in its ancient Near Eastern context but also with how these texts are related to the history of ancient Israel/Palestine in the first millennium before our era and how such a history is elaborated by modern historiography.

Philip R. Davies (1992) argued that "ancient Israel" is a distinctive historiographical construct of modern biblical studies, a combination of biblical narratives with data from the archaeology and epigraphy (the study and interpretation of ancient inscriptions) of Iron Age Palestine blended in a rather uncritical fashion according to historical epistemological and methodological standards. If we accept this view, most "histories of ancient Israel" are somewhat sophisticated examples of a predominantly *emic* interpretation of the biblical text in modern times that fail ultimately to adopt or follow a properly *etic* approach to all the data. The *etic* perspective of the biblical narrative and of the history of Israel/Palestine in antiquity is, therefore, the main analytical contribution that sociocultural anthropology makes to the investigation of the historical processes in the ancient southern Levant. It explores the biblical narrative as a textual source needing evaluation rather than as the first draft of a modern historical account to which the historian or the archaeologist can make corrections or additions.

First, the *etic* perspective identifies and characterizes a native or indigenous discourse about such a past in the biblical text (*emic*), which has to be subjected to the expected criticism as a historical textual source. This native or indigenous discourse can be read ethnographically—in a rather forensic manner, following a sort of ethnography of a dead culture—by integrating the logic of the mythical depictions in the biblical texts with the wider cultural traits of the Levant.

Second, the *etic* perspective also creates the categories through which we will grant coherence and form to this past as social structure and world view, political and economic organization, and religious practices, for example. This research orientation permits results that are less dependent on the biblical images of the land and its historical processes and more on sophisticated multidisciplinary approaches.

Finally, in light of the changes in interests and anthropological analyses, it is now clear that anthropological approaches to the Hebrew Bible provide a useful set of theoretical frameworks and research questions for both the history of Israel/Palestine and the interpretation of the biblical narrative. Using the Hebrew Bible to identify "what really happened" ought now to be considered much too narrow a historical perspective. Postmodern approaches to history recognize its constructed nature and allow for a range of topics to be investigated. As a result, there is a significant overlap in interests, themes, and problems to be researched between anthropological studies of an ancient culture and historical investigations of the cultures of ancient Israel and Judah. Biblical scholars who choose to investigate any such overlapping topics need to be aware that their work will benefit from the integration of anthropological categories and methods in their study of biblical texts.

About the Author

Emanuel Pfoh holds a PhD in history from the University of Buenos Aires. He is a researcher at Argentina's National Research Council and at the Centre of Excellence in Ancient Near Eastern Empires, University of Helsinki. He is the author of *The Emergence of Israel in Ancient Palestine: Historical and Anthropological Perspectives* (London: Equinox 2009); "Anthropology and Biblical Studies: A Critical Manifesto," pages 15–35 in *Anthropology and the Bible: Critical Perspectives*, edited by Emanuel Pfoh (Piscataway, NJ: Gorgias, 2010); *Syria-Palestine in the Late Bronze Age: An Anthropology of Politics and Power* (London: Routledge, 2016); and "Introduction: Social and Cultural Anthropology and the Hebrew Bible in Perspective," pages 1–16 in *T&T Clark Handbook of Anthropology and the Hebrew Bible*, edited by Emanuel Pfoh (London: Bloomsbury T&T Clark, 2023).

Suggestions for Further Reading

In This Book
See also chapters 1 (scholarly perspective), 13 (genres), 20 (genealogies), 22 (periodization), 24 (Kings and Chronicles), 26 (conquest of Canaan), 28–32 (archaeology), and 56 (polemics).

Elsewhere
Davies, Philip R. *In Search of "Ancient Israel": A Study in Biblical Origins.* Sheffield, UK: Sheffield Academic, 1992.

Esler, Philip F., editor. *Ancient Israel: The Old Testament in Its Social Context.* Minneapolis: Fortress, 2006.

Frazer, James G. *Folk-Lore in the Old Testament: Studies in Comparative Religion, Legend and Law.* London: Macmillan, 1918.

Gottwald, Norman K. *The Tribes of Yahweh: A Sociology of the Religion of Liberated Israel, 1250–1050 B.C.E.* New York: Maryknoll, 1979.

Harris, Marvin. *The Rise of Anthropological Theory: A History of Theories of Culture.* New York: Thomas Y. Crowell, 1968.

Lang, Bernhard, editor. *Anthropological Approaches to the Old Testament.* Philadelphia: Fortress, 1985.

Lemche, Niels Peter. *Early Israel: Anthropological and Historical Studies on the Israelite Society before the Monarchy.* Leiden: Brill, 1985.

Mendenhall, George E. "The Hebrew Conquest of Palestine." *Biblical Archaeologist* 25(3) (1962): 66–87.

Overholt, Thomas W. *Cultural Anthropology and the Old Testament*. Minneapolis: Fortress, 1996.

Pitt-Rivers, Julian. *The Fate of Shechem, or, The Politics of Sex: Essays in the Anthropology of the Mediterranean*. Cambridge: Cambridge University Press, 1977.

Quick, Laura. *Dress, Adornment, and the Body in the Hebrew Bible*. Oxford: Oxford University Press, 2021.

Rogerson, John W. *Anthropology and the Old Testament*. Oxford: Basil Blackwell, 1978.

Smith, William Robertson. *Kinship and Marriage in Early Arabia*. Cambridge: Cambridge University Press, 1885.

81

How Are Gender Approaches Used in the Study of the Hebrew Bible?

Rhiannon Graybill

What does gender have to do with the Bible? How do contemporary ideas about gender, sexuality, and gender identity help us understand ancient biblical texts? And what is the significance of the Bible for contemporary debates about gender and sexuality? These are the kinds of questions that gender approaches to the Hebrew Bible help us ask and answer. The phrase "gender approaches" describes several related approaches, including feminist interpretation, womanist interpretation, LGBTQ interpretation, and masculinity studies, which share a focus on gender as a category of analysis.

In everyday usage, "gender" is often taken to mean "male" or "female." While sometimes it is treated as a synonym for biological sex, there is increasing awareness that gender and sex are not the same. While sex has to do with the body, its genitals, and its chromosomes (though this can quickly get complicated!), gender is *socially constructed*—that is, it is created by society. Furthermore, the specifics of gender construction are culturally and historically dependent: what the category of "woman" looks like in the contemporary United States, for example, is different from in ancient Israel. While gender approaches have traditionally focused on women, masculinity studies is a rapidly growing field both within and outside of biblical studies. Another set of gender approaches considers "gender identity," which describes how individual people experience their gender. The terms "transgender," "cisgender," and "nonbinary" all refer to gender identity.

In biblical studies, gender approaches remain closely associated with feminist biblical interpretation. As a scholarly movement, feminist interpretation emerged in the 1970s. Biblical scholar Phyllis Trible (1973) tackles the assumption that the Bible and feminism are irreconcilably at odds with each other. Trible argues that a feminist reading of the Bible is not only possible but desirable. She focuses on three areas of analysis: the presence of feminine imagery for God in the Bible, antisexist readings of the creation of man and woman in Genesis 1 and 2, and female agency and love in the Song of Songs. Trible's article, expanded into a book, was soon followed by many others, and feminist biblical interpretation emerged as a significant field of study.

While Trible's work was groundbreaking, there were precursors. In the late nineteenth century, suffragettes and other "first wave" feminists often tried their hand at biblical interpretation. Elizabeth Cady Stanton, a leading advocate for women's suffrage, also oversaw the creation of *The Woman's Bible*, a work of commentary that offered feminist perspectives on the Bible. An even older example is by the French noblewoman Christine de Pizan. Her *Book of the City of Ladies* was written in the fifteenth century. These early female interpreters are, like Trible, concerned with questions of gender and with finding ways of reading that resist or rebuke the apparent sexism of the biblical text. Feminist theology was another important conversation partner for early feminist biblical interpretation, as feminist theologians like Mary Daly, Rosemary Radford Ruether, and Sallie McFague began asking questions about gender, God, and misogyny.

Since the 1980s, feminist biblical interpretation has flourished, and multiple distinct feminist approaches have emerged. Some feminist scholars are most interested in questions of gender in ancient Israel, such as "What was everyday life like for women in ancient Israel?" or even "How did ancient Israelites understand their 'gender'?" In order to answer these questions, they use the tools of archaeology and historical reconstruction with an explicit focus on gender. Often, feminist frameworks—such as a theory of what it means to do feminist archaeology—can help guide this work. Other feminist scholars are less interested in the world behind the text than in how gender is represented *in* the text. These researchers may focus their analysis on female characters; on gendered metaphors like the "marriage metaphor," which describes God as male and as married to a feminized Israel; on laws concerning the gendered body; or on other ways the text "constructs" gender. Sometimes this work endeavors to find more positive ways of reading texts that seem to represent women or the female body negatively. Trible's readings of Eve and the Song of Songs are two examples of this approach. At other times, feminist critics seek to document the misogyny and patriarchy in the texts. A final approach is to consider the *reception* of texts—what happens to the Bible after it is written, when it reaches the hands of religious communities and other interpreters. In all of these approaches, feminist criticism of the Hebrew Bible resembles other modes of feminist criticism applied to texts, though biblical studies remains somewhat more inclined to judge texts as "good" or "bad" for women than, for example, feminist literary criticism.

Feminist interpretation seeks to address all forms of injustice and to take seriously how gender interacts with other categories of identity, including sexuality, race and ethnicity, and social class. However, in practice, feminist interpretation has often privileged the experiences of a certain kind of woman: white, straight, and middle class. Black and other feminists of color have often critiqued white feminism for its ignorance, silencing, and even racism. In biblical studies, one important development has been the rise of womanist biblical interpretation.

The term "womanist" comes from writer, activist, and novelist Alice Walker, who offers it as a richer alternative to "feminism." Womanist biblical interpretation, like womanism more broadly, centers Black women. It emphasizes the intersections of race and ethnicity with gender and sexuality, both in biblical texts and in the history of interpretation. Women of color in the biblical text, such as the Shulammite ("I am black and beautiful"; Song of Songs 1:5) and Moses's Cushite wife (Numbers 12:1) have attracted womanist attention. Other womanists use the categories of race, gender, and enslavement to unpack the working of power in biblical texts. Womanist methods are informed by Black feminist and womanist thought, especially as these disciplines develop in the US academy. As a result, womanism is most closely associated with American biblical scholarship. However, scholars around the world have developed methods of interpretation that direct attention to the interplay of gender and race or ethnicity.

Postcolonial feminists emphasize how colonialism and colonial relations influence gender and other factors of identity. They stress the importance of race and ethnicity, social class, and historical relations of domination. Often, it turns out, Global North feminists want to "save" women and queer people in the Global South; this is a move that postcolonial feminism critiques. With respect to the Hebrew Bible, postcolonial feminist interpreters often cast a critical eye on how non-Israelite women such as Jael (Judges 4–5), Rahab (Joshua 2), or the Queen of Sheba (1 Kings 10) are represented, both in the text and in their reception by scholars. Postcolonial feminist interpretation also directs attention to questions of indigeneity and colonization, reminding us that the Israelites are colonizers and the Canaanites are threatened indigenous peoples. The intersection of colonization with gender is rich ground for critique.

Postcolonial feminist approaches often travel under additional names. In Africa, postcolonial feminist interpretation of the Bible often uses the label "womanist," but with a focus on the experiences of African women rather than the Africana diaspora. In Latin America, the term *mujerista*, a Spanish translation of "womanist," enjoyed some currency but has more recently been replaced by "Latinx," including Latinx feminisms. "Mestiza," a term introduced by queer feminist theorist, poet, and essayist Gloria Anzaldúa, highlights the crossing of borders as a key feminist practice. In biblical interpretation, this has translated into inquiries about eunuchs, transgressive and wounded bodies, and geographical borders as figurations of the boundaries of the body. These questions are consistent with feminist concerns but also push them further.

Another useful descriptor, especially for more contemporary feminist and other gender approaches, is "intersectional." The term "intersectionality" was first coined by Kimberlé Crenshaw to describe the compounded racial, gender, and class oppression faced by Black women working in the auto industry. The term has since come into widespread use as a general descriptor of intersecting categories of identity and their compounding effects. For example, the oppression of working-class Black lesbians cannot be reduced to gender + class + sexuality + race. Intersectional gender approaches, which include feminist, womanist, mujerista, and postcolonial feminist interpretations, analyze gender with attention to race and ethnicity, disability, class, sexuality, and other markers of identity.

Sexuality is the focus of a wide range of LGBTQ approaches, which include lesbian critique, gay critique, and queer critique (a broader, more flexible, and often more political category). Just as the range of feminist approaches focus on gender and the gendered body, LGBTQ approaches emphasize sexuality and sexual orientation—in the text, in the ancient world, and in reception history. While transgender approaches largely originated in queer biblical interpretation, their object of inquiry is not sexuality but rather gender in the form of gender identity. As such, they perhaps fit better with "gender approaches." However, currently, transgender approaches to the Bible remain rather rare (though interest is growing). As the scholarship develops, it will no doubt make an important contribution to gender studies more broadly.

A final gender approach that deserves mention is masculinity studies. As the name suggests, this approach counterbalances the traditional emphasis of gender studies on women (and, to a lesser degree, nonbinary and gender-nonconforming subjects) with a focus on men, male bodies, and the social category of masculinity. The first scholarship in this area often focused on the masculinity of heroic men, such as King David. A common analytical framework was the idea of "hegemonic masculinity," a term borrowed from sociology that describes the socially dominant form of masculinity in a given culture. My students frequently offer Dwayne "the Rock" Johnson as an example of hegemonic masculinity in the contemporary United States, for example. As scholarship on biblical masculinities has grown, the understanding of both hegemonic and nonconforming masculinities in the Hebrew Bible and in ancient Israel has developed accordingly. The masculinity of the God of the Hebrew Bible has been another area of analysis, with scholars debating whether divine masculinity is idealized, excessive, or unstable—or perhaps, all three.

Gender approaches to the Hebrew Bible are flourishing. From feminist interpretation to masculinity studies, from womanist critique to the emerging field of transgender biblical interpretation, gender approaches help us understand biblical texts more deeply and richly. They also facilitate connections between the ancient texts and our own present moment, where questions of gender and gendered bodies remain important, pressing, and passionate issues.

About the Author

Rhiannon Graybill holds a PhD in Near Eastern studies from the University of California, Berkeley. Her research interests include feminist, queer, and literary approaches to biblical texts. She is the author of *Are We Not Men? Unstable Masculinity in the Hebrew Prophets* (Oxford: Oxford University Press, 2016) and coeditor with Lynn R. Huber of *The Bible, Gender, and Sexuality: Critical Readings* (London: T&T Clark, 2020) and with Philippe Guillaume of the *Ruth* volume for the new series Themes and Issues in Biblical Studies (Sheffield, UK: Equinox, forthcoming).

Suggestions for Further Reading

In This Book
See also chapters 54 (genocide), 55 (patriarchalism), 57 (pro-choice), 64 (Ruth), 65 (King David), 82 (postcolonial studies), and 83 (reception criticism).

Elsewhere
Graybill, Rhiannon, and Lynn R. Huber. "Introduction." Pages 1–13 in *The Bible, Gender, and Sexuality: Critical Readings*. Edited by Rhiannon Graybill and Lynn R. Huber. London: T&T Clark, 2020.

Junior, Nyasha. *An Introduction to Womanist Biblical Interpretation*. Louisville, KY: Westminster John Knox, 2015.

Trible, Phyllis. "Depatriarchalizing in Biblical Interpretation." *Journal of the American Academy of Religion* 41 (1973): 30–48.

82

What Is Postcolonial Studies and How Is It Applied to the Hebrew Bible / Old Testament?

Sonia Kwok Wong

In the past three decades, postcolonial studies has been a vibrant partner in the study of the Hebrew Bible. The production, transmission, and canonization of the biblical texts happened within the imperial contexts of the Assyrian, Babylonian, Persian, and Hellenistic Empires. These imperial cultures conditioned the practices of the biblical writers and left their traces in the biblical texts. The motifs postcolonial critics frequently analyze, like ethnicity, identity, hybridity, exile, diaspora, displacement, homecoming, transculturation, and othering, appear in the Hebrew Bible, making postcolonialism an indispensable tool for unraveling the imperial ideologies and resistance to such ideologies in the Hebrew texts.

The prefix "post-" in the term "postcolonialism" is often used ambiguously to designate the period after or since the onset of colonialism, which has brought more confusion than clarity. Though many once colonized countries have declared independence and undergone decolonization, colonial effects persist in these polities. There exists no decisive time that marks the death of colonialism. Homi Bhabha (2004) proposes a spatial concept of "post-" as "beyond." This "beyond," according to Bhabha, is the site of resistance to, and critique of, colonialism. It is a site in which its aftermath, its effects, and various contemporary disguises are unmasked, challenged, and contested.

Following Michel Foucault (1978, 3–35), postcolonial critics define "discourse" in relation to power and knowledge as a historically conditioned and ideologically charged social domain that controls the effectiveness of a text and the intelligibility of both the author and the reader. This discursive power controls our comprehension of the world and shapes the larger discursive structure. We are limited by discourse but, at the same time, participate in its perpetuation and evolution. Even anticolonial discourse is inseparable from the power structure it resists.

To unravel this hidden discursive mechanism, a text produced in an imperial culture must be read, interpreted, analyzed, and critiqued specifically with respect to imperialism. This involves the analysis of imperial ideologies; the dismantling of representations, stereotypes, and othering in the text; and a description of how opposition and resistance to imperialism happens within the discourse conditioned by imperialism.

The Bible is often described by cultural critics as a colonial document used by the colonizer to legitimate territorial conquest and the subjugation of the people of the Two-Thirds World. The Hebrew Bible has been a convenient and multivocal ideological weapon that can easily be manipulated and interpreted in a way that promotes colonialism. The view of the Hebrew Bible as a colonial document is contingent on the colonizer's employment of the biblical texts in recent centuries. However, the Bible has also been interpreted to rebuke colonial ideologies and is thus no more colonial than anticolonial. It all depends on who holds the interpretive right. Most texts in the Hebrew Bible are written not by the imperialist but by scribes who were imperialized collaborators with the dominant imperial regime. This situation contributes to the ambivalence and ambiguity of the Hebrew Bible as a colonial document.

Rasiah Sugirtharajah (2006) lays out the threefold task of postcolonial biblical criticism as follows: First, it seeks to situate colonialism at the center of the Bible and biblical interpretation, which requires an interpreter to search out colonial assumptions, imperial impulses, power relations, hegemonic intentions, the treatment of subalterns, the stigmatization of women and the marginalized, land appropriation, and the violation of minority cultures embedded within the biblical texts. Simultaneously, it typically seeks to revive and reclaim silenced voices, sidelined issues, and lost causes. Second, it aims to expose the hidden ideological content in biblical interpretations. Finally, it endeavors to reread the Bible in the light of postcolonial concerns and conditions.

Postcolonial biblical criticism is not a homogenous project that employs a single method. Postcolonial critics use different critical lenses, reading strategies, and aims, but they all show a preoccupation with postcolonial concerns and motifs. Besides works that explicitly use postcolonial theory, there are latent postcolonial biblical works employing other critical methods that are influenced by postcolonial studies. Examples in the suggested reading include the works of Danna Nolan Fewell (2001), Ada María Isasi-Díaz (1995), Jason M. Silverman (2020), and Robert Warrior (2006). In addition, there are hyphenated works that use postcolonialism in conjunction with other critical lenses in biblical studies, such as the post-colonial feminist readings edited by L. Juliana Claassens, Christl M. Maier, and Funlola Olojede (2021).

Works on postcolonial biblical criticism may be grouped into three categories. First, postcolonial rereadings open up alternative hermeneutics that were precluded in traditional white, Eurocentric, and male-dominated biblical scholarship. The ancient biblical text is reread with respect to today's postcolonial concerns. A good sample of essays of this type appears in the edited volume by Sugirtharajah (2006).

Second, postcolonial critiques of biblical interpretations may be produced by those doing reception history from a postcolonial perspective. Postcolonial biblical critics scrutinize the Eurocentric interpretations of biblical texts in all cultural forms to unravel hidden imperial ideologies, such as white and monotheistic supremacy; to describe how they serve to legitimize colonial domination; to explore ways that biblical texts are used as a means of cultural hegemony; and to theorize the representations of the colonized and the colonizer. Besides Sugirtharajah's pioneering approach, Elsa Tamez (2006) deals with the use of the Bible for the colonial domination of the Americas in recent centuries, while Roland Boer (2008) espouses a postcolonial-cum-Marxist critical lens to identify the appropriation of the Hebrew Bible as an ideological tool by both the immigrants and the Aborigines in the colonial history of Australia.

The third type is postcolonial criticism of biblical texts from a historical-critical perspective. Steed V. Davidson (2017), David Janzen (2013), and Leo G. Perdue (2002) have published works that situate biblical texts in their ancient imperial contexts, looking at how ancient imperialism conditioned their ideological content.

Postcolonial biblical criticism is not just about reading biblical texts from the perspective of the (once) colonized or the marginalized or unraveling the imperializing content in Western-dominated biblical scholarship. As part of the discursive practices carried in imperial contexts, the Hebrew Bible is rich in postcolonial motifs. Therefore, postcolonialism provides a fresh perspective on the history of the Hebrew Bible with respect to the imperial cultures of the time. Biblical texts were produced under the influence and possible censorship of the imperializer, and they are likely to have been written or edited by imperial collaborators. How the hybrid identity of the biblical writers affected their literary production remains to be probed.

About the Author

Sonia Kwok Wong holds a PhD in religious studies from Vanderbilt University. Her research includes the postcolonial-psychoanalytic criticism of the Deuteronomistic (Hi)Story, cross-textual hermeneutics, and feminist criticism. Her publications include *The Solomonic Fantasy of the Imperialized Yehudites* (Tübingen: Mohr Siebeck, forthcoming); and "Signifying the Empire against the Empire, or Doing Historical Criticism with Postcolonial Theories," pages 125–142 in *Heilige Schriften in der Kritik: XVII. Europäischer Kongress für Theologie (5.–8. September 2021 in Zürich)*, edited by Konrad Schmid (Leipzig: Evangelische Verlagsanstalt, 2022).

Suggestions for Further Reading

In This Book
See also chapters 26 (conquest of Canaan), 75 (historical criticism), 78 (ideological criticism), 80 (social anthropology), 81 (gender studies), and 83 (reception criticism).

Elsewhere
<small>STUDIES USING POSTCOLONIAL THEORY</small>

Bhabha, Homi. *The Location of Culture*. London: Routledge, 2004.

Boer, Roland. *Last Stop before Antarctica: The Bible and Postcolonialism in Australia* (2nd edition). Leiden: Brill, 2008.

Foucault, Michel. *The History of Sexuality: An Introduction* (volume 1). New York: Pantheon, 1978.

Sugirtharajah, Rasiah S. "Postcolonial Biblical Interpretation." Pages 64–85 in *Voices from the Margin: Interpreting the Bible in the Third World*. Edited by Rasiah S. Sugirtharajah. Maryknoll, NY: Orbis, 2006.

Tamez, Elsa. "The Bible and Five Hundred Years of Conquest." Pages 13–26 in *Voices from the Margin: Interpreting the Bible in the Third World*. Edited by Rasiah S. Sugirtharajah. Maryknoll, NY: Orbis, 2006.

<small>STUDIES INFLUENCED BY POSTCOLONIAL STUDIES</small>
Claassens, Juliana L., Christl M. Maier, and Funlola Olojede, editors. *Transgression and Transformation: Feminist, Postcolonial and Queer Biblical Interpretation as Creative Interventions*. London: T&T Clark, 2021.

Fewell, Danna Nolan. "Building Babel." Pages 1–15 in *Postmodern Interpretations of the Bible: A Reader*. Edited by A. K. M. Adam. St. Louis, MO: Chalice, 2001.

Isasi-Díaz, Ada María. "'By the Rivers of Babylon': Exile as a Way of Life." Pages 149–163 in *Reading from This Place*. Edited by Fernando F. Segovia and Mary Ann Tolbert. Minneapolis: Fortress, 1995.

Silverman, Jason M. *Persian Royal-Judaean Elite Engagements in the Early Teispid and Achaemenid Empire: The King's Acolytes*. London: Bloomsbury, 2020.

Warrior, Robert. "A Native American Perspective: Canaanites, Cowboys, and Indians." Pages 235–241 in *Voices from the Margin: Interpreting the Bible in the Third World*. Edited by Rasiah S. Sugirtharajah. Maryknoll, NY: Orbis, 2006.

POSTCOLONIAL STUDIES FROM A HISTORICAL-CRITICAL PERSPECTIVE

Davidson, Steed Vernyl. *Writing/Reading the Bible in Postcolonial Perspective*. Leiden: Brill, 2017.

Janzen, David. *The Necessary King: A Postcolonial Reading of the Deuteronomistic Portrait of the Monarchy*. HBM 57. Sheffield, UK: Sheffield Phoenix, 2013.

Perdue, Leo G. "The Rhetoric of Wisdom and Postcolonial Hermeneutics." *Scriptura* 81 (2002): 437–452.

83

What Is Reception Criticism and How Is It Practiced in Hebrew Bible Scholarship?

Erin Runions

One of the first things you learn in class on the Hebrew Bible is that the text does not always say what you think it says. Genesis 3 does not mention an original sin. Eve is not solely responsible for the expulsion from the garden. The Babel story does not speak about "hubris."

Where do these ideas come from? How are they propagated? How are they amplified in art, literature, music, film, and advertising? How do politicians take them up? When you see an allusion to the Hebrew Bible in culture or politics, you might ask, What histories does it reflect? What philosophies, theologies, aesthetics, and politics does it combine? How has the ancient Israelite text been interpreted differently through Jewish and Christian lenses? Frequently, you'll find, Christian ideas are overlaid onto these ancient Israelite texts. But there are influences as well, for instance, from sexism and racism. Sometimes there is also resistance to dominant ideas.

Biblical reception criticism unpacks influences and traditions of biblical interpretation as they develop and circulate in any given historical moment. Scholars study how histories of interpretation congeal in citations of the Tanak. Reception criticism allows us to consider what stowaway ideas a biblical citation brings with it. Further, it analyzes the effect of biblical citations on their contexts (past or present). An allusion to the Hebrew Bible in culture or politics is probably not neutral. It is likely there to add weight to an idea or support a particular position.

Timothy Beal (2011) argues that the twentieth-century philosophies of Hans Gadamer and his student Hans Robert Jauss changed the way scholars thought about the biblical text. Instead of approaching interpretation as the search for the text's original intent, they began to see it as the *production* of meaning, influenced by the interpreter. They sought to understand the interaction of text and context. They began to see the "meaning" of a text as a cumulation of past interpretations. The tradition of interpretation overtly and covertly affects the way the Hebrew Bible is understood and deployed. Scholars now accept that we cannot "just read the biblical text" as though it exists apart from centuries—indeed, millennia—of interpretation.

The exciting thing about reception criticism is that it can integrate many kinds of expertise. Are you interested in art, film, music, literature, interreligious dialogue, advertising, gender, sexuality, or race? Dive in. It won't be long before you find a citation of the Hebrew Bible, and I guarantee, there will be something to study.

For instance, exclusively blaming Eve for sin in the garden was introduced by the early Christian author of 1 Timothy. He instructs women to dress modestly and to be submissive to men because "Adam was not the one deceived" (1 Timothy 2:14). Eve's sinfulness was significantly amplified in the second century CE by the early Christian theologian Tertullian, who called Eve the "devil's gateway" in *On the Apparel of Women*. Like the author of 1 Timothy, Tertullian wanted women to be modest. Similarly, the idea that Genesis 3 describes original sin passed down to every human was based on the writings of second century BCE Ben Sira (also named Ecclesiasticus), who explained that "from a woman sin had its beginning, and because of her we all die" (25:24). This idea was passed on to Augustine, who also blames Eve in his *City of God* (fifth century CE). The connections among Eve, women, and sinfulness have endured through art and literature. Caroline Blyth (2015) impressively illustrates the connections among theology, misogyny, and artwork. She shows image after image in which blame rests primarily, or solely, on Eve.

Even the serpent is sometimes represented as a woman in artwork, intensifying a connection between women and temptation. Brennan Breed (n.d.) points to the theology of Peter Comestor as an originator for this idea. Art historian Jane Schuyler (1990) looks at the female serpent in Michelangelo's Sistine Chapel and posits that Michelangelo had come into contact with Jewish Kabbalist teaching about Adam's powerful first wife, Lilith, originally thought to be a goddess or demoness of the night. Michelangelo appropriates Lilith into a misogynistic Christian context. In contemporary culture, women, apples, and snakes often appear together to represent sexual allure. Katie Edwards (2012) provides many examples of how Eve's sinfulness and sexuality are used in advertisements. Sometimes women seem liberated in these images, but Edwards questions how far that analysis can go given the misogynist history of interpretation and the continuing masculinist impulses of advertising.

Or consider that the interpretation of the Babel story as a warning about pride was introduced by the early Jewish historian Josephus (first century CE). In *Antiquities of the Jews*, Josephus retold it as a story about "hubris" and tyranny, as part of a pro-Roman political agenda about the Jewish rebels fighting Rome. He accused the rebels of being too democratic, against the priesthood (he came from a priestly family), and thus tending toward tyranny. He followed Plato's ideal of philosopher rulers.

Flash forward to 2013. Italian archbishop Vincenzo Paglia, president of the Pontifical Council for the Family, drew on Josephus's famous reinterpretation when he said of same-sex marriage, "The problem is to avoid Babel. . . . We cannot surrender to a sick egalitarianism that abolishes every difference" (Speciale 2013). US Supreme Court Justice Antonin Scalia made a similar point in his dissent when the Court ruled in favor of same-sex marriage in *Obergefell vs. Hodges* (2015). Scalia said of the ruling, "Hubris is sometimes defined as o'erweening pride; and pride, we know, goeth before a fall" (Phelps 2015). Scalia's citation of Proverbs 16:18 alludes to Josephus's reading of the Babel story. Scalia's gloss on Proverbs is startlingly similar to Leland Ryken, James C. Wilhoit, and Tremper Longman III's (1998, 66) description of the Tower of Babel as an "image of human aspiration and pride. . . . Lurking in the background is the classical notion of *hubris*— overweening human pride." Scalia's accusation of same-sex marriage as dangerous pride draws on Josephus's interpretation of Babel. It subtly draws in a Platonic worry about democracy as a form of tyranny and suggests, like Archbishop Paglia, that same-sex relations represent an ungodly egalitarianism.

More recently, biblical reception critics have started to interrogate how the racialization of biblical characters has had real effects on the lives of racialized people. Joel B. Kemp (2021) shows, for instance, how the reinterpretation of Cain (Genesis 4) has fed into racist interpretations of African Americans as dangerous, deviant, and depraved. In early Christian Scriptures, Cain's murder of Abel is read not as a response to God's arbitrary favor of Abel but as a result of inherent evil. In the Middle Ages, the "mark" God places on Cain is interpreted as Blackness. In the nineteenth century, however, the mark is read as whiteness in African American communities (see Junior 2020). On the contrary, some white readers used Cain's Blackness to justify slavery. These ideas, Kemp suggests, continue into the twentieth and twenty-first centuries with the ongoing police murders of African Americans. Hence, for these readers, the Cain story explains why white people are violent. Reception critics in the future might consider how such histories of the racialization, or counterracialization, of Cain might appear in cultural productions like film, music, or literature.

Similarly, Nyasha Junior and Jeremy Schipper (2020) trace how African Americans turn to Samson to voice a revolutionary biblical imagination and to convey the struggle against racial oppression. The biblical Samson—who is captured yet finds divine strength to pull down the Philistine temple in Judges 16—appears in the writing of many revolutionary and literary figures. Fredrick Douglass and Ida B. Wells-Barnett use Samson to express resistance and inspire revolt against the systems of slavery and lynching. In the 1930s and 1950s, Langston Hughes and Ralph Ellison used the figure of Samson to discuss labor exploitation and structures of exclusion. Poet Lucille Clifton uses the story to express anger over the police bombing of the radical Black group MOVE in Philadelphia in 1985. Junior and Schipper successfully show that the Samson tradition represents an important avenue of struggle against white supremacy.

In sum, reception criticism is an expansive and exciting form of biblical criticism that gives us a greater understanding of the politics or philosophies of a cultural discourse. It shows how the Bible still holds sway in a secular world. It analyzes how biblical texts continue to amplify systems of power. It unearths counterreadings. It will take you on a journey.

About the Author

Erin Runions is the Nancy J. Lyon Professor of Biblical History and Literature in the Department of Religious Studies at Pomona College. Her publications include "Rebel Trash, Bad Objects, Prison Hell: Isaiah 66 and the Affect of Discard," *Postscripts: A Journal of Sacred Texts and Contemporary Worlds* 13(1) (2022): 27–62; *The Babylon Complex: Theopolitical Fantasies of War, Sex and Sovereignty* (New York: Fordham University Press, 2014); *How Hysterical: Identification and Resistance in the Bible and Film* (New York: Palgrave Macmillan, 2003); and "Babel and the Fear of Same-Sex Marriage: Mapping Conservative Constellations," *Journal of Biblical Reception* 1(1) (2014): 47–65.

Suggestions for Further Reading

In This Book

Elsewhere

Beal, Timothy. "Reception History and Beyond: Toward the Cultural History of Scriptures." *Biblical Interpretation* 19(4–5) (2011): 357–372.

Blyth, Caroline. "Danger and Desire—Edenic Reflections." *Auckland Theology and Religious Studies* (blog), March 27, 2015. https://aucklandtheology.wordpress.com/2015/03/27/danger-and-desire-edenic-reflections/.

Breed, Brennan. "What Is Reception History?" Bible Odyssey. https://www.bibleodyssey.org/bible-basics/what-is-reception-history/.

Burnette-Bletsch, Rhonda, editor. *The Bible in Motion: A Handbook of the Bible and Its Reception in Film* (2 volumes). Berlin: De Gruyter, 2016.

Edwards, Katie. *Admen and Eve: The Bible in Contemporary Advertising.* Sheffield, UK: Sheffield Phoenix, 2012.

Furey, Constance M., Peter Gemeinhardt, Joel Marcus LeMon, Thomas Römer, Jens Schröter, Barry Dov Walfish, and Eric Ziolkowski, editors. *Encyclopedia of the Bible and Its Reception* (30 volumes). Berlin: De Gruyter, 2009.

Junior, Nyasha. "The Mark of Cain and White Violence." *Journal of Biblical Literature* 139(4) (2020): 661–673.

Junior, Nyasha, and Jeremy Schipper. *Black Samson: The Untold Story of an American Icon.* New York: Oxford University Press, 2020.

Kemp, Joel B. "Racializing Cain, Demonizing Blackness, and Legalizing Discrimination: Proposal for Reception of Cain and America's Racial Caste System." *Perspectives in Religious Studies* 48(4) (2021): 377–399.

Lieb, Michael, Emma Mason, and Jonathan Roberts, editors. *The Oxford Handbook of the Reception History of the Bible.* Oxford: Oxford University Press, 2011.

Phelps, Timothy M. "Analysis: Antonin Scalia's Dissent in Same-Sex Marriage Ruling Even More Scornful Than Usual." *Los Angeles Times*, June 26, 2015. https://www.latimes.com/nation/la-na-gay-marriage-scalia-dissent-20150626-story.html.

Ryken, Leland, James C. Wilhoit, and Tremper Longman III, editors. "Babel, Tower Of." Pages 66–67 in *Dictionary of Biblical Imagery.* Downers Grove, IL: InterVarsity, 1998.

Schuyler, Jane. "Michelangelo's Serpent with Two Tails." *Source: Notes in the History of Art* 9(2) (1990): 23–29.

Speciale, Alessandro. "Vatican Signals Options for Protecting Gay Couples." Religion News Service, February 4, 2013. http://www.religionnews.com/2013/02/04/vatican-signals-options-for-protecting-gay-couples/.

Scripture Index

Hebrew Bible / Old Testament

429

Deuterocanonical Books

Pseudepigrapha

New Testament

Classical Greek Authors

Rabbinic Works

Early Christian Writings

Qur'an

Subject Index

9 781800 504523